SEA
LITHUANIA

E.
PRUSSIA
Danzig

• Warsaw

POLAND

U   S   S   R

• Kiev

WITHDRAWN

• Krakow

CZECHOSLOVAKIA

Odessa

• Budapest
HUNGARY

RUMANIA

Tulcea
Galatz   Sulina

Belgrade
Kladovo   Bucharest

BLACK SEA

DANUBE R.
YUGOSLAVIA   Balchik   Constanța

BULGARIA
• Sofia

ALBANIA

Istanbul   BOSPORUS
GREECE

• Ankara

SEA OF
MARMARA
DARDANELLES

TURKEY

AEGEAN
SEA

Athens

RHODES
CYPRUS   SYRIA

CRETE

MEDITERRANEAN SEA

Haifa
Netanya
Tel Aviv
Jerusalem

TRANSJORDAN

• Alexandria
PALESTINE

EGYPT
Cairo
RED SEA

palacios

THE
FOUR-FRONT
WAR

THE FOUR-FRONT WAR

FROM THE HOLOCAUST TO THE PROMISED LAND

BY WILLIAM R. PERL

CROWN PUBLISHERS, INC.   NEW YORK

TO THOSE WHO DARED AND LIVED

AND TO THOSE

WHO PERISHED IN THE FOUR-FRONT WAR

Jacket photograph courtesy Jabotinsky Institute

Credits for picture insert: Page 1, Jabotinsky Institute with exception of author's passport. Page 2, Jabotinsky Institute. Page 3, photo at top left, Jabotinsky Institute; document top right, Betar, Austria; document at bottom, author's collection. Page 4, photo at bottom by Emil Patlaschenco. Page 5, Jabotinsky Institute. Page 6, photo at top, Jabotinsky Institute; documents middle and bottom, author's collection. Page 7, letter at top, author's collection; document at bottom, Public Records Office, London. Page 8, author's collection.

Designed by Shari de Miskey

Library of Congress Cataloging in Publication Data

Perl, William R
The four front war.

Includes index.

1. Holocaust, Jewish (1939-1945)—Personal
narratives.   2. Palestine—Emigration and immigration.
3. Perl, Wiliam R.   I. Title.
D810.J4P477   1979   940.53'1503'924   79-16255
ISBN 0-517-53837-7

CONTENTS

FOREWORD

In memory of the great horrible days

The thirties . . . the saddest period in mankind's history: the thirtieth of January 1933. A great nation which called itself with pride "the nation of poets and philosophers" turns, almost in toto, into a bloodthirsty mob, thirsty first of all for Jewish blood. Some naïve people, amongst them many Jews, including philosophers, assumed that as head of government, that embodiment of all evil in mankind, to use a famous phrase of Winston Churchill, will be responsible, will not put into practice the barbaric measures of his infamous "program." There was one man in those dark, indescribable days, who warned that the first part of that so-called program, which will be completely realized, is that concerning the Jews. The name of the prophet who understood reality was Zeev Jabotinsky. Alas, the people and the nations did not heed his warning and relied on—nobody knows whom.

In those days, the whole wrath of persecution and humiliation "legislated" by a mighty gangster state was brought on the heads of a defenseless, helpless minority. The Jewish people were trapped. In Europe, the beast of prey attacked the Jews, and Palestine, the national home, was denied to them. Jabotinsky called it later "the frozen stampede."

In those horrible days there were young people who took upon themselves the grave dangerous task to save the Jews from the beast's clutches and bring them to their home, Palestine. They had to overcome odds, break the law (that "law" which becomes foolish, antihuman in the face of persecution and death), endanger their own freedom, even their lives in order to save the doomed ones and bring them to the shores of their ancestors' land.

One of those young men was William Perl. He himself tells the story, gives the facts, describes the agony. The reader of this book will learn and know that I wrote these words of introduction in order to pay tribute to the author, not for what he wrote but for what he did.

Your deeds, Dr. Perl, will be remembered forever by the Jewish people, indeed, by all men of goodwill.

—MENACHEM BEGIN
Prime Minister of Israel

ACKNOWLEDGMENTS

Whatever merit this book possesses is to a large degree due to the assistance given the author by a large number of persons. Participants of the voyages contributed their experiences, some in writing, others in taped interviews. Several of the organizers, some in group meetings, recalled relevant incidents, and all these data permitted a by far more comprehensive report than the author's own diary, notes, correspondence, and memory could have produced. It would be unfeasible to name all who assisted. Special thanks, however, are due to Moshe Chasan, Mila Epstein, Eliyahu Even, Dr. Reuben Hecht, Mordechai Katz, Yoseph Kremin, Eliyahu Lankin, Shabtai Nadiv, Yoseph Navon, Emil Patlaschenko, Dov Rubinstein, and Eliyahu Tamarkin, all of Israel. Charles Gross of Chicago, Illinois, provided valuable data about Eichmann's actions in Prague; Bata Gedalja assisted with information about Yugoslavia. My son Raphael was untiring in procuring documentation and my son Solomon in sifting and organizing the mass of incoming data.

With unending patience Natalie Gawdiak read and reread the manuscript and made suggestions to the benefit of the final product.

Thanks are also expressed to the staff of the Jabotinsky Institute in Tel Aviv, the Central Zionist Archives, and the Yad Vashem in Jerusalem, the Public Records Office in London, the Library of Congress in Washington, D.C., and the Institut fuer Zeitgeschichte in Munich.

These supportive efforts were at all times accompanied by the never-ending assistance of the one who ever since we met in 1937 has inspired and encouraged me. Lore, my wife, who suffered so much showed herself just as committed as I to letting the world know the near unbelievable happenings reported and documented here. From the moment I started gathering the material to the writing of the last line, she shared with me the labor, the frustrations, and the joys of writing this book.

INTRODUCTION

We have endured fire and water
And you have brought us through.

Psalm 66:12

While millions of Jews were driven into Nazi gas chambers in Hitler's Germany, more than 40,000 fled the holocaust in a dramatic series of daring, illegal voyages to Palestine between 1937 and 1944, aboard often unseaworthy vessels supplied and manned by the Greek underworld. This is the story of these perilous trips and of the desperate planning for them that went on furiously day and night in the face of daily setbacks and appalling odds.

Told by the main organizer of the entire operation, it is a story of underground warfare, intelligence and counterintelligence action by the major powers; and by the Betar and Irgun, Jewish activist organizations which, to rescue the hunted, had to dupe not only the Germans but the Allied powers as well. The story unfolds against a backdrop of increasing danger and persecution, with the Gestapo arbitrarily allowing some Jews to depart, while sending others to Dachau, as Nazi policy moved from expulsion to genocide. It culminates in triumphant success with the breaking of the British blockade of the Palestine coast as one after another of the "illegal" refugee ships unloaded its desperate cargo. But hand in hand with triumph came crushing tragedy for many. Not all of those—mostly young people—who packed their rucksacks in Nazi countries made it through the closed borders and across the seas to the Promised Land. Thousands perished on the way, victims of the raging seas, of the bullets of Nazi slaughterers, of hunger, of cold, of epidemics. Many also died on the fever-ridden island of Mauritius in the Indian Ocean after deportation there by the British Navy for trying to reach British-occupied Palestine.

The official British statistics list 20,180 refugees of Nazi terror as having reached Palestine illegally prior to the end of the war. But

1

the Jews know better. They know that those "officially" counted by the British were matched by an almost equal number of illegal immigrants about whom the colonial authorities never learned.

Looking at the overall situation, one has to ask oneself how it could have happened that the Germans succeeded almost entirely in exterminating European Jewry. Why didn't more try to escape?

Although Hitler was in power as early as 1933, Jewish leadership, both in Europe and elsewhere, had failed to perceive the real danger ahead and thus had failed to prepare the Jews. Efforts to organize mass emigration prior to the start of the mass killings late in the thirties were belittled, and the peril was minimized.

The Jews had known persecution for millennia, but they had always been able to escape to another country. Never in their history had they faced an attempt to murder not just many but *all* European Jews. In addition, they were totally unprepared to deal with the German genius for organization which mobilized modern technology—communication, including propaganda barrage by radio, movies, pamphlets, and speeches, all based on up-to-date communication theory; chemical know-how; medical "science"; mass transportation—to achieve the "Final Solution."

As far as the Jews were concerned, the world at that time was divided into two groups. First were countries which openly persecuted the Jews, namely, Germany and the countries allied with or occupied by it. The second group included those countries which looked on and did nothing except, at best, to admit a token number.

Even the United States followed the general trend. She made a farce of the principle inscribed on the Statue of Liberty. Eleanor Roosevelt's efforts to awaken the American public to the inhumanity of the U.S. immigration policy had failed too. In her syndicated column, "My Day," of July 19, 1939, she charged that 4,487 more aliens had left the United States than had entered it in the six years since Hitler had come to power!

Certainly there were exceptions: a trickle of lucky ones who had friends or relatives overseas succeeded in both getting out of Germany and getting into another country. But the story of the underground railroad by which 40,000 Jews escaped to Palestine still remains largely unknown.

In our operation, absurd as the case may seem when one looks back at it today, we had to fight a four-front war. One front was, of course, the Nazis, who were bound first on persecuting and later on exterminating Jews. They could arrest us at any time, send us to a concentration camp, or kill any of us on the spot.

The second front, and for us the most active, was the British. They did not want a Jewish majority in Palestine. They did not view the Jews as likely to remain colonial subjects for long and saw in Jewish Palestine a danger to their principle of "Rule Britannia." Thus, the hapless Jews found themselves caught between the principles of *Deutschland, Deutschland, ueber alles* and "Rule Britannia."

Only recently has it become possible to report the story of British involvement in all the details. In the 1970s, after thirty years had elapsed, the secret files of the Colonial and Foreign offices had become, according to British law, accessible to interested parties. The intelligence service files themselves still remain closed. However, the Foreign and Colonial offices failed to remove from their own records many communications from the intelligence services before opening up these files. This author has studied thousands of pages contained in the Foreign Office and Colonial Office archives and has photographed many of the relevant documents.

During World War I, in the year 1917, Britain was in need of widespread support. She had suffered a shattering defeat at Gallipoli and was being driven out of the Dardanelles. British troops were stalled at Salonika; German East Africa continued to hold out against the British onslaught; and German submarine attacks and mines had caused many a disaster to British shipping. The only success to which the British could look back was the capture of Jerusalem from the Turks, an operation in which the Jewish Legion, consisting of volunteers from the United States and London's Whitechapel district, had played a major part. With the collapse of their Russian ally in 1917, the danger for the British became even graver since the Germans were now free to turn many of their troops from the eastern to the western front.

Britain had to look for support from every possible source, even the Jews. But most Jews had never been enthusiastic about backing any power fighting on the side of hated Russia—land of the pogroms and the czars. This feeling was shared by influential Jews in the United States. To gain the sympathy and aid of Jews generally, therefore, the British government, on November 2, 1917, issued the Balfour Declaration. Therein the British state:

> His Majesty's Government views with favour the reestablishment in
> Palestine of a national home for the Jewish people . . . and will use
> their best endeavours to facilitate the achievement of this object.

This pledge in the Balfour Declaration was made a preamble to the
Mandate for Palestine which Britain subsequently obtained from
the League of Nations. On the strength of this promise—to help
reestablish a Jewish national home—Britain had been ruling Palestine since the collapse of the Ottoman Empire in 1918.

But in their hundreds of years of political ascendency, the
British had learned to manipulate words and elude political obligations. Ruling Palestine was for the British Empire of paramount
importance because of the Suez Canal, Britain's lifeline to India and
to her other Asian colonies. At the Cairo Conference in 1921,
attended by, among others, Churchill and T. E. Lawrence ("Lawrence of Arabia"), therefore, the main thrust of British Middle East
policy was clearly defined: Churchill stated that it was of no
importance what the Arab sheiks thought or were called by title "so
long as they do what we want when we want it." But with the Jews,
one could not be sure that they would fit so well into a colonial
pattern. A Jewish majority in Palestine seemed undesirable for
British colonial aims.

Consequently, as soon as the British had received the "mandate" to facilitate the reestablishment of the Jewish national home
in Palestine, they began to renege on this obligation. Among the
British aristocrats most loyal to British imperialism, they found one
who happened to be of the Jewish faith but who could be depended
upon to put his British patriotism above all. They made him, Sir
Herbert Samuel, high commissioner of Palestine. He rewarded their
expectations well: one of his first acts was to pressure the Jews into
ceding all of Palestine east of the Jordan River to the Arabs. The
Jordan had never been the border of Palestine, just as the Rhine is
not the border of Germany, nor the Mississippi the border of the
United States: the Jordan had always flowed right through Palestine. Under the pressure of the Jewish high commissioner, and in
exchange for promises of eternal peace with the Arabs, the Jews finally agreed to cede the eastern part of Palestine. This amounted to
85 percent of the land covered by the original Balfour Declaration
and the Mandate. The British hastened to move their troops into
this territory. They gave Eastern Palestine a new name, "Trans-Jor-

dan," and placed a satellite sheik at its head. This sheik was a member of the Hashemite family which still rules in that part of the country today. In 1948, after occupying part of the Jordan River's western bank as well, the sheik proclaimed himself king of these lands, all originally destined to be part of the Jewish national home. And he renamed the lands Jordan.

As the rapidly deteriorating League of Nations became less and less effective, the British acted more and more blatantly in default of their Mandate. The rise of Nazism in Germany would have provided the perfect chance to reestablish the Jewish national home, as the British had promised and had been charged to do. The Jews claimed the birthright and, based on the Balfour Declaration and Mandate, the political right to enter Palestine just as freely as any American can enter the United States. But Britain blocked mass immigration while making excuses for her failure to act as promised. First of these was the excuse that the Arabs—whose opposition the British intelligence service had itself organized— were opposed to Jewish immigration. Another rationale offered was that Palestine supposedly could not absorb large numbers of immigrants however qualified they might be. The latter argument was disproved in 1937 by Britain's own Royal Commission which stated:

> Far from reducing the absorptive capacity, immigration increases it. The more immigrants came in, the more work they created for local industries to meet their needs, especially in building; and more work meant more work for immigrants under the labor schedule. Unless, therefore, the Government adopted a more restrictive labor policy or unless there were some economic or financial setback, there seemed no reason why the rate of immigration should not go on climbing up and up.

But this was not to be the policy that was to come out of Cairo, the center of British intrigue operations for the Mideast. While hundreds, thousands, and finally millions were fleeing for their lives, the British held the number of official immigration visas granted to minimal figures. Furthermore, in 1939, when the need was the most crucial, the British announced officially that they were breaking their obligation to uphold the Balfour Declaration and the

Mandate. In their White Paper of May 17, 1939, they made it known that after the admission of altogether 75,000 Jews during the next five years, the gates of Palestine would be closed to Jews for good. Fifteen thousand a year—1,250 a month—might not sound very meager, but this would throw millions to the Nazis and would relegate the Jews in Palestine to a permanent minority. And even this was only theory. What their immigration policy in practice was, however, may be demonstrated by the number of immigration certificates available the day the Nazis moved into Vienna: for Austria's more than 200,000 Jews, there were 16 certificates. And much later when we were already moving hundreds of young Jews out of Austria "illegally" while their more fearful elders still waited for a legal way to get to Palestine, the much-awaited emissary of the Jewish Agency came from London with "many" official immigration permits. The man was Mr. Moshe Shapiro, later minister of religion for the State of Israel. But more than religious faith was needed to believe that the 60 certificates he brought with him would have come even close to touching the problem.

The Jews could not bring themselves to accept this closing of the gates of Palestine, and *we* flatly refused to. Thus, from the beginning of our rescue action, Britain had become our second front. To protect what she viewed as her colonial interests, she mobilized against us. She fought us with her intelligence and counterintelligence services, with her diplomatic apparatus, and by applying financial pressures. Moreover, she brought her armed forces to bear against us, on land, on the sea, and in the air, and she conducted this war against us as ruthlessly as any war could be conducted. It is little known in this regard that the first person killed in World War II by a British bullet was not one of Hitler's soldiers. Hans Schneider, a Jewish refugee on an overcrowded refugee ship, the *Tiger Hill*, was the first to die at the hands of the British on September 1, 1939, the first day of the war. As unbelievable as it must sound, in fact, there was even a British plan to deport helpless "captured" survivors of the Nazi persecutions to neighboring Arab countries, a convenient way of having them murdered without soiling British hands. This plan, entitled *Possible Methods of Combatting Illegal Jewish Immigration to Palestine* is contained in the British Foreign Office File 371/25241 register W 7514-38/48, p. 247. It is dated January 1940 and was registered

on May 3, 1940. The plan was not adopted for immediate implementation, and it was decided on March 22, 1940, that:

As regards the possibility of *removing immigrants into neighboring
Arab countries,* there is nothing that need be done about it at the
moment. All that is necessary is that *the possibility should be borne in
mind** should circumstances oblige us to adopt a course of despair.

Unlikely as it may seem, the third front we had to face during
the war was the Jewish establishment itself. Most of the Jewish
leaders held our youth and lack of experience against us. They
judged our undertakings as too risky. They did not realize that the
perfect is so often the enemy of the good, and the good might be the
enemy of the necessary. Furthermore, the official leaders of world
Jewry were so concerned with propriety and obedience to the law,
and especially British law, that they not only condemned our rescue
efforts but actively worked against them, as we shall fully document.

Many Jewish leaders were Anglophiles who found it impossible to stand up to the British, even though the British were blocking
the escape of those who fled Hitler's firing squads and gas ovens.
The man in the Jewish Agency responsible for coordinating the
rescue activities of the captive European Jews, Mr. Richard
Lichtheim, a German refugee himself, referred to us mockingly as
"the Jewish admirals" who tried to fool the all-powerful British
Navy.† Yet at the same time he could offer no positive solution
himself.

The fourth front we had to fight was that of the elements. In
the long history of human development man has become increasingly independent of them. The uprooted Jews, however, fleeing
without any possessions and caught in the cross fire of so many
factions, found themselves so far removed from much of what
civilization had achieved, that the forces of nature became for them
almost as threatening as the elements had been to primitive man.

*Author's italics.
†Letter to Mr. Henry Montor, the executive vice-president of the United Palestine Appeal in
New York, dated October 29, 1940.

They were at the mercy of storms and rough seas and easily fell prey to the effects of cold, hunger, and epidemics.

If the emigrés of our story overcame the obstacles of the four fronts mentioned above, they still had the conditions aboard ship to withstand. Never during the height of the Negro slave trade were any of the traders' ships so overcrowded nor so unseaworthy as those into which the Jews had to cram themselves during the later phases of the illegal immigration to Palestine. The slave traders had a capital investment to protect, but to most of the world, these Jewish lives represented little value then.

With most unequal means we fought this four-front war, and as may be expected in war, even on the victorious side, many of the combatants lost their lives. They did not perish only in the concentration and extermination camps where they had been sent by the whim of some disapproving SS official. They also fell before the bullets of the British. Their necks were broken on British gallows. They drowned or died of exposure. They were machine-gunned to death while struggling in the high seas, after abandoning their torpedoed refugee ship. Particularly tragic was the end met by 40 of our best young men in Rumania, half of them still in their teens. Having secured the departure of some 2,176 fleeing Jews, they watched the ship weigh anchor. Staying behind, they perished to the last man in a subsequent attempt to save another 800.

Thus ours is a story not only of blockade-running through minefields but also one of ruse and counterruse. It tells of a gray freighter which had one smokestack, flew the Panama flag, and had been spotted by the Royal Air Force as carrying "illegals" and which at nighttime slipped into a bay in one of the numerous Greek islands, to emerge the next morning, not gray but black now, with two smokestacks, and flying the flag of Portugal. It is most of all the story of the hunted who refused to be marched like cattle into concentration camps and gas chambers, but who, against the "law," took their lives into their own hands trying to reach the land they viewed as their natural home, promised to them by God, and confirmed as theirs by the international community through the League of Nations.

Although the British held in their hands the key to the gates of Palestine, we, too, had a key to that very land from which they barred us. Our key to Palestine, the one which finally prevailed, was not made of metal. It was not backed up by warships, guns, and military aircraft. It was a key to the hearts and the minds of the downtrodden and persecuted. For almost two thousand years, Jews had dreamed of returning to their biblical homeland from which they had been driven by the Romans. For almost two thousand years they continued to celebrate harvest festivals and other local events as if they were still living there. One of my unforgettable childhood experiences was seeing my father and other Jews on the ninth of Ab, the anniversary of the Roman destruction of Jerusalem, sitting on the floor lamenting and crying, ashes in their hair, bemoaning the fall of their capital—nineteen hundred years after the event. Three times daily for almost two thousand years Jews have been praying for the reestablishment of the Jewish state. For them, Palestine, all of it, on both sides of the Jordan River, remained the Holy Land, promised to them by God. They continued to call it the land of Israel, although, to mock the vanquished Jews, the Romans had made Caesarea instead of Jerusalem the capital, and, as though to taunt them further, had named the land of Israel "Palestine" after the Jews' perennial enemy, the Philistines.

Thus our key was the power of human dignity which survives even in the most wretched of souls. It was the Jews' desire to live in freedom in their own country. In all our ships, the starved, decrepit, almost dying people were singing and praying the words which are part of the Jewish national anthem, "to return to the land of our fathers." This anthem is called the *"Hatikvah,"* or "The Hope." And hope proved to be the spark which was probably more encouraging as such than the individual successes of landing and landing again. This persistent hope was proof that human pride and dignity are not easily killed and can be called to life even in the worst of times.

But we did much more than save some 40,000 Jews from Nazi lands. Millennia of living in fear behind ghetto walls had twisted the Jewish soul and robbed most Jews of the courage to stand up and fight for survival. Our determination not to let ourselves be marched to our deaths became a spark for the Jews in Palestine itself. Our four-front war against annihilation became an integral part of that revolutionary change which, in Palestine, transformed the ghetto Jew into an Israeli. By working and traveling with us, many a European Jew who had been just one of the *Kaffeehausjuden* in pre-World War II years was awakened to this spirit of fighting on, despite all hardships. We created a different self-image for those whom we helped to brave the persecutions, and they in turn contributed to the change in the Jewish self-image from which reemerged the State of Israel. Imbued with self-respect, Jews showed themselves to be capable not only in commerce and science but also when it came to fighting for their freedom.

The numerical results of the actions described in this book are also of historical importance. The 40,000 who entered Palestine illegally during the period of Nazi persecution were not to be the only "illegals." After the war, when no longer threatened by firing squads and gas chambers, Jews, still barred by the British, continued the illegal immigration into Palestine. Now tens of thousands from Nazi concentration camps and from displaced persons camps flooded the country "illegally." Ship after ship, using our proven methods, broke through the British blockade, the story of the S.S. *Exodus* becoming the most widely known of these postwar adventures. Then finally, in 1948, the declaration of independence of the State of Israel was proclaimed. According to official Jewish estimates, of the 400,000 immigrants who had reached the shores of what used to be Palestine, one-half had reached the country "illegally." Most of them were young people, and without their strength the Israeli war of survival against invaders from thirteen Arab countries might well have ended with just another massacre.

Thus those who in Nazi times opened up and traveled the "illegal" way to Palestine did much more than save their own skins. Each of those "illegals" was a rebel against doom, a pathfinder for the upcoming reestablishment of the Jewish State.

chapter 1

THE ACTION

The room was small. About ten by twelve. The young man stood with his back to the wall. Facing him, a man in black uniform. The skull and crossbones on the lapel of the SS uniform impressed upon the young Jew the thought that these insignia might well be the last thing he might ever see.

The man in the uniform before the Jew was not just an

ordinary SS slugger and killer. He was a highly intelligent, efficient, and ambitious young officer, a second lieutenant, by the name of Adolf Eichmann. Within the Nazi hierarchy, he was as yet unknown to the higher and even to the middle echelons. But the Jews of Vienna, who had by then been under his rule for only a few weeks, referred to him already as *Des Teufel's Stellvertreter*—the Devil's Deputy.

Standing with his black boots spread wide apart, he demanded that the Jew tell him the whereabouts of a man named Blumenfeld. The young man before him denied knowing anything: "I know no one by that name." At the second denial, Eichmann drew his gun.

"Watch out, Jew! You are bargaining for a second belly button." He repeated his question, but the young man could still tell him nothing.

"About face!" As the Jew turned around to face the wall, he could feel the gun barrel jam into the small of his back. On the bare white wall, projected against it by the light behind, he could see, vague in outline but huge in proportion, the shadow of the man in the uniform behind him. Enjoying the display of his soon-to-become-notorious morbid sense of humor, Eichmann sneered: "Maybe a second asshole, one somewhat higher up is what you need."

He did not yell—Eichmann's power lay not in the decibels of his voice but in the tone: "You have exactly five seconds," he hissed, "to tell me where Blumenfeld is hiding. When I reach five"—and at that he jammed the gun a little toward the left of the young man's spine—"I shall provide the nearest pigsty with a little kosher meat. Now, where is Blumenfeld? One—two—"

The young Jew tried desperately to speak out, to say anything. But though a lawyer and seldom at a loss for words, to his horror, he felt that his voice was frozen. He could not get out one syllable.

I know how that nightmarish paralysis felt, the incapacity to utter the saving words. I know—I am that man.

"Three," Eichmann announced impassively. Just as he was about to say "Four," I crashed through the spell and the words came out in a torrent: "I have political information, much more important for you than this Blumenfeld of whom I know nothing."

Again the gun jammed still harder into my ribs. "A Jewish trick!"

"I am not just trying to gain a few seconds more of life; I am trying to tell you of a large-scale political plan."

"Like what, dirty Jew?"

"I have the means to help you make Vienna rapidly *juden-rein*"—pure of Jews—this was the expression used by the Nazis for "cleansing" an area of all Jewish inhabitants.

Eichmann hesitated. Then: "Fast!" he snarled. "Your pipe-dream. Without any Jewish verbiage! Telegram style!"

When I started talking, as well as I could "in telegram style," he obviously became interested. Still in a threateningly low voice but with his military intonation, he barked again, "About face!" It was clear that Eichmann's allowing me to face him instead of the wall had not been done for my comfort. He apparently could not understand me well enough when I was talking with my back to him. He must be interested. He was.

I told him in truncated sentences not just of projected plans but of others already in motion. I quickly outlined the workings of our—as yet small-scale—smuggling operation of European Jews into Palestine and of the recent successful landings of Jews there. As I saw that he listened, I went on to describe our small group which called itself *Die Aktion*—The Action—and told him that we were poised now, as Jews had to leave anyhow, to expand our work to proportions that would enable Jews to leave in rapidly increasing numbers. Our Aktion could help Eichmann make Vienna *judenrein* in a span shorter than could have been anticipated by anyone.

His curiosity, even more important, Lieutenant Eichmann's ambition was aroused. He did listen to the Jew.

I pointed out that the Germans wanted to get all the Jews out of Austria, but that none of the other countries would take more than token numbers. I told him that our group could arrange to send large numbers of Jews into Palestine. We had proven this with three experimental vessels. Two ships in 1937 had gone with 16 people in the first and 68 in the second. A third one had disembarked 120 Jews by way of our "visaless immigration" plan just two months before, in January 1938.

"Anyone else from your group here?"

"Yes, three more."

"Who are they?"

"Erich Deutsch, Otto Seidmann, and Erich Wolf." As I saw that he seemed interested, I was about to say more, to go into detail, when Eichmann cut me short:

"Eingabe machen!" ("Written presentation to be submitted!")
he ordered.

I told him I would get the presentation to him within forty-eight hours. Obviously, the interrogation was over. As I was getting ready to leave, Eichmann said, again in his clipped voice, "None of you four leaves. You are all under arrest."

I was terrified, startled by this sudden shift from auspicious questions and the order to submit my plan in writing to not only being myself under Nazi arrest but to having three of our best co-workers dragged along as well. But when Erich Deutsch, whom everybody called by his nickname "Tury," Seidmann, Wolf, and I soon found ourselves together in an adjoining room, "awaiting disposition," we agreed that the arrest, though fraught with danger for us, quite likely showed the seriousness with which Eichmann regarded our plan. Arrest was probably the Nazi way of finding out more about us. As it turned out, we were right about his interest in Die Aktion, yet we underestimated the danger of having been arrested and come into the focus of Nazi attention.

During a good part of the time while we were waiting, before the SS men herded us into a van, I thought about what I would put into the written presentation, which I still hoped to submit. How much of the story which preceded the interrogation could I put in and still keep it concise?

There was so much to tell. How much of it could I let the Gestapo know?

The illegal migration of Jews to Palestine began in 1922, after Britain had placed restrictions on the influx of immigrants. But this movement had involved only a minute trickle of individuals or small groups who made their way across Europe and through Syria, living from hand to mouth and often being arrested at various points en route. The first successful larger-scale and sustained, organized illegal immigration into Palestine had started with our work in 1936.* Early in the fall of that year, when I was a lawyer in

---

*A single successful attempt to land Jews illegally in Palestine had been made in 1934. The S.S. *Velos,* a tiny ship, landed people, but when another attempt was made, the *Velos* was stopped and ordered to return. The British command was meekly obeyed. The intended immigrants were returned to Europe and the organizers, in concurrence with the Zionist Organization, decided to discontinue any such further action.

Vienna, a young man appeared in my law office with a letter from Dr. Wolfgang von Weisl. The latter was a well-known journalist and writer, the Mideast correspondent for the Ullstein papers, the largest German-language newspaper chain. Dr. von Weisl was a well-known Jewish patriot and a very colorful personality. He was a man of original thought and effective action. In his letter, von Weisl urged me to listen to this young man before me. Mr. Moses Krivoshein had a provocative plan. Von Weisl had sent him to speak to me because I had been active in the *Brit Trumpeldor*, also called the *Betar*, a militant Jewish youth group, and was at that time co-chairman of its adult arm, the Zionist Revisionists.

I found Krivoshein to be a fascinating person. Dark-haired, olive-skinned, stocky, and at best of average height, he was built like a tank. His movements were rapid yet controlled. His shining eyes assumed a nearly fanatic gleam as he started to expound upon his plan. Born in Russia and living at that time in Palestine, he was an adventurer and was full of ideas on how to help his fellow Jews. He told me that he had some connections with Greek smugglers. These were people who had "worked" with Americans during Prohibition, but with Prohibition days over, they were now looking for new activities. He had explained to these acquaintances that smuggling Jews out of Germany into Palestine would be the upcoming business for them. They had agreed and were ready to give the idea a try.

Krivoshein unfolded the following specifics of his plan: in a few months, there would be the Fiera di Tripoli, an international fair. Tripoli was then Italian, and for economic and political reasons, Mussolini tried very hard to make this fair the major tourist event in the Mediterranean. Krivoshein had already spoken with some of his Greek smuggler friends about supplying a small ship to sail from an Italian port to Tripoli with "tourists." The "tourists" would, in fact, be members of the Betar. On the way to Tripoli, these "tourists"—actually armed Betarim—would hijack the ship to Palestine. In the 1930s, unlike today, piracy on the high seas had not been heard of for many decades. He said that because the "pirates" were not Blackbeards but Jewish youngsters from middle-class families, people all over the world would ask "Why?" Thereby attention would be called to the injustice Britain was committing. As a result, there would be tremendous publicity given to the fact that Britain had all but closed the borders of Palestine, thus blocking the escape of Hitler's victims. Besides, such an action would be relatively danger-free as the captain would be in on the game. The captain could further exploit the situation to the fullest by the kind of SOS's he would send and by his statements. He would do everything within his power to attract the maximum amount of publicity.

My reaction was that if we had this connection with the smugglers, we should first try to get into Palestine clandestinely as many Jews as possible. When the British finally caught up with us, we could then let loose with the publicity barrage. Krivoshein, as much as he liked fanfare and publicity, agreed with me that the actual smuggling of immigrants in large numbers was more important for Jewish survival at this stage. I told him that I wanted to discuss the whole plan with our group, Die Aktion.

Die Aktion had been founded by a Viennese journalist, Paul Haller, a genius in political thinking. Haller's logic was crystal clear; his knowledge of history was both deep and encyclopedic. I called Haller and we met with his small group that same evening in a little restaurant. Over a glass of beer, we discussed Krivoshein's plan and my modification of it. My own enthusiasm set Haller on fire, and he in turn had us all so excited that he soon had to calm us down and channel our energies into action. Die Aktion decided to put itself entirely behind the idea. In the spirited atmosphere of that night's meeting, we even thought up a motto. It was one that was soon to inspire thousands of Jews who wanted to save themselves by escaping to Palestine but found the way barred by the British. Because we would act in spite of the overwhelming odds, we adopted the rallying cry AF AL PI!—"In Spite of Everything!"

To get the first ship out, we needed the people who would dare the initial attempt to break the British blockade—and we needed money. Initially we thought that the travelers themselves might be able to supply the low cost of the trip. However, almost no one from Austria, where most Jews belonged to the middle class, was ready to go. It was all too experimental and too hazy. Die Aktion, therefore, decided that the first participants would have to come from Eastern Europe, where Jews lived in extreme poverty and where, therefore, the desire to emigrate to Palestine was strengthened by actual urgent need.

We informed some Betar groups in Eastern Slovakia and Carpathorussia, the most eastern part of Czechoslovakia, of our plan. We also sent word to one or two Betar chapters in Poland.

Within a couple of weeks, people started to arrive in Vienna. Hardly any of them had a passport, and several had been arrested on the Austrian border for traveling without documents. We arranged with the very cooperative Vienna police department for those so arrested to be handed over to us in exchange for our promise to get them out of Austria within a fixed time.

Of course, none of the refugees had any money. But a wealthy Jewish businessman, Mr. Hans Perutz, provided the major part of the initial funds. The Vienna Jewish community, with the help of a radical assemblyman, Mr. Graubart, and the Jewish community's vice-president, Robert Stricker, arranged for some more money. Mr. Stricker knew of our plans in detail; the rest of the community did not—and did not want to know—any particulars. Officially, funds were provided in support of transients on their way to Palestine.

The next thing needed after getting the money was someplace where the emigrants could gather. Bertschi Kornmehl, a human dynamo who had belonged to the Aktion from its first days, and Iser Reifer and his wife Frieda, who had joined more recently, were put in charge of this task. They found an old dilapidated mansion, south of Vienna, where the immigrants could be temporarily housed. It was located in Kottingbrunn where the prospective "pirates" were gathered after arrival in Vienna from their villages and towns in Eastern Europe. To keep the whole undertaking as quiet as possible, never more than three were brought in together. Instructions in Jewish history, in militant Jewish philosophy, and in Hebrew were conducted at the Kottingbrunn "castle." In anticipation of the final battle against the British occupiers of Palestine, close order drill and the use of small weapons were also taught.

Meanwhile, Krivoshein had left for Greece to make definite arrangements there.

Early in 1937, our first trial balloon—or trial boat—was launched. Sixteen young men went by train to Athens and from there, under Krivoshein's leadership, on a moonless night as planned, the boat brought them to the coast of Palestine, near Haifa's electric power station. At that point, Krivoshein jumped into the ocean and swam ashore, while the boat anchored nearby in the darkness.

There had been no prior arrangements in Palestine. In the middle of the night, Krivoshein, soaking wet, knocked at the doors of the Jewish settlers in nearby houses and whispered, "We have escapees from Hitler! They are offshore! Come and help us!!"

The next day, we had a telegram from one of the trustees in the group, announcing their safe arrival in Haifa, and several days later there came postcards with pictures of Mount Carmel from almost every one of the participants. Krivoshein, and with him Die Aktion, had passed the test.

But such haphazard planning, the chance that one might find residents on the coastline right at the landing point who were able to help with hiding and dispersing the newcomers before the British discovered them, might be good enough for a boat of sixteen. For our large-scale design, however, definite arrangements and detailed preparations were imperative. Krivoshein, an excellent organizer, was fully aware of that need. After he had landed the sixteen, he contacted representatives of the Irgun Zvai Leumi to make arrangements for future landings. The Irgun, as it was generally called, was the self-defense arm in Palestine of the Zionist Revisionist group. Prior to leaving Palestine for his next venture, Krivoshein had agreed with the Irgun as to particulars of aid for future landings.

With the first boat a success, with future landings not left to mere chance anymore, we had no difficulty in organizing a second transport. In August 1937, 68 young people left Vienna with Krivoshein to be smuggled into Palestine. Of these there were only four Betarim from Vienna; the others were again from Eastern Europe. Although Hitler had by then repeatedly threatened Austria, the Jews there still did not feel the urgency to leave, nor did German Jews yet realize the danger of their position, a situation which would soon change dramatically.

After he had successfully smuggled the 68 of the second group into Palestine, Krivoshein announced that he had changed his name to a Hebrew one and wanted from now on to be known as Moshe Galili. In doing so, he preceded many others who later on changed their European, German-sounding names to Hebrew ones. This phenomenon occurred to such an extent that in order to find anyone in Israel today, it is jokingly said, one must look in *Who Was Who*.

Eleven weeks before the cataclysm engulfed Austrian and German Jewry, we succeeded in getting one more transport out and into Palestine. But still, most of the 120 in the group that left Vienna late in December 1937 were neither Austrian nor German Jews.

With the sword over their heads and ready to fall, they could not believe that their centuries of prosperous living in these countries were now coming to an end.

It all changed abruptly on Friday, March 11, 1938. For the Jews of Vienna it was the blackest Friday, the worst day ever. On that evening, I was with my friend Dr. David Bukspan at his parents' home to which I had been invited for the Sabbath meal as I often was. He, his parents, and I, together with all of Austria and much of the world, were waiting for Austrian Chancellor Schuschnigg's radio address. The chancellor had received an ultimatum from Hitler demanding his country's surrender. Many Austrians were outright Nazis, and the Nazi program of anti-Semitism appealed to many more. Austrian Jews therefore greatly feared Schuschnigg's answer to the threat of an invasion by the Nazi army.

When Schuschnigg concluded his radio speech, announcing his country's surrender with the words "God save Austria," a death sentence was handed down against the community of approximately 200,000 Austrian Jews.

Many hastened to the nearest taxi stand in an attempt to reach the railroad station. Most of them never made it. Jubilant, marauding crowds of Austrians stopped the taxis and pulled the Jews out. Of those who did make it to the station, and even onto a train, most were turned back at the border crossings because neighboring countries had immediately closed their gates to Jews, afraid that too many people without means of support would flood across and remain stuck there.

With the Nazi troops marching into Austria and goose-stepping through the streets of Vienna, came also the Gestapo. And with the Gestapo came Adolf Eichmann.

When the Nazis marched into Austria, Adolf Eichmann was just an Untersturmfuehrer, a second lieutenant, in the SS, but, cleverly, he had prepared himself to be a specialist in the Nazi movement. His specialty was Jews—and this is not a joke. Up to then, the final aim of anti-Semitism had been vague. It manifested itself mainly in hatred, general persecution, and a program of *Juden hinaus*—out with the Jews. The Nazis knew little about Jews. Their plans for the future of Jews, while virulent and brutal, were hazy. This gave Eichmann a chance. Eichmann, deciding early what his role in the expanding Nazi empire should be, intimately familiarized himself with Jewish history, Jewish sociological conditions, with names, groups, parties, currents and undercurrents in Zionism, with every aspect of Jewish existence. He possessed an amazing overall grasp of Jewish life. It was said that he even spoke Hebrew. Though relatively low in rank, he was put in charge of the *Entjudung* program, the "de-Judaization," of Austria. Adolf Eichmann certainly did use this chance to advance his career.

Until her union with Austria, Germany's "problem" with the Jews had been entirely different. In Germany, with its approximately 64,000,000 inhabitants, there were only about 560,000 Jews. In contrast to this, Austria, with its 6,000,000 inhabitants, was the home of more than 200,000 Jews. Even more relevant, German Jews were distributed all over the country, and many lived in smaller towns. But more than one-third of all Austrians lived in Vienna—which gave Vienna a dominant position in the country's affairs—and almost all Austrian Jews lived in Vienna. Artistic and cultural life, journalism, and the professions were strongly influenced by Jewish intellectuals. In Austria, the "Jewish problem" for the Nazis, therefore, was much more extensive than in Germany.

But Eichmann proved a match for it all.

He lost no time. Immediately following the Germans' march into Austria, he began his measures for "the solution of the Jewish problem." One of his first orders was to command all Jewish leaders to assemble in the offices of the Austrian Zionist Organization. Approximately 20 of us went there to be questioned by Eichmann.

Dr. von Weisl, the president of the Zionist Revisionist Organization, was not among us. By clever planning, he had succeeded in escaping on the very first night. Most Jews who wanted to flee tried to make the nearby Czechoslovakian or Hungarian borders, which they found closed to escapees. As the German columns were marching into Austria, von Weisl and his family passed by them on the train in the opposite direction—straight into the lion's den. Because there was no longer a border between Austria and Germany, he had no problem entering that country. Then he traveled straight on through Germany to France where he entered easily, as the French did not yet have Austrian Jews besieging their border. One could still enter France with an Austrian passport and without a visa. Within a day after Hitler's march into Austria, Dr. von Weisl was in Paris, safe, at least for the time being.

Dr. Edmund Schechter, another leader in the Zionist Revisionist Organization, had escaped by using similar tactics. He crossed into Italy—much farther from Vienna than the Hungarian or Czech borders—shortly before a large flow of refugees caused the Italians to adopt the same "humane" manners which Austria's other neighbors displayed for the Jews.

Vienna's Jewish leaders had been made to understand that unless they appeared before Eichmann, the entire organization's membership would be made responsible for their disobeying the order to come and assemble. The Germans had immediately gone to the offices of Jewish organizations, had closed them, and had confiscated membership lists containing names and addresses. Therefore, as previously arranged with Dr. von Weisl and Dr. Schechter, Erich Deutsch and I went as representatives of the Zionist Revisionist Organization to this meeting with Eichmann. Otto Seidmann and Erich Wolf represented our youth branch, the Betar. We recognized the danger in the summons, but we viewed it also as possibly providing us with the opportunity to bring up the subject of emigration to Palestine and of trying to obtain permission to proceed even under Nazi rule—with our *AF AL PI* undertaking.

As the most militant Jewish group, the Zionist Revisionists were especially endangered because they had organized and led the Austrian boycott of German goods, an activity that the Germans considered particularly perfidious. If a citizen of Germany—or Austria, which the Nazis had always considered "theirs"—had engaged in this boycott, this would be viewed as "treason."

Of our group, I was the first to be called into the room where Eichmann was holding his interrogations. After the first questions, I become convinced that he was unaware that we were the ones who had organized the boycott of German goods. Instead of probing into the boycott as I had expected, he then focused on the whereabouts of the mysterious Mr. Blumenfeld. I had no idea then who Blumenfeld was, but I learned later that he had been a member of the Betar, and one of the main organizers of the boycott of German goods in the Baltic countries. Eichmann erroneously thought he had trapped this man in Austria. Perceptive and clever hunter that he was, Eichmann must have finally realized that I truly did not know where Blumenfeld was or anything about him. He thus decided to allow his interest to be diverted by my description of our plans for illegal immigration, but his interest did not prevent the four of us from being arrested.

As we were getting into the paddy wagon after a wait of about two hours, one of the SS men who were coming along ordered the driver to take us all to Biberstrasse, to the offices of the Revisionist party. Eichmann arrived shortly thereafter and began right away to conduct his personal search. It seems we had underestimated the Nazis. We had thought that they had not suspected us of having organized the boycott of German goods sold in Austria, but we had been mistaken. This boycott had actually been conducted from the very offices which were now being searched, and large quantities of pamphlets referring to that boycott had been stored there. Part of the material had been secretly supplied by the Austrian Commerce Department, which, prior to the German march into Austria, had tried to divert part of the German foreign trade to Austria. This connection with the just overthrown government made our action particularly "treasonable" and finding out about any of these activities of ours could have only one result for us.

Tury Deutsch had been the party's secretary, and as soon as he had learned that the Germans were marching in, he went to our office to see whether he could get rid of the boycott material. To carry it all away would have aroused the suspicion of some unfriendly neighbors. The burning of so much paper was impossible for the same reason. Von Weisl, in his book *The Jews of Austria*, describes how Tury remedied the situation:

> The secretary, T. Deutsch, therefore not finding a better solution, had all compromising printed material put on the stairway landing, and there it was lying openly. According to the pattern of the best crime thrillers, Eichmann searched everywhere, only the parcels lying on the staircase did not earn his attention. As nothing incriminating had been found, the arrested ones were freed; a small miracle saved them.*

Eichmann, who had felt this mission was important enough to handle it personally, had indeed made a thorough search of our office, but due to Tury's ingeniousness, *Des Teufel's Stellvertreter* had missed the most conspicuous and most damaging evidence against us.

After we were all set free, I returned to my office and immediately started composing the memorandum to Eichmann which I hoped would persuade him to grant us permission to organize large-

*Wolfgang von Weisl, *The Jews of Austria*, J. Fraenkel, ed., London: Mitchell, 1967, p. 169.

scale "visaless" emigration to Palestine. By using the term *visaless,* we avoided the word *illegal,* and in this way hoped to make the whole idea more palatable. All day and late into the night, I worked on the short presentation on which I knew so much depended. The next morning I showed my draft to Erich Wolf, who was an exceedingly bright law student at the time and is today a respected judge in Israel. One or two more friends were consulted; a few minor changes were made, and forty-three hours after Eichmann had told me to present my suggestions in writing, I was on my way with memo in hand to Vienna's most dreaded building. The Hotel Metropol had been taken over by the Gestapo to become its headquarters. We had decided that the document should be delivered in person to enable me to answer questions, if any, right away. In addition, we feared that if we mailed our presentation, it would not only be delayed by the mail delivery but might also end up displaced on someone's desk. While I went to the Metropol, Paul Haller and Tury Deutsch waited in a nearby coffeehouse for me. They were worried about whether or not I would get out of the building alive and if I did—they were anxious to find out how the memo had been received.

At the Metropol, I had no difficulty in getting into Eichmann's office. There I saw a Mr. Kuchmann, Eichmann's right-hand man who was later to become one of the most notorious and wanted war criminals in his own right. He read the memo while he had me stand at attention in front of him. "You can go" was his only reaction upon reading it, but I had no doubts that he would show the memo to Eichmann. Though we had worded it cautiously and referred to "visaless" emigration, we had to make it clear that we were talking about smuggling Jews into Palestine. The power of the message, we hoped, was in the inherent appeal to an SS officer's desire to excel before his Fuehrer by making the city for whose *Judenproblem* he was responsible, the first area to be *judenrein.*

The days that followed were filled with the tension of our almost unendurable impatience as we waited for an answer to our request. Daily new arrests were reported. Because the Zionist Revisionists and the Betar were known as action groups and because word had spread quickly in the existing emergency that we had organized illegal transports to Palestine before, Jews from all walks of life began to besiege us with letters, phone calls, and visits, pleading with us to help them get out. In my office I tried to keep the telephone lines open for the vital call from Eichmann's office. Every time the phone rang, we all jumped for the receiver. The postman's delivery had become the most important event of every day for us. But there was no word from Eichmann.

Nevertheless, we started preparing. We were aware that however large the program might become, we would be able to save only a part of Vienna's Jewish population. For this reason, Die Aktion formally adopted a resolution to take only young people. It stated: "For the upcoming battle for the liberation of our Jewish homeland from the British colonial yoke, the first ones to be saved must be Jews able and willing to carry arms." This was a hard decision. Generally it meant that we were taking teenagers and people in their twenties and early thirties. As a rule, this involved the separation of families, but in most cases we stuck to it. Holding to this decision, however, burdened the conscience to the breaking point when one had to say "no."

In proceeding with our plans, we told the young people in our own organization, the members of the Betar, to get passports. My law office, on the fashionable #14 Stubenring, was turned now solely into a headquarters for illegal immigration. We never called it "illegal immigration," however, because for us no Jew could immigrate into his homeland any other way than legally. We referred to it as "free immigration."

One day Dr. I. H. Koerner, an assemblyman in Vienna's Jewish community, and I happened to be waiting in the anteroom of the community's president when Eichmann and two of his underlings suddenly burst in. Brushing past us, Eichmann spotted Dr. Koerner and me and remarked, *"Aus diesen Transporten wird nichts. Wir brauchen keine Verbrecherzentrale in Palaestina, die Juden werden atomisiert."* ("These transports are out. We don't need a center for criminals in Palestine. The Jews will be atomized.") With this, he barged into the office of the president, of course without knocking.

We knew now where we stood with Eichmann. We also knew how dangerous an enemy he was, that he really understood what Zionism was. Generally, the slogan of European anti-Semites had been, "Out with the Jews. Pack them up for Palestine" or "One way to Palestine." Eichmann was not just emotionally anti-Semitic; he was a cool, calculating planner of a "solution to the Jewish problem." He understood that the more Jews there were in Palestine, the more surviving power there would be for Jewry. His comment on "atomizing" could not have implied what its meaning would be after the invention of the atomic bomb; we interpreted his words as meaning the pulverization of Jewry by chasing the Jews and scattering them in all directions.

We were quite downhearted after this. But that same afternoon while walking through the streets of Vienna, so lovely in the spring, I regained perspective and courage. It was Galili who changed my despair into defiance. *AF AL PI!* When I told him of Eichmann's statement, Galili immediately retorted that history had put us into a position which we had to live up to, whether we succeeded or failed.

I do not recall whether it was his suggestion or mine, but in blissful ignorance of the way the Nazis operated, we decided during this talk to go to Berlin to complain to Eichmann's superiors that he was standing in the way of a major evacuation scheme for Jews. We would go over his head and try in Berlin to obtain the permission that Eichmann had refused us.

Galili and I were on the train to Berlin the next day. Our compartment was crowded with six other passengers. Galili, who looked "foreign" with his deep tan, his burning black eyes, heavy jawbones, and round head, had a small British flag on his lapel. He was not actually traveling under a "false" flag, as he possessed a British passport. However, on it was printed "Palestine" to indicate that he was not a "real" Britisher but just a colonial. In those days, most foreigners in Nazi Germany used to wear such little flags. Such a pin, and particularly a British one, provided protection against harassment. On the other hand, many Austrians, even more than Germans, recognized a Jew when they saw one. I, in this odd Britisher's company, with neither of us participating in the discussions of the other passengers about the great future of Austria, created an obvious discomfort to them.

There was no checkpoint on what had been the border between Austria and Germany, but several times during the trip, patrols of stormtroopers checked travelers' identity papers. Each time I was amused to observe the respect with which they reached for Galili's brown British passport—and the astonishment they showed when they read beneath the words "United Kingdom" the word "Palestine." They were very primitive fellows. Not only did they not know that Palestine was a British mandate, it very likely did not occur to them that Palestine actually existed: it was more a joke to harass Jews with!

Because I was traveling in a "Britisher's" shadow, the first such control asked me no questions. The second one asked me if I was Jewish. I said yes, and I was traveling to Berlin to arrange for the mass emigration of Jews from Austria. This made me a potato too hot for these little guys to touch. The experience, though, was a valuable one. It strengthened Galili's and my decision to apply this principle in Berlin.

In Berlin, we headed for the home of Dr. Kareski, who was the chairman of the Zionist Revisionists in Germany. We intended to ask him for advice on how to proceed. The Nazis had been in power for five years by then. The persecution of Jews from 1933 to 1938 had not been as intense as the persecution that started in Austria immediately after the annexation. Yet, riding in the bus to Dr. Kareski's home, we saw for the first time, in parks and along the boulevards, benches on which were written the words *Nicht fuer Juden.* ("Not for Jews.")*

We reached Dr. Kareski's house in the early evening. A huge, intelligent man, Dr. Kareski possessed penetrating political understanding and realized the importance of our mission. That so many more Jews had come under Germany's rule created not only dangers but also possibilities. But he made it clear to us that if we thought we could go over Eichmann's head, we were totally ignorant of how the Nazi hierarchy operated. "You will never leave the Gestapo building alive if you try to do that," he told us.

We stayed overnight in Dr. Kareski's house and talked into the small hours of the morning. During our night-long conversation, another point evolved. Galili said that his Greek smugglers would not accept German marks. They would have to be paid in a "free" currency, either in dollars or British pounds. And foreign currency was *the* commodity of which Germany was short. Whatever of it Germany had was needed to increase its arsenal. How would we pay our smugglers? Even if some Jews had foreign currency, they could not admit it because possession of foreign money was a major crime.

Galili and I decided to try to obtain permission from the

*Within two or three days after the *Anschluss*, or "incorporation," many Viennese stores had signs in their windows, "No entry to dogs and Jews," or, "Jews and dogs not desired." I was very upset to see these signs in the window of the very restaurant in which I used to take my supper two or three nights a week, and in which many of our Jewish meetings had taken place.

German Ministry of Finance to change German marks into foreign currency for the purpose of paying the transportation. Although Kareski thought that this incredible scheme would prove an impossible task, he agreed that, as we were in Berlin and were ready to dare it, we should do so.

As we were short of money, we took a bus to the vicinity of the German Ministry of Finance, and then we took a taxi in order to drive up in style. At the gate stood an armed guard. We asked him on which floor Dr. Pachtmann had his office. Actually, Dr. Pachtmann was a fraternity brother of mine, a Jewish lawyer in Vienna, who of course had no office in this building. The guard told us to go inside the ministry to the information window.

Instead, we passed the information window and went into the elevator as if we belonged there. We got out on one of the floors, looked at the name signs that indicated rank and title, and knocked at the door of a man who seemed to be important. "Come in," he called. We entered and saw a jovial man in his forties sitting behind a desk. He invited us to sit down and asked how he could help us.

I told him that we had been sent from Vienna in regard to the task of making Vienna *judenrein.* He was enthusiastic because the newsreels and the newspapers had played up Hitler's entry into Vienna and the popular reaction of the jubilant masses there. Here were two people who had really experienced it!

When we made it clear that we were Jews who had come for the purpose of working out the details of mass emigration, his enthusiasm dampened. He became visibly less friendly, but he was still polite and certainly very alert to what we had to say. After all, to make Vienna *judenrein* was a most important task. We told him that "we were sent" to work out the financial details. He apparently assumed, and this was our intention, that we had been sent by the German authorities—but we never really claimed this.

He listened patiently to all we had to say, then told us that although this matter was very important and interesting, he had nothing to do with it; we had been sent to his office by error. We apologized and asked to whom we should talk. Our jovial friend looked into a small directory on his table and gave us a name and a room number on another floor.

Now we were one up! We already had an "in" to refer to. We went to this other man, told him that we had been sent from

Vienna, that we had already spoken with Mr. "A," who had sent us to him, and repeated our whole story. He listened to it and told us that the right man was in another building.

Now we were two up! We went to the third man—who was the right one. And he was a big wheel! We told him that we had been "sent from Vienna" and that we had already spoken with Messrs. "A" and "B." We explained to him—as if this were the thinking of the German authorities in Vienna—that these transports would amount to a double score for Germany: (1) The illegal transports would get rid of the Jews, and (2) due to the increased number of immigrants there would be trouble for the British in Palestine because (a) these Jews were a militant element (therefore twice as undesirable in Germany), and (b) the Arabs would charge the British with not having prevented the immigration.

He asked a few relevant questions, including, of course, how much money would be needed for each person. We told him, correctly, that we had to pay the Greek smugglers 12 British pounds for each person. At that time, 12 pounds was equivalent to $60 or 240 marks. We said that we had 5,000 people ready to go, and after the first 5,000 we would return to discuss further plans with him. Without committing himself in any way, he told us to give him the request in writing.

Just across from the ministry building was a *Schreibstube,* a secretarial-dictation office. That I was a lawyer and used to dictating briefs and other presentations came in quite handy: I dictated the request to a secretary who typed as I spoke. I highlighted the points that seemed to have impressed the last man we saw. On the afternoon of the same day on which we had, with much uncertainty, passed the guard at the gate, we handed to the appropriate high-ranking German official a request to smuggle Jews from Nazi-occupied Austria into British-held Palestine.

Within two days—I recall it was a Thursday—we had in our hands a document from the German Ministry of Finance advising the Austrian National Bank in Vienna to permit us to exchange German marks into British pounds at the official exchange rate of 20 marks to a pound for the purpose of the emigration of Jews from Vienna. The black market rate was eleven times as high. The permission was for 2,000 Jews—24,000 pounds or $120,000—and not for 5,000 Jews as we had grandly requested.

Little did any of these Germans know, however, that at that time we were far from being ready to ship any Jews at all, let alone 2,000!

Back in Vienna, we held another meeting of Die Aktion. Some of the dust that had been stirred up with the coming of the Nazis had settled. A number of Jews had left Austria individually. It was permissible to leave—individually—if you had a valid passport and an exit permit. Passports and exit permits were refused only to prominent persons or to those who were well-to-do. These people were blackmailed before they were allowed to leave. In some cases their exit permits were denied unless relatives from abroad paid a ransom, which was usually called an "exit tax," the same formulation the Soviets use nowadays.

One could not get an exit permit at all if one owed taxes. My aunt, Mrs. Irma Kohn, the widow of the uncle who had first inspired me to strive toward attempting to make Jews change themselves from frightened ghetto-creatures into proud men, owned a movie theater in Vienna. On the day after the Nazis took over, the usher boy told her that he was a Nazi, that he was taking over the theater, and she should get the hell out. She did. The boy did not keep the movie long; a more influential Nazi took it from him. This new "owner" took in all the receipts but did not pay any of his bills—not royalties to the film company, not rent to the landlord, and not taxes to the government. Because my aunt was still the formal owner, she was required to pay it all. She could not—and was therefore refused an exit visa for owing money to Aryans.

Fortunately, our young people in the Betar, in their teens and early twenties, did not owe taxes or anything else. We spread the word that each of our youngsters should try to obtain a passport and an exit visa. Most of them did. They then brought these documents to my office where they soon accumulated. We wanted to keep all passports so we could know for certain that each person had one and to make sure that his passport would not be stolen or lost.

At the same time, Tury Deutsch and I went to the Austrian National Bank. On the strength of the certificate from Berlin, we exchanged for British currency the marks obtained from those who had registered with us for emigration to Palestine. We purchased only 2,000 pounds ($10,000) then, the amount that Galili told us he needed to get a ship to wait for us in Athens for smuggling our passengers into Palestine. This was a down payment, the rest to be paid on embarkation, depending on the number of passengers. With these 2,000 pounds, Galili now left for Athens to procure the ship.

More and more passports were brought into my office as days went by. The number of telephone calls received from people begging to be taken along multiplied, and our phones rang day and night. Well-to-do Jews came to the office and offered money and jewelry if we would take them along. But we continued to adhere to our policy of young potential combatants only.

We still had no word from Galili, and the mailman's visit again became for us the most important event of each day. As no news came, we all became frightened. We did not know Galili well and had given him what was then a fortune—2,000 pounds. If he did not come back, we would be declared criminals for having cheated the German government out of foreign currency. Not only would we be tortured to death, but everyone in any way connected with us would certainly be killed. We became increasingly anxious.

Daily, scores of people came to my office to inquire when we would be leaving or to plead to be put on our list. All this activity created much coming and going at our headquarters. Because so many young people were hanging around in the corridors and in groups on the street outside—in spite of all our warnings not to do this—one afternoon the police raided the place. A "friendly" neighbor had reported that a Communist conspiracy was in the making, as Jews were holding "secret assemblies."

At first we thought that the illegal immigration movement was finished, that Eichmann had found out about our operation and had acted to end it. But I suddenly realized that this was the *federal* police—Austrian, not German. Indignantly, I told them that, as arranged with Berlin authorities, we were organizing the mass emigration of Jews, and they had better not interfere with it! I supported my statement with documentary evidence. The permission of the German Ministry of Finance, with its big letterhead, rubber stamp, and large signatures with "Heil Hitler" (this phrase was used in place of "Sincerely yours") was as authentic as it looked. The Austrian police thought that they had blundered and withdrew. One more danger point had been overcome.

Early in the morning on the last Friday in May—about a week after this first raid—one of Tury Deutsch's neighbors called me and told me that Tury had just been arrested and had been led away. I immediately left my home, which was in the same building as my office. I called two people from a telephone booth who, according to a prearranged plan, were to call others to warn them to leave their homes—yet be available at certain telephone numbers in certain coffeehouses.

The coffeehouse was central in Viennese life. Going from one to the other and using the public phones there, I soon found out that numerous Jews had already been arrested and that at that very hour still more were being hauled away. Those arrested included persons who had been active in Jewish life as well as names which were completely unknown to us.

Several times I called my office. Around noon, my secretary told me that two men who said they were policemen, but who wore civilian clothes, had been there and had asked for me, leaving a message that when I returned I should come to the police station "to supply some information." It had not been immediately evident that this was a generalized Jew hunt. But slowly the picture emerged confirming it. Most likely, I thought, the police had come to my office to arrest me as they would arrest any other Jew.

But there was a possibility that the visit had something to do with the transports. If this were the case and I did not go to the police station, I might endanger the emigration. By telephone, I called a meeting of several of those who had worked with us on the illegal immigration. We met in the house of Harry Schneidman, now Mr. Harry Shadmon, owner of a hotel in Herzlia Beach, Israel. Paul Haller, Bertschie Kornmehl, Paul Lustig,* Otto Seidmann, Israel Waksberg, and Erich Wolf took part.

We all thought that the police had most likely come to arrest me just like anyone else. Hundreds of Jews had by then been hauled to the overcrowded jails. But we also thought that it was possible that Galili had been stopped on the border as he was coming back with the fervently looked-for information regarding the ship, and that he had referred to me, and to the all-important Berlin document I possessed. If I did not go to the police station, it was possible that the whole action might be endangered. And so for this reason, I decided to go to the police anyhow. I did. And I was promptly arrested.

---

*After the war, Lustig became the treasurer of Hebrew University.

Like offices of minor police officials all over the world, the room to which I was led for questioning was bare and impersonal. Four identical tables stood equidistant from one another and from the wall. Each had a chair beside it. Two of these chairs were occupied by Jews being questioned; a third man was just being led away. The second chair on the left was waiting for me.

The brute whom I expected to interrogate me turned out to be just an overworked toiler. The worries of inadequate pay and a joyless life were expressed in his face and posture, his weary gestures, his monotonous tone. Like others in the room, he spoke in a low voice. He read the questions from a printed questionnaire as I sat down. He did not bother to look up from the paper in his hand. This made me feel better than I had felt since the moment I had learned that Tury Deutsch had been arrested, early that morning. Now I knew that my arrest was not due to a Gestapo sweep against our undertaking.

"Did you, during the last five years, have an affair with an Aryan girl?"

"Do you belong to a Free Mason's Lodge?"

"Are you ready to state under oath that you never did anything of possible harm to the German people?"

After I had answered all these absurd questions satisfactorily, there came the finale to this weird charade.

"Why were you arrested?"

The routine queries ended, I was shoved into a cell barely more than eight by ten feet, into which 15 persons had already been crammed. It seemed impossible, but after me, two more men were pushed in. I knew one of my cellmates, a Dr. Sperber, one of the top criminal lawyers of Austria. Normally anyone in jail would have been happy to have Dr. Sperber's advice available. One would have gladly paid a fortune for it. But here he was, just one of us, a persecuted, frightened Jew. Where there is no law, there are no lawyers.

From time to time a uniform with a swastika armband opened the door. With a sharp twang in its voice, it read a name or two. Those called up followed the uniform and did not return. What became of them? When would my own name be called?

In here, one was no longer a lawyer, regularly mentioned in the news; one was not now a journalist, a worried tailor, a little salesman, or a teacher. One was just a Jew, the grandchild of those who for millennia found themselves facing persecution, with the

world, if not actually applauding, certainly not stopping the perse-
cutors. Doubtlessly there must have been some among us who were
not strong, who in daily life were rather weak personalities. But
now no one wailed, nobody cried out. One waited for his name to be
called and then, without complaint, sometimes even with a little
joke, one followed the uniform, just as the fathers did.

Now another police officer opened the door. He called Dr.
Sperber and told him that he could go home. One of his clients, for
whom he had gained acquittal, was a Nazi and this Nazi had
obtained his former lawyer's release. But there were always other
high-ranking Nazis who could not be moved to help, even by
substantial pecuniary assistance. Little did Dr. Sperber know that
when he left our rank cell, he would walk in freedom for just a few
days. He would soon be rearrested and murdered in Dachau.*

Finally a small, mousy-looking man was called; then I heard
my name. We walked after the policeman to a green paddy wagon
parked outside. I was still dazzled by the sunlight, but as I waited in
front of the paddy wagon, I recognized Benno Lie, the king of the
Vienna entertainment world. Benno Lie was the man who had arranged for the entire cultural exchange program, tours for the Vienna Philharmonic Orchestra and other artists abroad, and those of
famous music halls. He was a little on the heavy side and had trouble stepping up and through the paddy wagon's narrow door, but
he, too, appeared calm, and nothing in his behavior indicated that
he had lost any of his stateliness.

As I was watching him a heavy boot kicked my behind.

"Hurry up, Jew!"

But I could not squeeze into the crowded vehicle. A second
kick and I could. The door was slammed shut behind me. We were
so packed in that even at sharp turns we did not fall or even sway.

The van had no window. Where would this trip lead? It took a
long time. . . . A man said, "I think they are taking us outside of
town, to the Vienna Woods." Even at that, no one lamented, no one
sighed.

Finally we halted. We could not have been out of the city yet.
A man called "Karajangasse." We all knew this means that we were
being delivered to the Gestapo makeshift prison. It had been con-

---

*Rumor had it that one or the other district attorney whom Sperber had beaten at the law
courts was behind his killing.

verted from an ancient school in the heart of Vienna's Jewish district to cope with the many arrests. No Gestapo prison can be good, but still, it is better to be brought here than to be dumped somewhere in the woods—one knows what the woods mean: a few salvos with submachine guns and the paddy wagon returns empty to fetch the next load. Everybody felt relieved. We were being committed to a Gestapo *Notgefaengnis*—emergency prison. For the moment we were "safe."

With 31 others, I found myself locked up on the top floor in what only a few weeks ago was a classroom. Although there were no furnishings whatsoever, the room appeared comfortable compared to the cell in the police station. Large windows admitted light, and while we had to sit or lie on the bare floor to rest, we were not crowded. All this conveyed, after the previous experience, a feeling of relative freedom, the more so as the Nazis had not bothered to put bars on the windows ... if a Jew wanted to jump down from so high up, the pleasure was his. From the floor below, we learned, one had already made use of the privilege.

The guards in this building were Viennese policemen. Though each of them now wore the swastika armband, some of the officers were still quite human. With many the dehumanization process takes time. And the Viennese police could not yet master the new, mammoth task of mass arrests. Prussian organization was still absent, and although the Karajangasse prison was run under Gestapo supervision, confusion still reigned.

I looked down from the top floor window into the school yard. Groups of prisoners were there for cleaning work, but now they had finished and were standing around in clusters, some pretending to be busy. Among those in the yard I noticed Erich Deutsch. In the general confusion I shouted "Tury!"

"Large general arrest action," he shouted back, wanting to calm my fears about our project, though I already knew this. He gestured that I should try to get downstairs; he wanted to talk to me right away.

Only when I was already away from the window and others were standing there shouting messages, did I remember that I did, of course, know what Tury wanted to talk about. It was about the money. This question was bound to be foremost on his mind and had, for most valid reasons, to worry him badly.

What had happened to the money was this: all the cash we had collected from the people who were registered with us had been handed to Tury, who was to hide it in his apartment. We did not dare keep it in my office which, with Eichmann against us, might have been raided at any moment. Even if on the strength of the Berlin currency authorization we should have finally been released, the large amount of money could have just disappeared during the mass arrest accompanying such a raid. We were responsible for this money and would never have been able to replace it. Although we had been accepting money only after an individual had his passport stamped with an exit permit, we had already collected some 60,000 marks, then equivalent to $15,000.

What Tury did not know was that right after his arrest at dawn on Friday, Aktion members had decided that we had to find out whether the arresting officer had or had not confiscated this money. If it had been confiscated, was it done "officially" and recorded, or had the huge amount found its way into the pockets of the raiding party?

Because we had anticipated a possible sudden imprisonment from the beginning, we had asked Tury well before his arrest where he was keeping the money, and he had told us that part was hidden in a little hole in the wall of his living room. This hole could be reached through a large crack in the window frame. A smaller part of the money was hidden in the silk shade of the lamp in his bedroom. Unless the police had searched the house at the time of Tury's arrest, the money was probably safe from the authorities. They were too busy now with their mass arrests to return for a search of each apartment. But there was still danger from one of the ever-alert neighbors. Frequently, after a Jew had been arrested the neighbors broke into his home and "searched" it on their own initiative, helping themselves to whatever they liked.

With Tury already arrested, and we still free to save the money, I knew that we had to act fast, but how could we get into the apartment? Tury was subletting the apartment from a woman who had the only other key to it. We could not break in, for anything unusual might cause a neighbor to call the police. We immediately contacted Dr. Schij. He was one of the Aktion's devoted supporters, fully committed to the idea of helping in the rescue work but too busy as a physician in the Jewish Community Hospital to take an active part in organizing the transports. His hospital had been on twenty-four-hour alert ever since the Anschluss, because of the many suicides and suicide attempts, and because of the numerous Jews brought into the emergency room after beatings. As Dr. Schij was not known to be an Aktion supporter, we hastened to enlist his help now. With him and Otto Seidmann, the leader of the Austrian Betar, I worked out the following plan.

In case the money had been found by the police, they would most likely have left a man behind to arrest anyone coming to visit this person who had hidden such an exorbitant fund. If Tury's arrest had been routine, just part of the mass raids against Vienna's Jews, possession of such a sum would be even less understandable, especially by a person living in such a modest apartment as Tury's. But if, on the other hand, the arrest had not been routine, leaving behind a police official was even more likely, whether or not the money had been found, for they would surely be looking for others connected with our undertaking. Therefore, Dr. Schij, a physician, and unconnected with Aktion, would go up first, and if the place was staked out, he would just continue walking on to the next floor above, or, depending on the situation, he could claim that he had come to visit Tury on a house call. If Dr. Schij did not see police outside Tury's door, he was to signal me. I would come and ask the woman from whom Tury was subletting the apartment to give me the key. She knew me to be one of Tury's closest friends, but she did not know Dr. Schij. If there were no police, I would have no difficulty obtaining that key.

Racing against time, Dr. Schij and I headed for Tury's. We almost collided with one of our co-workers who told us that he too was to be arrested that morning but had been warned by his concierge, and while the arresting officers were busy on the floor below his place, he made it out of there clad only in his pajamas and an overcoat. He had rushed to his relatives for clothing and was told that another young man who had been working on our rescue action had been arrested. Certainly not encouraging news.

With very mixed feelings we hurried on our way to Tury's. Our pockets were full of "emergency articles"—a second pair of underwear, a toothbrush, a bar of soap. Anyone who anticipated possible arrest carried such articles at all times, for it was known from the few letters smuggled to the outside that people arrested in the streets were not issued these items in Nazi prisons.

Approximately 1,500 feet from Tury's apartment, we separated, I following Dr. Schij by a few paces. In my arms I carried a large briefcase in which we hoped to put the money—if it was still there. Tury's apartment was on the "Donnaukanal"—the Danube estuary, which circled the Jewish quarters. As inconspicuously as possible, I sat down on the grass of the canal bank to wait for Dr. Schij's signal. Several minutes later, it came.

As I had expected, the landlady gave me the key with no trouble. Dr. Schij and I entered Tury's apartment and locked the door. We were both shaking as Dr. Schij reached for the lampshade. The money was there! Now to the hole in the wall. We barely touched the window frame, and it fell apart. But the money was there in the crack! If Tury's arresting officers had just leaned against the window, all would have been lost! We grabbed the money, stuffed it into the briefcase, locked the door behind us, and walked sedately to the landlady's to return the key. Hailing a taxi, we rode directly to a Jewish lawyer in whose safe we felt the money would be relatively secure.

All this I recalled now when imprisoned myself, and I realized how Tury must be worrying about that money. I went back to the window to reassure him that all of it was safe, but he was already gone from the yard.

Suddenly a policeman opened the door to the room and asked for volunteers for kitchen work. I was one of those who stepped forward. The kitchen was two floors below, nearer to Tury. Prisoners working in the kitchen were scooping some kind of soup from huge kettles into bowls. I joined them, and while we worked, we ate some of this soup ourselves. It did not taste bad, probably because I had eaten nothing since a quick breakfast at about six that morning. All the while I was anxious to get downstairs to Tury. He had been in here longer than I and might have something important to tell me, possibly in connection with some upcoming interrogation.

As I stood near the kitchen door, three prisoners passed me carrying a jumbo straw mattress. Taking a large step toward this group, I joined it. Our group entered a smaller room that seemed to have been some kind of office. A policeman there checked the mattress. I was kicked again, this time hard on the shin. The mattress was not full enough. We had to go and put more straw in it. My shin hurt badly. I started to regret that I had joined this group. I wanted to explain that I was actually assigned to the kitchen and that someone had ordered me to help with this one mattress because it was too heavy for the group. I wanted to say that I may have been needed in my kitchen assignment and that I

was afraid I might be punished for not being there. But before I had
the chance to say anything, the mattress detail was ordered "Downstairs! On the double!" We carried the bulky load into the basement,
where the straw was stored and where all the mattresses were being
filled.

The air in these underground rooms was suffocating. The small
cellar compartments, the long narrow corridors were certainly not
designed to have scores of hard-breathing, sweating people working
here. In the corners were piles of straw that prisoners, elbow to
elbow, were stuffing into filthy, fetid bags. With each breath, small
particles of straw were drawn into the mouth and lungs. That none
of those working there had ever had any experience filling straw
mattresses created even more of this ugly, biting dust than would
normally have been necessary.

I saw several people I knew, but I had to find Tury first. The
room was too dark and dusty, but I hesitated to call his name.
Suddenly somebody embraced me. Tury! He had figured that I
would soon find out that the basement was the only place in which
prisoners assigned to different floors could meet, and he therefore
had promptly volunteered for the mattress-stuffing detail.

Now we could talk. With so much going on here, and as the
dim gaslight hardly penetrated through the dust, control was almost nonexistent. The guards assumed that with working conditions down there what they were, the routine "Hurry up, Jews,
faster!" was not needed, as everyone would try to get the job over as
fast as possible.

"The money?" Tury whispered.

"Safe! All of it," I responded, smiling.

"I hoped, but I couldn't be sure. I asked the arresting officer
and, again at the precinct station, why they arrested me, and you
don't know how happy I was to hear them say 'You're a Jew, aren't
you?' because then I knew it had nothing to do with Aktion. But the
neighbors?"

"Nothing. No one touched it. It's all safe, relax."

"So, Willy, they got you, too, in the general roundup. But
that's bad, everyone might start to think that they picked us up for
special reasons. You know, Kotek Goldstein is in here, too. We
have to find a way to get word to headquarters about the truth, that
we were just caught in the general arrests. They may panic, and the
work will stop."

Tury had a plan. Although there were no outlets to the outside whatsoever, some of these cellar compartments had small, grated windows high up in the walls at street level. As Karajangasse is located in the center of the Jewish district, those who passed by were almost certainly Jews. One of us would have to climb up to one of these narrow windows, and when he saw a passerby's legs, would call to him and push a message through the bars.

The two of us sneaked into an empty compartment. No straw here, no prisoners. There was a window, high up. We stood on tiptoe to watch the traffic outside. Not many were walking by. At regular intervals we could see a pair of uniformed legs firmly marching past. We counted the seconds to the policeman's return and divided the time in half. When he was close to half the time away—and still facing away from the window—would be the best time to deliver the message.

Tury took out a pencil. To this day I do not know how it survived the frisking. In the trash heaped into one of the corridor's corners, we found a piece of torn wrapping paper. In beautifully printed, large block letters we wrote Erich Wolf's name, address, and phone number. He was the leader of the Vienna Betar and if he was not home, his parents certainly would be. We printed that the unknown recipient of the written message was to call Erich Wolf or to ride to him by taxi and to tell him that we were all right, that our arrest had nothing to do with "the store" and that he should go on with "business." In equally clear penmanship, we told the unknown deliverer that all his expenses, including the taxi, would be paid immediately on delivering the message. I wrote a second message. It was directed to my brother Walter and told him where I was, that I was all right, and that he too should call the Wolf family with the same information.

By the time we finished our slow printing job, the cell, empty before, had filled with other prisoners. Becoming aware of what we were doing, they also wanted to send out messages. These prisoners had been arrested in the streets, in their businesses, or in the street-cars on their way to work, and, of course, their relatives did not know if they were still alive.

All our messages were rolled into one paper ball about two inches in diameter. Tury, who was 6 feet 1 inch tall and particularly strong, positioned himself under the window. A small, thin, but wiry and agile fellow climbed up on Tury's back and waited for the right moment. Each time the uniformed legs passed, one of the men in the cell started counting aloud until "half-time." He then waited for the policeman's reappearance to start counting again. Several civilian legs passed by, but each time it was too close to half-time. Now came the chance. A pair of women's legs right at the best time.

"*Yiddine*" ("Jewish woman"), called "Tiny" in a subdued yet clear voice. "*Yiddine!*"

The legs stopped still.

"*Helft ins*" ("Help us"), our friend up there on Tury's back called out through the bars as he threw the paper ball out.

A short hesitation. Then a hand appeared, scooped up the paper ball, and the legs continued walking.

It all happened very fast; the policeman must still have been facing the other way. Hopefully, the Betar would soon know that the work must go on; my brother and all the other relatives informed via the paper ball would at least have heard from their loved ones. Within the hour, both our messages were delivered by phone by this good woman, who, unfortunately to this day, remains unknown to us.

Tury and I returned to the job of filling straw mattresses. The dust and the altogether miserable air did not concern us now. We had our important message out. For several hours we worked side by side. Then Tury suddenly asked me, "Didn't someone call your name?" I had heard nothing, but moments later a policeman came into the cellar compartment and shouted, "*Schutzhaftjude* Perl!" ("Protective Custody Jew Perl!"). Arrests were called "protective custody," and prisoners so titled.

"Here." I was being led up to the ground floor to the man in charge of the prison. A name plate showed his surname and rank: Oberleutnant Plachter—First Lieutenant Plachter.

"Do you know a certain Diamant?"

"I know several Diamants, sir."

"One who lives in Laxenburgerstrasse?"

"No, sir, at least I do not recall a man of that name and address."

"But he knows you," said Oberleutnant Plachter.

"This is quite possible," I said. "Like probably many others, I do know lots of people by sight, without knowing their names and addresses." During this questioning I wondered what the story might be behind this certain Diamant whom I truly did not remember. But the next question made it all clear.

"This Diamant claims that you have his passport in your possession. What are you doing with other people's passports? Are you trying to get away with somebody else's documents?"

Now I understood. This Diamant was obviously one of the youngsters registered with us for the illegal transport. The police must have wanted to take his passport away and he had stated that he had left it with me. He must have seen me in here and, when interrogated, apparently referred to it.

The man questioning me was obviously in charge of this emergency prison. His soft, slightly nasal German showed him to be an Austrian. From the way he questioned me, he did not seem to be one of those only too numerous Austrians who, immediately after the German Anschluss, emerged as real bloodhounds. I quickly decided to dare a major coup.

"I have at home not two, but more than three hundred passports," I told this officer quietly. Startled, he asked, "Three hundred passports? What are they for? Are you a forger of passports?"

"I am sorry if you do not know," I said. "I am organizing the mass exodus of Jews to Palestine. All these people have procured their legal exit permits, and I have been making the arrangements for the trip and the entry into Palestine."

"When are these Jews supposed to leave?"

"They should be leaving this Monday," I lied.

"Are they leaving or not?"

"With me here and unable to put the final touches on it all, they will not be able to go." That was a hit. Jews are supposed to leave. Oberleutnant Plachter must know more, otherwise he might be in hot water with the Germans.

"What will be done to clear these Jews out, anyhow?"

I answer bluntly, "Sir, this is all up to you."

"Up to me?"

"Sir, if you are holding me here, I cannot get things done."

But he could not let me go. He was just in charge of this prison. He could not release anyone. Yet he certainly did not want to tangle with the Gestapo endeavor to make Vienna *judenrein*. He lifted the telephone receiver, dialed, and asked for Obersturmfuehrer Eichmann.

Obersturmfuehrer! So! Eichmann in these few weeks had been promoted to the rank of an SS First Lieutenant. But the rank was not the issue. My heart almost stopped beating when I heard

Plachter ask for Eichmann. No doubt Eichmann would tell him that he did not know of any such emigration or worse, that a plan submitted by me had been disapproved by him. We were finished!

"Then give me Dr. Lange, please," Oberleutnant Plachter said into the phone. I started breathing again. Eichmann was not in. Dr. Lange was the chief of the Vienna Gestapo, Eichmann's superior, and was not as well informed about Jewish problems as his Jewish Affairs expert.

"I understand that several hundred Jews are to emigrate to Palestine on Monday. They apparently all have their passports ready and their Gestapo exit permits. I just established that the main organizer of all that has been committed to my custody, and he claims that without him, the transport cannot leave."

A pause.

"What time are they leaving?" Oberleutnant Plachter asked me. I now became more specific in my great lie. "Monday evening, at 2010 hours," I said.

He repeated this into the phone. Several "yes, sirs" followed, and the phone conversation concluded with the obligatory "Heil, Hitler." Plachter turned to me.

"You will be leaving here but will not be released. You will be out just until the transport leaves. If you do not come back, or if these Jews do not leave on time, we shall get you and your family and friends. Understood?"

"Yes, sir. But—I think I would rather stay here."

"You what?"

"I think I prefer to stay here. Of course I shall return if released temporarily only. But with my two main assistants here too, a snag could develop, the departure might be delayed, even endangered, and in this case you would say that I cheated my way out. I prefer to stay here."

"What assistants? You didn't mention any before."

"Sir, you didn't ask me, and I thought I was not permitted to speak unless spoken to."

Plachter was in a fix. He had called the highest headquarters before first having gathered all the facts.

"Who are these so-called assistants of yours?"

"Mr. Erich Deutsch, my closest co-worker, and Mr. Karl Kotek Goldstein, who is familiar with many important details."

"You want to empty my whole place. No Goldbergs, no

Goldsteins. That's out." Turning to a guard, he ordered, "Bring Deutsch in." They brought Tury in. Questioningly he looked at me.

"Do you know this man?" Plachter asked Tury.

"Yes."

"What's his name? What do you know about him?"

"He is Dr. Perl and he is a lawyer," Tury said hesitantly.

"Don't waste my time. What, if anything, does he have to do with Palestine?"

"He's a Zionist . . ." Tury muttered cautiously. At this point I interrupted by saying, "Tell the truth about what we are preparing for Monday."

"Dr. Perl and I are in charge of organizing the mass emigration of Jews from Vienna, and if we are in here, nothing will happen on Monday," said Tury.

"Get out, both of you. But if you are not back here on the dot of ten Monday night, we shall get you and all your family."

The formalities were quick. We signed that we were aware that we had not been released and were just on "temporary absence" until Monday at ten P.M. Both of us had also to list five names and addresses of our closest relatives before we could go.

As we were walking out the door, I met Walter, my brother. He had received my message and had brought an extra pair of underwear and a little Torah, hoping to find the basement window behind which he thought I was still locked up.

At home, on my desk was the fervently awaited letter from Galili. It had been mailed in Rome and reported that matters in Greece had been straightened out. What ups and downs in one day!

It had been an unbelievable stroke of luck that Eichmann, with his vicious theory of "atomizing" the Jews, had not been in. It was not only that Tury and I were free, even if just temporarily. The all-important fact was that we were out to complete, on orders of the chief of the entire Vienna Gestapo, the preparations for our transport. That Monday date would have to be taken care of, but this should be possible as the Gestapo now wanted our action to succeed. Official permission, unobtainable through Eichmann, had been received as a result of our arrest!

Seventy-two hours were left till Monday night, and there was, of course, not the slightest chance to get the transport ready, even within a week. We must obtain an extension of the Monday deadline. Fortunately, Saturday was then even for government offices half a working day, and as everyone felt the increased pressure of the times, important matters were handled at all hours, by all people—authorities, civilians, Jews, and "Aryans."

As soon as we were released, Tury and I, accompanied by my brother Walter, went directly to my home. This night my brother would sleep here, as it was safer for him than staying at his place. I was the only male resident registered with the police as living in my household, and since I was already under arrest, it was unlikely the police would return here. Actually, from Friday night to Sunday, Jews from several apartments in the same building were hauled away, but none of the ominous hard knocks hit my door. By Sunday, four more people were sleeping over to escape the mass arrests. But that night, ignoring the sound of boots on the stairs, the pounding of fists on doors around us, we devised a plan of how to extend the Monday deadline.

We decided that the only way was to take a chance on Mr. Gildemeester. Shortly after the Anschluss, it became known among Vienna Jews that a non-Jew, Mr. Gildemeester, who claimed to represent some American or British organization, had come to Vienna supposedly to help the Jews. Rumor had it that he was actually a Gestapo man put up to elicit information from Jews that they would otherwise not give. The Betar had looked into this matter as thoroughly as possible, and we learned that Mr. Gildemeester claimed to represent the Quakers, an organization unknown to most Viennese Jews. We had also found out that one of Mr. Gildemeester's men, a Mr. Kofler, tried to organize a special rescue action for "Non-Aryan Christians"—the word for Jews who had converted to Christianity, but who, for racial reasons, were nevertheless persecuted by the Nazis just as if they had never changed their faith. There were many thousands of such converted Jews in Austria. A good number of them were actually born Christians from parents who had converted. Their lot was particularly tragic. The world in Nazi lands was then sharply divided: Aryans on one side, Jews on the other. Neither group recognized the baptized Jews as belonging to it.

A week before my arrest, the Aktion had discussed this Mr. Gildemeester.* At that meeting, Paul Haller, Otto Seidmann, Erich Wolf, Bertschi Kornmehl, Paul Lustig, Tury Deutsch, and I con-

---

*By this time, the whole undertaking was no longer just the Aktion section of the Zionist Revisionists. Iser Reifer and Max Schwartz, another businessman and a Vienna Jewish leader, had obtained the backing for our work from the London Zionist Revisionists and the World Betar.

cluded that there was no doubt that Gildemeester had suspiciously good connections with the Gestapo, but we felt that he was most likely genuine. If he were a Nazi spy, we figured, his efforts would not be to help baptized Jews, for this could not endear him to the Jewish community. It would serve only to reduce his trustworthiness in Jewish eyes.

Early Saturday morning Tury and I hastened to see Mr. Gildemeester. He was glad to meet with us as he knew of the suspicions against him. For us, meeting him was an experience we would never forget. In those times, when your closest Christian friends had turned against you or shrugged their shoulders because they "could not" help you, he proved to be a Christian who was truly concerned for all humans, whatever their faith or descent.

We told Mr. Gildemeester most of our story. Our version included the fact that, because of new problems, a delay had developed which required an extension of the transport's departure time by a week or maybe even two. We stressed that we had already made arrangements for this first large transport of about 1,000 people, to be followed immediately by a second even larger one. We told him, of course, about Oberleutnant Plachter's conversation with Dr. Lange. Gildemeester asked whether we had our work coordinated with Eichmann, and we told him that we were under the impression that Eichmann might not realize the large scope of our efforts and therefore, were trying to avoid him. At this mention of Eichmann, Gildemeester made a gesture indicating that Eichmann was "small fry." He said he knew a man behind the scenes who wielded immense political power among the Nazis, far more important than Eichmann.

This man was Dr. Erich Rajakovitch, an ambitious young Vienna lawyer who had been a force in the underground Nazi movement in Austria long before the Anschluss. He was also said to be a friend of Ernst Kaltenbrunner, one of Hitler's closest trustees who eventually would become chief of Gestapo of the entire German Reich. Even more important, Gildemeester told us that Dr. Rajakovitch was the son-in-law of Dr. von Rintelen. Von Rintelen was one of the main figures behind an attempted Nazi coup in Austria in 1934 in which the Austrian chancellor, Dr. Dollfuss, had been murdered. Convicted for his complicity in the Dollfuss murder, von Rintelen had been sentenced to life imprisonment. Now, in 1938, as the Nazis had really come to power in Austria, von

Rintelen was a hero, but Rajakovitch, his son-in-law, had not yet found an assignment or task worth his efforts. For this reason, Mr. Gildemeester thought that it would be good to tie Dr. Rajakovitch's drive for power and fame to our emigration plans. In our presence he called Dr. Rajakovitch, described to him our already very advanced emigration undertaking, and stated that we needed some help to get it all running on a regular expanded basis. Dr. Rajakovitch told him that he was ready to see us on Monday.

This meeting with Rajakovitch might become a great break for our entire venture. But we knew that a man of his rank and ambition would have to be shown truly impressive facts, certainly something more than a few hundred passports.

For these "facts" we needed a special typewriter, one that matched Galili's letter from Rome. One of the Aktion members knew an expert in typewriters. On Sunday we took Galili's letter to him. He studied the envelope and told us what model typewriter had been used for it. None of the typewriters belonging to any of our closest co-workers was the same model, but Dr. Schij came up with one at the large hospital where he worked. We hurried to the hospital, and Dr. Schij led us to the proper machine. On typing paper that was standard all over Europe, we typed a letter to put inside Galili's envelope; we had to make it look as if it had been mailed from Rome prior to our arrest, to ensure authenticity of our "facts." In the letter, which we wrote as if it had been addressed from Galili to the Aktion, we had Galili inform us that he had succeeded in getting us a larger ship. It would take up to 1,000 people instead of the smaller boat originally planned. These people who were supplying the larger ship were big entrepreneurs, we claimed in the letter, and so a week or two after the first ship, we could have another one. He had made all arrangements; we had Galili tell us in this letter, to transport bimonthly, each time, 1,000 persons for the next six months. Thus we would be able to get 12,000 Jews out of Vienna within the next half year. Also in this letter of his—actually ours—Galili implored us not to let him down. He had done his part and would continue doing so, but we must do ours. These Greek smugglers meant business. They would stick to the arrangements, but if he failed, they would hunt him down and kill him, the letter asserted.

With this letter in the genuine envelope, and with the invaluable foreign currency permission of the Berlin Ministry of Finance, supported with some 300 passports—all stamped with the official exit permit—Tury and I knocked at the door of Rajakovitch's office at the appointed hour on Monday.

Dr. Rajakovitch received us cordially. Most unusual for a Nazi at this time, he addressed me as *"Herr Kollege"*—Mr. Colleague, the usual way for one lawyer to address another—unless one is a Jew. He asked us to state our case. I started out with the same arguments that we had used at the Berlin Ministry of Finance: that the Fuehrer has announced his intent to have Vienna *judenrein* as fast as possible, that as the refugees departed in destitution, no other country was ready to take them in large numbers, and that Britain had closed the doors of the country where the Jews belong. Of course, all this talk was blowing into the Nazi horn, "Jews out to Palestine." I mentioned that, to avoid arousing American Jewry, the British, who were facing a critical situation, would not seriously pursue the illegal immigrants, but if they did not, they would arouse the anger of the Arabs. I stressed that we had already landed three small transports in Palestine prior to the Anschluss and showed him some of the letters and postcards that we had received after the respective landings. As I spoke and produced our documentary "evidence," I handled the bag in such a clumsy way that almost 200 of the passports fell out on the floor. The sight of my picking up all those which had fallen out and of my trying to shovel them back into the bag—which appeared to contain many more—made the number of passports seem even more impressive. During the process of returning them to the bag, I handed some of the passports to Dr. Rajakovitch so he could see the exit permit stamps in them.

Tury later told me that all this was an excellent trick, but it had not been planned—the accident with the overnight bag was genuine.

Actually we did not really need all this heavy ammunition. Dr. Rajakovitch was apparently as eager to work with us on this project which could gain him glory in the Nazi movement as we were to get him involved with our undertaking.

Right in front of us he called the Gestapo and asked for Dr. Lange. He referred to our work as "interesting" and read Galili's letter to Dr. Lange, word for word.

"Yes, it is obviously genuine. I am holding it in my hand, together with the envelope which shows that it was mailed in Rome before these people's arrest." He asked Dr. Lange whether, in view of the chance of getting rid of so many Jews, Dr. Lange would not consider it best to have us released from Karajangasse from which we were now only on temporary leave, ending tonight.

"Yes, I will tell them." He concluded the conversation with other matters unknown to us and hung up with the usual "Heil Hitler."

"You will be released from confinement tonight," Dr. Rajakovitch told us, "but you must report at the Karajangasse Notgefaengnis tonight at ten, because you are still listed as under arrest there. The formalities should be short. Dr. Lange will be there at that time." We should report to Lange and refer to the conversation we had just heard.

As we left Dr. Rajakovitch's office, we realized we were free and our rescue action was clearly okayed by both Dr. Rajakovitch and the chief of the Vienna Gestapo. "Clear sailing from now on, Tury!" I could not resist the pun.

In the evening Tury and I took a taxi to Karajangasse. We were within a block of it at ten minutes to ten, but all the streets from there on were blocked by police. What was going on? The policemen claimed they did not know; in any case they had orders not to let unauthorized persons pass. This gave us the cue.

"We're authorized. What's more, we're expected. Dr. Lange, chief of the Vienna Gestapo, ordered us to report here at ten tonight." The policeman shook his head in a quizzical gesture and let us pass. Soon we understood what his gesture meant. "You poor fools!"

Police van after police van was lined up in those blocked-off streets. Either they were bringing new prisoners in—which was unlikely because we would have heard of any new mass arrests—or they were about to move the Karajangasse prisoners somewhere else.

They looked sinister and dismal, these long rows of paddy wagons in the dimly lit side streets of Vienna's poorest Jewish section. I knew how it felt to be in one of those vans.

On the dot of ten, we knocked at the door.

"What do you want?" asked the policeman as he opened the door a crack.

"We have to report to Dr. Lange."

"Tomorrow. He's busy tonight," he snarled. But we were of course afraid of Dr. Lange's reaction if we did not report on time;

the more so as we would have no proof that we actually were there and were punctual. In a demanding voice, not at all one expected to be used by a Jew toward a policeman, I stated that Dr. Lange specifically asked us to come here at this hour. "And I am certain he knows better than you do why he ordered this."

We were admitted, but we entered a Karajangasse prison very different from the one we had left only three nights ago. We were being admitted to hell.

On the staircase leading down into the foyer where we entered we saw—in the pale gaslight—a large group of prisoners. They were lined up in rows of two. Apparently they had been brought down from one of the upper floors to be loaded into the waiting vehicles. The nervous haggard faces looked almost ghostly in this old-fashioned gaslight. Each of them was wearing his coat and hat. Some were clutching tiny parcels, apparently the extra pair of underwear, or sweater, or a warm shawl that those who were arrested in their homes were permitted to take along. Right in the front row stood a colleague from my university days. He was looking at me wistfully. I had come from the outside. His eyes were asking me, "Do you know what is waiting for us out there, where they are going to take us?"

But I could not talk to him, not without certainly being battered to the ground. Already a policeman grabbed me and pushed me out of the entrance area into a neighboring room. The same tableau awaited us there. Jews, humans, in rows of two, ready to be marched out. Among these too I recognized several acquaintances. Tury and I had just entered this room when a policeman yelled at us to move on to the adjoining room. Before we could say a word, explain why we were here tonight, we were pushed into that next room. It was the school's gymnasium.

Here the prisoners had not yet been lined up in formation. They did not know what was happening in the other room, knew even less that outside the vans were already waiting. But they suspected it all, because it was late in the evening when they were unexpectedly driven from their straw mattresses in the former classrooms and former offices into which they had been crammed after their work shifts. And they had been told to take "all their belongings" along.

Tury and I were being besieged with questions. They had seen us come from the outside room; maybe we knew something.

"What is going on out there? Why all these mass arrests? One of the SS men said that Czechoslovakia has mobilized her troops against Germany. Is that the reason for these arrests? Is it a reprisal for Czechoslovakia's mobilization?"

And the most frequent question.

"What's to become of us, where are they taking us?"

Nobody pronounced it, but it was on everyone's mind, in everyone's eyes.

"Dachau?"

Neither Tury nor I knew, but we feared that the dreaded word might really denote their destination. Nazi rule was new in Austria, but some of the most prominent Jews had already been brought to Dachau, the infamous concentration camp outside Munich. Some of these people were known to be dead, including the Jewish councilman, Dr. Jacob Ehrlich, famous all over Austria for standing up for the rights of Jews in the often anti-Semitic Vienna City Council. A few days after Dr. Ehrlich's disappearance, the Vienna Jewish Community Council received a phone call from the Jewish Community Council of Munich. They had received Dr. Ehrlich's body from Dachau and did the Vienna community want him buried in Munich or in Vienna?

Nevertheless, although individuals had been brought to Dachau, so far no mass deportation to that or any other concentration camp had taken place from Austria. In spite of the air of dread and trepidation, Dachau seemed unlikely for such a large group. Maybe to some forced labor, road gang, or the like? It could not be Dachau.

Dachau was the worst one could think of, it was not just death, it meant torture, savagery, the German twentieth-century version of being put on the rack.

Now one man got it out, aloud, what all had been avoiding.

"It could only be Dachau," he said in a clear voice. After this, many crowded around Tury and me. Some had already written messages for their wives or children. We were taking notes of other requests. Suddenly a loud voice yelling a military order took command. It did not come from one of the policemen. A man in the terrifying black uniform of the SS barked, "Attention, Jews. Line up in rows of twos!" As the others scrambled to do so, Tury and I stepped back.

"You two! Get in line!" a policeman shouted. He swung his

billy club but stopped short just about two inches from Tury's skull. If we got into that line, we were lost, so I tried to start explaining. Immediately I had to pay for it by being hit with that same billy club, hard, but fortunately only across the shoulders. We were now lined up with the others.

"Shut up, no sound, no sound," the policemen bellowed. The still prevailing hum turned into dead silence as the door opened and three men wearing the dreaded black SS uniform marched in. Their grand entrance was led by a slim young man, strutting in, ramrod stiff, with a face expressing utter arrogance, as if he owned the whole world.

Adolf Eichmann.

The other two were noncommissioned SS officers who remained half a step behind him. Though no order was given, everyone stood at attention, even the policemen. The anxiety pervading the gymnasium was so heavy, one could almost touch it. One thought only came to my mind and certainly to many of those with me, standing there pale and terrified before Eichmann: "The Executioner!" No one moved.

As he stood there, his legs spread, twirling a swagger stick, the long row of twos turned toward him, and he now faced one long line with another behind it.

"Who volunteers for Dachau?"

Silence. Then an old Jew stepped forward.

"Why?" Eichmann was visibly amused.

"Because I want to get it all over with as fast as possible." The old man stood straight. Eichmann uttered a high whinny. Then, with a smirk, he added, in sugary tones, "Well, I would not want you to be lonely"—and in a changed voice, speaking very slowly, stressing every word, he hissed, "You—all—are—going—to Dachau." With this, he turned to the door and left.

A man dropped to the floor. Many of us knew him. He was an epileptic and writhed in convulsive contortions. One of the two SS men who had entered with Eichmann stepped over to him.

"Up!" he barked. The man's seizure continued unabated. The Nazi kicked the man with his heavy SS boot, once, twice. "Get up I said!" The second kick hit the head. The writhing of the man on the floor slowed. One more kick, this one into the stomach region. A thin stream of blood flowed from the man's mouth. He did not move anymore. The SS man gave an order to one of the policemen and walked out by the same door through which, less than half a minute before, Eichmann and the other SS man had left.

Tury and I were now being marched with the others back through the room through which we had come before we had entered the gymnasium. No SS men were here, but there was an Austrian police sergeant. I moved out of the formation, and when I was still far enough from the sergeant so that he could not, without moving forward, hit me with his club, I saluted and stated rapidly, "Most important political information for Dr. Lange. Immediate report required." The military-sounding sentence, which I had formulated while I stood in line in that room next door, and my military salute, startled the policeman. I noticed his hesitation and tried to exploit it immediately.

"Unless you report to Dr. Lange at once, you bear the consequences."

"If you are lying, Jew, you will not leave this building alive! Come along," the sergeant ordered.

"This man comes with me," I ordered in a commando voice, and Tury followed me and the confused policeman to Dr. Lange. The latter was standing in the lobby, close to the exit. He was even taller than Eichmann, even slimmer. The part of his forehead visible under the shield of his SS headgear showed two dueling scars. More such scars ran almost parallel across his left cheek, all wounds acquired in the German student sport of dueling with sharp sabres for the slightest offense against one's "honor."

The sergeant came to attention, saluted, and reported to Dr. Lange what we had told him. Dr. Lange, in an elegant, swift movement, turned toward us. "What Jewish fraud is this—political information?" he growled. Now I had to water down the "political" importance of the information.

"Dr. Rajakovitch thought that you, sir, might consider it politically worthwhile to have the mass emigration of Jews continue undisturbed. He told us that you ordered us to report to you tonight for discharge. We came here as ordered by you, and the lower-echelon police lined us up with the group that is leaving, though you wanted us to report to you."

He was still furious because of our cheek in pretending we had political information. But why should he, because of two dirty Jews, risk displeasure of the von Rintelen family? "Wait," he ordered us.

There was empty space around Dr. Lange, but our police

sergeant made us step back about six feet, so that our closeness should not offend this demigod. While we were waiting as ordered, prisoners in rows of two were being marched by, into a van, which could be seen through the open gate. Several times the slow-moving line came to a short standstill. The van was probably almost full already. At one such break in the movement, a man with a pale face who was standing close to me whispered, "Please tell my . . ."

"Move on!" a voice yelled before the prisoner could complete his sentence. This man's face was familiar to me. Later Tury told me it was Dr. Mandl, a well-known Viennese surgeon whom we both had met socially but whom I had not recognized because he looked so haggard and had a three-day beard.

When the van being loaded was full and was just departing, Dr. Lange looked suddenly at Tury and me and snarled, "Sign out and get out." He then turned to the sergeant and commanded, "You take care of it."

"Yes, sir!"

After a short release formality, Tury and I were shoved out of the office and into the hallway and, from there, into the entrance lobby. The sergeant accompanied us to make certain that we did get out. We moved slowly because the corridors were narrow, and priority of movement belonged to the prisoners who passed us in the continuing process of being loaded into the vans. Silently they marched, one row of two after another, of still live human bodies. Now they knew their destination, and with hope gone, their ability to plan and to make decisions had left them. Like automatons they put one foot ahead of the other and marched in step in neat formation.

Tury and I passed through the gate just as the loading of one of the paddy wagons had been completed. As we neared it, the door of the vehicle was slammed shut. The paddy wagon started moving, slowly following those in front of it, while another one positioned itself at the gate.

If anything could still strengthen our sense of urgency, of the necessity to succeed with our emigration project, this last hour had done it.

Days of most intensive activity followed. We had to get the first shipload of refugees out fast. The mass arrests, which lasted three days, produced in the Jews of Vienna two trends that opposed each other as far as our work was concerned. One trend, expected and probably intended by the Nazis, caused those who saw the danger now so much more clearly to do everything possible to get out anywhere, in any way possible.

But the effect of the mass arrests worked in the opposite direction, too. Many people, mainly older ones, were petrified at the thought of doing anything "illegal." They would dare nothing that might get them into any kinds of problems with the authorities. All their lives law-abiding, middle- and upper-class citizens, they simply refused to realize that their being Jewish was for the Nazis full justification for any kind of persecution. Some of these frightened people were—unfortunately—parents of youngsters who wanted to emigrate to Palestine with us. Now these parents, even more terrified than before, refused the permission needed to obtain a passport for their teenagers. In some cases the refusal by parents to agree to the issuing of passports hit us badly. It happened to a few of our most active and best-liked young people.

In mid-May, the problem of fearful parents had become even more serious. Word had spread that Zionist leaders abroad, who after all would "know better" than the captive Jews in Nazi-held lands, considered illegal immigration to Palestine too dangerous and damaging to the cause of Zionism. It would, these leaders believed, make the British angry, and we needed the British to "save us" from Nazi persecution.

Actually, even as late as August 1939, just days before the outbreak of World War II, there was little understanding among Jewish leaders abroad. When persecution was much worse than in the spring of 1938, when Jews were being murdered not in just one or two concentration camps but in half a dozen, Rabbi Hillel Silver of Cleveland, Ohio, unquestionably a leader of American Jewry, delivered at the Twenty-first Zionist Congress in Geneva a thunderous attack against these "illegal undertakings." On the twentieth of August 1939, as the Germans were already massing their Panzer divisions for the invasion of Poland, Rabbi Silver gave what the *New York Times* called "an impassioned speech" against "illegal" escape from Nazi hands. The same issue of the *Times*—in fact, the same page—reported "800 Refugees Seized off Palestine Coast: Jews in Rowboats Rounded Up As They Try to Land." Yet Rabbi

Silver stated charitably, "I am *not unmindful* of the plight of our poor refugees who are trying to get into Palestine, but I am worried about the possibility of our making a colossal blunder *at a time when circumstances do not warrant* our taking such an action."*

Certainly, although just as motivated to rescue the persecuted as we were, he had arrived at very different conclusions. He trusted the British and distrusted the young "irresponsible" people who tried to act outside the Zionist party machinery.

As word spread among Austrian Jews that leading Jews abroad disapproved of our undertaking, the number of parents refusing to cooperate with their children's plans to escape with us to Palestine grew. We had succeeded so far in overcoming Eichmann's opposition; in our initial, smaller transports, we had evaded the British patrol boats. We should also have been able to handle this obstacle, coming from Jews themselves, as frustrating as obstacles from that source were. One evening, Tury, exasperated about the fierce antagonism from within, gave vent to his anger. Paul Haller, Aktion's ideologist, who never spoke much, cut Tury short in a low but determined voice.

"Shut up, calm down, and listen." He reminded us then how it was in Jewish history so often the irresponsible ones who had acted against the judgment of the great majority and of the establishment and yet had succeeded.

"We might all end up as nameless victims of a concentration camp and," he added jokingly, "certainly no Chanukkah candles will ever be lit to commemorate what we are doing, as they are lit in memory of the Maccabee's fight and final victory for Israel's freedom from Syrian oppression. But we should recall that the Maccabees were compelled to fight not only the Syrians. They were first a small band of 'irresponsible' guerrillas condemned by the official Jewish leaders, who were only too ready to accept the imposed foreign culture and to offer sacrifices to the Syrian idols." In his quiet, firm voice, and in an often bitingly humorous way, Haller remarked that none of us was found in the bullrushes by an Egyptian princess and that the only fate which we might end up sharing with Moses was to bring Jews into the Promised Land without ever reaching it ourselves. We should remember something

*Author's italics.

else, too: that the pharaoh was Moses' main opponent but not his only one.

"Just think of all the troubles the majority of Jews themselves caused him. Remember how scared they were of the risks which went with the Exodus. How even before they had reached the Red Sea, the Children of Israel said to Moses, 'Because there were no graves in Egypt, hast thou taken us away to die in the wilderness?' And how, again and again during the march they revolted against him and wished they were back in Egypt with its fleshpots, which they forgot did not exist anymore for them. Just recall how, of the 12 spies Moses sent into Canaan, 10 returned with tales that the march had to be stopped, the risks were too great, the obstacles insurmountable. History decided in favor of the Maccabees and in favor of the two spies of Moses who had faith. The minority, those who had the courage to assume the risks, turned out to have been right. They had accepted odds which the circumstances necessitated. We are in good company," he concluded with a little smile.

Haller had never before spoken for so many minutes. He now exhorted us not to condemn the various Rabbis Silver because things looked very different when seen from Cleveland, Ohio, than when seen from a Gestapo prison. That we were a small group should only make us proud. There is a saying that nothing is as practical as a good theory. Looking back, Haller's talk sounded very theoretical. But though he had told us nothing we did not know, he had said the right thing at the right time and had provided us with the impetus to take more immediate, practical action. We had to counteract the silent Jewish obstruction and had to do it right then.

We had to. But how? One plan after another was suggested and rejected. Finally, after a brainstorming session that ended only well after we heard the first milk wagons rattle by, we decided how to dispel the hesitation many parents had to help in their children's rescue.

We could not let it be known that we now had the backing of high-ranking Nazi officials in Vienna—the suspicions already limiting the effectiveness of Mr. Gildemeester and his Quakers were only too well known to us. While we did not expect to become suspect as to our motivation, any known aid by the Nazis would have raised, among the established leaders of the Jewish community, the fear that we, the young, inexperienced, and too-bold ones, were falling for a Gestapo trick, and that our young people would be found traveling to a concentration camp instead of Palestine.

We had somehow to establish the impression among the Jews that although the Jewish community as such could not officially work with us, we actually had the council's full backing and blessing. To understand the importance that the Jewish Community Council as such played, one has to know that it was something entirely different from what any Jewish representation is nowadays in any country. The Vienna Jewish community was by law the official representative of all the Jews and in many ways constituted a legal state within a state. Every Jew in Austria was obliged, by law, to pay taxes not only to the Austrian government but also to the Jewish community. If these taxes were not paid, the same procedure applied as to nonpayment of federal taxes. Salaries could be attached and liens placed against property.

Some of the leaders of the Jewish community openly supported our undertaking, but as individuals only. The community as such took a different position toward the "Perl-Aktion"—as we now came to be called because headquarters were in my law offices. The community dubbed the Perl-Aktion irresponsible and held that it was reckless at such delicately critical times to engage in anything "illegal."

During that night of brainstorming, we decided that Dr. Maks, a leading staff member of the Jewish community, who had helped a good many of our youngsters on an individual basis, could provide us with the opportunity to end this "hide-and-seek" game of the official Jewish community. The preceding afternoon Dr. Maks had left word in our office that scores of young people were applying for financial support from the community so that they could emigrate with us. Money had been given to individuals by the community for that purpose but only confidentially. Now that so many more were applying for that aid, he must have our lists to ascertain that there was nobody getting money who was not really going with us. This was what gave us the "in."

According to our decision, I called Dr. Maks the next morning and told him that the enrollment lists were not what he wanted, as not all those who signed up could go, and that we neither asked for nor accepted money until an individual had procured a valid passport with an exit permit. Dr. Maks therefore asked us to send him the passports of accepted applicants with the exit permits in them so that members of the Jewish community could check the facts for themselves. I agreed to this, and we sent the passports over to the community in exchange for a written promise that these precious documents would be returned only to us.

Dr. Maks invited those who had applied for funds from the community and whose passports he had received to come to his office to discuss financial arrangements.

The day before the first of these appointments, Aktion members circulated the rumor that the Greek transit visas had arrived and would be issued that afternoon, and those whose passports were not available would risk losing their places to others. In times of crises, rumors spread like wildfire, especially when communications are under severe restrictions. All those who were to meet Dr. Maks the next day or two stormed to the offices of the Jewish community to demand their money and passports back immediately. They brought their friends, their relatives, anyone who, they hoped, could have influence with Dr. Maks. He saw the first few and tried to get in touch with us. He could not, for several hours. We were unavailable. At first Dr. Maks was unaware that those whom he refused to see before their scheduled appointments were congregating in numbers outside the building. The Jewish community was located in one of the narrow streets of the most ancient part of the city. Soon this street was filled with close to 200 shouting people, demanding their passports back.

Finally, Dr. Maks reached me. I went myself to the community and announced that the rumor was false; the people should leave their passports with the community.

The next day most of Vienna's Jews "knew" that passports handed over to the Perl-Aktion ended up in the Jewish community offices, that actually the Jewish community was behind the Perl-Aktion. From then on our young people found their parents much more ready to sign the required passport applications, and many were saved who, because of their parents' overcautiousness, might otherwise have perished. This ploy of ours also had another effect of weighty consequence. As the secret was out, and everybody now knew that there was some connection between us and Vienna's official Jewish community, the latter became less hesitant to support our travelers. As time went on and the pressures increased, there was almost open cooperation.

Several days after we succeeded in making it "known" to Vienna's Jews that we were not so "illegal" after all, Galili arrived in Vienna. His news was not nearly as good as his letter from Rome had led us to believe. Things were arranged but only as to the ship. The Greek transit visas, needed to get to the ship, were still "in the works." But we should not worry about the transit visas. He had assurances from some of the "most influential people" in Athens that these permits would be granted. The ship itself was small. Only large enough for 360. However, the next one, to leave shortly afterward, would hold three times as many.

We now had two main tasks: to make everything ready for the final selection of these first 360 and for their departure, and to obtain the Greek visas. But first, to reach Greece, we would have to travel through Yugoslavia. The Yugoslavs, however, would not dream of letting 360 Jews into their country without being fully assured that these destitute people would be just passing through. We obtained the definite promise from the Yugoslav Consulate General in Vienna that transit visas would be given for trainloads of up to 1,000 passengers if they possessed Greek visas, and with the stipulation that the cars be sealed to make certain that none of the passengers could stay in Yugoslavia.

Whenever, in the future, trains passed through Yugoslavia or Rumania, the cars were sealed. An example of a request for such transit is shown with the illustrations for this book.

As for the Greek visas, there was little we could do except wait for Galili's promises to come through. According to him the visas should arrive any day at the Greek Embassy in Vienna.

As soon as Galili arrived in Vienna, he insisted, "We must not lose another day. Send the foreign currency to Greece to the address I gave you; otherwise the boat might be late in coming, or we may even lose the trust of the Greek shippers altogether and the entire action will be endangered." We had gone so far in trusting Galili already, we could not stop now. Using the permit which we had obtained in Berlin, we exchanged 70,000 marks into foreign currency, and with much trepidation, but unable to do otherwise, we transferred this treasure abroad to the name and address in Athens given us by Galili. We now concentrated on other problems.

After the three days of mass arrests in May, Jews were in these days hauled in by the Gestapo on an individual basis. Usually a neighbor or someone who owed you money would claim that you had made a derogatory remark about Hitler or Nazism. Business-men who had sold goods on an installment basis and landlords were particularly subject to these accusations. One day the father of one of our chosen participants came to our office in tears and told us that his son, for whom he had made all the necessary arrangements for the trip, had been arrested that morning as a result of an anonymous accusation.

I then took a step that later proved to have been of great import for many who had been arrested. I informed Dr. Rajakovitch of this arrest and of two others that had been reported to me on this same day, also concerning people registered with us. I told Dr. Rajakovitch that these arrests of persons who were ready to leave brought quite some disarray into our planning and sched-ule. I asked him to intervene and to have these three set free. He did so successfully, and after that, we were able to have arrested people released almost without exception, on the written assurance that they would be leaving on the next transport. At first such releases were effected immediately; later those arrested transport-partici-pants were held in jail until a day or two prior to the actual departure. We could not obtain the release of those whose arrest had occurred on the accusation of a Nazi party member or against whom charges seemed somewhat substantiated. I recall that we tried in vain for the release of a brother of one of our Betarim. He was accused of having been engaged to an Aryan girl who, it was claimed, had occasionally spent the night in his apartment. The man whom this girl had jilted in favor of the Jew had reported the case, and he backed up his claim with affidavits from the Jew's neighbors.

"Hands off, Dr. Perl," Dr. Rajakovitch told me. "This is a proven case of *Rassenschande!*" Miscegenation was a very serious crime in Nazi Germany. Concentration camp for the man as well as for the woman was a matter of course. We were unable to save the brother of our Betari.

Our chance to have arrested people set free with our written obligation to take them along worked, however, at that time only if we learned about the arrest before the prisoner was taken from Vienna to a concentration camp. The lifting of the arrest was done by the Vienna Gestapo, and once the arrested person was removed from the city, the local authorities either could not free him or did not want to bother themselves to do so.

All this was actually possible because the Germans were, at

that time, less interested in filling up concentration camps than in getting the Jews cleared out.

I knew from my own experience what it meant to be set free once one is scheduled to go to Dachau, and nobody who did not live in Nazi lands can even imagine how one feels on stepping out into the streets after having seen oneself on the way to a concentration camp.

The tremendous power of arranging for the release of persons who had been arrested gave our organization a valuable high standing with the lower police authorities and raised immeasurably our status with the Jewish community.

Meanwhile our office work went on incessantly. We had to bring order again to our records, as the mass arrests had thrown everything into bad shape. Names of those chosen to go with us were indexed in a little filing box, but now many of the chosen ones were in Dachau. We had to pick others to take their place.

Determining who could come with us involved the most painful decision making. Picking one, we rejected many. And we knew what that meant. Priority went to members of our own Betar; almost without exception, these were boys and girls between the ages of sixteen and twenty. The Betar alone had more members than the 360 spaces on the ship, but not all Betarim were ready to go. There were not a few who could not bring themselves to leave their parents behind.

All kinds of pressures were exerted on us to take this or that person. There was a man who asked us to take his children who were of the proper age but did not belong to any Jewish youth organization. This man was very influential with the Jewish community and promised to put his full weight behind the next large transports if we took his children. Certainly not an easy decision. There was a couple who came with their twelve-year-old husky son. They brought his three most recent report cards, showing "A's" in physical education.

"He is strong. An athlete," the father said. "He plays soccer on the junior team of the Hakoah [a Vienna Jewish sport club]." We could not take this boy.

A mother showed us the report card of her seventeen-year-old daughter. "She is a good girl, a wonderful student. Let her go." As Jews attach so much importance to study, these were not the only cases in which parents tried to use report cards to save their children.

People who knew anyone in our office were beleaguered by acquaintances to exercise influence on us. Money was promised to the Aktion, to individuals; jewelry was brought to the office; promises to help one establish a future abroad abounded. But we had to stick to our principle of priority for Betar and next, to those whom we expected to stand the strain of the trip, to adjust to life in Palestine. One day these youngsters would have to be ready and be able to rise up in arms with the Betar for the establishment of the Jewish State against the British colonial power.

In spite of our determination to stick to the figure of 360 because this number already crammed the ship to the fullest, we could not stand by it. We felt we had to make compromises. One boy, Arthur, a young Betar volunteer in our office, was chosen to go. For years he had been one of our most active members, and he slaved in the *AF AL PI* office day and night. He did not accept the chance to go along because he could not bear to leave his married sister and her husband behind, since they had reared him. Nevertheless, he continued to work with the same enthusiasm. We felt we could not leave Arthur behind and took all three. Another case involved a robust young widow in her late thirties. Her son was a Betari, and she herself was a nurse. We knew that such a person would be of help both on the trip and in Palestine. We also took some strong and militant members of the Makabi Youth Organization and a few from a Zionist-Socialist group. We ended up with 386.

The pressure of events kept us going at a constantly feverish pitch. The office was bedlam. We had many more volunteers than we could use, as working with us provided some measure of safety from the Gestapo. The volunteers, however, often created more confusion than help for our regular workers, but each time we started to get tired and numb from overwork, news of arrests or the disappearance of someone we knew spurred us on.

The work was all done in our offices, which were my former law offices at #14 Stubenring. The premises were spacious and had a little ever-flowing fountain with an artificial grotto in the entrance hall. The water flowed down from a crevice in the rocks and collected in a little pool. A joker had put a child's toy boat into this pool. Someone else had written in Hebrew on the side of the little boat the name *Dror*, "Freedom," and the stern sported a tiny blue-and-white flag. The toy boat, when wound up, circled the tiny pool, and each time it successfully negotiated the turbulent waters of the little waterfall, those in the waiting room seemed to view this overcoming of danger as an omen. After each "success" they broke into applause. After a few days of travel, the toy's spring mechanism refused to keep up with our overloaded schedule and broke down. I had to remove the ship then, as, now broken, it might have seemed a bad omen. This looking for omens may sound childish, but in those desperate times, people grasped at straws in search of any hope they could find.

In these days, Bertschi Kornmehl and Paul Haller were in the office around the clock. Another whose energies seemed inexhaustible and whose role in our undertaking quickly grew to a major one, was Fritz Herrenfeld, the secretary of the Austrian-Zionist Revisionist Party, a former officer in the Austrian Imperial Army. He was then in his early forties and by far the oldest in our group. Being older and a former officer in Emperor Franz Joseph's cavalry, he was best equipped to calm the parents who thought it might be better to make no move at all, to wait it all out. Paul Elbogen, a young member of the Betar, was another human dynamo among us. While Fritz and Bertschi were handling internal organizational problems, keeping the records, adjusting the finances, answering the phone, dictating memos and letters, Paul Elbogen was forever racing around with Tury, negotiating for provisions, for the special sealed trains, and straightening out the many problems that kept popping up. Negotiations with the authorities were left to me and whomever I took along. Also, many of the problems of Haller, Fritz, and Tury ended up with me. Martha Hausner and Hertha Mandler helped with the clerical work and also with calming down the many unhappy women who came to the office.

At the same time, the Betar leaders, Otto Seidmann and Erich Wolf were working quietly and steadily with the youth. Meeting with groups of accepted participants, preparing them organizationally and ideologically, they molded them into small squads, each with its own esprit de corps. Otto and Erich were rarely in the office, but we knew they were as burdened and sleepless as we were.

Our office telephone rang at all hours of the day and night. Each call had to be answered because each might be an emergency. A large blue sofa provided me for many days in succession with the only place to which I could sometimes sneak away for a couple of hours of rest. Usually this was in the small hours of the night, but sometimes we just could not go on without rest in the daytime, too.

Just as things seemed to be going very well, our lingering fear regarding the Greek transit visa erupted into panic. We had already been to the Greek Consulate in Vienna to request that it ask Athens for the cause of the delay. We were now called and asked to come to see the consul. He told us that upon his enquiry, he had received an order not to issue the transit visa to us because we had no visa of destination.

Desperate, we returned to our office. We immediately put in a call to the people in Athens with whom Galili had been in contact and who had made such definite promises. We were not yet well informed about some of the practices used by this type of businessman, but we knew that the assurance of an error having been made by the authorities was, at best, wishful thinking.

The situation was nothing short of disastrous. Our 386 people were ready to go. Incomparably more important, the foreign currency that we had received from the German National Bank was now in Greece and could not be recovered, as the shippers had nothing to do with the visa. It wasn't even possible to go to Greece ourselves to straighten things out, because when we received the foreign currency, we were told, "We give you the foreign money now, even prior to the departure of the Jews, but you stay here as hostages until the Jews have departed." One of the worst crimes in Germany at this time was the violation of currency restrictions. And what a violation this would have been! People were sent to prison for many years on the mere accusation of having smuggled into foreign lands just a few pounds or dollars. All who had been connected in any way with our rescue undertaking—organizers, their families, the registered participants, even the friends and relatives of these young people—all were definitely destined for a concentration camp unless we got the Greek visa. It would all be labeled one mammoth Jewish conspiracy to defraud the German government of a huge sum of foreign currency if we failed to get that visa. The fact that we had arranged the release of arrested people registered with us, without them then really leaving, would only have served to compound matters further.

The Greek consul in Vienna was a very humane man. He knew exactly what was happening to the Jews and he would have liked to help us, but when we asked him to, he told us, "As much as I want to help, I cannot ask Athens for this visa. My position is such that I take orders from the higher-ups in the Foreign Ministry; I cannot give them advice."

We thought of sending somebody to Athens from the Zionist-Revisionist, or from the Betar headquarters, both in London, but this too was impossible. Only recently we had been ordered by the German authorities not to bring any more foreigners into the matter. The Nazis wanted to keep control entirely in their own hands. And, of course, no telephone calls to a foreign country could be made that were not listened to and immediately reported to the proper *Ge*heime *Sta*ats *Po*lizei—Gestapo—desk.

One of Galili's men in Athens, an attorney who seemed to be the most reliable and realistic, informed us that the Greek Ministry of the Interior had decided that there was no objection to the transit visa and had forwarded the matter to the Ministry of Foreign Affairs in Athens. Now "it was only depending on them." This sounded good but was, in fact, bad. The Greek Foreign Ministry would look at things very differently from the Ministry of the Interior; it would be afraid of complications with the British and either would immediately refuse the permission for a transit visa for people who had no visa of destination or, equally bad, would ask the British Embassy its opinion.

From our telephone conversations with Athens, we knew a name. It was the name of the high-ranking official in the Foreign Office who was handling the matter, and who might either make a decision himself or first ask the British. The very fact that we now had a name and did not have to deal with just an impersonal office provided possibilities. And we intended to use this to the hilt.

Members of the Betar cased the Greek Embassy in Vienna. Among other things, they found out that the porter used to go to a little *Gasthaus* (pub) after work to have a glass of wine or a snack. Dr. Schij, who took leave from the hospital for the "diplomatic" mission, and I went to this *Gasthaus* to explain to the porter how desperate we were and to ask his help.

Like most Greeks, he was friendly toward Jews.

"If I can help," he said in his heavily accented but fairly correct German, "I shall be honored to do so. But it must be all right [*sic*]."

"It is not really 'all right,' " I said, "but in these Nazi times one has to do things which are not 'all right' or one cannot help."

"What do you want me to do?"

"Something which would make you proud. All your life you will know that you, just you, saved not one, not ten, but hundreds of lives. From the human point, it is more than all right. From the legal point, not all right at all. But it could not be found out that you did something wrong, and if you make us happy, it is only fair that you, too, should be happy. We want you to share in our happiness with us and we want to give you two thousand marks for it."

The man was flabbergasted, then scared. Two thousand marks were the approximate equivalent of 100 pounds, or $500—a real fortune in 1938. And being with the Embassy, he would have ways to convert the German money into foreign currency. For us this amount was not so much. We would take an extra passenger, to be picked from one of the many wealthy Jews who were beleaguering our office and phone lines with offers to give us anything we wanted to get him out.

"What must I do for two thousand marks?" asked our Greek.

"A lot, but it can never be found out that it was you who did it. And don't forget—it is honorable, humane; you save hundreds of lives and get two thousand marks."

We told him what he would have to do.

"This is impossible! I cannot. I am risking my future."

We doubled the amount and again explained that even if things would go wrong, no one could prove who did it. He finally agreed and assured us that he did not do it for the money, but it would help with his children's education. We knew it was true that the money alone did not do it. We also knew how much the money helped.

We pulled out 1,500 marks as immediate down payment, the other 2,500 to be given to him after he had really done as planned.

Next morning at nine Vienna time, ten o'clock Athens time, the porter put in a *préavis* person-to-person call to the official in the Athens Foreign Ministry who was handling the visa matter. The *préavis* call advised the person called to be ready for a call from the Vienna Consulate General at eleven-thirty Athens time. Shortly before the appointed time, Dr. Schij and I arrived at the Greek

Embassy. The embassy switchboard was located downstairs in the entrance hall in a closetlike enclosure of one corner. Because now, after the Anschluss, the embassy had been reduced to a consulate general, many of the employees had been transferred, and the hall porter was doubling as a switchboard operator.

Shortly after ten-thirty, the long-distance operator informed the porter that he had his party in Athens on the line. The porter, talking in Greek, told the man in Athens that "we have here at the Vienna Consulate General an official of the British Consulate General in Vienna who wants to talk to you." I took the telephone and asked the man in Athens whether he spoke English. He did, but not too well. Most educated Greeks at that time spoke French fluently, and I inquired if he preferred to talk in French. He did. I told him in French that from our, the British, point of view, there was no objection to this transport because we did know the desperate situation of the Jews here and were acting in compliance with what we were unofficially told to do from London. He wanted to know who I was. The connection was poor. I spelled my name. *P-e-e-l.* William Peel. He asked to have something in writing. I told him that this was entirely impossible because of the delicate character of the matter, but that I was known to his consulate as an employee of the British Embassy who handled confidential matters of similar nature. The man in Athens wanted to speak to his consul here and I again gave him the porter.

The connection was now even poorer than before. The porter confirmed in Greek that the man to whom the Athens official had just spoken was known to "us" as a functionary of the British Embassy engaged in confidential work. The Athens official wanted to know to whom he was talking now. The bad phone connection was a blessing. The porter mumbled some name and stressed the urgency. The word *thanatos*—"death"—was understood by me. The porter then repeated my name, spelled the way I just had done over the phone. As suggested by us, the porter told the man in Athens that he could check on the authenticity of the whole matter by calling back right away.

The call from Athens to check whether the conversation was really being conducted with the consulate came not immediately, but in less than an hour. The porter took the call, pretended to connect it with the consul's desk and, in a different voice, became the consul himself. The connection was again very poor, which continued to help. The official in the Foreign Ministry said that he was making a note in the folder and taking down everything that was said over the phone. In view of the urgency of the matter, he would send out the order tomorrow to the Vienna Consulate General to issue the visas, but he requested a detailed report about the whole affair. "Yes, this will follow," the porter said in Greek.

We had achieved what we wanted. Tomorrow the order for the visas would be here, and we would somehow manage to get away without the expected report. Two days later the consul told us he had received a telegram from Athens, not with the order but with the permission to issue us the visa provided the Vienna Consulate General itself was convinced that there were no complications to be feared from any quarter.

The consul knew what was happening to the Viennese Jews, and from previous conversations, we knew that he was perturbed by it. He took the telegram from Athens and went to the chargé d'affaires, who was still present in Vienna, although there was no real embassy anymore. He told him that everything was okay, but he wanted the chargé d'affaires to know about the whole matter. The chargé d'affaires told us to come to the consul the next day with the passports and the small amount of money required for each of the visas.

Next morning we took the passports and the money, and we waited until all the visas were actually stamped into the passports.

The day after, we also obtained the promised Yugoslav transit visa. Now everything really was running smoothly. Up to now, every day, new difficulties had developed. One after another, they had been taken care of, and now there were no more stumbling blocks in our way.

During the next few days, everyone worked under even increased pressure. The telephone never stopped ringing. Whatever sleep we could get in came now in shorter and shorter snatches. No outsider can imagine how much detailed work the departure of such a large group requires. Everybody was now working around the clock to get our first large transport out.

Finally, on Thursday, June 9, 1938, hardly eleven weeks after the German march into Austria, we were ready! All the arrangements for the special train were made, all the passports were in full order, the ship in Athens was paid for—and with foreign currency obtained with useless German marks, exchanged with the explicit permission of the German government! Our young people were packed and ready to go.

I informed Dr. Rajakovitch that we intended to have a little ceremony at the railroad station before the departure. I said that I would deliver a talk, which would be a "pep talk" with of course no incrimination whatsoever of Germany. The purpose of the speech was to reassert control over the large group of young people, I explained, and to make certain that they understood how they were expected to behave during the trip. Dr. Rajakovitch consulted with Dr. Lange, who agreed, provided the speech be submitted to Dr. Rajakovitch for censorship.

In the future I was to see the departure of many more transports with many more young people in each of them, who were escaping from conditions much more perilous than even those that these 386 were leaving behind now. At none of these subsequent transports, although some of them required the overcoming of even greater obstacles, would I ever experience the deep and solemn bliss, the almost religious awe, which permeated me that evening. Leading up to this moment there had been many points at which one single wrong word, one wrong move, would have meant the end of the entire undertaking—and probably also of all of us. The audacity of youth, the knowledge that we had to act, our tenacity which did not permit despair, but most of all, miraculous luck, allowed us to pass all these danger points, often to our own surprised relief. Up to now, not a single group larger than a family of four or five had left Vienna. We had achieved this first large exodus, in the beginning against the opposition of Vienna's official Jewish establishment, later with its covert involvement, and only toward the end, with its hesitant cooperation. Here the "irresponsible" ones, the "young and wild" ones, were sending 386 humans to a new life. With no financial support whatsoever from any outside source, 386 were leaving this hell to go to their new homeland.

Again, as on the fateful eleventh of March, when Chancellor Schuschnigg had resigned, the railroad station was crowded. Again taxi after taxi drove up. But now, how different! From the cars this time jumped boys and girls with packs on their backs. No other luggage had been permitted, and therefore the parents had stuffed the rucksacks so that they were almost bursting at the seams. Though their packs were heavy, the youngsters chatted happily with their comrades, and, with each springy step conveying joyfulness, they entered the huge departure hall. Relatives had not been permitted to accompany them. The Nazis wanted as little commotion as possible—no attention should be focused on this first major exodus of Jews from Vienna.

Otto Seidmann, Erich Wolf, Hugo Lebenschuss, and other Betar leaders had all performed a banner organizational job. Each one of the young people knew in advance to which train car he was assigned, and had exact instructions on how to behave. They had all been ordered to come one hour prior to the departure, no earlier, no later, and here they were.

As the youngsters spilled over the sidewalk and into the train station, their excitement showed in their faces. In their happiness they had forgotten, as only youth can, that just minutes ago they had had to say farewell to their parents, brothers, sisters, their whole family, whom they likely would never see again. Following them into the station, I saw many policemen around and some who were obviously plainclothesmen. One of the latter was so broad-shouldered that from a distance he looked like a box. A press photographer who had sneaked by the police and plainclothesmen was grabbed, and the film was removed from his camera.

As soon as the boys and girls were inside the departure hall, they headed for the waiting train. Each of them went straight to the assigned car and within minutes after their arrival, the hall was empty again.

Approximately half an hour before the scheduled departure of the train, Dr. Lange arrived with Eichmann and two more uniformed SS men. They took their stand on the platform opposite the middle of the long train and were soon joined by Dr. Rajakovitch. As I walked alongside the train, I had to pass this group. I was in quite a quandary: if I did not greet them at all, this could be taken as impertinence. On the other hand, a greeting from a Jew was, of course, never returned. Besides, the obligatory greeting was "Heil Hitler," and Jews, even if they were ready to use this phrase, were not permitted to do so because they were not allowed to take the name of Hitler into their mouths. When referring to HIM they were obliged to speak of "the Fuehrer."

I greeted the Nazi officials with a "Good evening," and it had a most surprising result.

Dr. Rajakovitch stepped out of the group of three, extended his hand to me and replied, *"Guten Abend, Herr Kollege."* Of course I gave him my hand, and to the horror of Lange and Eichmann, he shook it—a truly courageous demonstration of humane spirit on the part of Dr. Rajakovitch.

Dr. Lange ordered me to tell him the exact number of those departing. Apparently he wanted it for his records. I told him there were still 386, just as I had advised him in the afternoon.

Right after I said this, while I was still standing with this group, a loud, commanding voice was heard.

"Amod Dom!" ("Attention!")

"Ahuza tzet!" ("Step outside!")

The Nazis were startled. The way it had been shouted, it was obviously a military command, but it was not German. The Betar had at all times prepared its members for their future life in Israel; this included not only training in the tilling of the land, as well as in Hebrew language and culture, but also training in military preparedness. These young people knew how to drill and how to handle a weapon. It stunned the Germans as, on the command, *"Ahuza tzet!"* all the young people streamed out of the railroad cars and, on the second command, *"B'tor reviot histader!"* ("Form columns of four!"), lined up as ordered. All these maneuvers had been prepared by us to show the Nazis that they were dealing with a well-organized group and thus to increase their readiness to work with us on the emigration.

"Yamin b'tor!" ("Column right face!") This was not a "horde of Jewboys and Jewgirls"—these were not frightened refugees, running frantically around in a cage with no exit. These were young Jews, all proud of the youth-group uniform they were wearing. These were not just individual girls and boys; this was an entire youth organization. What we had been ever dreaming had become a reality. Our Betar was moving to Israel!

Here they stood, lined up in front of the railroad cars, each of them with his or her squad, one squad next to the other, their squad pennants aloft. Those who belonged to other organizations had taken a short training course to comply with these few orders and they fell in very nicely.

After ordering them to stand at attention, Otto Seidmann

commanded, *"Amod noach!"* ("Parade rest!") I stepped before them to deliver the short talk approved by Dr. Rajakovitch.* Certainly neither Lange, nor Eichmann, nor any of the other SS people expected such a speech. It lasted exactly one minute.

"You are leaving, but you are also coming. You are leaving the country in which most of you were born, but in which you always were part of a minority, sometimes treated better, sometimes worse, but always as a minority. You are going home, to the country in which we will shape our own future. To the country which God promised us, in which we were great and heroic. To this land of which each inch is drenched with Jewish blood and which has never ceased to be the center of our dreams. The trip will not be easy, but the reward will be great. There must be strict discipline, and you are used to that. You will be proud humans in your own proud land, and one day you will make it your own state, the Jewish state. As you reenter these railroad cars, you leave behind a country and a people that do not want you, on the way to your brothers and sisters who are longing for you. A happy homecoming. Happy *Aliya!"*†

For a moment there was total silence after my speech.

Then a thin sound was heard. A girl started singing *"Hatikvah,"* ("The Hope"), the Jewish national anthem. In seconds the sound swelled into a truculent, then triumphant loud chorus. As they stood, now at attention, they raised their blue-and-white pennants and sang of the never-ending hope of rebuilding Jerusalem and the Jewish State. I could not keep quiet. Flanked by the three Nazis, come what may, I joined in.

And we were not arrested! Actually, nothing had been said against the Germans.

Otto's command, immediately as *"Hatikvah"* ended, ordered the boys and girls into the train; they rushed to their places, and the train started moving.

As this train, with its singing youngsters, rolled by, uniformed guards looking out from some of the windows, it left behind on the platform an odd little group:

---

*This was, to my knowledge, the only time that a Jewish patriotic speech was delivered at any of the departures in front of the Gestapo.

†*Aliya* is the word which Jews use for immigration into their homeland and translated, means "Ascent."

Dr. Lange, the powerful chief of the Vienna Gestapo, who soon would be working under Eichmann, now far below him in rank.

Eichmann, who would rise to the height of evil and infamy, and would one day dangle from a gallows in Israel.

Dr. Rajakovitch, who had helped us so much to get the transports going, who had just, in a demonstrative way, defied the Nazi code by greeting me and shaking my hand. He would rise in the Nazi ranks and in the process, would become so dehumanized by the Nazi spirit that he would one day stand accused and convicted as a war criminal before a court in this, his Vienna. He would be tried and convicted of war crimes by the Austrian War Crimes Court in March 1965. The Netherlands would seek his extradition for his role in the deportation of 100,000 Jews from Holland to Auschwitz, including a little girl called Anne Frank.

And I, who could be shot or tortured to death at the whim of any of the other three in the group here, but who would become an officer in the U.S. Military Intelligence Service, a lieutenant colonel, U.S. Army. And, in 1945–46, I would be a member of the prosecution team at the U.S. War Crimes Trials in Germany and in 1963 would be invited by the attorney general of Israel to come for the trial, conducted for the murder of 6 million Jews, against this arrogant, always viciously smiling first lieutenant SS who was standing next to me.

chapter 2

LONDON INTERLUDE: THE MARBLE-HEARTED AND THE FOOLS

While we were preparing the departure of our first major transport with 386 aboard in June of 1938, I had also made plans to obtain help abroad for what we were trying to turn into a rapidly increased evacuation effort. I was to leave the next morning for London by myself to organize Jewish and Christian support for our undertaking by presenting my eyewitness description of the Jewish situation in all its gruesome details. In preparing for this trip, Mr. Gildemeester, of the Friends, again proved helpful. He was a British subject, and through some connections at the British Consulate in Vienna, he was able to achieve the nearly impossible—he obtained a British visa for me. More than that, he gave me letters of introduction to George Lansbury, the leader of the British Labour Party, and to some politically influential Friends leaders in England.

This effort, however, took care of getting *into* England, but to leave Austria I still had to obtain an exit permit from the Gestapo. Because I was too well known a number for the Nazi authorities to grant such a permit without further investigation, my request was shunted by one bureaucrat after another all the way up to Eichmann. Although Eichmann was against any large-scale Jewish migration to Palestine, furthering our work was now Nazi official policy, and he had to comply with his superior's wishes. I was ordered to appear at his office in the Gestapo headquarters in the Hotel Metropol. There, Kuchmann, Eichmann's right-hand man, demanded to know exactly in what way would my leaving influence the flow of emigrants. I told him about the plans I had discussed with Mr. Gildemeester and stressed the expected financial aid from "World Jewry." With this information Kuchmann left me standing in front of his desk and disappeared into Eichmann's office. When he returned, he ordered: "Follow me, Jew."

As I was standing at attention before Eichmann, he smirkingly looked me over from head to toe. Suddenly he hissed: *"Haende an die Hosennaht!"* ("Hands glued to your side!") He then walked behind me, apparently enjoying the thought that I would be worried about what he might do to me from behind. Having completed his little promenade around me, he sat down behind his desk and demanded to know "what Jewish trick is this wanting to leave after you first said that you could get thousands out?" I explained to him the need for financial support from "World Jewry" and for establishing an ongoing landing procedure in Palestine. He wanted to know why the Palestinians could not come to Vienna to work all that out. I explained to him that while the people from the landing organization might dare to come, the financiers would certainly not travel to Vienna these days, and actions had to be coordinated if he wanted it all to grow into a really mass movement. I also assured him that in my absence the people now in the office of the Perl-Aktion would be well able to carry on.

Eichmann allowed me a maximum of two weeks abroad, after which I would have to return. In addition, he demanded that I supply the name of a person who would serve as a hostage for ensuring that I would return, or, as Eichmann expressed it, "For whom we can arrange a little necktie party if you don't come back." I promised to supply a hostage. From Eichmann's office, I went to see my close friend Dr. Eduard Pachtmann, a leading Viennese Zionist and well-known lawyer. Without hesitation, he agreed to serve as a hostage for me. He told me though, "I know you will not let me face the noose; still I also know that to have once been a hostage is not good. You don't get prominent with those people. They might use me later on without my consent for other cases. But we must give the alarm to the rest of the world abroad about what is going on here. We must involve Jews in the free world in our undertaking."

The day after, I called Eichmann's office and reported that I had a hostage and asked that they arrange for the exit permit and for the "right"—never before applied for by another Jew—to return to Germany. The man to whom I spoke, a Mr. Guenther, an assistant of Kuchmann's, kept me waiting on the line and then told me—apparently after he had verified my claim—that he would inform the police and that I should come to the police's Emigration Department in Dorotheergasse. There they would take care of the formalities. When I arrived at that office, I could bypass the long lines of Jews waiting there. And to the amazement of my fellow Jews, I was treated with respect. The officials at that office did not know what was going on, but Eichmann's office had called and I was to be given a permit to return.

German occupation of Austria was still new, and there were many administrative shortcomings, particularly in the communication between the new German and the old Austrian authorities. Passport matters were handled by former Austrian police officers, and fortunately a snafu occurred in the handling of my exit visa. The issuance of a return visa (to a Jew!) was so out of the ordinary that it somehow overshadowed the demand on me to supply a hostage. It was either misunderstood or, less likely, overlooked. It seemed to me that the Austrians thought that I had to supply—or had already supplied—the name of the hostage to the Germans, while the Germans thought that the Austrian police had taken care of the matter. Whatever the reason, I received an exit permit and a permit to return without ever having to supply any name. Now with the precious passport with the British visa, the German exit permit, and unique return permit in my pocket, I immediately proceeded to Dr. Pachtmann and told him, to his relief, that he was not a hostage and that his name had not been mentioned. No one but he and I knew of our conversation.* Of course, no Jew in his right mind would ask for a return visa. But because it was such an unusual document, it proved most valuable—possibly life-saving—soon enough.

June 9, the day of the departure of our first major transport with 386 aboard, had been a day of unabating excitement. Before we could experience the elation of seeing all these youngsters (among them my younger, only brother) leave for safety and a new life, dozens of seemingly insurmountable last-minute obstacles had suddenly appeared. But as filled as the day and evening had been with emotion, I knew that despite my being near total exhaustion, the upcoming night would not at all be one of rest or even of just "after the fact" relaxation. While getting my things together for the morning flight to London, I had to think of my family, most of whom I would never see again.

My parents were dead by then. We had been an extremely close-knit family, more a clan, guided by my eighty-one-year-old grandfather who was revered not only by his seven children but by their offspring as well—especially by me. He was a man of superior intellectual gifts who had played a major role in forming me, and I was aware that I would most probably never see him again, nor most of my aunts, uncles, and numerous cousins. My expectation, unfortunately, proved correct. Grandfather was soon murdered by the Nazis, preceded by some, and followed by others of his children and grandchildren.

I was taking leave that night not only of my family, however. This city, Vienna, after all, had been my home. I had gone to school there, had graduated from two of its colleges, and, young as I was, I had had a promising career as a lawyer there. The happy times that I had seen in this same city were now overshadowed by murderous hostility. Among my many Christian friends, among the clients—many of whom I had helped out of desperate situations—not one had come forward with an offer of help. One of my high school

---

*Dr. Pachtmann and his wife later made it safely to Palestine.

teachers, Dr. Franz Ahammer, whom I had held in high esteem and with whom I had kept contact during my university years, was a member of a German nationalistic fraternity and thus had excellent Nazi connections. I went to him to plead for his intervention on behalf of Kuno, a young cousin of mine, who had also been a student of this teacher's. Kuno had been arrested in the mass sweep of May 30 and had been deported to Dachau. Dr. Ahammer, the man whom I considered to be not only a friend but someone who stood above party lines, was embarrassed. His excuses came forth sheepishly at first, but as he spoke, he became more resolute: he could not do anything so risky as intervening for a Jew.

Hostility or—at best—complete lack of concern was every-where. There was no place to turn—the very building I lived in, the other houses on my street—all seemed to exude a feeling of animos-ity toward me. One might expect that under these circumstances parting from my old environment would have presented no conflict. Of course, I was happy to be able to leave, but I cannot deny that some ambivalence entered my feelings that last night in Vienna. During all my hectic last days I had not given myself a chance to identify and sort out my own emotions. Now they came suddenly rushing in on me, and I had to deal with everything at once—the total collapse of all that I had belonged to: my family, the city in which I had grown up, and the beginnings of a successful profes-sional career.

I was alone now and the night outside exacerbated the silence in the apartment. The quiet was the more impressive as it so contrasted with the hustle and bustle of the last weeks that had come to a climax this last afternoon before we all left for the railroad station. The hectic place—crowded with nervous, shouting people, with the telephone ringing and dozens of persons in the waiting room and on the stairs begging loudly to be taken along—had changed to a place of almost sinister silence.

A light knock came at the door. Furtively, a lone girl slipped into my apartment and immediately began helping me to pack. To have been seen coming into my apartment would have meant immediate arrest and deportation to a concentration camp for this girl because, it so happened, she was an "Aryan." Her name was Lore and she was known to my closest friends as a former girl friend of mine—one whom I had met before the Germans came into Austria.

Actually, she was not my girl friend but my bride of seven weeks—a fact unknown to anyone except her parents, my brother, and the chief rabbi of Vienna. I had literally "picked up" Lore in the park.

Nine months before the Nazis marched into Austria, I had gone to bed very early one evening, right after supper. I was a bachelor then and usually stayed up quite late. To catch up on my rest, I made one day each week a "sleep day," when I would sleep thirteen hours or so. The evening I met Lore I had gone to bed early but found it hard to fall asleep. It was early June and still daylight in balmy Vienna. The spring air and the hum of life coming in the windows made me long for life, not sleep. I tossed and turned and at last decided to get up and go down to the Stadtpark, the large city park one block away, to pick up some young lady there to bring her to my room for an hour or two before I finally retired for the night and went to sleep. The park was almost deserted but well lit. Across from the romantically illuminated trees and bushes was a long row of empty chairs, and on one of those chairs a girl was sitting. It was Lore, who had had an argument with her father and had come to the park alone to calm down, to do some crying, and to contemplate. I passed her, but as she was sitting, I could not see much of her figure and, as her head was bowed, not much of her face either. I did not know whether she was worthwhile my investing my time, but there was no one else around right then. So I returned, stepped close to her, and in front of the long row of empty chairs, I asked the most stupid question: "Is this seat free?"

It had the desired effect. Furiously, she said: "Idiot! Look at all these empty chairs! Take the one farthest away!" I had achieved the initial breakthrough; she had answered.

I sat down next to her and further lured her into talking. My immediate plans for the evening did not work out, but a date followed, then a second and a third. I found that I was in love as I had never been before. A few months later, we became engaged.

I knew that I would be leaving Vienna, and so we decided that it would not be safe for Lore to accompany me. But Nazis or not, we wanted to get married prior to my leaving. This seemed impossible. Yet it was not entirely. The Nuremberg Laws, which of course forbade marriage between Jews and Aryans, were actually in force from the day the Germans had marched in. But the new racial laws were not immediately officially promulgated. I went to see Dr.

Taglicht, the chief rabbi of Vienna's Jewish community, who knew me well. When I asked him to marry us, he believed that I was kidding. I pointed out to him that the Nuremberg Laws had not yet been officially announced and that according to old Austrian law, a religious ceremony alone sufficed to make a marriage valid. He would not have to record the ceremony anywhere, I told him; but Lore—who was about to begin conversion procedures—and I wanted to know that we were married according to Jewish laws. With much hesitation, the rabbi agreed, and the conversion and marriage ceremonies were performed in strict secrecy.

The coming of the Nazis had made even our talking to each other risky. We met secretly, and when we went anywhere together, one of us walked in front of the other. And now, in my apartment, we were packing for me to leave Vienna, probably forever. I could take only one valise along, but Jews were then still permitted to send one large piece of luggage abroad. While I was busy preparing our transport, Lore had purchased a large trunk. We were packing it to be sent to Jerusalem where it would be picked up by my brother who was now heading toward Palestine on our illegal transport. We packed all night and just as the sky started turning gray and the first horse-drawn milk wagons rode by, the packing was completed. After the exhaustion of the last days and nights, I fell onto the sofa for a short fitful sleep, while Lore sat next to me holding my hand. I woke up at about seven—my hands wet from her tears.

Shortly afterward, my aunt Vally, who was to accompany me to the airport, arrived. Lore, she, and I left in the same taxi, despite the danger inherent in Lore's being seen with us.

We arrived at the airport in plenty of time for the flight to London, which was to touch down in Prague and Rotterdam. We did not foresee any difficulty: all my documents were on me, I had only the one piece of luggage permitted, and in my wallet I knew I had a 10-mark bill—the only money one could take abroad.

When the customs' search began, my luggage was thoroughly examined. Everything was OK there.

"How much money do you have?"

"Ten marks," I said.

"Show me."

I reached for my wallet and pulled out the 10-mark bill.

"Give me your wallet." Without trepidation, I handed it to the uniformed official. It was one of the old-fashioned large European ones and was bulging with papers. Just before leaving home, I had checked it and taken out the 200 marks which I then had on me. As the customs official, in the presence of a police officer went slowly through the papers piece by piece, fear suddenly shot through me. Between the photographs of my deceased parents another 10-mark bill had become stuck. This was hardly more than $4, but it constituted a violation of the currency laws, and my flight would now be in question.

"You want to smuggle money out?"

I quickly pointed out to him the rush and excitement which go with leaving and remarked on the smallness of the amount for which I certainly would not risk my life. Both officials seemed convinced without saying so. But the customs man continued the search. I thought that my heart would stop beating when, folded into a small piece of paper on which I had written the address of an acquaintance in London, a 20-mark bill showed up. I had always been absentminded about money and seldom knew how much I had on hand. I had not attached the necessary importance to it to have made a thorough enough search through my wallet.

"You almost had us convinced, Jew, but now we see how tricky you all are. You, of course, are not flying. And we will now search everything."

While the plane was already warming up its engines, I assured the officials that if I wanted to smuggle, I would surely not try to get 30 marks out. Even if I could have changed them abroad—which was doubtful—this constituted a sum not worth the risk. It did not impress them. They took me to a separate room for a body search, external and internal. At the same time, my one piece of luggage was being rechecked. During the body search, I decided to use an approach other than one of imploring them.

I told the men that I was on a semiofficial mission, as could be seen from my return visa. I was going abroad on matters of Jewish mass emigration that had been previously coordinated with Gestapo action. Important people were waiting for me at the airport in London, and Jewish emigration—so important a program for the Reich—would be endangered if I missed this plane. They now looked closely at my passport, which they, being customs people, had checked previously only for details concerning my exit. They were quite taken aback when they saw the return visa. Nothing was found on my body, nothing in my shoes, and nothing sewn into my clothing. When I was brought out from the little room in which I had been searched, the examination of the luggage was not yet entirely completed. My aunt and Lore had in the meanwhile persuaded the people from the airline to wait until I came out. Yet even after I was out, I was not permitted to board, and the order was given for the plane to leave. But within seconds after the order, the man searching my luggage was through and stated "Nothing found."

As the customs official then indicated he would let me go, Lore and my aunt hurriedly threw my clothes, shoes, and papers back into the valise. I grabbed the suitcase and without having the chance to say good-bye to either my aunt or Lore—much less the time to embrace her—I made a dash for the plane. With some of my belongings trailing out of the partly opened valise, I raced up the stairs and jumped in, just as they were beginning to slam the door shut.

Even when the plane was in the air, I could not feel safe. We were still over German territory, and after the landing in Prague—Czechoslovakia was still free—we would fly over Germany again on our way to Rotterdam. At that time flying was not so safe, and emergency landings were not unusual. But everything went smoothly. After a short stop in Prague and a short flight over Germany, I could see that the countryside below was crisscrossed by canals: we were over Holland.

In London I went directly to the Hotel Russell on Russell Square. I was too exhausted and shaken by all that had just happened to feel up to calling anyone right away. It was not until the next morning that I called the office of the Zionist Revisionists and spoke to Vladimir Jabotinsky,* the leader of the movement, who had inspired in all of us the thinking and the philosophy which stood behind our organizing the large escape program. *"Baruch Habah!"* ("Blessed be your coming!") said Jabotinsky whom we lovingly called Jabo. "Come right over and report."

For four hours I talked and talked. It was the first eyewitness account Jabotinsky had received from Austria, and it was the first opportunity for me to describe in a free country, to a man who cared and understood, what was happening to our Jewish brothers

*Vladimir Jabotinsky was later more often referred to by his Jewish given name Zeev.

and sisters. I also showed Jabotinsky the letters of introduction from Mr. Gildemeester, and I strongly suggested that I act in England strictly as the representative of Die Aktion and not as a Revisionist. The Jewish establishment would be set even more against illegal immigration if it were so obviously a Revisionist undertaking. Jabotinsky first objected to this idea, but at my urging, he finally agreed. He noted at the time, however, "It won't help. It is acting and doing things without British permission and against their wishes to which the Jewish establishment will object. But try it if you feel you have to."

The following weeks saw me in the famous double-decker buses from early morning to evening crossing the sprawling city of London and its suburbs from one end to the other. First, I presented my letter of introduction to Mr. George Lansbury, who received me in the House of Commons, listened attentively to my report, asked relevant questions, and gave me letters of introduction to other important political figures. One of these was Lord Winterton, the head of the British delegation for the forthcoming International Conference on Refugees in Evian, France. He was a key figure and together with the other British politicians had within his power the possibility of saving many thousands, if not millions.

The British Empire was then huge, and parts of it were extremely thinly populated. Ties with the dominions were close. Although our main target for immigration was Palestine, there were many other places for which we had to seek entrance to cope with the emergency. Several of the territories of the British colonies, as well as the dominions of Australia, Canada, New Zealand, and South Africa were almost empty. When I met with the commissioners of the respective dominions, they all listened and expressed shock about what was happening. They voiced their intention to do "their best," but when I tried to nail anyone down to a specific promise, the answer I received was evasive. The commissioner for Australia was the only one who did not seem to be on the defensive. He told me that he would write to Canberra of our talk, but that, of course, any decision would rest with the Australian government. No answer could be expected for months. I tried to get across to him the idea that the situation was urgent, that he should ask for an emergency measure to admit 100,000 Jews immediately. The best he could do was to promise to forward this suggestion of mine.

Of all my visits with these marble-hearted British officials, the one with Lord Winterton was the most crushing to my hopes. To this day the memory of that meeting retains for me a nightmarish aura. He was the most powerful figure in the British delegation that was soon to leave for Evian on Lake Geneva for the International Conference on Refugees. As I entered Lord Winterton's office, I could almost smell the stuffiness that emanated from the man with the thin hair seated behind a huge desk.

Lord Winterton assured me of his government's "best efforts," a phrase used till today internationally to cloud an issue. His real intentions became clear to me when he expressed "concern" for the fate of Polish and Rumanian Jews. He told me, "You must not be too nationalistic and think of German and Austrian Jews only. You know that in Rumania and Poland, too, there are tendencies to drive the Jews out. If we open the gates of Palestine, or any other country, this would encourage Rumania and Poland to expel their Jews." Although this sounded humane, it was nothing but a fraud. It meant that Lord Winterton intended to follow, in Evian, a policy of bottling up all of Europe's imperiled Jews. And this is exactly what he did within a few weeks.

Many beautiful words were minced in lovely Evian on beautiful Lake Geneva, yet the conference was not just a failure, it was counterproductive. The United States had initiated that international meeting but apparently more for appearance's sake than for results. America shares with the other participating world power, Great Britain, the guilt for the failure, but most of the smaller countries cannot take pride, either, in the position they took. Several South American countries said that they were in principle ready to admit refugees . . . but they excluded professional people and businessmen, and thus most European Jews. Australia's announcement sounded promising at first. It stated that Australia knew no racial problem. But the conclusion Australia drew from it was different from what one could have expected. Because she had no racial problem, she did not want to create one by letting Jewish refugees in. France stated that she had already done so much that more could not be expected. New Zealand was concerned but not ready to change the immigration rules existing prior to the murderous Jew hunt going on in Europe. The United States was equally not ready to consider changes in its immigration quotas. But the United States was magnanimously ready to let those in who did qualify under the quotas established decades before. Three countries, two European

and one in the Western Hemisphere, in their humanitarianism put
the others to shame: Denmark, Holland, and Santo Domingo.
They declared themselves ready to take in those who had escaped
from Hitler Germany. But Holland and Denmark were threatened
themselves by Germany—and actually were soon to be invaded.
And Santo Domingo, as well-meaning as it was, had limited absorp-
tion capacity.

Yet there was one land where every Jew had hundreds of
thousands of friends who felt that they were brothers. The Jews of
Palestine were stretching out their arms to embrace those who were
suffering the age-old Jewish tragedy of persecution. Many of those
who had to flee had relatives in Palestine. But when Professor
Weizmann on behalf of the Jewish Agency wanted to address the
conference regarding emigration to Palestine, the British objected.
They endeavored, they said, to keep "political issues" out. The
American chief delegate, Mr. Myron Taylor, did not support Weizmann's demand to speak before the conference but suggested as a
compromise that Weizmann be permitted to address not the official
conference but a private meeting instead. The British turned this
down too. The American stand, if it can be called that at all, had
been for show only. The U.S. delegation agreed in the end with the
British that the request of Palestine's Jews to let their persecuted
brothers enter Palestine and the offer of a guarantee by World Jewry
to take care there of their needs, should not even be brought before
the conference.

No wonder the Nazi publication *Danziger Vorposten* (The
Danzig Advance Patrol) stated at the end of the Evian conference:
"We see . . . that no state is prepared [to accept] a few thousand
Jews. Thus the conference serves to justify Germany's policy
against Jewry."

To say that Lord Winterton's Evian conference had achieved
nothing would be an understatement. Determined as the Nazis were
to "purify" Europe of Jews, the Evian conference pushed the
Nazis into thinking of solutions other than emigration.

After six weeks in London, after making appointments and
running from the offices of one high official to another, I still had
gotten nowhere. True, I had seen some members of Parliament,
including the already sympathetic Captain Cazalet, who later on in
debates on illegal immigration in the House of Commons would

prove to be our friend, but there was no real relief for those whom I
had left behind and who had to get out now. The world was
watching with interest and maybe with some sympathy, but no one
in power was ready to move a finger to save his fellow human
beings from torture and murder in Nazi-held lands.

Full of despair, I returned to Mr. Lansbury who now arranged
an appointment with the all-powerful British secretary of state for
the colonies—Mr. Malcolm MacDonald. The minister of the colonies, whose office was located on Downing Street, received me with
the same hollow friendliness to which I was accustomed by now.
Next to his desk was a huge antique globe to remind him and his
visitors—so it seemed to me—how much of the real globe was then
under British control.

Again, I could just as well have spoken to a wall. Mr. Mac-
Donald did not even pretend to be interested in my plea. He shoved
the whole irksome matter off on Lord Winterton, whom I had already seen and who in turn passed it all off on the International
Conference on Refugees in Evian, which, as I correctly foresaw,
would bury the question of refugees by appointing committees to investigate the problem.

In contrast, Colonel Wedgwood, M.P., a firm believer in the
Bible and a great humanitarian, did not have to be convinced. A
great supporter of the Jewish people and one who believed that, in
accordance with the Holy Scriptures, the Jews were destined to
rebuild the Holy Land, he was also a personal friend of Mr.
Jabotinsky's. But wholehearted as his and the support of our other
friends was, it was not enough to alter the course of the British
administration. When humanitarian strivings collided with what
British statesmen felt to be the interest of their colonial empire,
most of them knew where they had to stand.

But the Jewish leaders were even worse. They did not even
pretend. Not even did they so much as offer the familiar "I'll see
what I can do for you." Their "no's" were categoric.

After the Holocaust, 6 million dead Jews later, when what had
happened was put into the final chilling figures, the Jews—rightly—
blamed the Nazis; they also blamed—but not enough—the British,
and all the nations that had stood by silently while the Germans did
the slaughtering and the British the bottling up in Europe of those
being slaughtered. Books were written and plays were produced
pointing out the culpability of the Pope for his general silence and
because he never excommunicated Hitler, though he had been born

and baptized a Catholic, and never threatened to excommunicate other Catholics who took part in the tortures and the massacres. But while this hardly diminished the guilt of others, the Jews have not pointed to the silence and inaction of their own leaders during these frightful years. And in the case of the Jews, it was more than inaction; it was at times outright interference with rescue efforts.

To involve the major Jewish organizations, I acted as diplomatically as I could. I knew that I was anathema to them, a wild "radical," and decided to establish a buffer between our illegal immigration efforts and the more "responsible" Jewish establishment. I went first to see the highly revered chief rabbi of the United Hebrew Congregations of the British Empire, Rabbi Joseph Herman Hertz, whose position, I thought, would place him above intra-Jewish factional warfare. Also I considered him a fighter for Jewish rights. I knew that in czarist times he had tried to organize public opinion against the "yellow-ticket system," according to which Jewish females could not be admitted to Russian universities unless they first registered as prostitutes.

But my research on his background had not been thorough enough. I had not been aware that Chief Rabbi Hertz was a fervent Anglophile. Previously he had been a rabbi in Transvaal in the Boer Republic, South Africa. After the diamond field discoveries in The Rand, when the British sent troops in and war broke out between Britain and the Orange Free State, the rabbi was expelled from the country by President Krueger of South Africa. In the South Africans' fight for freedom against expanding British colonialism, Rabbi Hertz had taken sides with the British even after Lord Kitchener, the British chief of staff, ordered noncombatants herded into what were then called concentration camps. After the British crushed the Boers, he returned to his post and was rewarded with a membership on the British high commissioner's consultative committee.

During our first talk, he did listen to me with obviously genuine compassion, and I left with the hope that through his powerful intervention I might swing official Jewish opinion to support the "illegal" rescue work. But I was mistaken. Apparently, those Jewish officials who opposed our action knew this committed rabbi's weak point. At my next appointment with him, I found that his attitude had become woefully negative. He "wished" he could help, but "after talking to the community leaders. . . ." And I now heard the old familiar arguments: to take other people's lives into one's own hands, one had to be "responsible" and "experienced";

one should leave things in the hands of the official Jewish organizations who would certainly "do whatever could be done," etc. But of all his arguments, I felt there was one he expressed with particular conviction: the British were traditionally the best friends the Jews had, and as they were so set against immigration to Palestine, the only way to handle the situation was by "quiet diplomacy" and by not doing anything that might ruffle them.

It was the first time I had heard this formulation—"quiet diplomacy." I learned later that the Jewish leadership continued this quiet diplomacy through the reign of terror in Auschwitz, Treblinka, Bergen-Belsen, and the other death camps. While in Auschwitz alone every day from dawn to dawn 12,000 humans were forced into the gas chambers, and smaller children were not even gassed but thrown into the stoves alive, the dabbling of these nondiplomats in "quiet diplomacy" continued.

Because it proved clearly impossible to gain the support of the Jewish organizations for the illegal immigration itself, we decided to try to obtain funds at least for the aid of those destitute ones whom we had already landed. But even this proved too daring a venture for the Jewish "leaders." The request for aid in settling those already landed was not made by me. It was submitted by the New Zionist Organization headquartered in London—the one founded by Mr. Vladimir Jabotinsky. The application for funds to aid at least those 386 whom we had already landed was directed to the powerful umbrella group created to coordinate activities on behalf of refugees from Nazi Germany, the "Council for German Jewry." The chairman of the council was the Right Honourable Viscount Samuel, P.C., etc., etc. He was that British Jew who had been high commissioner of Palestine and under whose "leadership" the Jews had ceded all of Palestine *east* of the Jordan, 85 percent of the originally allotted land, to the Arabs, in the hopes of thus obtaining a lasting peace. Viscount Samuel's council did not handle our request without the proper formalities. A decision that was very important in principle was to be made, and these people were very proper indeed. On July 26, 1938, the executive of the Council for German Jewry met and reached the following conclusion:

> The application for a grant to the 380 emigrants from Austria who recently reached Palestine was again considered with care. . . . The Executive of the Council [the answer to the application continues]

deprecates all emigration which is not properly organised and which does not make proper provisions for the welfare of the emigrants. The Executive cannot in any way encourage illegal immigration into Palestine and, for this reason, cannot make any contribution toward the object to which your letter refers. *

Well, here we had it, in black on white. The all-powerful council had not, of course, helped us with the rescue effort out of Germany and into Palestine, and now they even had the chutzpah to censure us for not having also prepared in advance for the "welfare" of those we saved, after their arrival in the homeland.

As disheartening as the meetings with the marble-hearted British politicians were and those with Jewish leaders who were too myopic to grasp the extent of the developing tragedy and to act accordingly, as reassuring for me was each day the arrival of the mailman. I had rented a small furnished room in Finchley Road in the Hampstead section of London, near the headquarters of the Revisionist organization. Every morning at close to eight o'clock the first mail delivery brought mail from abroad to Finchley Road, and the letters I received during breakfast often provided me with the happiest moments of the day. There was hardly one morning which did not bring me mail from one of the 386 who had escaped with the first large transport. Every one of these letters strengthened my determination to achieve on that day a breakthrough which not only would help to continue our work but would make it grow into a mass evacuation of the endangered. And Lore's letters were even more of a boost. She continued to live under her "Aryan" maiden name and was apparently safe. Her confidence in my ability to succeed with my mission was so unconditional that it too helped me to start each day with new hope.

But not all the news from abroad was good. No "bad" news could get out of Vienna, but the news from Palestine was marred by frightening information about British actions there. With the first large transport we had overcome the first front of our four-front war. We had gotten the 386 out of Germany. But when the British visualized that the Anschluss of Austria would heighten the persecution of the Jews in Germany and with it the dire urge on the part of the Jews to escape, they began feverishly building up their own

*Author's italics.

anti-Jewish action—our second front. Their effort was applied in three ways: by a sea blockade against illegal emigré transports along the Palestine coast; by an increase in their propaganda among Arabs to commit acts of terrorism against the Jews; and by direct British terror against the Jewish population, particularly against the "illegals."

One of these methods was the principle of inciting one part of a population against another. The British had secured and extended their colonial might by systematic application of that policy. In India, for example, when trouble erupted between the Hindus and the Moslems, the British assumed the position of objective arbiter for whose favor both sides had to compete. With the rise of Hitler and the likelihood of greatly increased Jewish immigration, the British stepped up their efforts to have the Arabs commit terrorist acts against the Jews. Ever since 1920 the British had organized terror, but now they pushed harder. Thus "spontaneous" Arab riots had broken out in Palestine on April 19, 1936. Numerous Jews were ambushed and slaughtered, and Jewish villages were attacked and set afire, but the British claimed the sole right to maintain law and order and interdicted any kind of self-defense by the Jews. At the same time, the Arab villages were infested with agitators who assured the population that *"a'dowlah ma'ana"*—the government is with us. How the British exercised the exclusive protective role they assumed and what actual risks rioting Arabs faced is best exemplified by the complaint of a British soldier whose job it was to fight Arab terrorism. He described his role in the prestigious London journal *New Statesman and Nation* on September 20, 1936:

> At night when we are guarding the line against the Arabs who come to blow it up, we often see them at work but are forbidden to fire on them. We may only fire into the air, and they, upon hearing the report, make their escape. But do you think we can give chase? Why, we must go on our hands and knees and find every spent cartridge case which must be handed in or woe betide us.

Rosh Pina is a Jewish village in the hills of northern Galilee. Its inhabitants are mostly small farmers. After numerous Arab attacks had occurred in various parts of the country, Rosh Pina heard that agitators in the nearby Arab village of Djani were

planning to attack this fairly isolated Jewish village, and this expected assault was the more fraught with danger because of Djani's
strategic position on Mount Canaan overlooking Rosh Pina. On
Thursday, April 21, 1938, while we were preparing our first large
transport, the saving of the 386, three young men were guarding the
road to Rosh Pina determined not to let strange Arabs into the
vicinity of their village. One of these three was twenty-one-year-old
Shalom Tabachnik who had fled Europe "illegally." After his
arrival, Tabachnik changed his name to the Hebrew one of
Shlomoh Ben Yosef. Also in the group of three was seventeen-year-
old Abraham Shein, who had come to Palestine as a child. Like
Shlomoh Ben Yosef, he was a native of Poland. The third one was
Shalom Dyuravin, nineteen, a native of Jerusalem. Around noon-
time, a bus full of Arabs of whom many were strange to this
neighborhood came down from Safed on the road to Rosh Pina.
The three young Jews stepped out onto the winding mountain road
and tried to stop the bus. A single warning shot was fired into the
air. Nobody was hurt, but although not one drop of blood had been
shed, the British saw here a chance to set a draconic example for
any Jew who engaged in self-defense, especially if he was an "illegal."

The trial started on May 24, 1938. It adjourned on Saturdays
and Sundays, but by June 3 the judges were ready to pass sentence.
These military officers who had served in India or other colonies
before, knew how to treat "troublesome natives." "Shlomoh Ben
Yosef," the presiding officer announced, "I sentence you to the
gallows, and you will hang until dead." As the judge completed his
sentence, Ben Yosef rose and called out: "Long live the Jewish State
on both sides of the Jordan." Unperturbed, the judge turned to
Shein, the seventeen-year-old, and announced: "Abraham Shein, I
sentence you to the gallows, and you will hang until dead." Shalom
Dyuravin, the only one of the three who was a native of Palestine,
was sentenced to life imprisonment until such time if and as a high
commissioner of Palestine should pardon him.

The general commanding the British forces in Palestine confirmed Ben Yosef's death sentence on June 25, two weeks after my
arrival in London, and commuted to life imprisonment the sentence
of the juvenile, Abraham Shein. The date of Ben Yosef's execution
was set for just four days later.

Within hours after the confirmation of Yosef's death sentence, blood was flowing in the streets of Tel Aviv. Throngs of young Jews demonstrated against the intended hanging. It would be the first hanging of a Jew in Palestine since 1,800 years earlier when the Romans executed the Jews who under Bar Kochbah's leadership rebelled against the iron-fisted Roman occupation of their country. Just as the Roman military, so did the British soldiers prevail. The well-trained troops using their guns charged the demonstrators of whom more than eighty were wounded.

The day prior to the execution date, a group of journalists obtained permission to visit Ben Yosef. In his cell, they saw that he had scratched into the wall the words: "To die or to conquer the Height." When one of the newsmen tried to console him, Ben Yosef answered: "Do not console me; I need no consolation. I am proud to be the first Jew to go to the gallows for the Land of Israel. . . . In dying, I shall do my people a greater service than in my life. . . . Let the world see that Jews are not afraid to face death."

Yzhak Gurion, a personal friend and an eyewitness to the execution, later wrote a book about the British use of the gallows in Palestine.* He describes Ben Yosef's last night in Acre prison, the ancient fortress built during the time of the Crusades and with walls so thick that Napoleon was unable to take it.

Calmly and with a smile on his lips, Shlomoh Ben Yosef stood in his red clothes behind the bars of his death cell and spoke with his close friends who had come to part with him. His was the smile of a person who had long since bid farewell to this earth and had already been transported to the heavens above . . . We wanted to tell him that all hope was not yet lost, but he pointed to the inscription which he had engraved on the wall of his death cell: *"Tov lamut b'ad hamoledet"*— it is good to die for the homeland . . . I told him that his aged mother had sent a telegram to the High Commissioner requesting that the execution be delayed because she wanted to embrace him once more before the hanging . . . For a moment he was overcome by grief. He loved his mother dearly . . . But soon his eyes lit up again. He loved the land of Israel and its freedom more than anything else, even more than his youthful life.

*Triumph on the Gallows. New York: American Memorial Committee, 1950.

At sunrise on June 29, Shlomoh Ben Yosef marched to the gallows. Those convicted with him heard him sing the *"Hatikvah,"* the Jewish national anthem, which asserts that wherever the Jews may have been living since the destruction of Jerusalem by the Romans, they carried Palestine with them and that the trust that it would be reestablished never died. They heard him shout, "To die or to conquer the Height," followed by *"Yechi Jabotinsky!"* ("Long live Jabotinsky!") Then there was silence.

Ben Yosef had been a friend of several people in our group and his death—we referred to it as a murder by the occupying colonial power—was a hard blow to all of us, but this was no time to give in to feelings of doom. Personally I felt even more strongly the duty to move British politicians toward some rescue action and to interest Jewish organizations in our cause. However, the execution of Ben Yosef had only increased the Jewish leadership's disdain for us and any like us who incurred British wrath with "illegal" acts.

On top of all that an unfortunate split occurred in our own group in Vienna. Those who had stayed behind decided that they could handle the situation without Krivoshein and pushed him out of the entire undertaking. Jabotinsky was furious about this and so was I. Krivoshein had proven during the arranging of the plans for the four transports that he was capable. He knew the ropes, knew who was who in the smuggling trade in the Balkans, and he had shown himself to be a match for those he was dealing with. It was clear to me that Paul Haller, who had taken command, was superior as an ideologist, but as far as practical matters went, Haller stood with both feet firmly in the air. I could not go back to Nazi Germany at this point, and so Jabotinsky decided to send Mordechai Katz, the secretary general of the World Betar Organization, to Vienna to make certain that the hoped-for large-scale immigration became a reality despite the split.

When Katz arrived, Haller obtained the permission from Eichmann to leave Vienna for Greece in order to procure more ships. In Athens, he was shown various ships and decided on one S.S. *Socrates,* for which he paid 2,000 pounds ($10,000) as a down payment. This ship was to proceed on a certain date to Fiume, an Italian seaport on the Adriatic, and to smuggle from there 1,000 immigrants to Palestine.

Two hundred and twenty tough, ideologically well-prepared

youngsters had already arrived in Fiume. Mordechai Katz had brought them there from Eastern Europe in a dramatic voyage which had involved several perilous border crossings. Most of the boys and girls had come from Poland, not yet occupied by the Germans but threatened almost daily by the Nazi media, with invasion by Hitler. In Poland a brilliant young man, Menachem Begin, had just become the commander of the 65,000-member Betar. He had selected and organized this group and had, with Katz, been instrumental in overcoming ever-arising difficulties with the authorities.

Emergency messages from Vienna reached us in London. The tone of the telephone calls and telegrams grew increasingly alarming. Something had gone wrong with the S.S. *Socrates.* Actually, everything had gone wrong with that ship. At a time when 220 youngsters whom Katz had brought from Poland and other Eastern European countries were already in Fiume, when all the preparations for the departure in Vienna had been completed, when the Gestapo threatened that any further delay would mean that not only the organizers but all those registered for the transport would be sent to Dachau, at that point, the catastrophic news broke. True, the ship Haller had been shown and inspected—the *Socrates*—was a good ship. There was just one hitch in the deal. Reminiscent of the proverbial sale of the Brooklyn Bridge, the *Socrates* did not belong to the people who had passed themselves off as her owners. They were plain Levantine crooks who had bribed somebody guarding the *Socrates* to let them aboard, and then they pocketed the down payment the greenhorns had given them. The disaster was all the worse because it involved foreign currency supplied by the German National Bank and would doubtlessly be construed by the Nazis as "another Jewish swindle involving foreign money."

Our people in Vienna did not even dare to make it known there that no ship was expected in Fiume, but neither could they stay any longer, as the Gestapo threatened to arrest all participants in case of any further delay. Except for a handful, the travelers did not know of the duplicity that had occurred. Most of the 800, therefore, showed much enthusiasm as they left in a special train "for Fiume" and for Palestine. On the Italian border, the train was, of course, stopped. There was no ship "yet" in Fiume. The 220 who were already in Fiume had gained their entrance into Italy only by the happy coincidence that the Italian commercial attaché in Warsaw, a

Dr. D'Cassio, had a beautiful Jewish secretary who influenced him to issue the transit visa without condition.

The border between Italy and Austria was near the little mountain village of Arnoldstein. There, high in the Alps, a tragedy was developing. The 800 people were crammed into a train, eight to a compartment. The train could not move forward into Italy and could not go back to Vienna. It was pushed onto a side track so as not to interfere with traffic while the 800 waited inside it for the S.S. *Socrates* to arrive in Fiume. Paul Haller and his brother Heinrich knew, of course, what was going on. They had come along, and all they could do was to alarm us abroad and ask us to get them either another ship as quickly as possible or permission from the Italians to enter Italy even though no ship was waiting for them.

Jabotinsky ordered me to fly to Italy immediately. There I was to meet Katz. An Italian Gentile writer, who was an admirer of Jabotinsky's, procured for me the Italian visa, and I was on the next plane out.

It was with a confusing mixture of feelings that I was sitting in that plane as it headed across the channel to bring me back to the perilous continent, to Mussolini's Italy. Hardly two months had passed since from the low altitude at which planes were then flying I had been looking down at the same waters. I had then been full of hopes and had experienced a sense of flying into freedom and safety. Now, after failure of my mission, I was heading back to try to disentangle a practically hopeless situation: no ship, no money, and the 800 crammed into a "special train" sitting on the border, still in German territory. If there was no solution—and how could there be one—the 800 would most likely be sent in a group to a concentration camp, the more so as the disappearance of foreign currency was involved. It would mean the end of not only those on the train. The Nazis might use "Jewish foreign currency fraud" as a reason for new mass arrests. It all would certainly spell the ignominious, disastrous end of our ambitious emigration plans. The irresponsibility with which the Jewish establishment had charged us would have been proven. Certainly, I could not go on living in safety when an action which I had initiated ended with the slaughter of 800 of our brothers and sisters who had entrusted themselves to the Perl-Aktion. I had thought about it before; now on the fateful way to Fiume, I determined: I could not live with myself if the 800 were sent to Dachau. I would have to join them.

chapter 3
THE BRITISH LION
AND THE GNAT

In Fiume we soon found out that Katz, Kornmehl, and I were not the only guests in our small hotel interested in the fate of the 800 in Arnoldstein. Two days after my arrival, we were tipped off that the heavy-set, olive-skinned "salesman" who occupied the room across the hallway from Katz's was a British agent. A Jewish visitor to the hotel, a Fiume businessman, had noticed the same man sitting in a café in the company of another Italian whom our friend knew to be in the employ of the local British Consulate. For the appropriate bribe, the hotel porter supplied us with the phone numbers this man had called. None of them was the Fiume British Consulate, but two calls had been made to Rome. The number in Rome was not that of the British Embassy, but when we called it, a voice with a heavy British accent answered. A tail put on the man showed that the "salesman" rarely left his room, and when he did, he spent most of his time in a shipping agency in the port.

The Italian authorities soon confirmed British intervention. There was not one official in Fiume with whom we had to deal who was not sympathetic. They all would have liked to help. Against their better knowledge, the Fiume police even advised the Italian border authorities that the ship was expected, so that the Italians on the border might be able to have their German counterparts delay the return of the train. But we were also told by the same officials in Fiume that there was no chance of getting the 800 into Italy unless there was proof that they were just passing through. There were orders from Rome. Britain then still maintained diplomatic relations with Mussolini, and she had, the Italian officials told us, strongly protested Italy's "supporting illegal activities directed against Britain." This protest had found willing ears in Rome, as it was the current practice for the world to close its gates to penniless refugees. Without a ship to get them out right away, the 800 would be stuck in Fiume. In fact as day after day passed and no *Socrates* arrived, the Italians insisted that the 220, who were not visible in the streets but whose presence was, of course, known, be sent back to Poland. This would mean not only tragedy for the refugees but also trouble for Dr. D'Cassio in Warsaw. However, clever negotiation by Katz and goodwill on the part of the local authorities resulted in several twenty-four- to forty-eight-hour postponements of the order.

Kornmehl had a contact in Athens, a Viennese refugee named Rosenzweig. We phoned Rosenzweig, and he in turn got us in touch by telephone with a big shipowner who, Rosenzweig thought, might be interested in going into the business of smuggling Jews into Palestine on a large scale. This man, whose name was Davaris, proved in time to be a blessing to our entire undertaking. He promised on the telephone to fly his representative to Fiume, and within forty-eight hours, his man arrived. I made it clear to him that we were talking here about activities which might yet grow into a multimillion-dollar business for his associates. I was ready to oblige myself to do business solely with Davaris, but only if he would send us a ship right away. However, when it came to price, I looked a fool, as we were short the substantial down payment Haller had made in Athens.

In Arnoldstein, meanwhile, the situation had considerably worsened, as Eichmann, who did not want an international scandal on the border, threatened daily to send the entire train to Dachau. Train after train passed by in Arnoldstein and saw the 800 crammed into their wagons. Not only could one see the train, one could smell it. Because for days no one had been permitted to leave his wagon, the feces beneath the train had accumulated into mountains. In addition, each immigrant had food in his rucksack for three weeks only, but this was slowly being eaten up. And there were problems of water. As the situation quickly developed into a health hazard for the local population, those who had to step out were finally permitted to go, under guard, up the hillside. Yet the stench in the whole area was unbearable.

After the train had been on the border a little over a week, Davaris's representative, Mr. Constantine Nikolopoulos, arrived in Fiume. Nikolopoulos was, as all agreed, the best-looking man they had ever seen. He looked like the Greek god Adonis. He had the manner of a great gentleman, and nobody would ever have guessed that this expensively clad man in the best hotel in Fiume was there to discuss any kind of smuggling. He, on Davaris's behalf, was extremely generous as far as money went, and I concluded with him a most unbelievable deal. He would send a ship right away. Our down payment to Davaris would be the 2,000 pounds that Haller had paid—and lost—to the crooks in Athens. "You have no chance of getting this money back," Nikolopoulos stated correctly. "But we have a much more powerful organization. We will get it from that small fry." From Fiume, Nikolopoulos called Athens and had the S.S. *Draga*, an old but good freighter of 230 tons immediately dispatched to Italy.

But Eichmann's patience did not last that long. Due to a delay in Malta, the *Draga* arrived one day after Eichmann had decided to end what he called "the comedy of Arnoldstein" and had ordered the train sent back. He again threatened to send it straight to Dachau "to teach you dirty Jews a lesson not to lie to us anymore." It was at that point that I threw the "Massada threat" at him.

Massada is the practically inaccessible rock on the Dead Sea which is today one of the main tourist attractions in Israel. Rising steeply to a height of 1,300 feet from the edge of the Dead Sea and surrounding desert land, it was in A.D. 73 the scene of a Jewish revolt against the Romans which followed the destruction of Jerusalem. Led by their commander Eleazar Ben Yair, 960 Jewish men, women, and children declared open rebellion against the Romans from this rock. They were well provided with food and drink and considered the Massada unconquerable. The Romans brought their engineers and in many months of work built a huge ramp in order to reach the Jews at the summit. On the day on which the Romans were ready to storm into the Jewish camp, they found to their horror no survivors except for an old woman who had been hiding in a cave with her grandchild. The Jews had decided that death by their own hand was preferable to death by the enemy or to a "life of infamy."

That Eichmann knew Jewish history helped to avert the tragedy of the entire train's being sent to Dachau. He knew of the Massada tradition, and his position in the Nazi hierarchy was not firm enough yet to let him risk the international scandal of hundreds of suicides.

When the train started moving back toward Vienna, and the 800 saw that their ordeal, two weeks in the cramped railroad cars, had been in vain, when they saw themselves rolling back to where they had escaped from, scenes of utter despair could be observed in every one of the wagons. Paul and Heinrich Haller had to be protected from physical attack as the unhappiness and frustration sought an outlet. Marshals had to be appointed to watch that nobody committed suicide by jumping out the window, although one young man did.

True, the train brought them to the Vienna railroad station and not to Dachau. But what then? Most of them had no home and no possessions anymore. Mrs. Berta Siegel, today of Tel Aviv, was one of those who was lucky enough to have a home to go to. Looking back, she describes her experience:

> The worst thing was to go up that staircase to face my mother again who had seen me already in Israel. As it was 6 A.M. when I knocked at the door, my family thought it was the Gestapo. They would have preferred to have been fetched from home themselves to seeing me back. My mother started crying and could not stop for a long time. "I saw at least you saved, and now this, the only way, does not work either."

The girl's father had in the meanwhile been beaten and several of his ribs were broken. The brother, who never got out of Nazi Germany and who later perished just as his parents did, tried to console them all. Berta continues:

> I felt not only unhappy, but guilty for having disappointed them, as if it had been all my fault.

As soon as they were back, our people in Vienna started to regroup and reorganize for an even larger shipment. I had, of course, informed the Gestapo of my new contact with the powerful Greek combine, and in their desire to get rid of the Jews, the Gestapo were ready to give it a try.

In the meanwhile, on September 20, 1938, with dozens of jubilant Jews and hundreds of sympathetic Italians standing on the pier, the *Draga* had arrived in Fiume. The 220 young people whom Katz had brought out from Poland, Lithuania, and Latvia, who only the day before had expected to be sent back, just as the Viennese had been, were marching in formation to the port. Accompanied by his wife, the prefect of the city, who had shown utmost understanding, stood in uniform with all his decorations at the pier. To the great delight of the youngsters, he saluted the Jewish flag which they were carrying in front of the marching troop. Within less than an hour, the embarkation was completed. In addition to Mordechai Katz's organized group of Betarim, 26 Jewish refugees were taken on the only half-filled ship. This additional group consisted of people who had heard the rumor that one could get away from Fiume. A Viennese Betari, a particularly clever operator named Max Stock who had escaped from the train in Arnoldstein and had made his way to the port, was also among those to sail.

Aboard the *Draga* was a young, inconspicuous man, rather small, on the thin side, and very taciturn. He wanted to be known as Johnny. But those who spoke English realized that his English was fair at best and those who spoke German that his German accent was a hard one, not often encountered in Germany, Austria, or Poland. Only when the boat approached the coast of Palestine did Johnny, from an almost unknown passenger, become the commander of the ship as far as the refugees were concerned. A native of Palestine, whose real name was Schmuel Tagansky, he was the representative of the Palestine Landing Organization, the Irgun Zvai Leumi, the militant underground group in Palestine, often referred to as EZEL from the Hebrew abbreviation of its full name. This group was also under Jabotinsky's command and was now organizing the last phase of the action: breaking the blockade, the actual smuggling ashore, and the safe distribution of the immigrants into the villages and cities. While the *Draga* was on her way, landing preparations were being made in Palestine.

Krivoshein-Galili's landing our first 16 without any preparations in the country itself had become the talk of the Jewish underground circles in Palestine. One day, two young men, one a member of the Irgun and the other just a friend of his, were walking along the deserted seashore near Benjamina. The Irgun member was Eliahu Lankin, later a member of the first Israel Parliament and now head of a prestigious law firm in Jerusalem. The other one, also in his twenties, was Mordechai Paikovich, the older brother of Yigdal Allon who was to become vice premier under both Golda Meir and Yitzhak Rabin. The two were talking about what was then on the mind of every Jew in the country: the plight of

European Jewry. Their conversation strayed to the daring landing of the 16, farther north, near Haifa. Looking at the landscape, Lankin's friend, Paikovich, mentioned, "Right here would be an ideal spot for large-scale illegal landings." Where they stood at that moment, they had at their backs the southern end of the Carmel Mountain chain, which just at that point breaks so abruptly that it looks "as if it had been cut by a knife." Suddenly the two realized that this feature was a landmark that was easily seen far out at sea by approaching ships and was therefore perfect for a rendezvous. Then Lankin noticed something else, "Look at these two sandbanks there!" They were the only two sandbanks in the area. Lankin and Paikovich were so excited by these distinctive landmarks—the cutoff in the mountain range and the sankbanks—that Lankin immediately informed his superior in the Irgun, Eliezer Raziel.* Contact among the Irgun, Jabotinsky in London, and our group in Vienna was then speedily established. Krivoshein-Galili, who did not know of this location, was told of the suitability of this landing place. The Irgun representatives met with Galili in Athens, and the next transports, the one with 68 and with 95 aboard, landed safely at this site after passing the sandbank on Tantura Beach near Benjamina.

By then, the communications system for our landing procedures had been established. From now on a representative of the Irgun would be on each ship, and from the port in Europe, he would send a coded cable announcing the expected arrival date of each ship to an unsuspected person in Palestine. On the night chosen—preferably a moonless one—the ship with the immigrants would approach the coast but would stay well outside the three-mile limit. Out there it would rendezvous with a smaller debarkation boat, which could get very close to the beach and which, because of its small size, would not constitute such a loss if captured by the British. The smaller boat was also supplied by the Greeks, as, of course, any movement by the few boats that Jews commanded at the time could be easily watched. Once the small boat came within a few miles of the coast where the mountains ended, it would send out light signals. The watchers on the beach would answer with their flashlight, but not with the same signal, so that a British patrol

---

*Raziel was later killed after becoming a legendary leader in the fight for liberation from the British.

noticing the signal could not lure any of the ships into a trap. The ship with the 68 aboard, for example, had a signal of three short flashes and one long one, the motif of the beginning of Beethoven's Fifth Symphony. Those on land had to answer with three long flashes and one short one, which stood for *"Hatikvah,"* or "The Hope," the way the word is sung in the Jewish national anthem. The code was different for each landing. How efficient this method was is described in a confidential Foreign Office memo dated January 17, 1940.*

The document described below is a "Memorandum prepared jointly by the Foreign Office and Colonial Office, December 1939–January 1940." It complains about the effectiveness of the landing procedures we had adopted:

> ... A sea-going patrol, supported by a coast guard service, has been organised for the purpose of detecting illegal immigrant ships and of preventing, if possible, them from approaching the coast. The patrol was operated in the first place temporarily by ships of the Royal Navy, and now by armed motor launches [*sic*] of the Palestine Government. The patrol launches cannot, of course, operate outside territorial waters, but within these limits, they have the power to stop and search ships, and to order them to leave Palestine waters if they are found to have illegal immigrants on board. They are empowered to use such force as is necessary, to the extent of firing into the ship, in order to compel it to obey orders.... Nowadays, however, the larger ships carrying illegal immigrants usually do not attempt to enter Palestine territorial waters. Instead they bring with them in tow or on board a number of small boats into which the passengers are unloaded outside Palestine territorial waters (sometimes as far as 60 miles out); the larger ship then returns to Europe and the small boats run ashore with the cooperation of the inhabitants of Jewish villages on the Palestine coast. Even if the small boats are intercepted by the patrol launches they cannot be turned back as this would mean the death of the passengers from starvation and thirst. Even if such orders were given the small boats would certainly refuse to obey, and there is no alternative but to seize the small boats (which is worthless) and arrest the passengers. A sea patrol and coast guard service

---

*File number W766/38/48. Documents referring to the war were filed under headings like "War (Germany)" or "War (Italian)." Characteristically, documents of British countermeasures against us, their war against the Jews, were also filed under such headings, and they were referred to as "War (General)."

cannot, therefore, *prevent* landing of illegal immigrants, and can only ensure that most of them are detected and arrested on arrival.

. . . Once an illegal immigrant has set foot on the Palestine coast, it is almost impossible to deport him. Illegal immigrants are commonly stateless, and those who are not, take care to destroy their passports and all other evidence of identity before they approach the coast. It is, therefore, impossible to establish their country of origin for the purpose of deportation under existing international practice. Attempts have been made, so far without success, to bring home the responsibility to the country which allowed the ship to sail.

Regularly, those just landed were appalled to see as the first humans two men on horseback, both in Arab attire. The two "Arabs" were men on our side named Navon and Paikovich. Dressed the way they were and speaking fluent Arabic, they were much safer from the British than without this disguise.

"We loved every one of our saved brothers and sisters," Navon told me years later, "but we had to act toward them like the pharaoh's slave drivers acted against us. 'Go! Faster! Don't stop!' I had to shout from my horse, riding up and down the long line. If the march had come to almost a standstill, we ordered a short standing rest. No one was allowed to sit down or to lie down; we knew these people were so exhausted that once sitting or lying, they could not get up again. And we had to have the whole operation completed before daybreak. Occasionally, I took a woman who could not walk anymore on my horse, and often I was carrying a baby or two, but the taking of an adult involved the risk that somebody else would say, 'So-and-so has been on the horse for half an hour, now take me on.' And we could not lose time by any discussions."

For the first few landings, small local rowing boats were used, but this was changed because some of the boats got stuck in the sand, and freeing them cost lots of time. Therefore, the immigrants usually had to wade through the water from a depth of about waist-high. I have interviewed dozens of immigrants, many who arrived in the middle of the winter and on stormy nights, and no one could recall whether the water was cold. They were all too excited. Later on, when older people and smaller children came to be more frequent among the immigrants, those totally incapacitated were carried to land on the backs of others.

Once past the perils of the actual landing, the immigrants had to be quickly dispersed to avoid the detection spoken of above. The next phase of the operation, therefore, was to find a place where buses to disperse them could safely await the arrival of the newly landed ones. As the buses could not park near the shoreline, the landing at Tantura Beach involved marching for several hours over the dunes. The immigrants were exhausted, and with every step, their feet sank deeply into the soft sand. In some places the march became dangerous as bushes in the dunes could hide British soldiers or Arab attackers. Burdened with their only belongings, the rucksack, many felt that they could not make it and just wanted to abandon this last piece of luggage. But the Irgun members could not permit that because it would have revealed in the daytime what had taken place during the night before on that beach.

Although detailed plans were worked out in advance, a landing rarely took place on the appointed day because of the many complications that often occurred between the leaving of the European port from where the coded cable had come and the actual arrival.

On the first trip of the *Draga*, for example, while en route, the crew increased its demand for salaries. Because Davaris did not grant them this, the ship anchored in a little harbor on one of the Greek islands, and there a power game was played at the expense of the passengers whose food was limited and whose water supply had given out. As this was the first trip with us, and as Davaris proved honorable in all his dealings with our organization, he fulfilled the demands of the crew to shorten the passengers' suffering, and after several days of delay, the *Draga* continued her voyage. To understand the difficulties that developed with our crews and captains, one has to be aware of what kinds of crews one could recruit for such trips. A sailor or a ship's officer could have ended up in jail in Palestine or as a victim of British guns or of torpedoes from German submarines. The ships, crammed with people from the hold to the deck, were frequent sources of disease, and there were almost no lifeboats. Escaping these problems, the crew members could have been jailed on their return to Greece, as British diplomatic pressure succeeded in persuading the Greek dictator Metaxas to punish by law with a long prison sentence anyone involved in smuggling Jews into Palestine. And, of course, any seaman involved in such trips risked the loss of his license, although this last possibility was not a threat to many of the crew. The crews into whose hands the immigrants had to place their lives often consisted of officers who had lost their licenses or of sailors who were wanted for murder or some other crime, and many of these had not been on a ship or worked on one for years.

Because of the delay resulting from the salary dispute on the *Draga*, "Johnny" sent from the last small Greek port a cable changing the originally appointed date of arrival, but this new date also proved to be incorrect. The small ship which was to meet the *Draga* out at sea approximately twenty miles from the point on land where the mountains suddenly ended, missed the *Draga*. This smaller craft, a motor ship called the *Artemisia*, broke the British blockade again and again and soon became the most hunted ship in the eastern Mediterranean. The *Artemisia*'s owner and captain was a fascinating character. I always knew him only by the name Kosta, and I believe that Kosta never in his life spoke one unnecessary word. He was tall, slim, and dark-haired, and his every motion expressed energy and determination. Many in Israel today owe their lives to his ability to handle both ship and crew while still evading the British, and I feel that Kosta certainly deserves a plaque for this to be placed on Tantura Beach or one of the other beaches we later used for landings.

Yet the rendezvous between the *Draga* and the *Artemisia* did not work out well on that trip. They missed each other on the first night, and again on the second, probably because of the delay in Greece. On the night planned for the arrival, everything had been ready on land. The two Arab horseback riders were riding along the beach. The people with the flashlights were hiding in bushes on the dunes. Other members of the Irgun, dressed in civilian khakis, were waiting next to their saddled horses in one or the other of the stables in the vicinity. They too were needed, because for the expected number of immigrants, more than two on horseback were required to keep the line moving. Eged, which was and still is the official Jewish bus company in the country, had dispatched buses, which were waiting in the vicinity, each at a different location. The bus schedules were of course known to the British, and any bus out of schedule anywhere was suspect at that time; certainly no two buses could wait at one location without arousing suspicion. At one time during the first night of waiting for the *Draga* out on the sea, those in charge of communication were excited to see what they hoped was the expected ship. They gave the signal as agreed, but the same signal came back. This was against the arrangements. For a moment, our people with the flashlight hesitated. Could it be that Johnny had misunderstood the directions? They waited a short while and then saw a British launch speeding toward them. Quickly they turned and signaled toward the others on land, giving the order to disappear, and everyone dispersed. Fortunately, the *Draga* did not arrive that night.

Neither did it come the second night. The following night most of the people had to be sent home. Obviously, something had gone wrong with the ship. Besides, the following night was the start of *Yom Kippur.* On this day almost every Jew all over the world is in a synagogue, and everyone wants to be with his family.

This occasion, because our people had stayed away from home for several nights without being able to tell their wives what they were doing, created a fifth front for us. The wives were suspicious and had they known the name of the ship, they would have been more inclined to believe that the *Draga* was a young attractive girl rather than a forty-year-old crate.

Eliahu Lankin was in charge of the skeleton crew, which, *Yom Kippur* or not, had to keep watch on the beach. And this was the night the *Draga* came.

"I remember exactly," he says, "how I slipped out of the synagogue in Benjamina, and how I heard as I moved to the beach the chanting of the *Kol Nidrei,* which had started at the moment of the sunset. The people on board may have lost the sense of time because the arrival on that date caused tremendous additional complications. Nothing moves in a Jewish village on *Yom Kippur.* Everything that happened outside a synagogue was suspect in these years. But on the *Yom Kippur* night of 1938, we got them all off and into our land.

"We found an abandoned building in one of the orange or- chards and moved the people into it. We brought food there and orange juice. Like all the previous arrivals, almost everyone, as soon as he was on dry land, had knelt down or thrown himself to the ground, and kissed the earth. Now in the dilapidated building, most of the arrivals, starved and parched as they were, refused to eat or to drink because it was *Yom Kippur.* They chose one in their midst to function as a rabbi and another one as cantor and went that night and the following day without food or drink, through the entire *Yom Kippur* service from the *Kol Nidrei* to the *Nileh* [final prayer].

They said that they were happy to add one day to their fasting. No doubt that prayers were rarely as full of thanks and more fervent than those which rose that night in that dilapidated, roofless building. As moving as it was to us, we were desperate because of the untimely landing. The risk of discovery had been unexpectedly heightened. Instead of keeping the new arrivals at one place for a few hours, we had to keep them that entire night and the entire next day until late in the evening. On *Yom Kippur*, when hardly anyone can be reached, we had to make the arrangements for the buses, which in turn could not leave from wherever they came before *Yom Kippur* ended. They could not arrive all at the same time at the same place. It had to move like clockwork. It did. By daybreak of the day following *Yom Kippur,* the new arrivals had been dispatched to their various locations, and an hour later, there was no trace that anyone had arrived."

As for me personally, the day following the *Draga*'s departure from Fiume on September 20, 1938, was probably the happiest birthday I ever celebrated. Another 246 had been saved. My wife arrived from Vienna to spend a few days with me in Fiume before returning to her parents in Vienna. She was still safe at that point— or so we both assumed. On the twenty-fourth of September 1938, I was on my way to Athens. Davaris had made certain that I got the necessary visas. It was a long journey in the slow train, which coughed its way from Italy through all of Yugoslavia into Greece. I had traveled third-class, of course, but once in Athens, I descended from a first-class car because Davaris's representative awaited me. He had made reservations for me in the Grand Hotel Bretagne, one of the top-class hotels of old Europe. Because I did not have the money to stay there, I told him that I would stay with friends, as my activities would be too exposed in any hotel. Thus, I fell into the modest apartment of Mr. Rosenzweig, and it took British intelligence quite some time to locate me there.

In Athens I made arrangements for an immediate return voyage of the *Draga*, plus one other ship, the S.S. *Ely.* Davaris would send the two ships wherever I decided in return for payment of 12 pounds ($60) per person. We also agreed that the old freighters would have to be rebuilt so that they could provide more accommodations than just those which allowed for passengers to lie on the bottom of the hold or on the deck.

But the most important talk, one which saved many thousands, occurred in a little café on Omonia Square. Our main problem, besides getting the ships and landing them, had been to get the emigrants to the port. I could still feel the Fiume scare in all my bones. How could one avoid transit visas? In a letter from Vienna, I was told that Dr. Paul Diamant, a historian, had suggested the use of the Danube River. I had not been very much impressed by it because the Danube, after leaving Vienna, flows through so many countries—Czechoslovakia, Hungary, Yugoslavia, and Bulgaria—before reaching the Black Sea in the Rumanian port of Sulina. Too many transit visas I figured. But my Greek partner literally jumped at the mention of the Danube. "Your doctor in Vienna knows what he is talking about: the Danube is by internationally ratified convention a free waterway; ships on the Danube are comparable to ships outside the three-mile limit on the high seas. You do not need transit visas anymore. You load them in Vienna on the Danube boats, and we just pick them up in Rumania. Eureka! We found the solution!"

When I left the café, it had been decided that, on its return trip from Palestine, the *Draga* would proceed to Galatz in Rumania, which is approximately one hundred thirty miles upstream from Sulina, but to which smaller seagoing ships can proceed. There the two Davaris ships would pick up 1,000 refugees to come down the Danube from Vienna. This gave us transportation for the 800 who had suffered in Arnoldstein, plus 200 more.

At that time, two small but elegant modern ocean liners, the *Transylvania* and the *Bessarabia* plowed weekly through waters from Constanṭa, Rumania, to Istanbul, Athens, Limasol, to Haifa, and back. Two days after the all-important meeting in the café on Omonia Square, I was on the *Bessarabia* on my way to Constanṭa. It was a beautiful trip. As we proceeded through the Sea of Marmara and the Dardanelles, dozens of dolphins played in the blue water around the ship; everything was so tranquil one could almost, but not really, forget what was going on 1,000 miles to the west.

Upon my arrival in Constanṭa, I learned fast that I was in an entirely new world, and I was given a lesson which I was certain to remember. I was one of the first ones off the ship and brought the two pieces of hand luggage which constituted my entire possessions to customs. The officer waited until the room was full. He had recognized me as just the man he needed. Aloud he asked me, "Do you have something to declare, or do you want to give me one hundred lei?" I was absolutely OK and was afraid that if I gave him the 100 lei (then about U.S. 20 cents) he might have thought that I wanted to smuggle something in. I answered, "I have nothing to declare. You can check me." In answer to my remark, the custom's officer smiled ominously. He then shouted, "This man did not want to pay me one hundred lei and asked me to check his baggage." At that, he opened both my valises and with hands which showed practice in this procedure, he threw all of the contents in rapid movements into the air, so that my underwear, my shirts, and other clothes, everything I had, descended like a fountain upon me and those who stood next to me.

I had learned my lesson. I gave the man 100 lei to help me put the things back. I got out as fast as possible but I was certain that I had functioned well as a guinea pig and that he received his 100 lei from all the other passengers.

This man's behavior did not necessarily indicate that he was mean. Graft was in Rumania at that time more common than anywhere in the Balkans. Most of all, the entire civil service system there was practically based upon baksheesh. Government jobs were valued, aside from their prestige, not for the salary but for the baksheesh opportunities they offered.

Working in Rumania was in many other ways entirely different from what I had done so far with Aliya Bet, "illegal" immigration. Contrary to Athens, Fiume, or London, we had numerous friends here. True, the official Zionist organization was against our "risky undertakings," but by 1938 the need for emigration was so great that there was no actual interference on the local level. To the contrary, although at that point help from the authorities could not be expected, if we needed food, technical advice on rebuilding a ship, a better price for the ship lumber supplies, and the like, we had it quickly offered to us. Jabotinsky's Zionist Revisionist Organization and its youth group, the Betar, were numerically quite strong, and we soon created a staff which worked closely together on the ever-upcoming problems. The most active members of this staff were Dr. Jacob Schieber, the leader of the Rumanian Betar; Dr. Edgar Kanner, a quiet, systematic-thinking, distinguished-looking lawyer; Mr. Gornstein, who was hard working and had valuable social connections; and Miss Mila Epstein, the niece of Mr. Jabotinsky. Her father was a respected surgeon in Bucharest, who on numerous occasions offered valuable suggestions. An odd couple of aides were assigned to me. One was a slim boy in his teens, fast-thinking and quick-acting. In spite of his youth, he got things done. One had only to complete half of a sentence and he knew what was wanted and was on his way out to do it. The other aide was as different as one can be. He was assigned to me as a bodyguard after our people found out that some shady characters, probably hired by the British, were tailing me. This bodyguard had a face like a pugilist. His body looked like a modern statue of Hercules hewn out of sheer rock. All together he gave one the impression that he could bend horseshoes and that he practiced karate by hitting the masts of ships and breaking them apart. He came from a small town near Kishinew in the Russian-speaking section of Rumania, now part of the Moldavian Soviet Republic. Some thirty years later when in *Fiddler on the Roof* I saw portrayed the life in Anatevka, David, my bodyguard, came again to my mind. The saving of Jews was for David a purpose for which he lived day and night. And that he could play such an "important" role in it was something he had never dreamed of. His shortcoming lay in the fact that his only argument was his fists.

Once we had a meeting with young Rumanian Jews who were to leave with the next ship and were to receive travel instructions. A young man whom I did not know but who, I later learned, was a youth leader employed by the Rumanian branch of the World Zionist Organization, asked to say a few words. I invited him to the platform, but, to my surprise, he gave a speech in which he exhorted those present not to entrust their lives to a reckless undertaking. The World Zionist Organization was, he said, opposing these dangerous trips because they were illegal and, therefore, gave the Jews a bad name, especially because the organizers put themselves in opposition to the powerful British Empire. I did not see David get up on the platform. When I first noticed him, he was already standing next to the speaker. At that point, he grabbed the man by the collar and threw him flying through the air into the audience, where he landed in the fourth or fifth row, fortunately neither hurting himself nor injuring anyone else as he came falling down on them. David was then firmly forbidden to use violence again unless told to do so or unless danger to someone's life or health demanded his own immediate action. "You are not a bouncer," he was told, "and you can do better than that."

Soon afterward, David did show that he could do better. That afternoon I was in Bucharest on my way to meet a man whose name and address friends of ours in Sofia, Bulgaria, had somehow scouted out among the hordes of Levantine spies and informers who were then hanging around the ports of the Black Sea, and the Mediterranean, and the strategically important Danube River. Some of them were in the employ of one or the other of the powers involved in the intelligence work, but most were "free-lancers" trying to make a fast buck. This man was a Turk who had connections with the Istanbul underworld and also with certain bribable police officials there. As we then had no local contacts in Istanbul, our meeting could be valuable. It was essential, of course, that my talking to this man not be found out. It was even more important for us, however, that neither the British nor the Rumanian police learn that the place where I was to meet him was one I used for all such secret contacts.

The place was a *casa de rendezvous*, a Rumanian equivalent for a high-class bordello. The system according to which these *casas de rendezvous* worked was quite ingenious, as it did not burden the madam with overhead. There were no girls domiciled there. Ladies—almost exclusively ones from out of town—who wanted to make some pocket money were on certain days either on call, sitting in one of Bucharest's elegant coffeehouses, or in a confiserie sipping their chocolate or tea and eating tiny sandwiches, or if a customer had made arrangements for a certain lady in advance, she often came straight from the railroad station to the *casa de rendezvous*. These women were "society ladies," wives of professionals, judges, university professors, and some even of high government employees. They told their husbands that they were traveling to the city for the afternoon or a day or two, to do some shopping or to visit a lady friend, who usually was in on the game, too. This way they made some good pocket money and escaped for a short while the boredom of the provincial city from which they came. As they were not well known in Bucharest and as the *casa* was always located in an unobtrusive private home in a good residential area, the risk of being found out was minimal. The house was usually the private home of the madam, with two or three of the rooms set aside for the purpose of "secret love." Financial arrangements were made with the "hostess"—that's what the madam called herself—and the women thus kept up the pretense of being ladies. To pay them directly would have been in the worst of taste. The madam kept part of the money as her cut. As her expenses were nil, this kind of operation must have been quite profitable. Her "guests" were expected not to be rude and not to treat the ladies as if they were purchasable. It was usual to start the acquaintance—or the reunion—with a bottle of champagne. One sipped the bubbling, intoxicating drink and ate some of the caviar sandwiches that were served with the champagne; as the lady started to succumb and one ate more of the sandwiches, the bill for the "champagne plate" rose higher.

Madame Le Blanc, our "hostess," owned one of the top-class *casas de rendezvous*. Her real name was Bergstein and, without asking for any remuneration, she lent her house as a place for us to meet people with whom we did not want to be seen. The police as well as the British Embassy were doubtlessly aware that I was an occasional visitor to Madame Le Blanc's *casa de rendezvous*, but they did not know that we used it as a place to meet there with men who had entered sometime before me. One afternoon I was on my way to Madame Le Blanc's. As soon as I was out of the hotel, I noticed that I was being tailed by a man who had followed me before and whom we suspected of being in the pay of the British. "Don't go to the taxi," David said. "Follow me." We walked along a few of Bucharest's main streets, and after a short walk, David, who knew the city well, said: "In the next block we turn right into the second alley." We passed one alley and about one hundred feet further on, turned into the next one. It was narrow and windowless. David pushed me in and after about thirty feet, another alley ran into this one at an angle of ninety degrees. David directed me into this alley and told me to walk on. It led to one parallel with the first one, which I followed. It brought me back into the main thoroughfare, where I waited for David. In less than a minute, he stood next to me with a bundle under his arm. "What happened?" I asked, worried about the life of the man who had been tailing us. "You will see," David said. "Just keep walking and look into the second alley." I did, and as we passed the alley into which we had first disappeared, I saw the man standing there, naked, with only his socks and shoes on. With his bright red sock-suspenders he really presented quite a spectacle. David had torn all his clothes from him and had carried the torn strips away, all that, as he assured me, without hurting the man in any way. "I just reduced his desire to follow us in the future." Neither David nor I worried about any legal consequences. The incident was much too humiliating to be followed up in the courts.

We were altogether not too apprehensive regarding interference by Rumanian authorities. True, every Rumanian public servant wanted money, but just because most of them were anti-Semitic, the Rumanians were "sympathetic" to our cause. In October 1938, Zeev Jabotinsky came to Rumania, contacted the all-powerful prime minister, Calinescu, and explained to him the "advantages" for Rumania of a large-scale Jewish emigration from and through that country. The Rumanians wanted the Jews out. To accommodate them, we promised to take a number of destitute Jews along on every ship and also foreign Jews who had come across illegally into Rumania and who, because they were now in jail, had to be fed at government expense.

Another reason the Rumanians were more or less cooperative was due to a ruse that we had invented. With the first transports in Vienna, we had claimed, in order to obtain the necessary Greek and Yugoslav transit visas, that although the British were officially protesting our illegal immigration, they actually favored it because they wanted many young Jews in Palestine in case of war with Germany. This sounded logical, and our claim seemed in time confirmed by the fact that our ships had managed to land. How could we have landed in Palestine if the British navy had really wanted to prevent it? Almost everyone in Europe at that time knew and probably believed the song "Britannia Rules the Waves." We, therefore, claimed that the complaints lodged by the British were for appearances' sake only and were meant to show the Arabs that Britain was "trying" to keep us out of Palestine. Thus, even when the British ambassador complained to the foreign minister of Bulgaria, Rumania, or some other country about its allowing us to prepare for our voyages there and to rebuild our ships in its ports, the officials of the respective Balkan country viewed such complaints as mostly *pro forma* diplomatic maneuvers.

As this worked so well, we decided to use the same tactic within the British bureaucracy itself so that the lower echelons would believe that certain orders from above had been made only for show and were actually to be disregarded. Most of the British officials were so certain of the unlimited capacity of their navy that our suggestions fell on very fertile ground.

Once, after the British Embassy in Bucharest had intervened with Rumanian authorities against us, I unabashedly walked into the lion's den. I demanded to see the British ambassador. Asked why, I stated that I wanted to lodge a complaint. I did not see the ambassador but met with the first secretary. Brazenly, I complained to him that he had interfered with our extralegal emigration plans. "I can't understand," he said. "Don't you know it is against our laws?"

"I can't understand you," I replied. "Don't you see that you are making fools of yourselves? The British Royal Navy is yours, not mine. Don't you believe in its ability? Look at our old crates, almost listing before they begin their trip. They have to cough and shake their way through the Black Sea, the Marmara, and the Mediterranean, and arrive limping and out of breath at the Palestine coast. Do you really think your navy cannot catch them if it wants to? Don't you trust your navy? These orders from London are issued only to show the Arabs that something is being done. But if your embassy really interferes with us, you'll be making fools of yourselves before your superiors."

The first secretary responded that he would write to London to clarify matters. I smiled. "London can only answer that you should refer to your orders. Your mere *inquiry* would show me, if I were sitting in the Foreign Office in London, that you are a clerk and not a diplomat and that you cannot read between the lines."

This was strong language for a homeless Jew with a German *J* passport to use against the representatives of His Majesty's government, but I had all the logic on my side. The very fact that I had the gall to complain about steps the British Embassy had taken seemed to support my claim that they were doing something they actually were not expected to and which ran counter to some secret understanding. The question whether they were really expected to act effectively against us plagued British authorities to varying degrees during all the years of our activities. Some officials, nevertheless, acted fully in accordance with the orders, but others remained most hesitant. The only ones whom we could not sway were the higher officials of the Middle East Intelligence Services located in Cairo. Lord Moyne, the highest British representative in the Mideast, and his predecessors knew the policy only too well.

Utilizing this method, we struck another blow by making British intelligence officials the very messengers for our policy of fermenting mutual distrust among the British themselves. At about the time I had started working in Rumania, while we were preparing there for the arrival of the 800 who had been returned from Arnoldstein plus 200 more, a man and his wife, who had arrived illegally in Palestine with the 386, appeared at a police station in Jerusalem. The man stated that he had had enough of living illegally and that he was ready to supply any information against us if he and his wife were given legal status. What they had to relate was sent by the high commissioner himself, Sir Harold MacMichael, to "the Right Honorable Malcolm MacDonald," P.C., M.P., His Majesty's principal secretary of state for the colonies, in a report classified "secret." In this report, he stated that Mr. A. Saunders, the inspector general of the Palestine police (whom the Palestinian Jews hated most) had succeeded in obtaining information an extract of which was being forwarded to the secretary of the colonies. In this extract, the British Consulate in Vienna is accused of cooperating with us:

> After the Anschluss, I wanted to leave Austria and come to Palestine. I sent a friend to the Consulate, but I was told that no certificates were available, but the man at the Consulate suggested that there were other methods of getting into Palestine. I got in touch with the man called Willy Perl, of 16 Stubenring, Vienna—*

The rest of the statement supplied information which we were certain the British knew anyhow. This "free admission" of an immigrant only confirmed to the British what they had been hearing from all their foreign representatives ever since we started working, because we had used this argument that the British were actually with us all the time.

Of course, the story that the British Consulate in Vienna had sent a man to me was a canard planted by us to sow distrust among the British officials themselves. As more and more ships arrived, an increasing number of British officials could not believe that such nobodies as we could really do what we did without British cooperation, and one official started to distrust the other in spite of all the vehement official denials from London.

---

*Foreign Office file number 371/23246/65273 dated 12 January 1937.

In a ciphered cable* marked both "Immediate" and "Secret," Sir S. Waterlow, British ambassador to Athens, informed Lord Halifax, the British secretary of foreign affairs, on the nineteenth of July 1938, that:

> Greek Minister for Foreign Affairs unofficially alleged that *Palestine officials connived at* [sic] *these illegal immigrants. I find it difficult to deny this categorically as I have heard the same from other sources* and feel definite action is necessary.†

Thus, we were succeeding in making the authorities in Palestine believe that the Foreign and Colonial offices were probably cooperating with us. At the same time, even the British ambassador to Athens found it "difficult to deny categorically" that the Palestine authorities were not indeed cooperating with us.

The Foreign Office in London started an investigation and informed its representatives abroad in a ciphered telegram that:

> No information is available here to show that any Palestine official has connived at [sic] these illegal immigrations, and it is to be hoped that Greek Government will not be influenced by such rumor.‡

A copy of this telegram was sent to Jerusalem, and the high commissioner there must have hit the ceiling, as it showed that his distrust of other British officials, which he felt was justified, had been thrown into his lap! It is interesting to note the wording of the telegram from the Foreign Office: it does not really acquit the Palestine authorities; it merely says "no information is available here."

We could play the game of divide and conquer too!

Actually, the British authorities, although distrustful of each other, were feverishly working to stop this ridiculous state of affairs. It was incredible that some young people, opposed by the leading Jews themselves, should nullify decisions of the British Cabinet, which after all had been responsible for so long for the White Man's Burden!

---

*Foreign Office file number 371/21888/8939, p. 280.
†Author's italics.
‡Foreign Office File 371/21888/8939, p. 282.

While we were making progress here on our second, the British front, news from our first, the Nazi front, grew more and more alarming. More people had been arrested and deported to concentration camps; others had disappeared without any arrests. One young woman, who had left her hometown in central Germany, described how the rabbi, an old man with a long beard, had been forced by the SS to dance in the street to the tune of a popular song. She was particularly horrified by the sight of not only the SS, but many ordinary citizens, some former neighbors included, being entertained by this "amusement." What was for us more important was the fact that all these barbaric measures were not only an outcome of Nazi sadism. They intended to force the Jews into faster emigration, yet the other countries took but a few of us. What would the Germans do when it became clear that, as the number who wanted to emigrate into other countries grew, the smaller the number of those allowed into these countries became.

But the news from our office in Vienna, at any rate, was encouraging. Certainly, even if our extralegal immigration into Palestine should grow ten times, it would still constitute only a small contribution toward alleviating the plight of European Jewry. However, in terms of the lives of thousands, possibly tens of thousands, to be saved, things seemed to be going well.

Oddly enough, it was Eichmann who helped, who in fact pushed us to get the transport ready. His rising star had been somewhat blemished by his inability to get those Jews through Arnoldstein and thereby to get rid of them. He ordered the Danube Steamshipping Company to assign priority rating to the "dejudaification" business. Two of our people were ordered to Gestapo headquarters. Standing at attention before one of Eichmann's black uniformed underlings, they were told that Eichmann would any day now decide that the "Arnoldsteiners, the organizers, and their families had by now too long poisoned the good German air of the city." The "Dismissed!" thundered after the one sentence pronouncement sounded to them like sweet melody. The two could go home—at least for the moment.

Paul and Heinrich Haller, Fritz Herrenfeld, Paul Elbogen, Dr. Felix Herzig, Moritz Pappenheim, Julius Steinfeld, and a few others worked efficiently and unceasingly in getting the next transport out, and on November 1 they were ready. When darkness fell on that day, just a few days prior to the great nationwide pogrom of the

Kristallnacht, 1,090 people (we always surpassed the allotted number), mostly youngsters, assembled, each with a rucksack at the Reichsbruecke, and descended into the two luxury sightseeing paddle-wheelers which were waiting there for them. For 800 of the emigrants it was the second attempt. They were the returnees from Arnoldstein. We were now taking all of them out plus an additional 290.

The riverboats belonged to the former Austrian, by then Nazi, Danube Steamshipping Company, which had the monstrous name of *Donaudampfschiffahrtsgesellschaft*. Though these ships were flying the flag with the swastika, all those interviewed state that as soon as they were aboard ship they felt as if they were already in Palestine. At this time the Germans had not yet begun to force us to take anyone else on board. On later occasions, some Jews who looked more dead than alive and whom for some reason unknown to us the Nazis wanted to get rid of in that way (we suspected some bribes) were brought to the departing paddle-wheeler. If we said the boat was already too full, we were told by the SS, *"Sie gehen entweder auf die Donau oder in die Donau."* ("Either they go on the Danube or into the Danube.")

On that November 1, 1938, the Danube Steamshipping Company had loaded her two paddle-wheelers, the *Minerva* and the *Grein*, to what the company felt was up to the brim. Still it was paradise for those who saw the landscape of Germany gliding by and with each additional mile saw themselves closer to the shores of Palestine. The mood on the ships was euphoric, and this was furthered by the triumphant welcome which the emigrants received at each of the short stops on the long way down. At every docking, there were hundreds of Jews hailing those who had escaped. Little did most of those who stood jubilantly on the piers know that in a short time their own country—Czechoslovakia, Hungary, Yugoslavia, Bulgaria, or Rumania—would be under the German heel too. The Jews at the various stops brought food and warm clothing. Most important were the medical supplies which they brought at our request. The latter were urgently needed because Germany, anticipating a war, had not permitted us to export anything that might be needed for medical purposes. At one place a rabbi handed our ship's commander a Torah. It was given and received in a moving ceremony with the ancient required blessings. As it turned out, this act probably saved the old scroll. Now in Israel, it would most likely have been burned shortly after our departure had it not joined us on the adventurous trip.

Discipline on both ships was soon established, and this permitted the regularity of life which helped to make the passengers feel secure. To visualize an illegal transport, one must be aware that these voyages did not require just loading the ships with large hordes of people. Organization and discipline were an absolute must, else chaos would have reigned. Assignment of space on the ship, the distribution of rations, arguments among the emigrants or with the crew, all required organization and the adherence to rules. A commanding officer who wielded absolute power was appointed by us prior to the departure of each ship. He was the only speaker for the group with the captain.* Well before the departure, the office in Vienna organized those on the list into manageable units of 50. The Hebrew name of such units was *plugah,* or platoon. Each *plugah* had a *rosh plugah,* a platoon leader, and was itself subdivided into five *zeroroth,* or squads. Each of the squads was commanded by a *rosh zeror,* or squad leader.

A definite timetable for each activity and for each *plugah* had been worked out in Vienna. Conditions on the ship always demanded subsequent changes of the original plans, but we felt that tentative plans were better than none.

At least one daily conference between the ship's commander and all platoon leaders was mandatory.

With the memory of sad farewells fresh in mind, worries about families and friends left behind, and having in addition to face the daily frustrations on board ship, the emigrants had tempers that often ran high once they were beyond the relatively pleasant Danube leg of their journey. Iron discipline became necessary to keep life functioning aboard ship. In summarized form, the following rules were to be observed on the trips:

1. Absolute, military discipline. Requests and complaints were to be submitted at daily roll call to the platoon leader. His decision could be appealed to the ship's commander, but until or unless changed, it was valid. A complaint had to be decided within 24 hours.

*On the second trip of the *Draga* (we referred to it as *Draga II*), the ship commanders of the *Draga* and the *Ely* found it necessary to appoint one assistant commander for each hold and one for the deck. This procedure was then made routine for future trips.

2. Strict enforcement of the no smoking rule below deck, due to the great fire hazard.

3. Separate sleeping places for men and women.

4. Individual possession of firearms was forbidden.

Occasionally, at an interim landing, someone would slip a gun on board to one or another of the passengers. Also, as sometimes happened, passengers were added along the way, and one of these might bring a gun with him. Any such weapon had to be handed to the ship's commander, who, as it often turned out, needed it to handle a blackmailing crew, to prevent sailors from molesting women passengers, to provide protection against intruders coming aboard at one of the ports on the way, or even possibly for defensive use at the landing site.

The ship's commander was given authority to decide on punishment, but he was also handed guidelines to which he had to adhere. Those breaking the rules were subject to: (1) receiving a reprimand in private; (2) having their reprimand publicly announced; (3) assignment to a special work detail; (4) being tied to a post up to a maximum of twelve hours; or (5) having to, at the next stop, if any, debark; if none: being sent back on the same ship when the others debarked in Palestine. The latter punishment was never applied, but its threat was a powerful deterrent.

Most of the participants accepted these rules. They meant liberty to them, as these were their own regulations. After having come out of Germany, emigrants experienced our rules as lenient. The ones who broke them were felt to have acted against the community and its common purpose.

While the *Minerva* and the *Grein* were gliding down the Danube from Vienna all the way to the Black Sea, we experienced hectic days in Rumania. The seagoing vessels had to be refitted, provisions procured, and permission had to be obtained to transfer the emigrants in the middle of the Danube onto the seagoing vessels. Although no country could legally interfere because the Danube was an international waterway, any country could still find some reason to intervene. Because Rumania was then, prior to the outbreak of the war, an ally of France and therefore of Britain, she yielded to some of the pressure by the British ambassador to prevent the transfers. As a result, the Rumanian government stated that, although Rumania had no right to interfere with shipping, it was her duty to make certain that for humanitarian reasons there would be no health hazard connected with any trip for which a seagoing ship left any mooring in Rumania.

Fortunately, Galatz, where the first transfer was to take place, is about one hundred forty miles from Bucharest, and with civil service being what it was in Rumania, there were ways of circumventing orders from the capital. In Galatz, Dr. Schieber conducted the necessary negotiations with the chief of police, and after the preliminaries, Schieber and I met with him in his office. Dr. Schieber, as a Rumanian, had to be more diplomatic, but I—as a foreigner without any rights due to my German Jewish passport—used the hatchet. I asked the police chief whether he knew that other illegal transports had already arrived in Palestine. He said he had heard about it. I pulled out newspaper clippings to that effect and said, "Do you think these landings would have been possible if the British had not really cooperated with us? Who do you think controls the waves? Britannia or our decrepit, barely moving, hardly seaworthy hulks?" I told him that this order from Bucharest was not really meant to be applied, that they had to issue such an order there, but that he would appear the fool if he were to enforce it. "If you do not let us transfer, it is your neck," I said. The power of the bluff was strengthened by the simultaneous offer of a bribe if he did not cause any delays. He could not delay us more than a day or two anyhow, I said, and if he did make trouble, it would be good neither for us nor for him.

That night Jacob Schieber and I met in an unlit park at an appointed time with a dark figure and handed this figure—the chief of police—20,000 lei, the equivalent of $40 U.S. money with which he had to take care of all those below him including the port captain, who had approached me separately. Unknown to the police chief, this port captain had already received 5,000 lei, $10 U.S. money, from us. Another obstacle had been taken care of.

Freezing because I was not dressed for the cold Rumanian November weather, I stood on the pier in Galatz several hours before the arrival of the Danube paddle-wheelers. We thought that we knew the approximate time of their arrival because we had been receiving telephone communications from towns along the way, but the ships were overdue. One hour, two hours, two and a half. What had happened to them? Suddenly, a thin trail of smoke appeared beyond the river bend, and within seconds the *Minerva*, followed within half a mile by the *Grein*, came elegantly gliding down. I doubt whether any ships flying the Nazi flag were ever as anxiously awaited or as lovingly received by anyone as those paddle-wheelers were when they arrived in Rumania, ready to spill their precious human cargo. In a graceful arc, the two snow-white ships turned on the Danube, which is at that point so wide that it looks almost like a lake. Within less than two hours, the transfer to the *Draga II* and the *Ely* began. And in another hour, the two German ships were ready to go back. The 1,090 emigrants had become immigrants. Along with those boarding the *Draga II* and the *Ely*, we added— much to the satisfaction of the Rumanian authorities—60 Jews from Rumania. They included 46 Betarim and 14 Jews from other countries who had been in Rumanian jails for having lacked passports or visas when they crossed the border in an effort to reach Palestine.

The *Draga II* and the *Ely* were ready for them all. About a week before the expected emigrants gathered at the Reichs Bridge in Vienna, the two Davaris seagoing ships that were to bring them to Palestine, had arrived in Rumania to be specially outfitted for the trip.

"Johnny" Tagansky had not traveled the sea before he brought the *Draga* to a safe landing on her first trip. Now an experienced seafarer, at least as far as the requirements for an illegal trip were concerned, he had been ordered by the Irgun commander to stay on board. He knew better than any of us what was needed for the *Draga* and the *Ely* in terms of food, water, medical supplies, and other items. Johnny also saw to it that the *Draga*, although only a small ship, 230 tons, should now on her second voyage take on 550 emigrants, which meant cramming the ship to the last available square inch and utilizing every nook and cranny.

Large wooden platforms had been built along the walls of the holds to make the maximum use of the empty space below deck. As one reached each platform by a ladder, one stood on a wooden gangway which led all along that "floor." Toward the wall were the triple "bunks," which were actually just shelves. The space between each such shelf and the one above it was only one meter. The immigrants had even less head room than that, however, because we had provided them with thin straw mats, and everyone was required to bring a blanket along. In the beginning, we had two such "bunks" next to each other, although there was no division between the two. During these earlier transports, we had figured the width at 75 centimeters, or about 2½ feet, for each person and his rucksack. As the extermination program in Germany and German-occupied lands went into high gear, however, this space was narrowed down even further with each trip. The central gangway, which originally served not only for moving around on that platform but also as "living room" for the respective floor, became more and more narrow until, when it was certain that whoever did not make a ship would have been surely gassed or otherwise murdered, there was just a deep, dark row of "bunks," with only a few feet of gangway left for air and movement. That meant that those close to the wall of the hold might have to crawl over five or six others before they reached their own place. And only three feet above them was the next shelf.

Most of the immigrants had not traveled the seas before and so became seasick, but even experienced seafarers would probably have become ill in such enclosed places as these. During the later voyages, the conditions within the hold were savagely inhumane. If one were seasick, one could not get out to the deck in time. Vomit was all over, and the stench, with insufficient air coming in anyhow, was suffocating. Yet there was no other place to escape to. Many of those whom I interviewed in 1974–75 stated that only the hope of soon being a free person in one's own country prevented them from committing suicide. In any case, marshals were on duty at all times on deck, and they had to prevent more than one passenger from shortening his voyage by jumping overboard.

But at this time, in November 1938, although the ships were immensely crowded, conditions on the *Draga* and the *Ely* were not yet so devastating.

On the *Ely* and *Draga* were 150 people who had come straight out of the Dachau concentration camp. At that time the Germans were still more intent on driving the Jews out than on having them all killed, and if we certified that a certain inmate of a prison or concentration camp would leave with us, that person might be released. Just prior to our departure, such a person would usually be brought directly to the paddle-wheeler. Sometimes he was even released a few days earlier with the threat—to him and to us—of immediate arrest if he did not leave within a certain number of days. The British Colonial Office files contain a copy of such a certificate together with the British confirmation that these certificates, issued by Dr. W. Perl's office and certifying that a certain person had been "noted" for the next Palestine transport, were "often used to obtain a release from concentration camps."*

But not only the 150 who had come straight from Dachau to the *Minerva* and the *Grein* had escaped. All those who were on those two riverboats missed by just a few days a mass pogrom that sent tens of thousands to Buchenwald, to Dachau, to Oranjenburg, or to their immediate deaths.

All during October 1938, frightening rumors—unfortunately later proven true—had been circulating. It had become known that inmates in the concentration camps were preparing thousands of uniforms with the yellow Star of Zion on them, that additional barracks were hastily being built, and that supplies were being prepared for many more than were at that time in the camps. A large pogrom was being planned with thousands to be sent to concentration camps, apparently in order to force the other countries to open their borders to the Jews.

Ever since World War I, many Jews, from what became Poland after 1918, had been living in Germany and Austria. They had fled the war, running from the advancing Russians, and had stayed on during peacetime, but could not become German or Austrian citizens. On October 26, 1938, six days before the departure of the *Minerva* and the *Grein* from the Reichs Bridge, all Jews holding Polish citizenship were ordered to leave Germany—which by then included Austria and the Sudetenland region of Czechoslovakia—within twenty-four hours. Twelve thousand of them were packed into trains and shipped to the Polish border. The Poles immediately issued a decree that any Polish citizen who had lived abroad for more than five years could not enter Poland without special permission. As Poland was not about to grant these special permissions, 12,000 Jews were stuck on the border—in no-man's-land—without food, without accommodations, without any protection against the icy November rains and the biting winds that sweep across Europe's northeastern plains.

Among those stranded was the family of Sendel Grynszpan. Sendel was a poor man who had fled Polish Russia in 1911 because a flood of pogroms was expected; he had settled in Hanover. He had eight children, and when the income from his small tailor shop no longer sufficed to feed them all, he had to close his shop and began

*Colonial Office File COF 6CO 733/396/75113/38/1459.

to trade in secondhand goods. For a short time Sendel had received welfare assistance—available then only to the very poor. But by 1938 he was able to reopen another small tailor shop. One of his sons, Herschel, had tried to run away from all the poverty and at fifteen had made his way to Paris to the house of his aunt and uncle.

Late in October of the same year, the Paris papers reported the tragedy on the Polish-German border. The Germans were driving the refugees into Poland with bayonets, and the Poles were driving them back. Herschel figured correctly that his whole family must be among those unfortunates. On November 3, 1938, his fears were confirmed. The mailman brought a letter from Herschel's oldest sister, Berta, which read:

> DEAR HERSCHEL,
>   You must have heard about the disaster. I shall tell you what has happened. On Thursday evening, rumors were circulating that Polish Jews in our city were being expelled. None of us believed it. At nine o'clock that evening a policeman came to our house to tell us to report to the police station with our passports. We all left as we were. Practically the whole neighborhood was already there. Almost immediately, we were taken to the city hall in a paddy wagon. Everybody else was too. No one told us what was happening, but we knew that this was the end. They shoved an expulsion order into our hands and said that we had to leave Germany before October 29, but we were not allowed to go home any more. I begged for permission to still pick up a few possessions, and the policeman went with me. I packed the most important clothes, but it was all we could salvage. We are left without a cent. Could you send us something to Lodz?
> Love from all of us,
> BERTA

Years later when Sendel Grynszpan appeared at the Eichmann trial, he testified that these homeless Jews, after being unloaded, were told by the SS that they would have to walk about two kilometers to the border.

> Those who could not walk were beaten until the road was wet with their blood. Their baggage was taken away. We were dealt with cruelly and barbarously. It was the first time that I realized how barbarous the Germans really are. They made us run while they

shouted, "Run! Run!" I was struck down at the roadside, but my son Marcus took me by the hand and said, "Come on, Papa, run. They'll kill you if you don't."

The news in the papers and then Berta's letter depressed Herschel badly. Four days after its receipt, on the morning of November 7, Herschel, then age seventeen, arose and went out early. On the table of his small room in his uncle's apartment he left a small card:

MY DEAR PARENTS:
    I could not act differently. May God forgive me. My heart bleeds at the reports of the suffering of 12,000 Jews. I have to protest in such a way that the world will hear me. I have to do it. Forgive me,

                                                           HERSCHEL

At half past nine A.M., he walked into the German Embassy. In his pocket was a small pistol he had just purchased. When an underling wanted to know the purpose of Herschel's visit, Herschel claimed to have a document that he could hand only to somebody higher up, at least at the rank of embassy secretary. Because it sounded as if he had some confidential information, he was led into the office of third secretary, Ernst Vom Rath. When Vom Rath asked to see the document, Herschel Grynszpan pulled the gun from his pocket and cried, "Here in the name of 12,000 persecuted Jews is your document!" There were five bullets in the gun, and Herschel shot five times. Only two of the bullets hit, but Vom Rath died two days later.

Herschel was arrested on the spot. After describing the nightmare of the Polish Jews, he told the French magistrate: "To be Jewish is not a crime. We are not animals. The Jewish people have a right to live."

This killing of a German diplomat, who in addition had been a member of the Nazi party even before Hitler's ascent to power in 1933, provided the Nazis with the pretext for the large-scale pogrom which was in the making anyhow. Hitler himself decided that "The SA should be allowed to have a fling."* And a fling they had.

*Recorded by the International Military Tribunal in Nuremberg, Volume XII, p. 381.

What happened on the night of November 9, 1938, and all during the day of November 10, while the *Draga* and the *Ely* were plowing the waters of the Black Sea, sent our own operations hurtling full steam ahead. It made the Jews in German-occupied lands assume any risk whatsoever just to get away. From the North Sea to the Brenner Pass, from the French border to the Polish boundary, the largest-scale pogrom Europe had ever seen took place. The German genius for organization excelled. In every little village, every town, and every city the great Jew hunt was on. The skies all over were red from the arson that took place everywhere, and torture and murder were carried out with systematic planning. And as imaginative as they were, the Nazis gave to this pogrom, the poetic name *Kristallnacht*, or "Crystal Night," in reference to the mountains of shattered glass from Jewish shops and apartment windows that littered the streets the next morning. The happenings leading to and during the Crystal Night are described most impressively in Rita Thalmann's and Emanuel Feinermann's book *Crystal Night.**

The Germans had ordered the "spontaneous" burning to the ground of all synagogues, the destruction of all Jewish shops, mass arrests, and deportation of Jews to concentration camps. Two hundred sixty-seven synagogues were gutted that night. Every one of the 7,500 Jewish-owned shops that had escaped earlier destruction or "Aryanization" was now ransacked, and what could not be taken away was hacked to pieces. Close to 31,000 Jews were herded into trains and deported to concentration camps. There the uniforms with the yellow Star of Zion, apparently "spontaneously" produced, were waiting for them. If one of the SA or SS butchers suspected that a Jew might have a weapon and might reach for it, he would kill him on the spot. It was fun to suspect many people that way.

The parents of my friend Sigfried Diamand, who had been respected owners of a small department store in Innsbruck-Tyrol, together with other Innsbruck Jews, were driven into the icy waters of the Inn River. Those who could swim and made it back to shore were murderously beaten before being thrown back in again to drown. Similar scenes took place all over Germany. Wherever there

*London: Thames and Hudson, 1974.

was a body of water, it was used in the same way. This is corroborated by a report of the then U.S. consul in Leipzig, Mr. David H. Buffum, from which the following example is taken:*

> Having demolished dwellings and hurled most of the movable effects to the streets, the insatiably sadistic perpetrators threw many of the trembling inmates into a small stream that flows through the Zoological Park, commanding horrified spectators to spit at them, defile them with mud and jeer at their plight.

The consul's report drew upon events in Leipzig, a large city. But villages with only a few Jewish citizens were just as much part of the nationwide pogrom. The progress of the pogrom in the small village of Lesum, near Bremen, was typical. The mayor of the village received orders from the SA company group commander that all Jews had to be "wiped out" and their stores destroyed. He checked the order with the SA command in Bremen and was told that in fact he was behind schedule—the synagogue in Bremen was already on fire. This was, as Bremen confirmed, The Night of the Long Knives. The latter phrase was taken from a popular Nazi song, *"Wenn's Judenblut vom Messer spritzt"* ("When the Jew's Blood Splashes from the Knife").

Everybody knew the few Jews in Lesum township. Bruno Mahlstedt and August Fruehling, both noncommissioned officers in the SA, were the heroes of Lesum that night. They hurried to the Goldberg home. Mr. and Mrs. Goldberg heard the heavy SA boots storming up the stairs. They stood at their bedside as the SA men entered. Fruehling, a well-mannered murderer, with gun in hand, announced: "I am fulfilling a difficult mission." Mrs. Goldberg told him: "Please aim carefully." A quick death was a bonanza then. Fruehling aimed and fired; Mahlstedt fired too. They had aimed well. There was another Jew in the village, Mr. Sinaisohn. His name, son of Sinai, had been the cause of much taunting. But now the taunting was over—he was assassinated that night as well.

And the rest of the world? How did people react? They did what they would do even later when conditions became much worse. When later, every day from sunrise to sunset, 12,000 people

---

*Report to the U.S. Consul General as recorded in Document L202 in *Nazi Conspiracy and Aggression*, Berlin, November 21, 1938. Washington, D.C.: U.S. Government Printing Office, 1946.

were marched into the gas chambers and thousands were assassinated daily in open-air killings, the nations of the world stood idly
by. The big powers with their elaborate intelligence network most
likely knew about the pogrom even earlier, but on November 9, in
the morning, the Jewish Agency in London knew for certain what
was to start that night. Dr. Weizmann, the agency's executive
chairman, urgently requested the Foreign Office in London to
approach the Nazi leaders immediately. It seemed fortunate that Sir
Neville Henderson, the British ambassador to Berlin, was in London that day, but he advised against such a step.

The Jewish congregation in Berlin also acted directly to obtain
British support against the impending pogrom. Sir Michael Bruce, a
former but still influential British diplomat, was just then in Berlin
at the request of Chief Rabbi Hertz of Great Britain. Sir Bruce was
approached by Berlin's Jews, and as he reports in his autobiography, he went

> at once to the British Embassy . . . I told Sir George Ogilvie-Forbes
> everything I knew and urged him to contact Hitler and express
> Britain's displeasure. He told me he could do nothing. The Ambassa-
> dor Sir Neville Henderson was in London and the Foreign Office,
> acting on instructions from Lord Halifax, had told him to do nothing
> that might offend Hitler and his minions.*

Listening to foreign broadcasts was then in Germany a major
crime. Yet because these programs were almost the only source of
uncensored news in Nazi Germany, almost everyone took the risk
of listening to them. If only the BBC had broadcast a warning,
hundreds, if not thousands, could have saved themselves. They
could have tried to go into hiding until at least this one storm was
over. Those near a border could have tried to cross into a neighboring country. Of course, such crossings would have been illegal
because the neighboring countries, in support of the Nazi terror,
had closed their borders to all but a token few of the hunted. Even
neutral Switzerland, the traditional haven of refugees of war, must
bear its burden of shame. Shortly after the Germans had annexed
Austria, Switzerland informed Germany that German Jews would
be refused entry into Switzerland. Switzerland, which had welcomed Jewish German tourists as long as they had money to spend,

---

*Michael Bruce, *Tramp Royal* (London, New York: Elek, 1954), pp. 335–40.

did not care whether these Jews perished in Germany or not. Notwithstanding their loudly proclaimed humanitarian principles, the Swiss did not want to be swamped with now penniless Jews. Only a few weeks prior to the *Kristallnacht* pogrom, the Swiss had concluded a deal with the Nazi government. Dr. Heinrich Rothmund, chief of the Swiss Federal Police, went to Germany with a brilliant idea to help keep the Jews out: the passports of the Jews would be specially marked. Everyone of Jewish descent, even if the family had been of the Christian faith for generations, would have a large red *J* stamped on the front page of his passport. The Germans went even further. Every Jewish man had the name Israel added to his first name on every document. Thus, my former German passport shows my name to be Willy Israel Perl, even though my name had never been Israel. This was supposed to degrade the bearer of the passport. Jewish women were treated equally. They had the name Sarah added to their passports.

Thus, the infamous *J* passport system was formed, which allowed Nazis to cross the borders of other countries at will, while Jews found themselves trapped.

And the Jewish establishment? Its reaction to the pogrom of the *Kristallnacht* was consistent with its policy of silence, which it would maintain during the ever-increasing ferocity of the Holocaust. Jewish organizations had been in the forefront of the fight for the rights of the oppressed everywhere. They continued this tradition after the war when they marched in America for the rights of the oppressed blacks, the underpaid grape pickers, the exploited gravediggers and garbage collectors. But they were so eager to demonstrate their "objectivity" that the murderous persecution of their own kind evinced no more than meek protests. In America, with its large influential Jewish population, the Nazi flag continued to fly provocatively over the German Embassy, while inside the luxurious building, Dr. Walter Thompson, Hitler's ambassador, could continue unimpeded to spread his Nazi views and his cheeky defense of what was being done to those subhumans, the Jews. When French Jews demanded that France protest the bestiality of the *Kristallnacht* to reduce the danger of its recurrence, Chief Rabbi Julien Weill of France stated in an interview in the Paris daily, *Le Matin*, on November 19, 1938: "We cannot at this moment endorse any initiative which would endanger Franco-German relations." The whole world, Jewish leaders included, tried to appease Hitler and to avoid anything that might displease him.

For those on the *Draga II* and the *Ely*—with fires raging in their former homelands—there was certainly no return. Except for those who would help them in Netanya, they were now on their own. For the British and the rest of the world, the Jews were expendable. This was the world from which those on the *Draga II* and the *Ely* who had just missed the *Kristallnacht* by a hairsbreadth tried to escape as they sailed toward the British blockade and the chance for a new life in their old-new land. But at that point, they were still far away from their goal.

Despite my having bribed the Rumanian newspapers, the *Vocea*, the Galatz daily, published a story on the eighth of November which was a compromise between not writing at all and reporting correctly. The paper reported about the *Draga* only, not about the *Ely*, thus indicating that if I wanted complete silence, I would have to pay more the next time.

The following day two Rumanian papers carried headlines that Rumania, though not bordering Germany, had apparently, via the Danube, become one of the escape routes. One editorial pointed out that Rumania did not want to be drawn into any controversy with powerful Germany.

Although I stayed in Galatz in *the* hotel, it was one that would have caused jurisdictional dispute in America. The fire department would have wanted to close it down as a firetrap; the health department, because the hotel constituted an overall health hazard; the building department, because it feared the collapse of the structure; and the vice squad, because the hotel provided a diversity of accommodations.

The morning after the hostile editorial there was a knock at my door. Still in my pajamas, in the glare of an unshaded light bulb, I faced a tall man with a powerful frame. He wore a fur coat with a beaver collar, an impressive-looking piece of clothing, but on closer examination it showed wear. "I am Jonel Popescu," he said. To my question of what I could do for him, he answered that my not knowing of him showed how inexperienced I was in handling matters in Rumania. In a voice that was just at the right pitch and powerfully resonant, he asserted that everybody in Bucharest knew him as the man with the best connections, both in government circles and with other people whom I might need because they engaged in shady business. He had read in the papers about the beginning of the flow of refugees through Rumania, and said, "You don't know Rumania; I am exactly the man you need. Happily for you, I completed my last major assignment and decided that I am now your attaché for personal and internal affairs."

It was clear to me that this man was blustering but also that he may have been right, that with his aggressiveness and self-confidence he may have been the man I would need to deal with all the currents and undercurrents I might encounter from Rumanian officials as well as from the underground, which might try to blackmail me. My outright question of how I could be certain that he would not blackmail me himself, he answered by beating his chest: "My honor, my reputation guarantees it. Everyone in Rumania knows that Jonel Popescu is to his friends as loyal as a dog . . . just as he is a tiger to his opponents," he added.

A short telephone inquiry with Jewish leaders in Bucharest showed that Popescu was a widely known figure, largely because there were few people to whom he did not owe money. He was renowned for his unbelievable ability to obtain more money from persons to whom he already owed some and to get them involved in financial adventures which, while not clearly crooked, usually resulted in a big bust for the investor as well as for poor Popescu. He was, however, also known as a live dynamo who worked with obsessive tenacity on the project with which he identified himself. He knew how to bribe which government official and with how much, and although part of the bribe money ended in Popescu's pocket, he was good at "contacts."

We did need government officials because it had already been hinted to me that the transfer from the paddle-wheelers to the seagoing vessels required the cooperation of various port authorities. I decided to hire Popescu as my "special assistant," and he immediately had business cards printed that read below his name: "Attaché for Personal and Internal Affairs, Jewish Emigration Office." Having him work for us proved to be the right step. He was efficient in his own way. Observing him as he went after his target with an amazing combination of go-getting, finesse, bluntness, and perpetual enthusiasm, constituted for me a source of pleasure, frustration, and amusement, often all three feelings simultaneously.

The way he bribed without risking trouble may be illustrated by the sentence he once used when bluntly putting a bundle of money on a high official's table: "If this can be done, we shall be happy to contribute right now twenty thousand lei for charity, the money to be used, of course, entirely according to your own discretion."

One day Popescu and I left for Tulcea, a much smaller town some sixty miles farther down the Danube delta, because the bribes to be paid in Galatz for the transfer permits had become intolerably excessive. In Tulcea, we expected the small—800 ton—oceangoing ship *Gepo*, which was to receive 750 refugees who were on the way down from Vienna on one of the paddle-wheelers. When I suggested renting a car with a driver to bring Popescu and me from Galatz to Tulcea, Popescu was indignant. "One car for both of us? You don't know Rumania. We have to travel each in a separate car, else the authorities will be down on us and will be impertinent." My chauffeur-driven, rented car left a little before Popescu's; he still had not had his manicure finished in the local beauty shop. On the way down, I noticed an unusual, lovely landscape. Many birds, at home in this region only, and not afraid of the automobile at all, inhabited the marshy delta area. I signaled to the driver to stop, went out, and took photographs.

At my second or third such stop, a soldier stepped out of the underbrush and, pointing his gun at me, indicated that I was arrested. With my arms raised over my head, I had to march with him for about half a mile to a wooden shack, also located on this single-lane dirt road.

There was a second soldier, a corporal, the first soldier's superior. My knowledge of the Rumanian language was at this time still quite poor, but I understood that I had been arrested for being a "spy." When I protested that I was not a spy, the corporal, with a contemptuous expression of superiority and convincing logic, "proved" to me that I was one. "The way you talk, it is clear that you are not a Rumanian. As you are not a Rumanian, you are a Russian. And Russians are spies." At that time, Rumania was still a kingdom and, bordering Soviet Russia, lived in permanent fear of this powerful neighbor. When I showed the man my Austrian passport, he knew the answer right away. "Austrians are not Rumanians; they are Russians, too." I was not worried because I knew that Jonel Popescu was on his way. Within a few minutes I saw a cloud of dust approaching. In the rear of the open convertible, in regal posture, with a big cigar in his mouth, sat the attaché for personal and internal affairs.

He asked me what had happened and I told him. When the corporal, impressed anyhow by Popescu's stature and fur coat, tried to explain, Popescu snarled at him. "When you talk to me, you address me as 'Your Excellency.'" The corporal, already on the defensive, explained that I was obviously a Russian and that he had to arrest me. I had taken photographs of the landscape and photographs are taken of either one's girl or one's mother, but why should anyone want to photograph scenery, unless he is a spy?

Popescu now asked him, in a quiet voice, if he could see a nearby tree. "Yes, Your Excellency," answered the corporal. Suddenly Popescu broke into a thunderous voice, which reminded me of what I had learned in high school about what Zeus's voice was supposed to have been. "Look at your watch! What time is it?" "I don't have a watch, Your Excellency," the soldier replied. Popescu then showed him his golden one, pulling it from his vest pocket. "Look at it. When the hand moves to 'here' "—he showed ten minutes—"you will both be hanging from this tree."

"And now you connect me, with your telephone, with Bucharest, with my cousin, His Majesty the King!"

At this, the younger of the soldiers started begging for his life. The corporal joined in. Both explained that their families would be left bereft, and at my persuasion, Popescu decided not to have them hanged. We continued on our trip.

Sailing for the *Draga* and the *Ely* was smooth. Of course, each time another ship appeared on the horizon, our commanding officer blew the whistle, and everybody had to leave the deck so that the ship should look just like a regular cargo vessel and not arouse anyone's suspicions. The immigrants, therefore, saw nothing of the beautiful Bosporus and nothing of Istanbul. But spirits remained high. The various platoons had their roll call when it was their time to go on deck to stay for a few hours in the open air. On these occasions, not only old Jewish folk songs and the Jewish national anthem could be heard but also the new "Song of the Illegal Immigrant." Set in a powerful C-minor key, the march melody was both exciting and inspiring. There were several verses to this song, and on each trip one or more new verses were created and became

the "property" of that particular ship. Translated from the Hebrew,
the "Song of the Illegal Immigrant" went something like this:

It does not matter, brother,
From where you came or why
To board this moving deck.
Crammed from hole to smokestack,
It's a battleship—this wreck—
Though it has no guns.
We warriors thereon,
Though we have no arms of iron,
Yet we have an iron will
Against all odds
To build the future of our land.
Win we shall.
Our nation and our land
We shall make them live again.

Very much to the chagrin of "Johnny," who was familiar with
the landing at Tantura Beach, the Irgun had decided that the region
near Benjamina had become too "hot," as the police were watching
it more closely all the time. A new landing site at Netanya, only
twenty miles north of Tel Aviv, was decided upon. This place was
not as easily discernible from the sea, but it had other advantages
that made it ideal for the purpose. The town and all the surrounding land lie high above the ocean. For this reason, one cannot see
from the land what is happening on the narrow beach below the
steep rocks. In addition, aside from thus being protected from view,
the immigrants, once they had climbed the dune and the rocks,
found themselves right in the middle of an entirely Jewish town.

Only a few hundred feet from where the climb ends was, and
still is, Netanya's movie house. The owner of the theater offered to
hide all the new immigrants landing there until they could move on.
Pedestrian movement on the square in front of the theater was, of
course, not suspect. Still another advantage over Tantura was that
there were no Arab villages close by from which the approach of an
unknown vessel could be reported to the British. Also, although the
climb was steep—a rise of about 150 feet on rocks that cut one's

soles—it was short and much less strenuous than the hours of hiking in the dunes at Benjamina.

For these reasons, most of the later ships landed at Netanya, then a sleepy little country town, now a resort city of 90,000 people and also the center of the diamond trade in modern Israel. It prides itself today on being the place at which more "illegals" entered the country than at any other. The landing operations at Netanya, carried out under the able leadership of Moshe Chasan, were organized quite differently from those in Tantura near Benjamina.

On the nights ships were expected to arrive, at least three people were hidden among the rocks below Netanya. This observer team was in an incomparably better position than had been the "Bedouin" horsemen near Benjamina because they could scan the beach and sea through their binoculars from lookout points in the rocks not visible from inland. When they sighted a ship giving the agreed-upon signals, they returned the signals, and at the same time, one of the three climbed up the remaining part of the cliff, which brought him right into the middle of town. According to a plan carefully worked out in advance, messengers were then sent out to various houses, and, one by one, those involved in the operation went down to the beach.

There was also a contingency plan worked out to have dozens of Jewish families come out en masse if required. The idea behind this plan—which did not have to be put into effect with the *Draga II* and the *Ely* landings but did later with other ships—was the following: if the British noticed what was going on, all the immigrants were given the order to rush the hill. Up there, hundreds of townspeople were milling around. The British then could not pick out the immigrants from the villagers, and any questioning they did gave others the chance to slip away.

Although this plan was not needed with the *Ely* and *Draga II*, their debarkation did not go smoothly. In fact, if anything ever went smoothly with our operations, it seemed like a miracle, so plentiful and serious were the possibilities for something to go wrong.

The newspaper article in the Galatz *Vorea* reporting about the *Draga*'s departure had exposed that ship more than the *Ely*. For this reason, the two did not travel together. The *Draga* changed its name to *Libertad* and flew, instead of the Panamanian flag, the flag of Spain. Her captain found the new place for the rendezvous, and the debarkation boat, the *Artemesia*, was ready. As always, women and children were allowed to disembark first. Next in line were the "older" people; at that time, these were still anyone approximately over thirty. While the *Artemesia* was smuggling 300 of the 544 aboard the *Draga II* to shore, the *Draga II* was discovered by a British warship and had to weigh anchor immediately. Although she was outside the three-mile limit and thus could not be arrested, the British ship pursued her. As soon as the *Draga*'s captain saw that he had been noticed, he started to sail in zigzag fashion away from the coast. The chance to avoid the incomparably faster British ship was, of course, nil, but the captain hoped to make the *Draga* appear suspicious in order to divert attention from the *Artemesia*, which was within the continental waters and full of refugees.

The maneuver succeeded, but because the British warship continued to follow the *Draga* for two whole days, a catastrophe almost occurred: with almost half of her passengers still on board, she was about to run out of coal. She had been forced to cruise for so long that she could no longer return for refueling to any of the Greek islands and had to sail into a Turkish port. The Greeks and Turks had not been friends for many years. Turkey was allied with Britain at that time, and the British consul there had no difficulty in making certain that the captain received, instead of coal, a warrant for the arrest of the ship. The 250 immigrants still on the *Draga* were distraught. They had seen the coast of Palestine; some of their friends, in many cases members of their immediate family, a wife or child, were already there.

Fortunately for the immigrants, the Turks did not want any Jews, so they too were in a bind. On the second night, after two fearful days in the Turkish port, the immigrants were awakened by Johnny's whistle. The signal he had whistled meant: "Attention, debarkation imminent." Panic gripped those in the holds, but those on deck were first to know the good news. First with apprehension, they saw a ship approaching the port. Suddenly somebody shouted, "The *Ely!*" It actually was the *Ely*, dispatched there by Mr. Davaris. She docked next to the *Draga*. Although the *Ely* still had all her 620 passengers on board, several gangplanks were laid across the two ships. Accompanied by encouraging shouts from friends on the *Ely*, one after another of the *Draga* immigrants crossed over. A few fell into the water, more rucksacks were lost, but nobody drowned. Before dawn, the *Ely* left, and two days later Moshe

Chasan and his people—again with the help of the faithful little *Artemesia*—smuggled everybody from the *Ely*, which had hardly any standing room, right into the main square of Netanya.

The roles each one in the landing organization had to play in helping the immigrants disperse quickly after their arrival in Netanya had been decided upon beforehand. The milkman came with his horse-drawn wagon and delivered milk to the movie; others delivered food; still others brought blankets for the wet ones if supplies on hand were not sufficient. Not many blankets could be kept in the movie house because few in Palestine at the time had more than one blanket, and this they needed for themselves. Oddly enough, the owner of a shoe store was on call, too. Many of the immigrants arrived without shoes. How this happened is probably best explained by the story of Berta Siegel, the eighteen-year-old who had been in Arnoldstein and had so dreaded facing her parents upon her return home. She had been originally scheduled to go with her young husband on the first large transport with 386 abroad. But she received her passport too late, and her husband had left with the 386. After the Arnoldstein experience, she had now finally made it too: "As I was lowering myself from the *Artemesia* into the water to wade ashore, I had taken my shoes off so that they would not get wet, too. A Greek sailor helped me, and I thought he was very nice to hold my shoes; but as it turned out, he kept them! As I was wading toward the land, I looked back and saw that he was similarly helpful to another girl. These people must have been able to open a small shoe store on their return to the Piraeus."

Her husband, with whom she was soon to be reunited and who had been in the country four months by then, also had a "shoe story" to tell:

We had been told that [after our arrival in Palestine] we must not look conspicuous and wear regular work clothes. As we knew that we would soon be transferred to the small ship, I started shaving the beard which I had grown on the trip. I had just finished shaving the left side and had still no shoes on when the command sounded "Transfer." When we landed, and I was asked where I wanted to go, I said, "Tel Aviv." I knew nobody there, but figured that I could more easily disappear in a large city. The bus deposited me on a square, and there I stood. Absolute inconspicuous: half my face shaven, the other side of my face covered with a matted beard; one foot bare, and one in a new, firm hiking shoe. I felt like a clown! It

was early in the morning and a man with a three-wheeler bike loaded
with milk cans peddled by. As he saw me, he stopped. He asked me
in Yiddish, "*Ihr kimmt fin Hitlern?*" ["Did you come from Hitler?"].

Upon my, "yes," he put me next to the milk cans and peddled
me to his house. I was starved and parched. His wife brought food,
orange juice and coffee, more than enough for three. But do you
know what I enjoyed most? Sitting in a chair. I hadn't sat in one for
so long, and this chair symbolized for me that I was human again.

The happenings of the *Kristallnacht,* the despair of those who
had seen their fathers, husbands, or brothers carted away to the
concentration camps all propelled the thought of illegal immigration into the plans of even those who had been too afraid to take the
risk before. Our office in Vienna, our new one in Prague, and our
group in Bucharest were being overrun. Anybody who knew anyone
who might know somebody working with us was besieged with
pleas for intervention and help. There was nothing which was not
offered to those of us who really had a say. Money, jewelry, women.
I was offered a little house in Brooklyn, if I got one man's parents
and two sisters out; one lady in Bucharest showed me a notarized
statement according to which her brother would make me a 50
percent partner in his soda fountain in the Bronx if I took her
family on the next ship. To these people we appeared to be God, yet
we were at the mercy of a thousand complications. Almost every
day, new panic befell us because of sudden changes in the complex
situation as to ships, authorities, food supplies, etc. When one had
to say no to a person who wanted only to save himself and his
family, one felt like an executioner. I decided that I had to exclude
my heart; only if I succeeded in freezing it or in turning it into stone
could I make the decisions that had to be made. We continued to
adhere to the principle of taking young people first and among the
older ones only those who seemed the healthiest and most likely to
abide by the strict discipline on board. The latter were hard to
judge. I recall the violinist who had performed many concerts in
Europe whom I did not want to take because I thought he would
"break" too easily. With many reservations, we accepted him. On
the boat, he surprised us all by proving himself to be a source of
great strength. Always in a hopeful mood, he made friends with the
most despondent ones, and some of them gained so much courage
that they in turn formed little circles who sang together, developed

mutual plans for the future, and aided in spreading the feeling that this was all temporary and would in the future be a great memory of heroic times to relate to one's children and grandchildren.

The pressure in our offices in Vienna and Prague was the stronger because the knowledge had spread that the *Ely* and *Draga* had carried 150 who had come straight from Dachau, and that for the next ships we would again be permitted to take people out of concentration camps.

Unfortunately, because the *Draga* on her second trip had been sighted by the British off the coast of Palestine and, along with the *Ely*, was observed and photographed during the transfer in the Turkish port by agents of the local British Consulate and by the RAF, the cover of the two ships had been blown. After having been remodeled with so much labor and at such expense, they were now known in every detail. The *Draga* could, therefore, not come back for a third trip, and neither could the *Ely* return. Instead, Mr. Davaris promised to send a different ship, the S.S. *Gepo*, a thirty-four-year-old coal ship which, in spite of its age, was well built. Davaris dispatched the *Gepo* as fast as he could, but not fast enough for our people in Vienna and Prague. In daily telegrams and phone calls, they complained about the slowness with which I was working. Finally, early in December of 1938, the *Gepo* entered the Danube. We did not have her come as far as Galatz but had decided to outfit her in Tulcea, the small town on the Danube close to the delta, which I had visited before with Popescu to explore its suitability for that purpose.

Rumanian winters are hard. This one had come earlier and was the hardest the Rumanians had had for years. The morning I set out with Mila for Tulcea, I learned that a soldier who was standing guard at night in the port area of Galatz had been attacked by wolves. In the morning, only his boots, his belt, rifle, and a few bones were found.

This time Popescu did not come along. During our first trip to Tulcea, we had arranged matters with the local authorities there, and he was now in Bucharest in an attempt to prevent the Rumanian government from issuing orders for health, safety, or some other reasons that would forbid the transfer at Tulcea.

To reach Tulcea, we had to cross the Danube at Galatz. The "ferry" consisted of a large float with a sputtering motor attached.

It could carry one oxcart. Sometimes it carried an automobile instead. It also had standing room for pedestrians.

After an icy, bumpy ride of more than six hours, we rode proudly into Tulcea. To our delight, we saw, in spite of the fog, that a black ship was tied to the small pier. Was it really the *Gepo*? It was.

As I had this time to spend at least one night there, the taxi brought us to the town square to Tulcea's only "hotel." A dirty wooden sign showed it even had a name: HOTEL IMPERIAL. Mila got what I jokingly called the "royal suite." Her iron bed had four legs, and there was a chair in the room. My bed's fourth leg was too short and was therefore supported by two bricks. I had no chair, and my "window" was actually an opening of frosted glass onto the corridor. A glance at the sheets showed me that they had been used before. When I mentioned this fact to the hotel owner, a fat woman blessed with no teeth and legs so short one had the feeling she was walking on her knees, she answered indignantly: "These sheets are almost fresh!" As an afterthought, to impress me further, she added, "And the only person who slept on them was a gentleman!" With a voice as if she were saying, "He was a king," she announced, "He was a traveling salesman!" She added, and she was right, that hers was the best hotel east of Galatz, or, as she expressed it, "between Galatz and either Odessa or Istanbul." My attempt to bribe her into giving me new sheets taught me that people have their pride. If her Hotel Imperial was not good enough for me, I could sleep in the street! Unfortunately, I found out that her statement that this bed had been used only by the traveling salesman was incorrect. Scores of bedbugs, each one thirsty for my blood, crawled out of the mattress, out of the pillow; they came from everywhere. And if I killed one, a whole clan came to the funeral! A small iron stove in the corner was literally red hot, but its door had the annoying trait of opening up when one of the pieces of wood inside changed its position. Besides, the little beast had to be fed every hour or less to keep the fire going. Each time I had to attend to the stove, the thought irked me that I was so obviously in the minority in this room and that I was watching and feeding the stove largely to keep the bedbugs warm.

First thing the next morning, we walked—and slid—down to the pier and onto the ship. There Mila and I had a pleasant surprise:

Davaris had loaded all the lumber considered necessary for equipping the *Gepo* before it had left Greece. And all during the trip from Greece to Rumania, workmen had been busy on board building platforms and, on them, the shelves for the bunks. I assume that most fire marshals in civilized countries would have paled had they seen the coal stoves standing on the wooden platforms inside those ships. But the stoves were needed to keep the people from freezing to death—particularly those not lucky enough to have a blanket or a straw mat to lie on. A special crew was assigned to guard the stoves on a twenty-four-hour basis. There were always two watching, and during all our trips, there was never a fire caused by one of the stoves.

In converting the freighter for its intended use, we had included practically no toilets. Mila, therefore, spent the entire day on the *Gepo* supervising the building of the wooden enclosures which were to serve as additional toilets, and watching so that none of the supplies brought aboard might disappear. The pace was hectic, and despite our low finances, we had to pay the workers double time for night work in order for the ship to be ready in time for the emigrants.

We knew by then that 694 emigrants had already passed Budapest—good news! Five hundred and forty-four of them had come from Vienna and Prague, and 150 from Dachau. But along with these good tidings we heard bad news as well—as always seemed the case with us: those coming from Czechoslovakia had been robbed of their belongings by the Slovak militia in the Slovakian Danube port of Bratislava. Most important, everyone in this group had lost his blanket, and we needed close to 200 blankets.

The tiny telephone office in Tulcea finally got through to Bucharest again, and Schieber, together with Dr. Kanner, the systematic, hard-working chairman of the Revisionist organization in Rumania, procured these blankets too.

When the emigrants arrived, the transfer was immediately begun. Before any supplies, came the people. They were anxious to get off those ships flying the Nazi flags as fast as possible.

Standing on the plank and having the emigrants pass me one after the other was an experience of strong yet contrasting emotions. On the one hand, every face I saw meant one more person saved. On the other hand, most of these faces I saw reflected the tragedy clouding this moment of felicity. There was a girl whom I had dated in Vienna and whom I knew as an elegantly dressed, poised young lady. Now, she came down the plank from the Nazi riverboat, squalid, her hair matted, walking heavily as she lugged the unfamiliar weight of a rucksack with her. When she saw me, she burst into tears. Her brother had been arrested during the *Kristallnacht* and shipped to Dachau. She had thought that because she was friends with some of the people in our Vienna office, she would be able to take her parents along to Palestine. Before she tried to arrange for that, she discussed it with her mother and father. But they refused to leave because their son was still in Dachau. As I learned later, the son never returned and the parents never got out.

Another face I saw was that of a stretcher case. A man who had been a urologist, I believe the chief of urology at the Hospital of the Vienna Jewish Community. I cannot recall why he was so ill, but he had been taken along because his wife was one of the most experienced nurses at the same hospital, and we, of course, needed experienced nurses badly. One man, on his wife's arm, followed by two teenage daughters, had a faraway look in his eyes and apparently knew little of what was going on. He was a physicist whose research papers, the result of years of work, hope, and planning had all been destroyed by some Nazi troopers who had invaded his home and had gone from there to his office.

After everyone was aboard, the stronger of the emigrants helped to transfer the supplies from one ship to the other. Within four hours after their arrival, the riverboats were ready to return. On the *Gepo* itself, work had not yet been finished, and some 50 of the new passengers were detailed to help the workers on the ship. One more day and the *Gepo* was ready to sail. At that point, Mila remembered something: there was by far not enough toilet paper on board! We had figured on three weeks at sea; we had food supplies for that long and enough water to make it to one of the Greek islands for watering up. But the toilet paper! The best we could come up with was old newspapers. Not everybody around Tulcea was literate, and of those who were, few subscribed to a newspaper. A telephone call to Bucharest put into motion there a taxi which arrived that evening loaded with old newspapers.

The final figure on board the *Gepo* was: 540 "regulars" from Vienna and Prague, 4 smuggled on board by the Vienna crew, 150 from Dachau, 25 Betarim from Rumania, and 15 "chosen" from those who were in Rumanian jails for having fled illegally into Rumania. Thus, all told, we had 734 emigrants on board.

At last, two days after their arrival in Tulcea, the emigrants were on their way.

None of the voyages of our blockade breakers were uneventful, but comparing the ventures still ahead of us with the ships to follow, the *Gepo*'s first running of the British blockade was relatively smooth and fast. After she had passed through the Dardanelles, the captain evaded the British by clever crisscrossing, interrupted by occasional hiding in one of the countless little inlets of the many Greek islands. Finally, on a moonless, slightly foggy night, the transfer to the landing ships was effected rather smoothly, and before daybreak all the passengers of the *Gepo* stood on the soil which was, to them, their ancient-new home.

But there was no respite for us because there was no respite in the persecution. When we returned to Bucharest from Tulcea, after just having dispatched the *Gepo*, we found messages waiting for us from all over Europe. "More ships," they demanded. "More ships!" In telephone calls, telegrams, and special delivery letters, Vienna, as well as our office in Prague, and the Betar headquarters in Budapest, Warsaw, and Danzig pleaded for more transportation. Davaris sent the *Gepo* back right after her stop in Greece to take on fresh provisions and new supplies of coal and water. There was also a partial change of crew at that time because some members of the original crew had become frightened by the risks involved in the trips. Finding replacements was no problem for Davaris, however, because many Greek sailors could not wait to go to sea, as the police were after them for one reason or another. Besides the *Gepo*, which for its second voyage we renamed *Gepo II*, Davaris sent a ship still new to our service, the S.S. *Katina,* that would now have to be outfitted for our purposes.

Our immediate obstacle right then was not a scarcity of ships, therefore. With the coming of winter, the freezing of the Danube rendered the river unnavigable from the Bulgarian border. This meant that we had to fall back on transit visas, a procedure which had caused so much trouble and tragedy before. The British were, of course, well aware of our need for transit visas, and they, in effect, tried to bottle up those being hunted down in Nazi Germany. However, Zeev Jabotinsky's visit to the Balkans in October 1938, during which he intervened with Mr. Calinescu, the Rumanian

prime minister, and other Balkan statesmen, had created in these
countries a more favorable climate for us. Yet to let us through
without a visa of destination would have been interpreted as an
overt rejection of a legally founded British request. But by giving
assurances that the refugees had not the slightest intention of really
traveling there, one or the other of the diplomats of a faraway
country could be bribed into issuing visas of destination.

Our offices in Vienna and in Prague, therefore, undertook to
provide these destination visas, or end visas as we called them. In
Vienna, Heinrich Haller, Paul Haller's brother, Fritz Herrenfeld,
and Paul Elbogen started negotiating with the consuls of various
Latin American nations as well as with the consul of Liberia. In
Prague, similar negotiations were undertaken by my cousin Robert
Mandler and by two Betar leaders, Eliyahu Gleser and Emil Faltyn.
We also put our feelers out with the Berlin diplomatic representa-
tives of Latin American countries and of Chiang Kai-shek's China.
Several of these representatives of faraway countries agreed to
"grant" invalid visas in exchange for, in their eyes, an "appropri-
ate" consideration.

End visas were a must. They permitted the countries of transit
to claim that according to the documents our people were not
headed "illegally" for Palestine, as the British maintained, but were
traveling to San Salvador, China, or some other out of the way
country. By promising these countries of transit that we would
relieve them of some of their refugees and by making it clear that
without our activities all these people might come flooding across
the borders anyway, we thus succeeded in obtaining transit visas for
up to another 1,500 who were to go on the second trip of the *Gepo*
and on the S.S. *Katina.*

The Hungarians specifically demanded that at least 100 Hungarian Jews leave the country with the two transports applied for
right then, and that, in addition, at least 50 foreign Jews, who were
being held in Hungarian jails for having fled into Hungary illegally,
be taken off their hands. We promised them we would do so, and
we explained to the Hungarians and the officials of the other transit
countries which wanted to rid themselves of Jews that our operation
had started only a short time ago. We pointed out that within a year
the numbers of Jews we could take along from their country would
multiply as our operation grew.

The refugees came this time in sealed trains. Straight to

Constanța, the Rumanian seaport. On January 18, 1939, the *Katina* left for Palestine with 775 immigrants on board; on February 28, the *Gepo II* steamed out of port with another 750.

The *Gepo II* sailed from Constanța, but for the *Katina* we chose an entirely new location, quite out of the way, a town which had not seen any refugees before and no action associated with illegal immigration. It was the tiny, colorful Rumanian Black Sea port of Balchik, some 70 miles south of Constanța. I have never seen a town more picturesque. Perched against a hill, its little church, a mosque, and a charming small castle looked down upon a miniature port that was the center of activity.

It was at Balchik that I met Moishe Kapitaen. Shortly before the *Katina*'s departure, one of the marshals appointed to keep order on the ship, formerly a well-known Viennese corporation lawyer, brought to me a boy of about fifteen who was dressed in rags. The old boots he wore were obviously several sizes too large for him. The youngster was not a member of the group and had somehow smuggled himself on board. He had learned in his hometown of Cernauti—then in Rumania, now "annexed" by the USSR—that an illegal ship was leaving for Palestine from Balchik, and he had made his way to that town. Quite experienced in the art of stowing away on ships, he had found it very easy to get on board. I soon learned that he was a well-known figure among young Rumanian Zionists. He was commonly known as Moishe Kapitaen. His first name was Moses, and he was referred to as Captain because on six previous occasions he had stowed away on ships traveling from Rumania to Palestine, only to be returned each time.

In these days, two modern Rumanian passenger liners, the *Transylvania* and the *Bessarabia*, were on regular weekly schedules from Constanța, Rumania, to Haifa. Our young Moses, in his yearning to go "home" to Palestine, had succeeded six times in getting on board. On one occasion, he was found hiding in the ship's water tank. The crew was concerned that the passengers might find out that this dirty boy had been found in the tank from which they got their drinking water. The captain of the liner promised Moses to see to it that he got on land in Haifa if he did not tell anybody where he had been hiding on the ship. The crew got him on land supposedly as a crew member, but within minutes he was reported or recognized as suspicious by the British. The port police arrested him. And again he was returned to Rumania.

"This time," he told me, beaming with pride and happiness, "I am going for the first time legally." I had to agree with his logic, and, of course, Moishe Kapitaen came along. As I learned later, he became active in Irgun when it, together with the even more militant Stern group, started and continued to the ultimate liberation, the armed revolt against the occupying colonial power.

On both *Gepo II* and the *Katina*, discipline was good in spite of the misery which the immigrants on those two ships had to endure. The keeping up of morale and discipline was largely due to the leadership qualities of the commanding officers, whom the Irgun had sent for those two boats. Our commanding officer on the *Gepo II* went by the name of Mordochay Navon. His real name is Josef Kremin; he is now a builder in Ashkelon, Israel. The commanding officer sent by the Irgun for the *Katina* was Moshe Chasan. Both Irgun commanders had been active in the landing organization and were well qualified to bring their ship to the rendezvous and to supervise, this time from the ship's side, the landing operation. Contrary to the procedure used by Johnny, who had assumed command at landing time only, Kremin ("Navon") and Moshe Chasan took control as soon as their ship was on the high seas. This change had become necessary because we did not have enough leaders left in Germany and in the countries occupied by it. Many of our Betarim and most others with leadership training had gone as commanders or just as passengers on our rescue ships, and leadership during the voyage had deteriorated.

By the time of the *Katina* and the *Gepo II* sailings, the British were fully determined to explode the myth that their navy did not really try to prevent the illegal landings. Due to sharply increased British patrolling, the *Katina* had to turn back twice when she approached the Palestine coast. The signals from land had informed her that she would run into a trap if she tried the unloading then. Equally, the *Gepo* was advised to keep away. On both these ships conditions became daily more unbearable. The already sparse food and supplies had to be reduced to "iron rations," and the number of sick rose to alarming proportions. It was, therefore, determined that the *Katina* would have to leave her hideout in a small inlet on one of the Greek isles and try a landing, although all the odds were against it. On February 5, as she approached the coast, the signals again flashed "Keep out," but the captain and Kremin decided that whatever the risk, they had to take it because of the conditions on board.

That night was to become one of the most exciting of all

the nights during which landing operations were set into motion. The little *Artemisia* had been dispatched by Davaris and was waiting at the appointed place. Because this time the risks were particularly high, the immigrants had to discard their rucksacks, their only remaining possession, so that more people could be crammed into the *Artemisia*. With 300 immigrants standing shoulder to shoulder on the deck of the small landing craft, many with their arms raised so as to provide a little more space, the *Artemisia* took off while the *Katina* waited at a safe distance, well outside territorial waters. When the landing ship was about two miles from shore, the almost complete darkness around her turned suddenly into dazzling bright light. A powerful searchlight had its beam focused on her, and everyone and everything on board was almost shining in the radiance of that cone of brilliance. The landing craft's captain had now to decide whether simply to surrender, to try to make it back outside the three-mile zone, or to proceed anyhow. He knew the conditions on the *Katina* and ordered: "Full steam ahead for the coast."

Followed by the beam of light and the patrol boat from which it came, the *Artemisia* raced toward the shore. As soon as she was close enough for the immigrants to wade or swim ashore, the order was given: "All who can swim or who will risk to wade in the waves for a hundred to hundred fifty feet, JUMP!" Two hundred and eighty-three jumped—and they all made it. Only 17, mostly elderly or sick people, stayed on board, and when the *Artemisia* tried to run back to the open sea, they were captured by the British together with the landing boat and its crew.

In a cypher telegram, sent on February 11 by the high commissioner for Palestine to the secretary of state for the colonies, the high commissioner gives the British version of what happened, a fairly correct one, although he believed that we had landed 400 while the actual figure was 283. This telegram reads:

> Important. No. 166 Secret
> Addressed to the Colonial Office No. 155,
> repeated to His Majesty's Minister at
> Athens No. 62
> On the night of 5th February, Police surprised Greek steamer *Artemisia* of the Piraeus landing illegal immigrants some ten kilometers north of Tel Aviv. *Artemisia* was boarded and taken to Haifa

where proceedings are being taken against the crew of twelve, all Greeks and against 17 Jewish passengers. Preliminary investigations reveal that the *Artemisia* left the Greek archipelagos on February 2nd accompanied by the steamer *Katina* which had 900 Jews on board. On arrival near the coast the *Katina* lay some 20 miles off shore and the *Artemisia* which is a vessel of 221 tons gross was used as a ferry and had landed 400 illegal immigrants from the *Katina* before discovery.*

The British were never certain of our actual figures and while the high commissioner thought that we had landed 400, the London *Times* on February 9, reporting on the glorious capture, shows that the *Times* correspondent had no idea how many we had landed and successfully dispersed. The *Times* writes:

SMUGGLING JEWS TO PALESTINE. GREEK STEAMER SEIZED . . . There were 17 would-be immigrants on board the ship without passports or permits to enter Palestine, but it is supposed that 30 or 40 others and four crew members had been able to land.

These wretched 17 who could not make it into the water were the first ones to be captured out of thousands whom we had successfully smuggled in. They were, therefore, the subject of much discussion among the British. In a note classified SECRET, the Foreign Office reveals that it too did not have the correct figures and comments sarcastically, "It is something that the Palestine authorities have at least managed to arrest some of these illegal immigrants, even if it is only 17 out of a shipload of 400."

We were pleased to know how little the British knew about what had actually happened: the figure of those who had landed varied from one report to the other, and with the exception of the 17, all their figures were incorrect.

But in spite of this partial success, the landing of 283, the *Katina* was left with 475 passengers. At the same time, the *Gepo II* was cruising among the Greek isles. On both these ships, food supplies for the immigrants were down to almost zero. Crew members, particularly on the *Gepo II*, took advantage of this situation, although the captains tried to prevent it. The crew remained relatively better supplied, and crew members sold their own food or

*FO 371/23246/P249 Feb. 20, 1939.

part of it for anything an immigrant might have. Usually the items of such trade were wedding rings, the only jewelry the Jews had been permitted to take out. Younger couples found this parting not difficult. However, the older a couple was, the more memories were symbolized by the ring, and many preferred to go through the worst of hunger and thirst rather than separate themselves from even one of the rings.

But worse than hunger and thirst was in store for those on the *Gepo II*. In the midst of a foggy, storm-whipped, and moonless night, about a week after the *Katina* had reduced her load to 475 and the *Gepo II* was still zigzagging south of Crete, the catastrophe struck. A frightening, grinding noise from below awoke those crammed into the *Gepo*'s holds. For a few seconds there was silence—and then everybody knew. The ship had steered into a reef, which had torn a large hole in her bottom. The alarm siren sounded and within another two minutes the signal changed from "Alarm" to "Abandon Ship." The captain expected the ship to sink fast. Only people who had been facing death for many months could keep the stoic composure that the starved and parched passengers of the *Gepo II* displayed during the ship's sinking. Fortunately, the death of the ship did not come as rapidly as first expected. Women and children were loaded in an orderly way into the two lifeboats and were all shuttled to a small uninhabited island, which was less than a mile away. But this was a slow process. While the crew and some of the passengers were hectically working on the pumps, the radioman was steadily sending the SOS. As the ship started slowly to list, the Greeks told those on board on which side to assembly to delay the inevitable sinking.

As the sky was turning gray, a ship that had heard the SOS appeared on the horizon. Was it a British ship that would "capture" the immigrants and likely bring them back to Europe? As the ship approached the sinking *Gepo*, it became clear that the vessel was at least not a warship. It was a freighter. But what nationality would it be? Did it fly the flag of one of the axis countries, or, potentially even worse, was it British? When the immigrants were told by the *Gepo*'s crew the nationality and the name of the approaching ship they felt that a miracle had occurred. The rescue vessel was, the crew asserted, the *Katina!*

But was it the *Katina?* True, one could already see that the deck was crammed with hundreds of waving refugees—but the ship did not look at all like the *Katina.*

After she had discharged part of her passengers, and because she had been noted and certainly photographed by some of the planes which followed her for some time as she was steaming away from the Palestine coast, the *Katina* had entered one of the numerous inlets on one of the smaller Greek isles. There Davaris had made preparations in case one of his ships would have to "blow its cover." As soon as the *Katina* had entered the inlet, a contraption, built on that island and ready for just such an occasion, was brought on board. It was a sham smokestack. While the contrivance was erected, a dozen or so of the islanders together with members of the ship's crew went feverishly to work on still another task. They were painting the ship. And when the *Katina* left the inlet, she was a ship with not one but two smokestacks, not gray but black, and she was flying not the Greek flag but that of Portugal.

Davaris had held his two ships in relative proximity so that one could help the other. But the *Katina* still had 475 passengers of her own on board, and now she had to take on another 750. She had been able after the partial landing to obtain some water, but she was still without food. In fact, her captain had hoped to get some food from the *Gepo II.* But whatever the conditions on board would be, first those from the sinking ship had to be saved—and this had to be done fast. During the transfer, one could see the *Gepo II* listing more and more, and just as the last ones climbed aboard the *Katina,* the faithful *Gepo* tipped completely on her side and quietly went under. A few bubbles and her life ended.

Now with 1,225 immigrants on board and nothing to eat, there was only one way left for the *Katina.* Whatever the risks, the immediate breaking of the blockade and the rapid landing of all immigrants had to be dared. She steamed straight for the Palestine coast, and so did a landing ship which Davaris, reliable as always, had dispatched in place of the captured *Artemisia.*

All previous landings had been made when the sea was relatively calm. This time the night was stormy. One man and two women fell into the water during the transfer to the small landing ship, but they were saved. One of the women had already disappeared in the waves but was picked up by the landing ship, and though she was unconscious, she was revived. Actually, that the night was stormy turned out to be a blessing. The British knew that we had always landed when the waters were calm, and they "knew" that it was impossible to use the little boats in such a storm. Their vigil was reduced. This was one night when, they figured, they could take it easy.

During that night, the *Katina* unloaded 1,225 immigrants, 475 of her own and the 750 rescued from the *Gepo II*. Next day, it was known in all the jubilant Jewish villages, towns, cities, and *kibbutzim* that another 1,225 brothers and sisters had escaped persecution, torture, and murder.

As happy as the Jews were about this rescue, the British were infuriated when they found out that we had again run through their blockade and that, except for the 17 whom they had captured during the *Katina*'s first landing attempt, we had smuggled into Palestine every single person on the *Gepo II* and on the *Katina*. The Colonial and Foreign offices in London decided to increase their efforts to stop us in Europe at the points of origin. For that purpose, they persuaded or pushed foreign governments to arrest us, the organizers. In short sequence, I was arrested once in Rumania, once in Yugoslavia, and twice in Greece, but each time I managed to get out and to continue our work. The major infractions had all been committed, not by me, but by a Mr. Teff. Of course, each time when interrogated, I was asked the whereabouts of this Mr. Teff.

For the more delicate operations, I used the code name of "Teff," and each questioning showed me that the authorities were aware of the existence of the mysterious Teff but did not know that Dr. Perl and Teff were one and the same. My real name was unavoidably known to local police everywhere I went, because whenever one registered in a hotel in Europe, one had to hand one's passport to the hotel porter who then gave it to the police for a day.

All Balkan police and even the British possessed a photo of the mysterious Teff. As one of our moves in the chess game which we were forced to play with British intelligence, we had made certain that their error as to Teff's identity be "well documented." I had arranged that a letter be sent to me in Bucharest from Fiume, Italy. Like all my letters, this one had been opened by the Bucharest police for aliens' affairs and then again carefully resealed. The letter was written in a rather childish handwriting, apparently by a girl who was not the brightest. Included in the letter were three photographs. A professional one of "her," which, however, did not show the name of the photographer and had been taken in another city.

On the back it read in the same handwriting, "In memory of a beautiful time. Do you remember it ALL?" The other two photos were obviously taken by an amateur with a cheap camera. One showed me and the girl together at the hotel in Susak in which I stayed when I was there. The back of the photo read, "You, bad boy, and me having breakfast on the terrace of the Park Hotel." The third picture showed the S.S. *Draga* being loaded in Fiume, the refugees, each with a knapsack on his back, walking up the gangplank. A slim man in his early thirties, with sharp features and bushy hair stood at the bottom of the gangplank. His arms were raised as if he were vividly gesticulating and explaining something to a younger man who stood in front of him. In the right front I was just blowing my nose into a hankie. Clearly an action picture. Although the photo showed the slim man and me from three-quarters profile only, our features were distinct. The back read, "You, during the loading of the ship, and Teff bawling out that boy. You did not even see me shoot it. Ha Ha!" Actually, the man in the photo was a Warsaw insurance broker, a longtime member of ours. He had come with Katz's group, and we had put him in charge of the passengers on the *Draga*'s first voyage. By the time I received the letter he had been in Israel for several months, working as a waiter. The girl, too, was safe from investigation. Only her likeness became known. She did not live in Fiume but in Zagreb, Yugoslavia, where she was active in the Betar. She had come to see what we could do to include Yugoslavian Jews in our transports.

The day after I received the letter with the photos, the clerk in the police for aliens' affairs, whom Popescu had paid to become our informer, came to me with the bad news that the police had a photo of Teff. To verify his claim he had an enlarged copy of Teff's photo with him. It had been distributed to police stations in all Rumanian ports. I showed myself appropriately disturbed, and knowing my good friend's methods, to make certain that he knew what to do next, I inquired worriedly whether the British Embassy had received the photo, too. No doubt he ran right from me to the British and sold them Teff's photograph for good money—unless another police official had beaten him to it.

On one occasion the Bucharest police learned, correctly, that Teff and Mr. Andronikos, the Greek owner of the S.S. *Liesel*, which was soon to smuggle 906 refugees into Palestine, were about to meet in the little cottage on Cercului Street, which I had rented.

Living for weeks in a hotel had become too expensive and too conspicuous, I had told the rental agent that I was looking for something small on a quiet street. He recommended the bungalow on Cercului Street because "if the King visits a mistress, he could not have a place with more privacy. Do you know who used this cottage before you? Our minister for religious affairs, to meet his women here!"

When I moved in, I met the owner, a countess. She was of striking appearance—in a dramatic way—white-haired; her voice was resounding and deep. In my first and only encounter with her, she was smoking a cigar, and in her other hand she held an ebony cane with an ivory handle, although the cane was apparently for indicating authority rather than serving a physical need. In her *basso profundo* voice she said, *"Monsieur le docteur,* enjoy every minute here, and if any woman ever resists, you are authorized to tell her that the Countess Carageu stated 'Chastity is vulgar!' "

On the night I was meeting in the cottage with Andronikos, the rain came down in buckets. It must not have rained like that since Noah. Two hard knocks at the door, and in came, dripping wet, a raiding party, as if just saved from the river. Four uniformed policemen and two plainclothesmen. With every step, they left a rivulet of water behind, and when the plainclothesmen took off their hats, it was as if they had emptied pitchers onto the rug.

With Teff's features firmly impressed on their minds, some of them with his photo in their pockets, the policemen searched the cottage, and when they found only me with Andronikos, they rushed out the other door, up to the cottage's roof, into the yard, the neighboring yards, and onto the roofs of the neighboring cottages. The officer in charge of the raiding party showed me Teff's picture and lied, saying that Teff had been seen by them entering the house; I must know where he was hiding. I insisted that to the best of my knowledge Teff was probably in Athens or in Sofia.

According to routine police procedures in the Balkans, I should have been taken along to the precinct and pressured to reveal all I knew about Teff. But Popescu had spread the information that I was an immensely rich Jew who organized the financial end of the undertaking. Rich people are treated differently by police almost everywhere. After finding out that his raid was a failure, therefore, the officer in charge called the police and then told me to report at headquarters the next day at eleven A.M. I would meet there with the chief of police for aliens' affairs. As the raiding party left, the man in charge stayed behind, and I knew what that meant. "I am sorry you had to come on such a rainy night and on false information, too," I said. "Your men are soaking wet, and certainly they will appreciate it if you take them into a pub for hot grog. Certainly you should not have to pay for that." With these words I put 500 lei into his pocket. It was good to have another friend in that office.

Next morning at eleven, actually twelve according to Balkan custom, I was sitting across the desk from a middle-sized, hawkish-looking man.

The beginning of police interrogations everywhere—probably through the ages—follows one of two principles. One is the sudden switch from a sweet or unconcerned manner to a tough one. The other principle is to rapidly "break" the one interrogated in the first confusing moments of the encounter, before he has time to collect himself. Probably because I was "rich" the sweet approach had been chosen for me. It started out literally sweet. A pretty secretary brought in some dulceata, traditionally served as a symbol of welcome. With a friendly smile, she put a little plate with the jam and a glass of water next to me before she served the dulceata to her boss.

In a syrupy voice, the man, who reminded me of a spider, asked me how long I had been in Rumania, which of course he knew, and how I liked it. But he was not the person who, to anyone with any knowledge of the world, could successfully pretend sweetness, and apparently aware of this, he soon started building up his attack. He asked me whether I would not like Rumania even better if I had stayed at the Athenee Palace or the Ambassador Hotel instead of having lived so long at the modest Majestic. With this question, we had entered serious talk. Obviously, it had puzzled the police why, if I were really so rich, I would be staying at the Majestic. I knew that the Majestic's manager had already been questioned.

All other appearances supported Popescu's claim of my wealth. When I left Vienna, I was permitted only one suitcase. Of course, I filled it with the best of clothing because I felt that appearing prosperous would help with authorities abroad as well as with shipowners—as it did. I had even tried to get in at Knize's, the famous Viennese tailor. His firm had worked for a century for the Hapsburgs and other selected aristocrats. From Paris to Constantinople the noble and the rich vied with one another to have their orders accepted by Knize's. He was for men's clothing what Dior or Caron was for women's couture or Cartier for jewelry. The wives and mistresses of Knize-clad men were usually Dior- or Caron-clad and Cartier-bejeweled. Well, I did not get in at Knize's, but my suits were made by another top-class Viennese tailor, and a Jewish friend of ours, a label manufacturer, provided some Knize labels. When the Balkan police came snooping into my hotel room, as they doubtlessly did as soon as I left it for the first time, they must have seen my two "Knize" suits and knew that Popescu was speaking in understatements.

I stayed at the Majestic because I just could not afford a luxury hotel, but my answer seemed logical enough to the Spider. "I hate that flophouse, but I am not here for comfort. I want within all my means to help my unfortunate Jewish brethren. In a small hotel like the Majestic we could better observe the comings and goings and anything unusual. Besides, some of the people I have to meet dress and look such that they would have been quite conspicuous in the Athenee Palace or the Ambassador."

But all this was still the preliminaries. On his next move, the dagger was really drawn. "How about Teff? Don't you have at least a photo of him?"

This was a dangerous question. They knew I had one. But if I surrendered it, it might make them suspicious whether this was really Teff.

"No, I don't. I had one, received in a letter a few days ago from a girl who has been throwing herself at me. But I flushed the whole thing down the drain." I actually had disposed of the letter and photos right away. With the police surveying my apartment and finding no trace of the letter or of Teff's photo, they would be even more certain that their mail surveillance had hit the jackpot.

After I had asserted that I had no contact with Teff, the Spider across the desk asked me, "What do you think of the idea of my providing you with some solitude for better recollection?" To his surprise, I answered, "This would cause a lot of trouble, which neither you nor I want." "Trouble?" he said. "You are carrying a German passport. Have you heard of a man called Hitler? Do you think he would protect you? Would he declare war on Rumania if"—and now he sank the dagger up to the hilt—"something should happen to you in case you decide to escape?"

That was more than a blunt hint. It was a clear-cut threat of murder.

This man was used to seeing his victims cringe. The only way of countering his attack was to come back with heavy artillery, too.

"Since you asked me so bluntly about Hitler, I hope you will not mind, sir, if I ask you equally openly: have you ever heard of the name Roosevelt?" There was a short pause before his, "Oh."

The pause told me that one of my ruses had worked. I had gotten for myself a fake reporter's identification card with my photo on it and my name spelled "William Peel." The top of the ID showed the name of the newspaper in the same print which the paper actually used. It read, NEW YORK HERALD TRIBUNE. Beneath was stated that I was a reporter on a special mission. As soon as I had this "identification," I ordered confidential mail to be spelled Peel and to be sent care of the U.S. Embassy in Bucharest. The first time I came to the embassy and the girl asked for my passport, I showed her my newsman's identification card. From then on, I had gone at least twice a week to the embassy for my mail. The Spider's hesitation when I mentioned Roosevelt showed me that he was aware of my visits to the U.S. Embassy and had probably been wondering about it.

"You are a German citizen, aren't you?"

"Yes, I am, but I am working for one of the largest American newspapers, which is very interested in what happens to its representatives." I displayed my fake reporter card. "Besides," I added, "some financial circles in America are supporting our rescue action."

The Spider let me go, but I knew he was not at all finished with me.

Two nights later, the familiar two bangs on the door, I was arrested. Two plainclothesmen, one of whom was so fish-eyed that I wondered how he could survive on land, brought me "in." That I was—again—not handcuffed gave me hope that there might still be some doubt about my American connections. I was kept in solitary for the rest of the night. Solitary was supposed to be "better" than sharing a cell with the riffraff—but it was not. It made me the sole source of food supply for the armies of lice and bedbugs. I would have needed fifty fingers to scratch at all the places from which they decided to draw their food. It was winter and ice cold in the cell, but I undressed completely to see the enemies before they could draw so much blood that the bites would continue to itch for hours after the vermin had been squashed. How could I be alert next morning at an interrogation? The police had searched me for weapons only. Anticipating arrest anew as soon as the Spider would find out more about my ID card, I had a few strong sleeping pills on me and I took one. It made things only worse. Each time I fell asleep for a few seconds, I was awakened by some bedbug dropping down from the ceiling onto my face or by one crawling across it.

Next morning at seven I was told to wash and shave because I would see the boss at eight. Actually, it was past nine before I entered my Spider's room. That he met me at such an early hour indicated that he expected the interrogation to last long. It did not.

He received me with a smile that reminded me of the way Eichmann had smiled when, in the Karajangasse prison, the old Jew had volunteered for Dachau. As the interrogation proceeded, the smile came to contain an element of perplexity before it faded entirely and his features displayed plain, natural rancor.

"We have checked on your claim about the New York newspaper and of course you know it is a lie. Now we want to know everything about Teff."

I told him that he could not have checked, as he would have found that it was true. But he had checked. His people had asked several foreign correspondents, including Americans, and nobody had ever heard of me. Now I knew his source of information and could attack it.

"Of course they don't know me. Don't you see, it says special correspondent. Ask any one of them if he is a special correspondent. My sole mission with the paper is to bring in a good story covering the illegal immigration. And for this, I must be known to as few people as possible." As I found out later, through our informer in the police for aliens' affairs office, they had also inquired at the U.S. Embassy whether I was known there. Negative. Not even the girl who handled the mail knew Dr. Willy Perl. She knew only a Mr. William Peel. The negative finding was good for me; after all, I had been seen by the Spider's agents entering the U.S. Embassy regularly. That the embassy now denied knowing me tended to corroborate my claim of being on a special mission.

"But you are actively involved in the illegal transports. Do you deny that?"

"Sir, do not think I take you for a fool. Of course, I am involved. As a financial backer. The assignment as a correspondent is genuine, but not my main purpose in being here. I know that and you know that. The assignment was provided for me for exactly what I'm using it now. For protection. And protection it is."

"The document is a fake. You have never been to America according to your passport. How did you get this card from the *New York Herald Tribune?*"

"Did you ever hear of a man called Fiorello La Guardia?" I asked the Spider. Of course, the Little Flower was known all over Europe as a staunch supporter of the Jews. He had attacked Hitler in the strongest words. It was also know that New York was "Jewish" and that Jews had considerable influence on the mayor.

"What do you have to do with La Guardia? You are just throwing around big names."

I had mentioned La Guardia because I had decided to use my knowledge of a little-known fact. "You may or may not know that I have some connections in financial circles," I lied. "There is a banker, a Jew, who is married to La Guardia's sister. His name is Glueck. They both live right next door to you in Budapest, and I am certain you know that. Hungarian Jews are in danger, too. Well, I think you are riding the wrong horse. It's time to let me go." I could see he did not know anything of what I had said about Mrs. Gemma La Guardia Glueck, but he did not admit his ignorance.

"We don't need the Americans. There is a continent between us and them. We need the British. And they are after us because of your illegal immigration. So we will give you time to recollect all you know about Teff."

"You are right. America is far and you need the British. They're about to give you a loan, aren't they? Well, I can tell you, they are not. Much of the money that you are expecting from England comes from American sources, and the Jewish bankers in America will make sure that the loan does not go through if you continue to harass us—not just me, us, I mean," I said in a demanding tone. "Remember, I admit that being a special correspondent is only a sideline for me, but if the loan does not come through because of you, you will find your name in all the papers."

It worked! I almost had lunch with him.

I knew that he would still check in Budapest on the widely unknown fact that La Guardia's sister lived there, married to a

Jewish banker, and this red herring would clinch my story. In the future, although many steps were taken against us, they were halfhearted. This changed only with the war and with the German march into Rumania.

All during this time conditions in Germany and in German-occupied countries had steadily worsened and were heading toward the point at which the Germans would decide on extermination instead of forced expulsion. This made our tasks during the trips much more difficult. There were still young disciplined people from the Betar and other youth organizations to be taken out, but, slowly, older, undisciplined people gained in numbers, and many of them caused serious problems during the torturous voyages. Typical of problems which could arise from such groups but also characteristic of the way with which we would handle the issues is the "revolt" which broke out on the S.S. *Astir*, one of the Revisionist ships.

Credit for the organization of the *Astir* is almost entirely due to Abraham Stavsky, one of the most active workers in free immigration and a specialist on conditions in Poland and the Baltic countries. The ship had left Rumania on March 6, 1939, with 720 on board. The core consisted of 200 Betarim, handpicked by Begin and his staff. There were many other young people from Poland, but there was also a large group from Danzig. Many of those from Danzig were older, undisciplined people with no ideological background. They were just refugees running for their lives. The *Astir* encountered many difficulties in trying to land the passengers in Palestine, and it was on the water for many weeks. Food and drinking water ran out. When the ship went into Piraeus for more supplies, the leaders of a group of dissatisfied ones smuggled a message on land to the captain of the port, saying that conditions on the ship were unbearable and that the passengers should all be taken off, preferably to be left in Greece (which was soon afterward overrun by the Axis) or sent back to Rumania. They felt that even Germany was preferable to conditions on the ship.

The harbor master announced that he would inspect the *Astir* the next afternoon. When he arrived, he found on deck 200 Betarim lined up in column after column, each one in his uniform, each platoon with its own pennant. When the Greek officers entered the ship, the trumpeter blew a salute. At the orders of our ship's commander, the 200 snapped to attention. The little band started playing the Greek national anthem, while the commander and his accompanying staff stood at attention and saluted throughout the playing of the Greek anthem and the following Jewish anthem. Then our ship's commander shouted *"Zita."* ("Long live.") The 200 answered by completing the sentence and shouting, "Kyrios Zacharaki [the commander's name]." After having done this three times, the trumpet was blown again, and our ship's commander now yelled, *"Zita."* And the 200 answered, "Hellas." This too was repeated twice more. The harbor master was impressed with the discipline. Together with our officers, he walked along the ramps, and when they passed one or another young man who had his uniform shirt not buttoned, his name was written down by our adjutant. When the harbor master asked why there were only 200 on deck, our men answered, "You see even with the 200, the deck is full." The Greek officer was then led to the bridge from where he directed a short speech in French to the assembled formations. This was the end of the revolt on the *Astir* which finally did unload everybody, including those fools who had been ready to go back to Rumania or even to Danzig.

Early in 1939 the British stepped up sharply the diplomatic phase of their offensive against us. The Foreign Office urged the British ambassadors in Hungary, Yugoslavia, Bulgaria, Rumania, and Greece to demand from the governments to which they were accredited that Jews who had no visa of destination—an "end visa"—should not be permitted to transit through their respective countries. This included transit via the Danube, too.

Therefore, although it could not be contested that the Danube was by international agreement a free waterway, the British ambassadors in Budapest, Belgrade, Sofia, Bucharest, and Athens pressured the governments to which they were accredited to insist that anyone transferred to a seagoing vessel on the Danube would first have to show a valid visa of destination. Our people in Vienna, in a countermove, succeeded at high cost in obtaining even more entrance visas into Paraguay. To the surprise of the protesting British, soon paddle-wheeler after paddle-wheeler arrived with immigrants who held seemingly valid Paraguayan visas. In vain the British officials pointed out that one hardly travels to Paraguay via the Danube and the Black Sea! But the formal requirement of a "valid visa of final destination" had been fulfilled. It apparently never occurred to anyone that one cannot sail to Paraguay any more than one can sail to Switzerland, as Paraguay is a landlocked country and at least one other South American visa would have been required to get there.

Despite the success of our Paraguayan ruse, we were forced to discontinue our connection with the Paraguayan consul and some of his equally willing colleagues. As the persecution increased in Germany, the prices for these visas doubled and tripled, and we just could not pay these exorbitant sums.

One evening Dr. Imre Kalman, a lawyer and the chairman of the Revisionist party in Hungary, and I were sitting in his living room in Budapest and were holding a brainstorming session about how we could overcome these blackmail prices for visas, which were not really valid anyway. I do not recall whether it was Dr. Kalman's idea or mine, but that night we cut the Gordian knot: I appointed myself consul for Liberia in Budapest. We did not intend to "forge" visas. This would not have been possible in an authoritarian country as Hungary was then. The day after my "appointment" into the diplomatic corps, Dr. Kalman, who had good connections with the police, went with me to pay a visit to the Budapest deputy police commissioner. We told him of our problem with the visas of destination, and we let him know that I would "function" from now on as consul of Liberia in Budapest. "You will want to know what is in it for you. On the first paddle-wheeler that comes through, we will put fifty Jews whom you now have in Budapest jails for having crossed over illegally from Germany or Czechslovakia. We will take another fifty Hungarian Jews, and with every paddle-wheeler that comes through, in addition to Hungarian Jews, you will get rid of more such prisoners whom you would otherwise have to feed." He left the room obviously to consult with the commissioner himself. When he returned, he told us, "Your plan would sound interesting if we knew anything about it, but we never heard of it." Dr. Kalman and the newly confirmed consul of Liberia left the office and went to a stamp maker. We showed him the Liberian visas issued by real consuls and were in business.

But we had to stay in business as long as possible. We had to prevent the British from complaining to the Hungarian authorities as soon as the first Budapest-issued Liberian visas showed up. After such a complaint, the Hungarians would have to investigate. The investigation would gain some time for us, but the later it started, the better. We, therefore, decided to divert the thrust of British countermeasures away from Budapest.

To do this successfully, we tried to put ourselves into the antagonist's shoes. We had to use his own way of thinking for the planned deception, and the system had worked with our claim that the British actually supported our activities. We had then built upon their conviction that the might of the British Navy, especially over our puny operation, was incontestable. Furthermore, we had offered them the logical explanation for the supposed British support of our plan as follows: Britain obviously wanted more young Jews in Palestine so that these Jews could be killed in defending the British Empire in Palestine against the Germans instead of being killed in Germany by the Nazis, thus denying the British from gaining anything from their death.

Now in the matter of the Liberian Consulate, we again had to feed them information which according to their own thinking was plausible and would therefore cause them to do as we wanted. The British knew that we had bought some consuls of smaller overseas countries, and so bribery was something they expected from us.

The day after we had ordered our Liberian visas from the stamp maker, I met with Lajos Fekete. He was a small-time operator to whom we paid petty sums for minor, usually correct information about the steps the British were taking with the Hungarians. He was also fairly well informed about the reaction of the police to these steps. I had no doubt that Fekete peddled information to anyone willing to pay for it. I met with him, therefore, under the pretense that I wanted to find out whom I should approach in the police department for visas permitting two of our staff members in Prague to come for a few days to Budapest for further planning. During the conversation, I hinted to Fekete that this meeting was necessary because a sharp increase of emigration from Prague, Vienna, and Berlin was in the cards. He started probing and I confided to him that a big thing had happened. Prices for visas to various smaller countries had risen so much that we decided to end it. We had bribed a government official in Liberia itself. It had cost us a large sum—but less than the price of continual bribes to various consuls for individual visas. As a result of that bribe in Monrovia, I would be officially appointed consul of Liberia in Budapest. I did not watch Fekete after he left and turned the corner, but I visualized him jumping into the nearest taxi and having the driver rush him to the British Embassy with this hot tip.

The Fekete story was bound to appear plausible to the British, and to strengthen its credibility, we leaked information to the British Embassy in Belgrade that soon Yugoslav Jews would be able to leave in large numbers because an important deal with some foreign government had been concluded. To make it all the more credible, we did not let on to the informant in this case the name of the particular foreign government supposedly involved.

The British were much too cautious, of course, to act right away. They had to see at least one such visa first. But from the moment the first Liberian visas issued in Budapest were found on emigrants, the question of the Liberian visas sent the British diplomatic wires buzzing. The British could see for themselves, in rubber stamp on the visa and above it in my own handwriting, my true, full name above the words: "Consul of Liberia, Budapest, Hungary." The night it all had become known, there was a little party in the hotel where I was staying, the Bristol, to celebrate my appointment. I was toasted by members of the Budapest Jewish community who really believed the story, and, of course, the waiters quickly spread the tale around even further. They, as well as the hatcheck girl, the desk clerk, and the people in the coffeehouse—everybody—called me "Herr Konsul Perl."

It apparently never occurred to the British to assume the so much simpler story that I was just forging the visas. A forger, after all, works secretly in some basement and does not strut proudly through the streets of the city the way I did. It was all quite far from British rules of crookedness.

As a result, they did as we wanted them to do. Instead of concentrating their efforts on Budapest, they complained to Monrovia. The Foreign Office had swallowed the red herring head and tail.

The Monrovia bureaucracy was not given to speedy action. The investigation of the British allegation took time, and by the time it was finally established that the Budapest Liberian visas were forgeries, one paddle-wheeler after another, loaded with emigrants holding Liberian visas issued by the Budapest Consulate, had already passed down the Danube.

After it had become official that there was no authorized

Liberian Consulate in Budapest, we just changed our stamp to read "Consul General of Liberia, Paris."

The old game, though played somewhat faster, started again. The British complained to Monrovia—although why they did not cable straight to Paris was never clear to me. The Liberians answered that there was no consulate in Paris either, only an embassy.* The Liberian government in Monrovia wanted to see such visas first before they made any statement, and so the British had to fly some of the visas to Liberia. Finally, many ships later, the Liberian government declared the visas to be forged. In the meantime, we had not been idle; for the sake of variety, we had opened a Paraguayan underground "consulate" in Prague run by Gleser and Faltyn, and whenever we needed transit visas, we simply made them ourselves. No more blackmail money to any consuls. This stroke took a great financial load off our backs and freed money which could be used for hiring ships and buying supplies.

By the spring of 1939, illegal immigration to Palestine had become enough of a problem to the British colonial regime to be brought up in debates in the House of Commons. A major debate took place on April 26, 1939. Mr. Malcolm MacDonald, Neville Chamberlain's secretary of state for the colonies, dealt flippantly with the issue. He stated that the ships were simply being turned back:

MR. NOEL-BAKER: What will happen to the refugees?
MR. MACDONALD: They have been sent back where they came from.
MR. NOEL-BAKER: Does this mean to concentration camps?
MR. MACDONALD: The responsibility rests with those responsible for organizing this illegal immigration.

The parliamentary debate and the rather weak opposition encountered did not change Mr. Chamberlain's determination to keep the gates of Palestine barred to Hitler's victims. As this policy of turning escapees "back where they came from" was being an-

*Foreign Office Document F.O. 371/25241/173/310. Classified "Secret," Cable No. 267 from the secretary of state for the colonies to the high commissioner of Palestine. "There is no Liberian Consul in Paris where they are represented by a Minister. It is therefore suggested that the visa may be [sic] bogus. I shall be grateful if I may be furnished with photostatic copies of some typical examples of the visas in question for transmission to Monrovia."

nounced, the British government was taking resolute steps to make it work. On April 14, the 1,325-ton British destroyer *Grenade* arrived in Haifa. It was soon to be replaced by a much mightier naval fighting force to "protect" the coast. To show the population that any kind of involvement with illegal immigration would land one in prison, the British placed the tough head of the Palestine police and prison service, Major Allen Saunders, in charge of the immigration service as well. The day after the reported House of Commons debate, April 27, 1939, an "Extraordinar Issue" of the official *Palestine Gazette* was published. It promulgated a drastic increase in penalties for illegal immigrants and those who aided them. From now on the captain of a "captured" ship could be imprisoned for up to five years and could be fined up to the immense sum of 10,000 British pounds, the equivalent of $50,000.

But all this did not stem the inflow of illegal immigrants. Three and a half months after the first increase in penalties, the *Palestine Gazette* had to announce a further sharpening of penalties against illegal immigration. The new ordinance provided for "summary trial before a British Magistrate who shall direct detention during the pleasure [*sic*] of the High Commissioner." This formulation meant that one could be held captive for an indeterminate period.

What the Jews loathed more than imprisonment was the indignity of being whipped. In Palestine, the British applied a mixture of Turkish and British colonial law, and flogging was a legally founded punishment. Sadistic whippers lashed the back of the victim with a large whip, each stroke leaving a bleeding welt. This punishment was not applied to illegal immigrants but was used against persons aiding them. On August 4, 1939, the media reported that even a child, a twelve-year-old boy, was sentenced by a British judge in Haifa to six lashes. But this seemed "too mild." On August 18 a fourteen-year-old boy was sentenced in Tel Aviv by a British court to receive twelve lashes for distributing illegal leaflets. These flyers had exhorted the population to protest the British immigration policy and to aid their Jewish brethren.

But none of these measures brought the results the British hoped for. Those who tried to save their lives "illegally" kept coming in ever-increasing numbers. They had to keep coming because it was their only way out. Thus, three months after he had presumptuously announced that he was turning back the illegal immigrants, Mr. MacDonald would no longer exhibit the self-assurance he had shown in the debate of April 26. By then he had to admit in fact that, like the lion in Aesop's fable, the British lion had been stung by the gnat. His report to the House of Commons on July 20, 1939, starts with small figures, leads to greater ones and ends with an impressive, but for MacDonald depressing, total.

> We took account of 1,300 illegal immigrants. They went into the country between first April and 24th May. Since 24th May some two months have elapsed and during that time our patrol vessels out at sea or our patrol forces on land have *captured** [sic] 3,500 illegal immigrants. In addition to that, because our patrols are not at their maximum efficiency yet, something between 500–1,000 have got into the country undetected. In addition, some 4,000 intending illegal immigrants are now in ships approaching the coast of Palestine and are intending to force their way into the country ... Therefore something like 8,000 illegal immigrants have either got into Palestine or are about to go into Palestine at the present time.

Mr. Noel-Baker concluded from the secretary's report, "I think it is probably true that within a short time illegal immigration which he [the secretary of state for the colonies] will not be able to stop, will be greater than legal immigration has ever been, even when the figure was 60,000 a year, as it was in 1936. . . ."

In spite of all British countermeasures, illegal immigration into Palestine was soaring. The gnat was really up the British lion's nostril!

After Mr. MacDonald had thus revealed the size of the problem to the House, he was asked how many ships the Royal Navy employed to prevent Jewish refugees from landing. He replied that it was a "Division of Destroyers" supported by five smaller launches. He was then asked whether, speaking of a division of destroyers, he referred to a flotilla, but he never answered this question. From intelligence documents obtained, we can answer the question that Mr. MacDonald evaded.

Those who had escaped the one great mustachioed destroyer were, at the other end of their flight, hunted down by four destroyers of His Majesty's Royal Navy: H.M.S. *Hero* (flagship), *Havock, Hereward,* and *Hotspur*! They were among Britain's newest and fastest fighting ships. All four of them, commissioned just two years

*Author's italics.

previously, were now charged to chase the refugees. These destroyers belonged to the famous "H" (Hero) class, named after the flagship. Each had a speed of 36 knots and was 323 feet long. Each of them carried a complement of 145. Thus, 580 combat-ready officers and men were to hound the escapees from Hitler. Each of the destroyers carried four 4.7-inch guns, plus six smaller guns and two quadruple-barreled 40-mm Bofors automatic cannons. Each also carried eight Mark IX torpedoes. Each refugee carried one knapsack.

At least one other destroyer, the *Ivanhoe*, was also used in this lopsided warfare. But how could such a small armada face those damned crates? It was supported, as Mr. MacDonald said, "by five smaller launches." They were the sister ships, *Sea Wolf* and *Sea Lion*, the *Shark*, the *Lorna*, and the *Morna*.

Thus nine, maybe even at times, ten heavily armed warships stalked the parched and starving refugees. These British ships were, of course, of a speed and maneuverability far superior to that of their adversaries. To hold, and even to encircle the refugee ships, to prevent any kind of undesired movement, would have been no problem for the British. But the military authorization went further. With the arrival of the flotilla in Palestine waters, came also the authority to shoot. The *Palestine Gazette*, in its " Extraordinar Issue" of April 27, 1939, announced the authorization to open fire "at or into" any ship that was suspected of having illegal immigrants on board, and that did not obey the warning to stand by.

The British have always been proud of their navy, and they have produced ample literature on its history. One of the books, *British Destroyers* by Edgar March, with a foreword by an admiral of the fleet, gives a history of each of the destroyers from 1892 to 1953. Although published as late as 1965, when some historical distance should have permitted objective treatment, not even this scholarly work recalls the ignoble mission of this "H" class flotilla. The admiral of the fleet, the Earl Mountbatten of Burma who wrote the foreword, had his name followed by a flood of titles that encompass almost the entire alphabet: "K.C., P.C., G.C.B., O.M., G.C.S.I., G.C.I.E., G.C.V.O., and D.S.O." These titles, however, did not suffice to make him aware of and to report on this heroic part of British history.

The debate on July 20, 1939, was the longest and probably the most impassioned of the discussions in the House of Commons dealing with illegal immigration. Quite unusual for parliamentary debates in Britain, it lasted until eleven P.M. The official records of that day's debate fill 122 pages (pp. 762–884). The secretary of state for the colonies defended his policies by claiming that they were in the British interest. He was assisted by the more conservative members of the House of Commons, including Colonel Ponsonby and, ironically, also by the representative in the House of Commons of a learned institution of worldwide reputation. Mr. Pickthorn, the member for Cambridge University, was one of the strongest supporters of the government's restrictive policy regarding Palestine and illegal immigration.

Some members of Parliament closely associated with the military also supported the government's policy, but not all did so. Captain Cazalet stated, "If there is anyone who under those conditions would turn back these people, he would deserve neither the title of British nor that of Christian."

The debate was not restricted to illegal immigration but encompassed British policy toward Palestine and the obligation of the British mandate to help create a Jewish national home there. Only two months previously, Britain, in the White Paper of May 17, 1939, had reneged on its obligation of the Balfour Declaration and the League of Nations Mandate to establish Palestine as the national home of Jews. In this White Paper, the Chamberlain government had announced its decision to end, within six years, Jewish immigration altogether.

Mr. Duff Cooper, who, later serving in Churchill's government, was to become minister of state for information, stated in defense of large-scale immigration into Palestine and in support of meeting the obligations of the Mandate:

> We should decide that it is our policy first and foremost to make a real home for the Jews in Palestine ... Before these Islands began their history, a thousand years before the Prophet Mohammed was born, the Jew, already exiled, sitting by the waters of Babylon, was singing, "If I forget thee, O Jerusalem, Let my right hand forget her cunning."

A dramatic moment developed when Mr. Noel-Baker asked Mr. MacDonald what he would do if he were a German Jew. Mr. MacDonald responded, "The Hon. Member for Derby [Mr. Noel-

Baker] has asked me one or two perfectly fair questions and I would like to answer them. He said to me if I were a German Jew, what would I do? I will tell him absolutely frankly. I would do my best to escape from Germany." But he continued that as a Britisher, he found it in the British interests to continue the blockade. That it was against British interests to save those who had escaped from Hitler was later more formally expressed in an official British ordinance. On November 20, 1940, the Palestine government denounced illegal immigration as "a serious menace to British interests in the Middle East."

In his "Rule, Britannia" policy advanced in this House of Commons debate of July 20, 1939, Mr. MacDonald's arguments for clamping down on the escape route to Palestine were strongly supported by the politically powerful Lord Winterton. When I had seen him in his office, he had clearly exhibited his hostility against any effective action, and now in the parliamentary debate, Lord Winterton continued his opposition to any rescue attempt. Backed by this "expert" on emigration, Mr. MacDonald endeavored to divert the discussion by throwing in a spurious issue conceived by Lord Winterton: "Polish and Rumanian vs. German Jews." Mac-Donald stated that many of the illegal immigrants were not German Jews but Jews from Poland and Rumania. This statement was correct. However, it did not take into account that many of the "Polish" and "Rumanian" Jews had been living all their lives in Germany or Austria, without being able to obtain German citizenship. Colonel Wedgwood interrupted: "Does the Right Hon. Gentleman think they are not refugees?" Mr. MacDonald answered: "The Hon. and Gallant Gentleman knows perfectly well that, when private authorities in this country make an appeal to the British public to be indulgent to this illegal immigration because it is an immigration of refugees, those authorities are not referring to Jews from Poland or from Rumania."

COLONEL WEDGWOOD: Certainly they are.
MR. MACDONALD: Certainly not.
COLONEL WEDGWOOD: Anyone who knows anything about Poland and Rumania knows that they must be.

The debate was taken up by Mr. Lansbury, who described the conditions in Poland and Rumania.

When I was in Poland two years ago—and we ought to keep this in mind when we are considering the attitude of European governments towards European Jews—I was told by the Polish authorities, that there were 3,500,000 people, mainly Jews, in Poland for whom the League must find a place. That was reported in a debate that took place at a meeting of the League of Nations Mandates Commission . . . In Rumania . . . I was told that it was quite impossible that a Jew could ever become a Rumanian citizen in the sense that a Rumanian national is.

In reference to people who had been living in Germany but were Polish citizens, Mr. Lansbury continued:

At the present moment the committee of which I am chairman has on its hands a problem in what is called no-man's-land, between Poland and Germany, of what to do with 17,000 to 20,000 men, women, and children. I could tell the most harrowing stories of what these people have endured during the last 15 to 18 months, how they have died of privation and semistarvation, how they have committed suicide and how again and again they have appealed for something to be done. We hold meetings in this country and the Jewish people and those who attend respond magnificently to appeals for funds, but those that we can get out are a drop in the ocean. Some of them have got out quite illegally . . . They have been taken to Palestine illegally . . . The Polish authorities have taken away their papers now and they have been chased to the border with the bayonets, the guns or the bludgeons of the German soldiers on the one side and the bar of the Polish authorities on the other. That condition of affairs is a scandal and a disgrace to the whole of Europe . . . I should like him [Mr. MacDonald] to realize that there is something higher than the law of man, and that is the law of humanity, which some people call the law of God.

How effectively the hearts and minds of politicians who are set upon a certain course can be moved from that course was demonstrated by the words with which the member for Cambridge University concluded his speech at 10:13 P.M., July 20, 1939. "The essence of it must be that, however much the hearts of any of us may bleed for the Jews . . . there must be limitation of immigration."

In that sentence, Mr. Pickthorn had summed up the whole debate and its "essence" quite correctly. Many words had been said, many headlines produced, but the "limitation of immigration" continued. And during the whole day of July 20 and during the whole night, and during all the coming days and nights, the British flotilla, "supported by five smaller launches," continued to roam the waters in its hunt for refugees. There was one minor fact that had never come up in the debate. Even while compassionate words were being said in the House of Commons, the much-admired Royal Air Force had joined in the chase.

The war between the British lion and the gnat stretched all over Europe and to all shores of the Mediterranean. British consulates everywhere were asked to keep an eye on anything possibly connected with illegal immigration into Palestine. This included such ports as Tripoli, Oran, Tangiers, and Beirut. Some of the ships to be put into our service were at the time of all in African ports; others, somewhere in Greece or on the Black Sea. British agents were hanging around the docks to find out from sailors and captains what they might know about their next destination.

However, debates in the House of Commons or not, the hunt continued. Six Coast Guard stations in Palestine, and two major Marine Division stations kept watch through radio contact with the flotilla and its support, as well as with the planes patrolling the coast. In addition, telescopes were manned day and night. But all this in no way stopped or even decreased the stream of illegal immigrants. The eight maritime stations on the coast had to be increased to twenty. On August 17, 1939, British authorities announced that twelve new Coast Guard stations were being added to the existing six and the two Main Division stations. With an ardor reminiscent of the German defenses on Normandy Beach, the British were determined to "defend" the beaches of Palestine against the emaciated refugees and their creaking crates.

Of course, the chase was not over once one had disembarked in Palestine. In 1936, when Hitler had already been in power in Germany for three years, illegal entrances of small groups by land, across the Syrian border, had increased and an ordinance was promulgated demanding that every legal resident of Palestine carry identification. Naturally, no Arab was expected to have any, but if a Jew had no ID, he was under suspicion. One could still be caught, therefore, after one had landed and had mingled with the local population. In addition to regular police forces, a special unit of 100 constables was formed for the task of apprehending illegal immigrants. Buses, movie theaters, eating places, and streets were searched for Jews lacking proper identification, and whenever a Jew applied to authorities for anything whatsoever, even when picking up a general delivery letter, he had to prove his legal residence status.

Street vendors were a special target for harassment. Because they had arrived without any means, many of the illegal immigrants became street vendors first. Thus, one could see former physicians, executives, and university professors call out their wares in the streets of Palestine. The occupation of street vendor became licensed. To obtain the permission to hawk, one had to produce identity documents. Supplying our people with such documents was a job beautifully done by the Jews of Palestine.

We followed the policy of destroying, on board ship, all passports, so that nobody could be deported to the land from whence he had come. The Betar instructed every immigrant that when questioned, he should simply answer, "My name is Ben Avraham"—son of Abraham. "My home is, always was, and will be, Jerusalem." This was stating in principle what Sir J. Haslam, in defense of an "open-the-gates-policy" had stated in the House of Commons shortly before the close of the debate of July 20, 1939. He had said:

> The Jews regard Palestine as their native land whether they were actually born there or not. Millions of them who have never been to Palestine at all, regard that country as their home, just as millions of people of the British race who have never set foot in this country regard this country as their home ... As long as I can remember, Palestine has been known as the Promised Land. Promised to whom? Promised by whom? It was promised to the Jews by Lord God Almighty. Almost every book of the Old Testament and many of the New Testament repeats that promise.

Often legal residents of Palestine, when asked for identification papers by a patrol, answered in the same way as the illegal immigrants: "My name is Ben Avraham, and my home was, is, and always will be Jerusalem." They, too, were arrested and frequently stayed in jail for several days before the British investigation showed their legal status. By doing this, they kept the British police busy chasing the wrong people and made them doubt whether every Ben Avraham was, in fact, illegal. But the eagerness of the Jews of

Palestine to help the immigrants was roused so readily that one could easily use it for personal advantage. Once an arrested pick-pocket, being marched to the police station, started screaming, "They're arresting me because I'm an illegal!" An angry crowd quickly gathered, freed him, and he strutted away.

To fight us, the British used means not always as crude as deportation, police patrols, the navy, and the air force. Political and economic pressures were applied, particularly against Rumania and Greece. This sometimes resulted in a last-moment revocation of a granted transit permit or a permit to transfer from a riverboat to an oceangoing ship. Even when the seagoing vessel was already loaded, permission to sail was sometimes refused because of a last-minute intervention by the British Consulate.

Our counterweapons were simple. In the Balkan countries, they consisted of mobilizing the shipowners to influence their government on behalf of their own financial interests. With the illegal immigration, large amounts of money flowed into Greece, Rumania, and, later on, Bulgaria. Others besides shipowners also profited from illegal immigration. The ships had to be provisioned. Installations had to be made to transform the holds into the many-layered sleeping quarters we needed. Shipowners, timber merchants, ship provisioners, carpenters, and other marine craftsmen all had vested interests in the continuation of illegal immigration and used their connections to void what had been decided on high government levels. Sometimes they succeeded, but something they did not—and the British pressure became increasingly heavy. If, for instance, a trip from Vienna, Bratislava, or Budapest had initially taken two months, we were later prepared to fight the ever newly arising problems for four or five months, before a successful landing.

A most efficient counterweapon against the British was the "sympathy" which we acquired from well-bribed officials. There were many such examples of sympathetic understanding purchased by us. An order from Bucharest had reached Constanța prohibiting the transfer of refugees from the sealed train to the waiting ship. The reason given for the order was that the immigrants intended to travel illegally into Palestine. When, e.g., this order had come for the S.S. *Katina,* we had 775 shivering refugees sitting in the train. It was January 1939, and the temperature was well below freezing. The train was not heated. The refugees had eaten up their last provisions. In the port, the *Katina* was ready. And here was the order from the capital to send the train back into Hitlerland.

The simplest way to handle such a situation was to kill it at the source. Such telegrams sometimes "never arrived," and for this some people at the telegraph office had to be made sympathetic. If this did not work, some snafu had to develop in the communication between the telegraph office and the port police. Of course, the port police were the next line of defense. They could, with some help, be convinced that the telegram from Bucharest referred to an entirely different train because the immigrants all clearly had visas for Liberia, Shanghai, or Santo Domingo, or some other place at the end of the world, and the ship's captain himself gave a sworn affidavit that this outlandish country was his destination. In the case of the *Katina*, as with similar cases, we had to run the gauntlet of all possible obstructions. The bribed official in the telegraph office immediately informed somebody at the port police of the chance to earn money, too, for which, of course, he got a kickback. And even after everything had been cleared with the port police, the pilot discovered that his tug motor needed some oiling with lei. Yet, in spite of all obstacles, the *Katina* finally did sail on January 19, 1939. Other ships encountered very similar difficulties prior to sailing.

Some of this might sound amusing today. It was not, then. Human lives were at stake, and each time, there were hundreds. If the train had to go back to Czechoslovakia after all, the 775 passengers, or most of them, would have been lost.

Next to mobilization of businessmen who profited from us, and almost as important, one of our most effective weapons was intelligence information obtained by the Jewish underground organizations in Palestine. We had also paid informers in the relevant ministerial offices in Bucharest, Athens, and also, on lower ranks, in Constanţa, Sulina, and Varna. Some of these contacts had been initiated by Popescu, who continued to use his apparently quite useful visiting card: "Jonel Popescu, Attaché for Personal and Internal Affairs." I liked to work with him; not only was he an efficient go-getter, he was also for me a source of amusement and in these tense days one needed a good laugh from time to time. Once, after he had opened the way for us to a higher-ranking official in the Rumanian Foreign Office, Popescu told me that he wanted to discuss a serious matter with me, but not right then; we should meet specifically for that purpose. He suggested Bucharest's most expensive restaurant, and I would be his guest. When we had finished eating, he pulled out of his wallet a 1,000-lei bill, $2.00, but then quite a bit of money in Rumania. He held the bill over the candle on our table and then lit his huge cigar with the burning banknote. "You think I am doing what I do because of the money," he said. "Jonel Popescu has utter contempt for money. I am working with you because I want to help these people and because of the honor." He wanted me to promise him that when the Jewish State would be created we would put up a monument—commemorating his activities. The monument would not have to be life-sized. "I have discussed the matter with Mr. Gregorianu, the famous artist, and this is what we have in mind." At that, Jonel, well prepared for the meeting, pulled out a drawing which showed him in a gesture of Napoleonic grandeur standing at what appeared to be the edge of water. One arm was reaching slightly to the rear, and the hand gave the impression of beckoning or inviting one to come. In the other hand he held a lifesaver, which he was apparently about to throw to a person in danger. Popescu was disappointed when I explained to him that Jews were forbidden to create any likeness of a man or animal and that there were no monuments of such kind in any Jewish town or village in Palestine. I promised that I would do my best to have him remembered in a plaque in Jerusalem at as central a location as could be found. I am sorry to confess, I was not able to follow through, and there is no plaque for Jonel anywhere.

Popescu was not the only one who helped us to have informers in various offices, but this was only part of our local "intelligence work." We also had to be watchful for possible British agents. Besides those in the ports, the British tried to smuggle spies posing as refugees on board our ships. To find persons who could pass themselves off as Jewish refugees was difficult for the British, and it appears that they gave up after we exposed two of them. We never encountered a Jew who acted as an informer against us. Twice the British sent Gentiles who had grown up in the London East End, were quite familiar with Jewish customs, looked Jewish, and spoke Yiddish. To their bad luck, both were smuggled aboard ships filled with German Jews—who did not speak Yiddish. The British agents stood out like sore thumbs as they could not speak German.

The first of the British agents had radio equipment on him, a most valuable and, in the future, much-used addition to our small arsenal. How little the British knew about conditions on the refugee ships, not to realize that there was hardly standing room and not a chance in a thousand to use such equipment unobserved!

It helped that the passengers themselves were suspicious and expected spies on board. Once a Betar leader was told by some of his youngsters that a man in his midtwenties was apparently a Nazi spy; he knew close to nothing about Jewish customs. I questioned this man and quickly established that he was not Jewish. When I asked him for his father's first name, he gave the same name as his own—probably the truth. He also said his father had died a few years ago. But Jews of Europe never named a child after a living relative. Well, this man was not a Nazi. He was a Gentile married to a Jewish woman who had feared that we would not allow him on board with his wife if we had known he was not Jewish. Of course, he continued the trip with us.

He and his wife had come on board with what we came to call "the last-minute rush." It was in Balchik that I experienced this rush for the first time. Just as our captain was giving the order to raise the gangplank, some policemen stepped on it and out from a little storage hut stormed 40 to 50 refugees. They rushed up the gangplank and, aided by the police, were crammed onto the over-crowded deck. They had purchased "tickets" from some fraudulent "travel agent" in Bucharest who had bribed the local police to help him with his scheme.

Such a "last-minute rush" became routine as the profits of the "travel agents" grew. Actually, we did not really mind. It permitted us to stuff even more people onto the ships than we ourselves could have done—and, thereby, to save more lives. A disadvantage was that we had no control of selection and the two British spies were both brought on board by this method.

Active operations by the Jewish underground against the British were still rare at that time. But on August 31, 1939, a new police launch, which was part of the patrol force hunting for illegal immigrants, was blown up by a time bomb and sank. The CID (Criminal Investigation Division) did not find out who had smuggled the bomb on board; however, a Jewish "supernumerary" guard was arrested and an Arab was put in to replace him.

But the mobilization of vested interests, bribery, the Jewish underground spy network, and even the inventiveness and courage of our immigrants were not our main weapon against the British lion. By far our most powerful weapon was the iron necessity of the situation. There was just no alternative. The refugees had to get out, whatever the risks. It was by then almost impossible to get into any other country; it was absolutely impossible for those who had no money. British lion or no, they had to try to get into Palestine.

chapter 4

THE KLADOVO INTELLIGENCE PLOT

One large group had to experience to the bitter end all the vicissitudes that resulted from being a pawn in a brilliant and ruthless British intelligence plot. The intrigue which made up the "Kladovo affair" was probably one of the most dramatic sabotage-diplomacy actions of World War II. Strangely enough, it went unnoticed at the time, and today is known in detail by only a few.

A most intensive "chess game" for the lives of a thousand escapees, the player on the one side was the British intelligence service. With the aid of the British diplomatic corps in a dozen countries, it maneuvered most actively to have those refugees murdered by the Nazis rather than to allow them to reach the only available haven, Palestine. The counterplayers were the organizers of the rescue action who desperately tried to thwart the British plans.

Move after move, the British improved their own position and worsened the chances for survival of the thousand humans for whose life the deadly game was being played and who grew increasingly frantic as month after month passed.

After we had landed, in 1938 and early 1939, the *Katina*, the *Gepo*, the *Astir*, the *Liesel*, the *Aghia Tsioni*, and some smaller ships,* the Zionist Socialists started preparing a large transport in Vienna. The passengers of this transport were to consist of immigrants most valuable for the future State of Israel: 1,000 young pio-

*See Appendix, "List of Voyages."

neers who had been on *hachscharah,* had undergone agricultural training, physical and ideological preparation for a future life on a *kibbutz.* The Zionist Socialist youth group from which these young people were drawn was the Hashomer Hazair. For these youngsters there would be no problem in settling in Israel as many of the *kibbutzim* had been founded and were populated by that organization. The organizers preparing this transport were referred to as the Mossad (organization) and closely cooperated with the Zionist Labor party, then the most influential group in Zionist politics.

There were great hopes for the success of this undertaking because the Mossad had just succeeded in landing a large ship, the S.S. *Tiger Hill.* This action had focused world attention on the unreasonableness of Britain's policy toward Palestine for the following reason: the first two persons to be killed in World War II by British bullets were not Nazis, they were Jewish escapees aboard the *Tiger Hill* refugee ship on its way to Palestine. On the very first day of World War II, September 1, 1939, while German dive-bombers rained death on Warsaw and a dozen other Polish cities, His Majesty's ship, the *Lorna,* opened fire on the rickety overcrowded *Tiger Hill* because, in her approach to unload her cargo of human misery on the coast of Palestine, she did not heed a British order to turn back toward Germany. This encounter between H.M.S. *Lorna* and the *Tiger Hill* had ended with a victory for the British Navy. Killed in the "encounter" were Dr. Robert Schneider, a physician from Czechoslovakia, and Zvi Binder, a young pioneer from Poland, whose hopes to till the land peacefully in a *kibbutz* died within sight of the land he had been longing for years to reach.

The killing of the two was admitted by the British and debated in the House of Commons. The results of the debate as far as British policy went were nil, but the cruel irony of these deaths had strengthened the determination of those working for illegal immigration. However, the resolution of the British to prevent future such scandalous shooting "engagements" between their warships and our limping refugee crates was also strengthened. The British decided to reorganize their efforts. With the war on, they could no longer afford before the eyes of the world to shoot at the wretched survivors of concentration camps. They, therefore, decided that the transports must be stopped at their source, before anyone could step on any seagoing vessel.

As early as July 7, 1939, when the outbreak of war was

imminent, Mr. Malcolm MacDonald, British secretary for the colonies, called and presided over a special meeting at which the minutes record the decision "to stop the flow of immigration at the source."*

These same documents note: "This question of illegal immigration into Palestine has as Mr. Reilly shows . . . become a question of first class political importance."

Still reflecting the distrust which we had planted among the British to make each department feel that the other actually favored illegal immigration, these minutes continue: "I am not certain that the Palestine Administration have done everything possible to bring about its [i.e., the illegal immigration's] cessation . . . Further action by us *in a number of directions* is to be taken."†

Three such "directions" were taken to achieve the action demanded by the British Cabinet: one was a sharply increased diplomatic offensive. The second was a brilliant, though ruthless plot by the British intelligence services. In its imaginative concept, it did honor to the best tradition of British secret service. If successful, it could with one coup deal a hard blow to the German war effort and finish all illegal immigration for good. These two moves were to be supported by a third direction: a propaganda drive in which BBC news broadcasts would have to play an important role.

The British, in their circumspect way, did not, of course, record this intelligence plan in the files of the Foreign Office. Their machinations, however, come to light in the series of official documents left behind, such as the above-cited and others to be mentioned below in the story of those 1,000 Jews who started assembling in Vienna in the early fall of 1939 for their intended illegal voyage to Palestine. An example of the British diplomatic efforts to stop the emigrants from leaving is recorded in the very minutes referred to above:

> Our latest action was on July 5th when the Secretary of State spoke *severely* to the Rumanian Minister. We should make sure that his *reprimand* reaches the Rumanian Government and instruct Bucha-

*Foreign Office Document W10846/1369/48268.
†Author's italics.

rest to drive home all our arguments . . . We should *use ever means* of impressing on the Rumanian Government the seriousness with which their conduct is regarded by H.M.G. and the damage it may do to relations with us.*

Similar interventions were undertaken with the governments of Bulgaria, Greece, and Yugoslavia. These governments did little enough anyhow to facilitate the escape of Jews from Hitler. But the British, against all international laws governing the Danube and the high seas and against all codes of humanity, demanded from those governments active cooperation in the blocking of the only escape route left.

Those who were in these days registering for escape with us did not realize how the British had intensified their war to keep prospective immigrants to Palestine bottled up in Nazi Germany. Yet I learned about it in general terms from an informer we had planted in the British Embassy in Athens. He told me that at the embassy, they even went so far as to talk about us in terms of real war: "The Greek front," "the Hungarian front," etc., and that "front reports" were received and went out as they did for the combat zones in which Britain was involved. I believed at that time that the man was exaggerating, but in the mid-1970s when I studied the files of the British Foreign Office, I found out that our informer was telling the truth: some of this talk about "fronts" had even slipped into official communiqués. Foreign Office File Number 371/25241† reveals, for example, the following information: ". . . concerning *the Bulgarian front*‡ of our campaign against illegal immigration." What a front! What combatants! The British Empire vs. a tortured, hunted people, men, women, children who had already lost most of their relatives and who tried to make it in barges and unseaworthy ships to the only land where loving hands would welcome them. But the British, in their desire to gain the good graces of the Arabs, most of whom were heavily pro-Hitler, truly considered their efforts to keep Jews from reaching Palestine to be one of their fronts.

The scope of the diplomatic offensive the British were under-

*Author's italics.
†Register Number WF0371/25241/5185/38/48.
‡Author's italics.

taking on all "fronts" may be seen in a five-page directive issued by the British secretary of state, Viscount Halifax, on July 21, 1939.* In this directive, Halifax demands that the ambassadors of the following countries stationed in London "be summoned" to the Foreign Office and "be spoken to on the subject." Although the net Britain spread all over Europe to achieve "cessation" of our rescue action was widespread enough, the ministers of Brazil, China, Iran, Liberia, Mexico, Panama, and Santo Domingo were to be summoned.

But even this thrust did not appear to be enough for the British secretary of foreign affairs. The "countries of origin" from which Jews started out in their flight from extermination by the Nazis also needed a reprimand. They should be enjoined not to permit such escapes. Mr. A.W.G. Randall, Viscount Halifax's right-hand man in the war against our rescue action, writes:

> . . . countries which . . . may be regarded as countries of origin. These are Poland, Hungary, Yugoslavia, Rumania and Bulgaria. In many cases one of these countries is the actual country of origin of the illegal immigrant. In all cases one or more of these countries must be crossed in transit before embarkation for Palestine. I am to enclose drafts of dispatches to His Majesty's representatives at Bucharest, Budapest, and Warsaw. Instructions have already been sent to His Majesty's Ministers at Belgrade and Sofia in telegrams of which copies are enclosed for convenience of reference.*

In the same document, the Foreign Office informs the Colonial Office:

> . . . Lord Halifax is of the opinion that it is urgently necessary that arrested illegal immigrants should be kept in custody, and not released . . . unless such arrangements are made it seems likely that it will be almost impossible to *arrange for the return to their country of origin of those illegal immigrants who can be proved to have come from Rumania, Poland, or other countries which can be induced and even compelled to readmit them.*†

Copies of this humanitarian document were sent to the Admiralty and to the Home Office.

---

*Foreign Office File FO371/24092/2829.
†Author's italics.

This brutal British war against Jews should be viewed in the light of the barbaric strategies conducted by the Nazis at the very same time against the hapless millions of European Jewry.

At the time the British were speaking of their fronts in their war against Jews, the German war against the Jews was going brilliantly well—for the Germans. As Eichmann's stupendous organizational talent unfolded, trainload after trainload went rolling east, with cattle cars full of Jews who were to be "resettled" there. The catastrophic juncture at which European Jewry found itself right then is probably best seen in the following description. It does not stem from a Jewish source, nor from one of the nationals of the invaded countries. Document No. 2832 ED 81 of the German Institut fuer Zeitgeschichte in Munich is the cool, matter-of-fact description of one Wilhelm Cornides, a sergeant in Hitler's army. With German exactness, noting not only the day and hour but even the minute of a happening, he records the final phase of a resettlement action, not in the notorious Auschwitz but rather in a little-known "resettlement" camp named Belzec altogether some 800 by 400 yards in extent:

INSTITUT FUER ZEITGESCHICHTE   File Number
MUNICH   2832 ED 81
OBSERVATIONS REGARDING THE "RESETTLEMENT"
OF JEWS IN THE GENERAL GOVERNMENT

1. Notes of a German Sergeant (Wilhelm Cornides) of August 31, 1942

Rawa Ruska (Galicia) German House, August 31, 1430 hours.

At ten minutes past noon I saw a transport train arrive on the railroad station. On the roof and on the running boards sat guards with rifles. One could see from a distance that the cars were crammed with people. I turned and walked along the entire train. It consisted of 35 cattle cars and one passenger car. In each of the cars were at least 60 Jews. (When enlisted men or prisoners are transported, 40 men are loaded into those cars, but benches had been removed and one could see that those who were locked in had to stand one jammed against the other.) Some of the doors were a tiny bit ajar, the windows were crisscrossed with barbed wire. Few of those locked in were men and of those most were old. Everything [sic] else was women, girls and children. Many children were pressing against the windows and the small open cracks in the doors. The youngest ones were certainly not older than 2 years.

As soon as the train had come to a halt the Jews tried to reach out with bottles to obtain water. However, the train was surrounded by SS guards so that no one could come near. It was at that moment that a train arrived from the direction of Jaroslav. The passengers streamed toward the exit without bothering about the transport. A few Jews who were in the process of loading an armed forces truck waved with their caps to the locked in people.

I talked to a policeman on duty at the railway station. To my question as to where these Jews came from, he answered: "Those are probably the last ones from Lemberg. This has been going on, without interruption, for three weeks. In Jaroslav only 8 were left." I asked: "How much farther are they going?" He replied, "To Belzec." "And then?" "Poison." I asked, "Gas?" He shrugged his shoulders, then he just added: "In the beginning, I believe, they always shot them."

Here in the German House I just talked to two soldiers from Front Stalag 325. They said that these transports had lately been passing through there every day, mostly at night. One with 70 cars is said to have passed through yesterday.

In the train from Rawa Ruska to Cholm 1730 hours:

Just as we were in the process of boarding at 1640 hrs. an empty transport train arrived. I walked along the train and counted. There were 56 cars. On the doors numbers had been written in chalk: 60, 70, once 90, a few times 40, obviously the number of Jews transported within.

In the compartment I spoke to the wife of a railway policeman. She is presently visiting her husband here. She tells me that these transports are through daily, at times also with German Jews. Yesterday 6 children's bodies were found along the track. The woman thinks that the Jews themselves have murdered these children, but they must have perished during the voyage. The railroad policeman who comes along as escort came into our compartment. He confirmed the woman's statement regarding the children's bodies found yesterday along the track. I asked: "Do the Jews know what is happening with them?" The woman answered: "Those who come from far away might know nothing, but in the area here they know it already. They then try to run away when they see that they are being fetched. So, e.g., in Cholm where 3 were shot to death on the way through the city." "In the railway paperwork these trains are named 'resettlement transports,'" the railway policeman commented. He then said that after the assassination of Heydrich* several transports with Czechs had passed through. The Belzec camp is said to be located right next to the railroad track and the woman promised to show it to me when we pass it.

1740 hours.

Short stop. On the other track another transport train is standing. I talk to the policemen who travel in the passenger car in front. I ask: "Going back home to the Reich?" One of them answers with a grin: "I suppose you know where we come from. Well, for us there is no end to the work." Then the transport train continued. The cars were empty now and swept clean. There were 35. Most likely this was the train which I had seen at 1 P.M. in the Rawa Ruska railroad station.

1820 hours.

We have passed the Belzec camp. Prior to that we traveled for some time through forests of tall pines. When the woman shouted: "Here it comes," all one could see was a high hedge of fir trees. A penetrating sweetish odor could be made out distinctly. "They stink already," said the woman. The railway policeman laughed: "Baloney, that's the gas, of course." Meanwhile we had moved another 200 meters and the sweetish odor had changed into the pungent smell of something burning. "This comes from the crematory," said the policeman. Shortly after the fence ended. In front of it one could see a guardhouse with an SS guard. A double track led into the camp. One track branched off from the main line. The other one led over a switch from the camp to a row of sheds about 250 meters further away. A freight car happened to stand on the turntable. Several Jews were busy turning the disk, SS guards, rifle under the arm, were standing by. One of the sheds was open. One could clearly see that it was heaped to the ceiling with bundles of clothes.

As we continued to move along I looked back toward the camp once more. The fence was too high to see anything. The woman said that sometimes, when going by, one can see smoke rising from the camp. But I could see nothing of the kind.

In my estimation the camp measures about 800 by 400 meters.

In the referred-to file of the Institut fuer Zeitgeschichte can be found two more eyewitness reports as to the "little" Belzec murder factory. Both of these additional eyewitnesses are German. Both

---

*Head of the German "Security Services." Also "Protector" of Bohemia and Moravia. Assassinated by Czech underground.

reports corroborate, each with more details, the one by Sergeant Wilhelm Cornides.

For the tens of thousands of Jews who were shipped there, Belzec was, of course, the horror of horrors: their lives did not just end there prematurely, though for the many young people and children it had hardly started. The victims of Belzec did not just die there; they were not simply killed. They were slaughtered. Yet, in the overall Nazi scheme, Belzec was just an insignificant little slaughterhouse. The following extract from the official German record of the infamous Wannsee Conference of January 20, 1942, at which Adolf Eichmann played a prominent role and at which the plan for the total annihilation of all the Jews the Nazis could get hold of was formally decided, reveals the ultimate aim of Nazi plans for the "Final Solution."*

Around 11 million Jews are involved in this final solution of the Jewish question. They are distributed as follows among individual countries:

Country	Number
A. Old Reich	131,800
Austria	43,700
Eastern Territories (Poland)	420,000
General Government (Poland)	2,284,000
Bialystok (Poland)	400,000
Protectorate of Bohemia and Moravia	74,200
Estonia—free of Jews	
Latvia	3,500
Lithuania	34,000
Belgium	43,000
Denmark	5,600
France/occupied territory	165,000
unoccupied territory	700,000
Greece	69,000
Netherlands	160,000
Norway	1,300
B. Bulgaria	48,000
England	330,000
Finland	2,300
Ireland	4,000
Italy, including Sardinia	58,000

*Nuremberg International War Crimes Trial Document.

PHONES: EUSTON { 3925. 3926.

TELEGRAPHIC ADDRESS:
INLAND: "MIGRATE, KINCROSS, LONDON."
CABLEGRAMS: "MIGRATE, LONDON."

THE COUNCIL FOR GERMAN JEWRY

CHAIRMAN:
(HON. VISCOUNT SAMUEL,
P.C., G.C.S.I., G.B.E.

JOINT SECRETARIES:
L. BAKSTANSKY, LL.B., B.SC.(ECON.).
M. STEPHANY, F.L.A.A.

MS/CL

WOBURN HOUSE.
UPPER WOBURN PLACE.
LONDON, W.C.1.

The New Zionist Organisation,   26th July, 1938.
47 Finchley Road,
N. W. 3.

Dear Sirs,

With further reference to your letter of the
5th instant and in continuation of mine of the
8th idem, I have been requested to inform you that,
at a Meeting of the Executive of the Council for
German Jewry held yesterday, the application for a
grant to the 380 emigrants from Austria who recently
reached Palestine was again considered with great
care.

The Executive of the Council strongly deprecates
all emigration which is not properly organised and
which does not make proper provision for the welfare
of the emigrants. The Executive cannot in any way
encourage illegal immigration into Palestine and, for
this reason, cannot make any contribution towards the
object to which your letter refers.

Yours faithfully,

Joint Secretary.

Above, left

Front page of "Jew Passport" on which author had to travel. The large red *J* in the upper left-hand corner stands for "Jew." To "shame" him, every Jewish male was given the middle name of Israel, and every Jewish female the middle name of Sarah.

Above, right

The official Jewish organization "deprecates all emigration which is not properly organised. . . . The Executive cannot in any way encourage illegal immigration into Palestine. . . ." (Author's underlining.)

The last fifty feet.

Debarking.

JQUE
IBUCAREST

Bucureşti, 30 decembrie 1938 .

Onor.

    M i n i s t e r u l   d e   I n t e r n e,

                                L o c o

    În urma cererii din partea Ministerului Ocrotirilor Sociale din Praha ne permitem a vă ruga să binevoiţi a aproba tranzit prin România al unui tren special cu vagoane plumbuite,care va pleca în prima jumătate a lunei Ianuarie 1939 cu emigranţii-evrei din Cehoslovacia în Republica St. Domingo.

    Toate lucrările în legătură cu transportul prin România sunt organizate de Dl. Dr. Willy P e r l .

    În speranţa că veţi binevoi a aproba cererea susmenţionată, binevoiţi a primi, vă rugăm, pe lângă mulţumirile noastre anticipate, încredinţarea deosebitei noastre consideraţiuni.

                            Ministru,

Letter from Czechoslovakian Embassy in Bucharest requesting the Rumanian Ministry of the Interior to permit passage in a special sealed train of Jewish refugees from Czechoslovakia, on their way to "Santo Domingo" in a transport organized by Dr. Willy Perl.

Trudging through the dunes.

In a sealed train.

00139
Sonderpersonenzug
Liberia
am 4. November 1938

Abfahrt

Wien Ostbf

21 Uhr

3. Kl.   0.30 ℛℳ

Keine Fahrtunterbrechung

Nicht übertragbar

00139

Zählkarte Nr. 834

Name:

Waggon Nr. XIV

Railroad ticket with place card for "Special Slow Train" from Vienna to Liberia. The reference to the "special slow train" shows the sort of humor Eichmann favored.

Private

London, 2·I·1939

Dear Dr Teff

Please forgive me last night's cancelled call. We had had to order it because of some urgent questions that had to be settled; but in the evening we spoke to another town and saw that the matter already _was_ settled, and talking to you might only complicate matters.

Let me seize this opportunity to congratulate you.

Yours
V.

My kindest regards to friend Sch.

A letter to "Dr. Teff"—the author's code name—from Vladimir Jabotinsky.

Contrary to general belief, it was not entirely impossible to obtain release from a concentration camp, at least well into 1940. Proof of the possibility of impending departure often achieved such a release. This document from a British intelligence file shows the kind of informal slip issued by the author's office in Vienna on the strength of which the release of numerous prisoners from Dachau and Buchenwald concentration camps was obtained.

Death of the *Rim.*

Right up the Tel Aviv beach. Unloading of the *Parita* after
she broke through the British blockade.

His Majesty's forces in action—battling survivors on an "illegal ship."

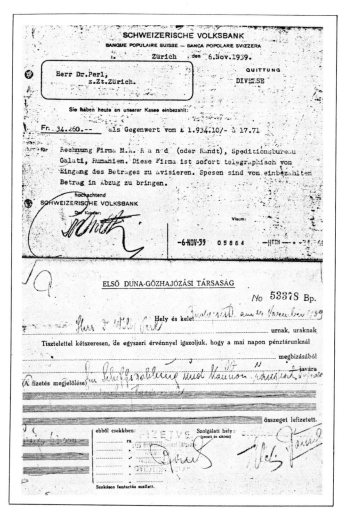

The risky advance payment for the *Sakarya.* Swiss bank statement confirming the transfer.

Receipt dated Budapest, November 27, 1939, confirming payment of 63,000 pengös to the Hungarian branch office of the Donaudampfschiffahrtsgesellschaft for the charter of the *Grein.*

7.8.40

Dear Dr Perl

You saved 2400 souls
from death by cold &
famine. You ought to
be a proud man and
I am very proud of your
friendship

Yours sincerely

Josiah C. Wedgwood

M.P., P.C.

Colonel Josiah C. Wedgwood, M.P., a
leader in the (minority) Labour Party, was
a strong supporter of our actions and initiated on their behalf several debates in the
House of Commons. Letter to the author
after arrival of the *Sakarya*.

Professor Weizmann promises the British
that action will be taken against the demonstrations planned by Jews in Palestine
and in the United States in protest against
deportation of the *Patria* disaster survivors
from Palestine to Mauritius.

No. 76021/40.

288

1201/38/48

Date 22.11.40

Reference

CYPHER TELEGRAM

TO   High Commissioner   PALESTINE

Sent 17th November, 1940. 16.00 hrs.

MOST IMMEDIATE.
SECRET. PRIVATE AND PERSONAL.

Illegal Immigrants. I saw Weizmann on 14th
November and explained to him why we considered it absolutely
essential in existing circumstances to proceed in manner
proposed. He admitted force of arguments and expressed
willingness to do his best to damp down Jewish agitation. He
has now asked us to give him facilities for telegraphing to
Shertok and to his friends in U.S.A. in following terms
Begins Lord Lloyd informs me ships now at Haifa are being
followed by another contingent about 1800 refugees now at
sea which may be followed by yet others. Government opinion
is that this action may be prelude to wider and more
systematic efforts by Nazis now in control of Roumanian ports.
This aims first at getting rid of Jews, second at embarrassing
Britain creating conflicts between Government and ourselves
by introduction of German agents provocateurs, and using this
for propaganda among Arabs. Doing my best to obtain
alleviation of situation. You must try prevent rise of
feeling which may complicate situation. Cable your own
suggestions. Ends.

I am giving Weizmann non-committal answer for the
moment. Meanwhile I should be glad to learn with least
possible delay whether you consider that message on above
lines would be useful to you as tending to allay Jewish
excitement and to facilitate task of Palestine Government.
I do not overlook risk that by encouraging Weizmann's
cooperation in this matter we may be laying up embarrassments
for ourselves hereafter if and when we have to take measures
(e.g. implementation of White Paper) to which Jews will
raise strong objection. Immediate needs of the moment have
to be weighed against these wider considerations. Please
telegraph your views urgently.

Gestapo arrest order for Lore, whose conversion and marriage to author remained unknown to the Germans. She was arrested because "she endangers the existence and security of the people and the state by having granted asylum to a Jewish woman in her [Lore's] apartment in order to protect her from an eventual resettlement and by in other ways, too, maintaining contact with Jews who had been resettled, and by all that exhibits a lack of the restraint which one has to keep as to Jews and by creating unrest and agitation by her dishonorable behavior."

Aftermath of the *Struma* disaster.

Geheime Staatspolizei
Reichssicherheitshauptamt
IV C 2 Haft Nr. R 12520

Berlin SW 11, den 9.Januar 19
Prinz-Albrecht-Straße 8

Schutzhaftbefehl

Vor- und Zuname: Leonore Maria R o l l i g

Geburtstag und -Ort: 15.3.1913 in Wien

Beruf: Privatbeamtin

Familienstand: ledig

Staatsangehörigkeit: DR.

Religion: röm.kath.,

Rasse (bei Nichtariern anzugeben): Arierin

Wohnort und Wohnung: Wien 12., Rosenhügelstrasse 31/1

wird in Schutzhaft genommen.

Gründe:

Sie — gefährdet nach dem Ergebnis der staatspolizeilichen Feststellungen ihr — Verhalten den Bestand und die Sicherheit des Volkes und Staates, i sie dadurch, dass sie einer Jüdin in ihrer Wohnung Unterschlupf gewährte, um sie vor einer eventuellen Aus siedlung zu schützen und auch sonst mit bereits ausgesiedelten Juden Verbindung unterhält, die gegenüber Juden gebotene Zurückhaltung vermissen lässt und durch ihr ehrvergessenes Treiben Unruhe und Erregung in die Oeffentlichkeit trägt .

Gezeichnet: M ü l l e r .

The author and his wife, Lore, at the time of the happenings

ר צ ח !
סיר האַרולד מק מײַקל
הידוע כנציב העליון לפלשתינה (א"י),
מבוקש עבור רצח
800 פליטים יהודים במימי הים השחור באניה "סטרומה"

MURDER!

SIR HAROLD MAC MICHAEL

Known as High Commissioner for Palestine

WANTED for MURDER

OF 800 REFUGEES DROWNED IN THE
BLACK SEA ON THE BOAT STRUMA

Country	Number
Albania	200
Croatia	40,000
Portugal	3,000
Roumania, including Bessarabia	342,000
Sweden	8,000
Switzerland	18,000
Serbia	10,000
Slovakia	88,000
Spain	6,000
Turkey (European portion)	55,500
Hungary	742,800
USSR	5,000,000
Ukraine	2,994,684
White Russia, excluding Bialystok	446,484
Total over	11,000,000*

Against these unbelievable odds, caught between Nazi barbarism, Britain's ruthless desire to hang onto its empire, and severely handicapped because of the complete lack of political understanding on the part of the Jewish establishment, the small group of organizers of illegal immigration went on with its work.

While the Revisionists prepared the largest illegal transport ever—the *Sakarya* with 2,200 on board—the Zionist socialists of the Hashomer Hazair and the Mossad proceeded, equally without hesitation, to assemble in Vienna many of their highest-qualified young people. These arrived in Vienna in well-disciplined groups from Czechoslovakia, Poland, and other Eastern European countries, and some also from Germany and Danzig. A contingent from Vienna was to come along as well.

The plan made in conjunction with the Association of Jewish Communities of Yugoslavia for the trip down the Danube had been well prepared. The thousand young people would leave Vienna on a large luxury riverboat, the *Uranus*, one of the two most modern ships owned by the official German Danube Steamshipping Company. To avoid any danger in case of a complication during the

*The above numbers show figures already substantially reduced by killings and by emigration of Jews at the time of the Wannsee Conference, January 20, 1942, e.g., 580,000 Jews lived in Germany at the time of Hitler's takeover in 1933; 200,000 Jews lived in Austria when the Germans marched in in 1938. Compare with above figures at the end of 1941.

river part of the voyage, the passengers would be transferred in
Bezdan, on the Hungarian-Yugoslav border, to three Yugoslav
riverboats hired by the Association of Jewish Communities of
Yugoslavia,* and owned by the government-controlled Yugoslav
Shipping Company, the Rezna Plovidba. From there they were to
continue their voyage on the Yugoslav ships down the Danube, all
the way to Sulina, where the Danube flows into the Black Sea.

In the highest of spirits, the 1,002 (in the last moment one
always had to add some extreme emergency cases) embarked in
Vienna. Happy Hebrew songs were sung in praise of working the
land in one's own country, of drying out the marshes, and of
making the desert bloom. Our country will again be the land of milk
and honey, they sang as they danced the traditional hora.

On the sixteenth of October 1939, shortly after midnight, the
Uranus arrived in Bezdan, where the Danube enters Yugoslavia.
Although the night was foggy and visibility on the river at that hour
was almost zero, a jubilant crowd transferred from the German ship
to the three ships flying the flag of Yugoslavia (Yugoslavia at that
time was still free). They had, of course, no inkling of what the
British had in store for them. Little did they know of the vast
preparations the British had been making to achieve a "cessation"
of their rescue action and all future ones. The reception was, in a
way, a royal one. A queen and two emperors were awaiting them:
they were the Yugoslav riverboats, the *Czar Nikola,* the *Czar
Dušan,* and *Kraliza* (i.e., Queen) *Maria.* Czar Dušan had been a
king of Yugoslavia and Czar Nikola an emperor of Russia known
for his Pan-Slavic sentiment. Maria was then queen of Yugoslavia.
Waiting with the ships for the pioneers was Mr. Naftali Gedalja, a
most capable and hard-working representative of the Association,
who saw to it that the 1,002 got through to Sulina so that the
voyage down the Danube would be as smooth as possible. Within a
couple of hours, Gedalja had the transfer from the German ship to
the Yugoslav ones effected, and the happy immigrants continued
their trip down the Danube.

In Vukovar a great deal of coal was loaded, and in Belgrade
there was another holdover, where Mr. Sime (Simon) Spitzer,
secretary general of the Association, gave an inspiring welcoming

*Hereafter referred to as the Association.

speech. As the gay little flotilla floated down the Danube the hardships of what we called "free immigration to Palestine," which the passengers had been duly warned about, seemed quite exaggerated.

The first news of trouble came at Prahovo. One important part of the contract with the Yugoslav Shipping Company had been that by the time the two Czars and the Queen arrived in Donji Milanovac, the last station in Yugoslavia on the Bulgarian border, a cable would be waiting there from the Rezna Plovidba's representative in Sulina, confirming that a seagoing vessel able to load them all was waiting there.

Prahovo was the first place after Belgrade, from which Mr. Gedalja, who was with the young people traveling on one of the three ships, could phone Belgrade again and report to Sime Spitzer that everything went fine. To his horror, Sime told him that in Sulina there was no word about the ship.

Worse than that: none was expected.

The news hit Gedalja "like a bombshell." He decided to tell only the leaders on each of the three ships about the complication. The four of them together decided, Gedalja reports, "to keep the news secret to avoid panic." Although there was actually no word about any seagoing vessel due for them in Sulina, the expected delay was described to the emigrants as "short." The three riverboats turned into the nearby tiny Danube port of Kladovo to wait for the green light.

As the two Czars and the Queen Maria were being lashed broadside to the pier, there was great disappointment on board. Some felt apprehensive, but certainly no one on the ships could have guessed at that point what Kladovo would come to mean in their lives.

The ships were essentially sightseeing vessels, equipped for short trips on the Danube, and though they also had cabins for those who on regular cruises could afford to pay for them, there was, of course, only very limited cabin space.

But days passed. After a week in Kladovo, the seagoing ship was still "delayed." Staying on the riverboat day and night and having to sleep on the crowded floor, as so many had to, caused tempers to become shorter and little of the originally jubilant mood could be still observed. At least there was no hunger, however. Mr.

Gedalja, who was in daily contact with the headquarters of the Association, saw to it that all passengers were fed well and at regular intervals.

But when two weeks had gone by, there was still no word about a ship in Sulina. After the third week, the first November fogs began to shroud the port area. As the days and nights grew colder, fear and a foreboding of danger started to creep into the hearts of those on board. True, they were in a free country, but how much longer would it remain so? They saw one small country after another fall into the hands of the Nazis. Yugoslavia's assertion that she would fight if attacked provided little feeling of security for those who counted the hours until they could continue on their voyage to Palestine.

With these feelings of insecurity, they had, of course, not the faintest notion that it was not only the Nazis but the British as well who were working hard on delivering the group and tens of thousands of others like them back to German concentration camps and firing squads. The escapees were unaware of the cables being exchanged between the London Foreign Office and its ambassadors in a dozen countries urging the ambassadors to pressure the respective governments to block the immigrants' escape.

Even the BBC—to which so many millions listened because it was supposedly the "voice of freedom and truth"—was being used for that sinister purpose, as the case of the S.S. *Hilda* documents. The *Hilda* was first destined to be the seagoing vessel to take the Kladovo party from Rumania to Palestine. On January 17, 1940, when more than three months after their arrival there, the 1,002 were still frozen on their icy ships in Kladovo, the British Foreign Office* reported with glee:

> The harbour authorities at Constanza [*sic*] have forbidden seamen registered in Roumania to sign on with ships bringing Jewish emigrants to Palestine. [Note: not just *illegal* emigrants but *Jewish* emigrants!] . . . this is good news.

The Rumanians had given "agitation" among their sailors as a reason for this inhuman measure. The Foreign Office document referred to continued boastingly:

*Registry Number W 1082/38/48/No311 Received in Registry twentieth January 1940. General: Refugees.

The agitation is probably an echo of our BBC Foreign News items. We should ask Mr. Downie to give us whenever possible material for BBC. SS Hilda case, if satisfactory, should provide excellent material. *

In the meanwhile, those who were to serve as that "excellent material," many of them by now human wrecks, huddled on their small riverboats on the icy Danube. There they lived in wintry isolation. Their number had by then increased to 1,004. Two babies had been born on the boats.

The pier to which the ice-bound vessels were tied was two miles outside Kladovo. The village itself, with only 3,000 inhabitants, is cut off in winter from the rest of Yugoslavia. There was no railroad there, the Danube was not navigable, and the nearest "larger" town, Prahovo, was separated from Kladovo by thirty miles of snow and ice. Every day Mr. Gedalja made his way through that snow to Kladovo, a four-mile hike that was often extremely strenuous. He had to walk that distance every day, however, to reach the nearest telephone to give his daily report, as demanded by Sime Spitzer. Travel to Prahovo, where supplies could be obtained was possible only by sleigh. If one of the snow storms—which at times raged across the plains—arose, the sleigh ride would be a dangerous undertaking. If a snow storm caught you in between, your body, the frozen horses, and the sleigh might well be pulled out only in spring when the snow melted.

In spite of it all, the emigrants tried to keep life going as normally as possible. There were marriages and more children were born. A pharmacist from Bratislava, a Mr. Klein, was one of the first ones to get married on the boats. At one time there was a flurry of weddings. It seemed that many were desperate to seize from life whatever it could still hold for them. Even Gedalja got married there, to a Viennese girl who had come down with the *Uranus* and was now on the ships. When a baby boy was born, the prescribed circumcision was performed. A small group of very orthodox Jews who stood out from the rest because of their beards and earlocks, saw to it that the ritual functions followed the prescribed tradition. The Association acted in the most devoted and generous manner. Through their indefatigable Mr. Gedalja, generally called by his nickname "Bata," they made certain not only that there was never

*Author's italics.

any hunger on board, but that those who wanted to could adhere to the dietary laws.

But the stranded had more to think about than their own well-being. Hardly one had not left behind parents, brothers, sisters, or other relatives. Back "home" every day railroad cars filled with Jews rumbled over the tracks eastward on the last journey those in the cattle cars would ever take. On awakening aboard those boats, one had to ask oneself every morning: will this be my father's or my mother's last day at home? Are they already in the train? Are they already dead? If our transport runs into such difficulty, will this escape route continue to function and will they, will at least some of my friends still get out?

If one could only do something. But here they were, the lucky ones—those who had "escaped"—frozen in and unable to do anything for either themselves or their loved ones.

One day there was great excitement: a representative of the American Joint Distribution Committee (JDC), a Mrs. Jacobson, was to come to visit the Kladovo group. Rumors flew that the JDC would purchase a ship and have it ready for the emigrants in Sulina as soon as the ice melted! Although she was certainly used to safer traveling conditions, Mrs. Jacobson courageously risked the winter voyage from Thurn Severin. She was impressed with the plight of the refugees, and the ensuing funds she arranged to have the JDC provide to the Association of Yugoslav Jewish communities helped to make their lives easier.

But, like all official Jewish organizations, the JDC shied away from something as improper as providing a ship for illegal immigration. Yet even the humanitarian role the JDC played was too much for the British. They intercepted a telegram that the JDC in Paris sent to one of its executives, Mr. Trooper, in which such strictly philanthropic aid was requested. In reaction to the intercepted cable, the British Foreign Office sent a cypher telegram to its minister in Belgrade* headed: "Assistance for Party of Immigrants to Palestine Marooned in the Danube." The cypher cable referred to the JDC's proposed assistance for 1,000 *chalutzim* ("pioneers") who had been blocked by ice on their passage down the Danube. It stated that "an effort should be made to prevent the assistance being given." It requested a confirmation of this report from "His Majes-

*Registry Number 1087/38/48 1940W 319/20 Jan. 1940.

ty's Minister at Belgrade." A handwritten note to the document in the files of the Foreign Office states: "The JDC certainly should be warned. Sir H. Emerson was asked on W 10038/1369/48 to warn them and reports having done so in W 10823." This is the same Sir H. Emerson, as we will document in the following chapter, who in cooperation with Mr. Arthur Lourie of the Jewish Agency obtained and related to the Foreign Office information harmful to the Holocaust survivors.

Poor 1,000 *chalutzim* in Kladovo! Poor millions of Jews in Europe who had to face such perverted alliance!

The British diplomatic offensive against those marooned in Kladovo was, of course, not restricted to this one step. Cables and admonishments were coming out from London in a stream, all intended to keep those marooned in Kladovo pinned down. On January 24, the Foreign Office, this time not only in cypher but in a cable specifically classified SECRET, inquired of its ambassador in Belgrade* in regard to the "party of Jewish intending immigrants marooned on a Yugoslav steamer in ice at Kladovo" what had become of the previous enquiry. In regard to the obstacle of the international status of the Danube, that Secret cypher telegram stressed that "Jurisdiction to impose such restrictions would derive not from any territorial rights over the Danube but from the Yugoslavian nationality of the steamers."

In the meantime, for those on the riverboats, October had turned into November. And November into December. There was a ship in Rumania in December which had been chartered by the Mossad and which could have taken them along, but the way via the internationalized Danube was by now blocked by ice, and to travel on land, they would have needed a transit visa. It was solely for traveling on the Danube that only a visa of destination was demanded by the country in which transfer was to take place. Though a ship was waiting for them, they could not get their hands on transit visas because the British had so far succeeded in stopping immigration at its source. The Foreign Office had sent dispatches for this purpose to "His Majesty's representatives at Bucharest, Budapest, and Warsaw" and "Instructions [had] already been sent to His Majesty's representatives at Belgrade and Sofia."

But nature was kinder than these humans were. Though it was

*Foreign Office File Number FO341/35238/1809 Registry W 1087/35/48 326RTEL.

wartime and every day could bring the invasion of Yugoslavia, it seemed that the day of freedom was moving closer as the cold abated and the first signs of spring appeared.

By March the river was navigable again. Yet there was no ship now, and so the danger grew daily. The war had then been on for half a year without a new major German offensive. The French and British were sitting behind their supposedly unconquerable Maginot line. Would the German war machinery not start up again as soon as spring was really here? The German *Drang nach dem Osten*—"Craving for the East"—was a well-established maxim of their geopolitical aims. As they were now allied with the Russians, the only way they could move East, many then argued, was into neighboring Yugoslavia and the rest of the Balkans.

April 9 was a day of panic. The German tiger had moved. At three A.M., Nazi troops had again attacked a neighbor of theirs, this time peaceful, little Denmark. As Denmark crumbled within hours before the German juggernaut, the air of gloom in Kladovo descended even more heavily. The day after Denmark, there was another victim, one which did not even border Germany: Norway, across the sea, supposedly under the control of the powerful British Navy.

Would Yugoslavia be next? And, if so, would those who had escaped from Germany not be among the very first to be murdered by the Nazis? Entering Kladovo, they would find already waiting there a ready dish of 1,000-plus Jews.

But Yugoslavia was not next—yet. On May 10 at three A.M., the Germans attacked neutral Belgium and the Netherlands, and just as they had done in World War I, they turned back the French left flank and proceeded to take the Maginot line from the undefended rear. The French army disintegrated, and the British, trapped in an iron-clad encirclement, were happy to leave all their equipment behind and to have their men escape home in an improvised evacuation from Dunkirk.

Would Yugoslavia now be next?

It was.

But before that, a number of happenings occurred which would have their impact on the final fate of the 1,004 refugees stranded in Kladovo.

While the Germans were drawing up their plans for the invasion of Yugoslavia and the other Balkans; while the members of the Mossad spent anxiety-laden days and sleepless nights trying to extricate these people, the British diplomatic service, and the more lethal British intelligence service worked as hard as they could to prevent the Kladovo people from escaping from the almost fully Nazi-controlled European continent.

The British master plan was nothing short of brilliant.

In its final version, it went like this: a ship that was chartered by Jews for illegal immigration to Palestine and was ostensibly on its way to pick up the Kladovo people would steam up the Danube. It would be loaded with thousands of crates containing scrap metal, largely old pipes, all filled with dynamite and with hundreds of metal barrels, also filled with explosives. At a place which had been previously pinpointed by the British, where the Danube was very narrow, the ship would be blown up and would sink with all the scrap metal on board. The sunken vessel would block all transport on the Danube, and thereby the flow of oil and grain from Rumania to Germany. It would take months and valuable German machinery and manpower to clear the Danube of this obstacle—a costly blow to the German war effort.

This plot's special—devilish—feature was that the Germans would attribute the sabotage, or cooperation in it to those involved in illegal immigration, especially to the Kladovo group. They would, of course, "liquidate" everyone in any way connected with these rescue actions—and the innocent British could wash their hands of it.

Naturally a major sabotage act against the Germans committed in wartime by "the Jews" would almost automatically start wide-scale pogroms all over German-occupied lands, a "spontaneous" outburst which would dwarf the outrage of the Kristallnacht.

A British advantage in all this would be that the atrocities in Germany would become incomparably more widely known than the quiet extermination at obscure places in Poland, and the BBC would be ready to publicize this horror in hopes of increasing the chances of getting the United States into the war.

Thus, if the scheme worked, a three-fold benefit would result for the British: the damage of the blocked Danube; the "cessation" of all illegal emigration into Palestine; and the reaction of the world to the resulting German outrage which the British could then use for their anti-German propaganda.

The British master plan to blow up a ship at that location was quite clever, but the truly ingenious part was the active involvement of illegal immigration in it. The involvement of the refugees had another advantage too. A ship going up the Danube in wartime might arouse the suspicions of the countries through which it had to pass. All these countries were frightened of Germany as each waited in paralyzed fear lest it be the next target. But the old crates transporting refugees were a familiar sight on the Danube. It was generally known in the Balkans that a large number of refugees had been stranded for many months in Yugoslavia, and a ship coming up to call for them was less likely to be closely checked. If the British could involve not just second- and third-echelon Jews but "responsible" Jewish leaders in the scheme, it would be particularly advantageous.

To have the intrigue work smoothly, the British had to arrange things so that the Jews not only were suspected of participation but were actually involved. If a few leading Jews could somehow be persuaded to cooperate in the scheme of blocking the Danube and having the ship sent up under their auspices, it would substantially reduce the risk for the British of a premature discovery that the ship was actually in their service. If, following the inevitable mass slaughter that would ensue, not only the Germans but the British too would be blamed, one could point a finger at the Jews who themselves had gone along with the scheme. And again, the British could wash their hands of the whole affair, probably defended by the Jewish leaders who had first agreed to it.

But whom among the Jews could the British persuade to go along?

Our group, the Revisionists, was best known to most Balkan authorities because we were not only the originators but also the ones who were most active in bringing ships up and down the Danube. "Our" ship would probably raise the least suspicion. The British knew this very well. Just at the time the Kladovo people were frozen in, in December 1939 and January 1940, the British Foreign Office and the Colonial Office prepared jointly and printed a four-page memorandum, classified CONFIDENTIAL, entitled: JEW-ISH ILLEGAL IMMIGRATION INTO PALESTINE.* Under the heading WAR [*sic!*] (GENERAL) it stated: "Various organizations and speculators are concerned in arranging illegal immigration. *The principal body concerned, is,* however, *the New Zionist Organization,* lately called *Revisionists . . .* † During the six months April to September

---

*Foreign Office File No. FO371/25241/253.
†Author's italics.

1939, over 11,000 illegal immigrants succeeded in entering Palestine." White Hall, the British War Office, and MI 2, the high-level intelligence unit, also had no doubts about it. In a memorandum making suggestions to the Colonial Office as to how to stop the illegal immigration into Palestine, MI 2 of the War Office stated: "The Revisionists are behind the whole business . . ."* Thus, the logical step would have been to try to involve us in their scheme. But they never did. Perhaps they felt that we might not have fallen for their tricks or that Jabotinsky would not permit us to play any game of intelligence with British professionals for whom we could be no match. Perhaps they wanted to implicate more important Jews than our most active but smaller group. Most likely, however, the reason for not approaching us was that the British intelligence had a ready-made Jewish official working with them. He was none other than David Hacohen, a member of the executive council of the Jewish Agency. The Jewish Agency, before the establishment of the Jewish State, was considered by Jews as the Jewish government in exile, and the coveted membership on the Jewish Agency's executive council was, in that sense, equivalent to Cabinet rank.

David Hacohen was a trusted friend of Dr. Chaim Weizmann, the president of the Jewish Agency and the World Zionist Organization. He worked closely with David Ben-Gurion (then the leader of the powerful Zionist Labor party) and even closer with Moshe Shertok, the Jewish Agency's expert on foreign affairs.† Hacohen‡ and his connections were most valuable for British intelligence. It might be possible, if need be, to gain support from one or the other of these influential personalities to force the British Danube plot down the throats of Jews who would not cooperate. Opposition against what we called "free immigration to Palestine" was strong among Jewish officials anyhow as they were anxious to appease England.

---

*War Office White Hall D.O. 936/MI 2. Note to J. S. Bennet, Esq. Colonial Office SW 1, Copy of that document also in Foreign Office File No. FO371/2540/277/128 and 278/129.
†Shertok later changed his name to Sharett. He became Israel's first foreign minister and served from 1953 to 1955 as prime minister of Israel.
‡Hacohen too continued to hold top positions in the Israel hierarchy. In 1949 he was elected a member of the Knesset—the Israeli Parliament—and served in that capacity until 1953. From that year to 1955, he was Israel's ambassador to Burma. Hacohen was a member of the Israel Delegation to the UN, in 1951, 1954, 1956, 1960, and 1962.

In 1974, thirty-four years after the Kladovo affair, at age seventy-six, Hacohen published his autobiography, *Et L'Saper** (*Time to Tell*) in which his various exploits with the British intelligence service play a major part. He worked and traveled for them not only in the Balkans but in various Middle Eastern countries too. There are indications in the book that he viewed his role in getting the *Darien II*, the ship destined by the Mossad for the Kladovo rescue, not as one of life or death for 1,004 humans. This was to be primarily a test he had to pass, a test, he felt, by the British of his "loyalty"—and that of Jews generally. The chapter about the complications which arose with the *Darien* is not entitled "The Plight of the Kladovo Group" or anything like that. Its heading is "The Test of the *Darien*."† Hacohen's role in the Kladovo tragedy is introduced in his autobiography with the sentence: "One occasion which almost cancelled all my cooperation and caused me‡ [*sic*!] a lot of dramatic trouble§ with the Special Department. . . ."

Had they known of his British connection, the Kladovo people would have most likely viewed Mr. Hacohen simply as a British spy or at best a double agent. In his autobiography, Hacohen does not view himself at all as acting contrary to Jewish interests. British intelligence had Hacohen—and we believe him—thoroughly convinced that Jewish cooperation in the *Darien* murder scheme was for the British a test of Jewish loyalty to the empire and that if the Jews would not cooperate with the British in their intrigue, British cooperation with the Jews—whatever that meant—during and after the war would not merely be endangered but would be lost. The question may be raised whether the end justifies the means. And this soul-searching question as far as the Kladovo group goes should have been asked not only by Hacohen but also by Jewish leaders who were in the Zionist hierarchy much higher placed than even he was. But independent of the moral issue, the notion many Jews hold that the long-range foreign policy of any country is decided by favors done and not by what power politics demand was

---

*David Hacohen, *Et L'Saper (Time to Tell)* (Tel Aviv: Hozet Am Bred, 1976).
†Ibid., p. 162.
‡Author's italics.
§In the course of his cooperation with British intelligence, he flew from Palestine to Cairo, center of all British anti-Jewish intelligence intrigue. He flew from Alexandria to London, from London to Istanbul. He traveled on the famous Orient Express from Bucharest to London, etc. He was, when required, equipped with a British passport and traveled as a British courier.

of course entirely naïve. It was a remnant of two thousand years of ghetto tradition during which the Jews could survive only by favors and were far removed from international politics. After the war, the British continued their policy of trying to prevent a Jewish majority in Palestine. They kept the doors of that country barred to the wretched skeletons who had miraculously survived Auschwitz, Bergen-Belsen, and other slaughterhouse complexes—places where the few remaining Jews had left their families and which many of them would never have seen in the first place had not Britain kept those hunted ones locked up on the continent.

Hacohen gives a detailed account of his role in the Kladovo tragedy—as he saw it. He also makes it clear that *the* top men in the Jewish leadership cooperated. Incredibly enough, Hacohen reports that Dr. Chaim Weizmann himself, then the president of the World Zionist Organization and up until his death the first president of the State of Israel, knew of the British plan regarding the British use of the "refugee" ship and finally became actively involved in trying to bring those Jews in line who refused to hand the *Darien*—so desperately needed for rescue—over to the British for their intelligence plot.*

Hacohen reports about his talks in Bucharest with a high-ranking British intelligence man and writes that he learned from him some details of the assignment:

> . . . and it was decided that I leave Bucharest and go to London on the Orient Express, a trip of two days on the train and we made that trip.
>
> *With further consultation in London with Ben-Gurion and Moshe Sharett and later with Dr. Weizmann it was decided that we will agree to this request without any further hesitation. It was decided that we would cooperate with the British with all the possibilities that we had.†*

One may ask how did Hacohen, how did the most respected Jewish leaders, become so involved with British intelligence that they could be used by them as their tools in the *Darien*-Kladovo intelligence plot. It all started relatively innocently enough. They were just no match for the old hands of the "Special Department,"

---

*Hacohen, op cit., pp. 163, 164.
†Ibid., pp. 136, 137. (Author's italics.)

and the Jewish leaders' desire to please the British and to establish valuable "connections" was exploited by the British to the hilt.

With the full knowledge of Mr. Shertok (Sharett) and more or less as a representative of the Jewish establishment, Hacohen had flown to London shortly before the outbreak of the war and had offered unconditionally to the British intelligence for the upcoming fight with Nazi Germany, the cooperation of the Zionist organization and its numerous members in more than a dozen European countries. This was done at a time when for many months the British intelligence service had been conducting its war against the Jews who tried to escape from the Nazis; when for many months the British Navy, the British diplomatic corps, and the British forces in Palestine had been hunting the Jews who tried to save their lives by fleeing to the country which Britain in the Balfour Declaration and subsequently again in the Mandate had promised them. No specific promises were made by Britain in return for that offer. Hacohen and those who sent him just maintained a hope of ingratiating themselves and of establishing valuable "connections," which in a vague way would help the Jews of Europe and which would be of value for the time after the war. Poorly prepared for the war, Britain was certainly in a squeeze, but according to Hacohen, who offered the help of thousands of spies all over Europe, no demand was made that in return Britain should relent in its war against the refugees. Even if Palestine was too hot a subject, Britain could have certainly at least opened for a temporary haven the gates of one of its numerous colonies and could have influenced some of its dominions to do likewise, such as then underpopulated places like Australia, South Africa, and Canada.

But instead the British accepted Hacohen's offer, and Hacohen himself reports how he supplied a Sir Charles Taggert of British intelligence with "information about Jewish Youth movements," about our Betar as well as about the Hashomer Hazair and Hechaluz,* the Zionist Socialist groups which were right then preparing the large transport that became known as the Kladovo group.

Of all this the hapless people on their ships in Kladovo had no inkling whatsoever. Month after month, they waited in vain for the ship which was not to come; the ship which, if everything worked according to the British-Hacohen plan, supported by Sharett and

*Ibid., p. 136.

Weizmann, would blow up before it could reach them. The Association of Yugoslav Jewish Communities also knew nothing of the game that was being played nor did the members of the Mossad, as they were not informed of the deal with the British until the very last moment. Hacohen thus had kept his own people in the dark.

Reports published later blamed the lack of transit visas for causing the failure of the flight of the 1,004. But if in October 1939, when the group came down from Vienna, a seagoing ship had been waiting, as they and the Yugoslav Jews had been told it would be, no transit visas would have been required, as the Danube was an international waterway, and not yet frozen. Thus, in winter, when the river was frozen, transit visas were needed, but not in October when the original 1,002 arrived, nor were such visas needed in the spring of 1940, after the ice had melted.

May 1940 saw the group still on their riverboats, but in that month their lot was improved somewhat; they were at least permitted to get off the boats in large numbers. However, soon another catastrophe was to befall them. One day they learned that they would leave Kladovo, but not to proceed closer to their goal. They had to go backward, close to three hundred miles in the direction of Germany instead of Palestine, to a city called Šabac, a place not located on the Danube River but on one of its tributaries, the Sava. The reason given by the Yugoslav authorities for this order was that Germans who were to be settled, at least temporarily, in nearby Prahovo, would object to this proximity of Germans and Jews.

Šabac, at least, was much larger than Kladovo. Life there was easier than on the ships. The city had a small Jewish community, and Mr. Gedalja, the Association's representative, fully supported by his organization in Belgrade, cared for the pioneers as if they were his own children. But for the people, temporary comfort was of little concern. They saw whatever was done to ease their lot as merely a tiny part of a fool's paradise. On the border, now so much nearer than in Kladovo, stood the German panzers. The Nazi monster was still digesting its latest conquest. And Hitler was promising his hysterically jubilant masses more victories. There was only one direction in which he could turn. It was not England. He had missed his chance there when he hesitated after the catastrophic defeat of the French and British forces in France, when the British had to leave all their equipment behind on the beaches at Dunkirk.

To the south was Mussolini's Italy. The only direction in which the Nazis could attack was southeast: Yugoslavia and the Balkans.

In was now late summer of 1940; more than three hundred days and nights of frustration and sleeplessness had elapsed since the 1,002 full of hope and youthful enthusiasm had left Vienna and had begun moving down the Danube. No shipwrecked person on a remote island could have wished more intensely for a ship to show up than every one of these stranded ones did. Letters went out by the hundreds, daily phone calls were made to Belgrade in an effort to mobilize Jewish leadership, particularly the Jewish Agency. But for some reason, not understandable to those in Šabac, no ship was made available. Always some new unexpected difficulty popped up—just for them.

And fall came again. Soon it would be a year since their voyage had been stopped in Prahovo. Soon the Danube would freeze for the second winter, while the Germans became more and more menacing and news about mass deportations and mass open-air killings became known. Many times a ship was promised, including visas and whatever appeared necessary. Many times an imminent departure appeared assured. But somehow it just never worked out.

Bitter disappointment with the information received from the Mossad developed, although the Mossad people in the field—for a long time in the dark themselves about the deal their superiors had struck with British intelligence—worked hard and passionately to get the Kladovo escapees out.

Those in the Kladovo group did not know that the British had to do their very best to keep the Kladovo people pinned down in Yugoslavia. Fighting in the west had ended. A second front, with the United States still out of the war, was far, far in the future. If the ship blocked the Danube too early, the Germans would have enough time to clear the passage before new fighting erupted and before they really needed the Rumanian oil and food badly. The British needed the people in Kladovo to have the pretext of a ship going up to call for them. And in order to do the utmost damage to the German transportation system, they needed them at the strategic moment when the anticipated major flare-up would take place in the Balkans.

The British went about this business in a manner worthy of the best past exploits of their own then-famous intelligence service.

While diplomatic interventions with the various Balkan governments were to keep the Kladovo people stranded in Yugoslavia, their intelligence service purchased through David Hacohen the only ship the Mossad owned. Never before had illegal Aliya owned any ship. Charter was the only way to get hold of a ship for our smuggling and blockade breaking purposes. Thus, one was always at the mercy of the shipowners who, as the war began and progressed, had many offers for well-paid, legal uses for their ships. By a stroke of luck, the Mossad succeeded in purchasing a ship which now would be their own. Or so they believed. This ship, the *Darien II*, originally a salvage vessel, was now being reconverted in the Piraeus for use as an illegal immigrants transport ship. Mr. Hacohen writes in his biography, however, that the *Darien II* was still anchored in that Greek port "without any use."* This was at a time when every hour and certainly every day could decide the lives of many hundreds. He further maintains that the Mossad sold the ship because they needed the ridiculously low sum of 15,000 pounds—the price for which he sold the *Darien II* to the British. He asserts that he received the okay from other Zionist leaders, including Mr. Eliahu Golomb, the commander of the Haganah and also a member of the Zionist executive council. Hacohen claims that the latter even pressured him into selling the *Darien II* to British intelligence. It is tragic to read in Hacohen's report how, while the cry "Save us, send us a ship!" went out from a dozen places in Eastern Europe, agents of the British intelligence inspected the *Darien II*, the hope of thousands, found her suitable for their sabotage plan, and purchased her. And all this was done without the knowledge of the Mossad members who were on the firing line. Kept in the dark, they made arrangements for the rescue of the Kladovo people and made bona-fide promises which they could not keep.

Ruth Klueger, one of the hardest workers in the Mossad, describes† how the *Darien II*, because she was small enough to go up the Danube, was to rescue "the 1,100 refugees stranded at Kladovo" and how amazed she was that the conversion in the Piraeus from a salvage vessel to an illegal immigrants ship could be obtained without any bribing of Greek officials. There was, of

*Ibid., p. 162.
†Ruth Klueger, *The Last Escape* (New York: Doubleday, 1973), p. 372.

course, a party more powerful than the Mossad which was interested in such a conversion, but this was unknown to those in the field.

For the British everything went smoothly. Thousands of tons of scrap iron, mainly old pipes and barrels, were bought and filled with explosives. All this had to be done in utmost secrecy in order not to arouse German suspicions.

It might seem odd, but the metal was being gathered and "filled" in Palestine. British intelligence was aware that in Palestine German spies might be right in British government ranks, such as Arabs who were either pro-German or merely spying for money— or both.* Yet, it was decided to launch the operation from Palestine. We feel that the order from the top, the Foreign and Colonial ministries, to smother illegal immigration at the point of origin might well have played a part in the decision to involve Palestine and with it the Jews as deeply as possible in the sabotage under way. Whether the plot succeeded and the ship exploded as planned, or whether it failed because it was prematurely discovered or due to some other cause, if the Germans found out that the metal and the explosives had come from Palestine, they would still have another reason for a super-*Kristallnacht*. However, we found no indication that the Zionist leaders protested that the sabotage material was being purchased in Palestine nor that they suggested Malta instead, Cyprus, or some other British colony.

For the time being, however, involvement of Palestine had to be covered up. Businessmen actually in the scrap-metal trade in Palestine and dealing with Greece were found in Athens. The metal purchased in Palestine was officially exported to Greece. Merchants who were trading with Hungary in scrap metal and who had shipped metal via the Danube in the past were located so that the papers to be made out for the "goods" would appear as inconspicuous as possible. Large sums of money and months of carefully planned and precisely executed preparations went into all that.

Just as things were going very well for their big coup, however, the British encountered to their surprise an obstacle at an essential juncture where they had believed that everything had been taken care of. Because Hacohen had made the deal regarding the *Darien II*, and other Zionist leaders knew about it, the British assumed that they had the Jews in their pocket. Unexpectedly, however, members

---

*Hacohen, op. cit., p. 143, 144.

of the Mossad, those who were on the spot in Rumania, Greece, Turkey, and Bulgaria doing the actual work, did not want to fall in line. The rescue work was for them as it was for us: not something to be regarded in the abstract; it was personally experienced human action and interaction. The refugees meant to all of us working on the "firing line" not numbers or lists of names but faces and tragedies of which we knew many details.

To break the news to the lower echelons that the *Darien II* had to be surrendered to British intelligence, Hacohen used a certain Yehuda Arazi. He is described by Ruth Klueger as a man of many faces, a person who "changed his mood and mien like a chameleon."* Like Hacohen, Arazi had undoubtedly convinced himself that what he as doing was in the long run beneficial for the Jews.†

When Arazi brought the order to the Mossad line workers to hand the ship over to British intelligence, they were aghast. Arazi did not appear to be moved by the argument that the *Darien II* had been definitely promised to Sime Spitzer for his Kladovo people. In response to this argument, he cited the major advantages which would, it was hoped, accrue if the Jews of Palestine showed the British how fully they were ready to cooperate with them in the present war.

Frustrated and pained, Mrs. Klueger yelled at Arazi that the mission of the refugee ships was to rescue the survivors of Hitler's persecution and not to help in some intelligence plot. She reminded Arazi that those engaged in rescue work were working against the British and not for them. As correct as this statement of hers was, it was incomplete. It was not that we all worked against the British but that they worked against us. Arazi was told that if he and his partners in British intelligence wanted to blow up a ship in the Danube, they should do it with some other one, not with one of the ships used by the Mossad. Ruth Klueger also pointed out that there must have been some faulty reasoning somewhere: it could not really have been that the British in a war against Hitler needed any proof that the Jews were not on Hitler's side! But Arazi stressed that the Jews of Palestine would have to show how much they could do for the British cause.

Arazi's arguments did not convince Mrs. Klueger nor the

---

*Klueger, op. cit., p. 375.
†After the war, after it had become patently obvious how he and how the "cooperating" Jews altogether had been used by the British, Arazi became a fervent and most imaginative underground fighter for free Jewish immigration to Palestine.

other members of the Mossad whom she contacted. To the contrary, she recounts that in a telephone conversation the same night she confirmed to Sime Spitzer in Belgrade that the *Darien II* was to take all the escapees in the Kladovo group.

The British plan seemed at least for the moment to be in trouble. But for David Hacohen, the members of the Mossad were small fry whom he intended to handle with orders from high up. Unfortunately, his hopes were, as it turned out, not unrealistic.

In the meantime, the original Kladovo people had increased in number to 1,080—others had found their way individually to that group and more children had been born. It was more than a year since the *Uranus* had left Nazi Vienna with the jubilant group aboard, almost half a year since they had to trek back closer to the German border, to Šabac. On behalf of the utterly despairing ones, Spitzer shouted many accusing words at the organizers over the telephone. He had written letters charging the Mossad that it was not keeping its promises, that the promised ship, for reasons that were incomprehensible to him, was delayed again and again.

The last annual report of the Association of Yugoslav Jewish Communities, stating the situation at the end of December 1940—approximately thirteen weeks before the German invasion of Yugoslavia—describes the last attempt of the Kladovo people to make it to the sea and the subsequent hopelessness when after all the delays and more delays this last attempt failed: the Association had finally established the fact that by early November 1940, the *Darien II* was already in Istanbul, and they had by then obtained a definitive promise from the Yugoslav ministries of the interior and of foreign affairs, that the ministries themselves would take care of "the undisturbed voyage on the Danube and the transfer in Sulina."

The ship seemed ready, and the voyage down the Danube and the transfer seemed assured when, to the utter surprise of the Jews in Yugoslavia, a new problem arose. This time the Yugoslav Shipping Company, which had until then been most cooperative, created the obstacle, at the urging, we assume, of British intelligence.

The Association reports:

When the ship arrived in Sulina, suddenly new difficulties arose with the Yugoslav Shipping Company, the only one which could be considered to make this trip. Suddenly the company raised its material demands so that we were unable to fulfill them. We had to negotiate with the help and pressure of the Prime Minister and this way we forced the company to agree to conditions which were bearable.

Departure was scheduled for December 2nd. The ships had arrived in Šabac. The boarding began. Suddenly the crushing decision arrived that the ships were not permitted to make this trip.

The Shipping Company had filed a new statement with the prime minister in which it made demands on him personally which he simply could not grant. His position shortly before the German invasion and with part of the population favoring separatism for various regions of Yugoslavia was already shaky. He had in addition done more for the refugees by that time than he could have done without being considered by the Germans a friend of the Jews. Now the Shipping Company demanded from the prime minister a written order to proceed with the voyage for the Jews. The company pointed out that the two riverboats which were to bring them to Sulina cost 15 million dinars and that if the weather changed, the ships could be frozen until the following spring.

The prime minister understood the implicit threat. If the anticipated German invasion found the two ships not in Yugoslavia but stuck in the ice somewhere farther down the Danube, he would appear to have sabotaged the German need for bottoms. Of course, he did not give a written order because it was clear that such an order was intended for use as possible future evidence against him. And the 1,080 who had—finally, finally—seen themselves on their way, had to disembark.

The Association's report continues:

It was a hard task for our President, Mr. Pops, and for Mr. Spitzer to apprise the severely tried humans of the new situation and to provide solace and new hope after hope had just collapsed.

It was heartrending to see how woefully the people pulled their last meager possessions back into their modest domiciles. How much longer would they have to wait for the so-long-yearned-for departure.

This was December 2, and it was not the last time that the Kladovo people saw themselves fooled in the most cruel way, by fate or incompetence or some unknown element.

The official report of the Association goes on:

... Tuesday, December 10th, 1940, Mr. Solomonides, President of the Jewish Community of Braila, informed us by phone that the same afternoon a Rumanian object was leaving for Prahovo and would arrive there in the night from Tuesday to Wednesday.

Prahovo was the last Yugoslav major Danube port, and the 1,080 were to be brought from Šabac to Prahovo by train and from there by the "object" down the Danube to transfer to the *Darien II.* But it was not to be. The report continues:

Because all preparations had been discussed and Solomonides insisted that our wards must arrive in Prahovo on Thursday, December 12th, we tried to organize the voyage from Sabac to Prahovo for Thursday.

The Yugoslav railroads could not provide a special train on such short notice:

A special train for Friday was ordered from the Directorate of Yugoslav Federal Railroads ... Wednesday, December 11th, our employee came to Prahovo and informed us that the expected object (which should have come in during the preceding night) had not arrived by 17 hours. Shortly afterward, a telegram arrived from Solomonides in which he advised us that the whole program was postponed by 24 hours. Immediately all steps had to be taken to cancel the special train and to order it anew for the following day, Saturday the 15th.

On Thursday, we received a new dispatch: the object would definitely arrive that evening.

As everything had been arranged in Belgrade, Mr. Spitzer traveled Thursday the night through to Šabac. And Friday was a day of helter-skelter packing.

Saturday morning a new message arrived: today the objects would absolutely, certainly be in Prahovo.

And again they did not come ... Tuesday (December 17th) at 10:20 our employee reported that the object had finally arrived.

Alarm in all directions. By noon the special train had been assured and all details arranged. Thursday morning (December 19th) departure from Šabac! On Tuesday still, by 3:00 P.M., 4 train cars, each 15 tons, full of food supplies were ready. Our people loaded until 3:00 A.M. and at 7:00 P.M., the railroad cars rolled out.

But it was not to be. One obstacle after another had been placed in the way of the departure. The voyage from Šabac first scheduled for December 2, which was rather a late date anyhow because of the danger of ice on the Danube, had to be postponed again and again. Now, seventeen critical days later, it was too late. There were reports that ice had started to form at a few places along the Danube, and the captain of the riverboat in Prahovo received orders to return immediately.

> Again it was our Mr. Spitzer who had the difficult task to explain to the unhappy people what had happened. This time it was already December 20th. . . .

It was during these crucial weeks described in the annual report of the Association, between December 2 and December 20, while the Jews of the Kladovo group made their last attempts to break out of the trap in which they were caught, that Hacohen applied the greatest pressure against those members of the Mossad who were not ready to fall in line. He told them that Shertok himself had issued this order because Shertok felt carrying out the plan was extremely important for future Zionist-British relations.* A main argument used by Hacohen was that if the British saw that our future foreign minister was not able to push through an order of his, how could they believe that the Jews would be capable of having a state of their own after the war.

But none of the refugees, shattered by their new defeat and trotting back to their hated quarters, had any idea of the fact that they were pawns in an intrigue which was rapidly moving toward a tragic conclusion.

The Association's report on the fate of the Kladovo people closes with a statement which indicates that the BBC in publicizing the plight of the illegal immigrants did a good job in discouraging rescue attempts and in demoralizing at least some into apathy.

> Whether, after the last experiences and the unequivocal decision of the British to deport people, these odysseys serve any purpose has first to be well considered. Just to travel in order to travel and to

---

*Klueger, op. cit., p. 456.

waste Jewish money in order to land in St. Mauritius or some other colony in the Indian Ocean can not be the purpose of all that work. In such cases it seems better that the people are given the opportunity to wait here for a reunion with their beloved ones. Altogether we want to see what the conditions in the spring will be . . .

This is the next to the last official report regarding the fate of the Kladovo people.

In the last days of March, when German troops started massing on the border, Bata Gedalja was called up to serve in the Yugoslav army.

On April 9, 1941, the German tanks smashed across the Yugoslav border and the Luftwaffe laid Belgrade and the country's other larger cities to ruin.

The Yugoslav Jewish community, which could not have been more concerned and helpful, had little political foresight, even after half a dozen countries had been swallowed up by the Nazis. The Association did not realize that even "St. Mauritius or some other colony in the Indian Ocean" would have constituted a lifesaving haven.

Just before the German invasion, altogether 185 of the Kladovo people—130 children, 30 young girls, and 25 accompanying adults—did receive legal entrance permits to Palestine and were saved literally in the very last moment.

Of the remaining 915, every single one was butchered.

The next official report about the fate of the Kladovo group after the above-cited annual report of the Association is a statement by Milorad Mica Jelesić, a Serbian farmer who took part in the massacre and who, on February 20, 1945, made the following deposition:

No: 849/45/80/66

DEPOSITION

Taken on February 20, 1945 at the County Investigation Office of the Serbian State Commission for War Crimes in Šabac. Present, properly summoned is Mr. Milorad Jelesić, farmer, from Majur, 40 years old. After having been reminded to speak the truth and of the consequences of false testimony, he makes the following statement: In the month of October 1941, when the German "Chastising Expedition" moved through the Macva, I followed the German orders to report with all adult farmers in order to receive an identity card. At that occasion, I was locked up in barracks in the Šabac camp. Prior to Mioldjan [holiday] I volunteered for work because there was a call for volunteers and I hoped that was to get a little out of the camp. Now a group of about 400 was led to Klenak and from there by train to Sremska Mitrovica . . .

In Sr. Mitrovica we remained for three days without food in a field in the railroad cars which had brought us there. On the fourth day one started to separate certain work details, but when those people returned from their work in the evening, they were not permitted to be with us. On Mioldjan an Orthodox church holiday of Saint Michael, on October 12, according to the Orthodox pravoslavic calendar on October 25, I myself was brought in a group of 40, to Macvanski Mitrovica and from there to Zasavica. On the way we expected to be shot. Our fear increased when we were led to a ditch which was about 200 meters long, 2.50 meters wide and 2.50 meters deep. Later on I learned that this ditch had been dug by the people who had been taken out from the railroad cars the previous days and had been led to work. We were driven to the Sava River. About 200–300 meters away from its bank we were ordered to sit down. But everything was under water there and full of puddles so that we begged we should not be tortured so long and should be killed right away . . . A German who spoke Serbian told us that they did not want to kill us, that we were workmen.

At that point I noticed that the Germans at a distance of about 3–4 meters from the ditch were driving about 50–70 stakes into the ground. The stakes were about 50–60 cm high and approximately 10 cm in diameter. Having this done, they led us to within 50–60 meters of the ditch. At that moment came a company of Germans and all ate. The food was brought to the Germans to that place.

After that meal a group of about 50 people in civilian clothes was marched in from behind a cornfield from the direction of Mitrovica, and I saw they were Jews. Each one of those brought in that way had to stand at one of the stakes which had been driven into the ground and which were about 1–2 meters apart. They had to stand in such a way that each had the stake between his legs and that they were facing the ditch.

After this had been completed the company was arranged in such a formation that each two soldiers were aiming at one Jew. The soldiers were at most 10 meters away from the Jews. We were about 50 meters behind the soldiers.

Now four German soldiers carrying a spread-out blanket went with it to every Jew and the Jew threw something into the blanket, probably money and other valuables. When this too had been done, an officer shouted a command and the Germans aimed at the neck, always two upon one Jew.

Immediately after we were ordered to double up ["on the double"] to the ditch and to throw the murdered people into the ditch. After that the Germans ordered us to examine their [the Jews'] pockets and take out any valuables, like money or gold. We were also ordered to pull any rings off the fingers. Because many of the rings could not be pulled off, the Germans gave me a pair of pliers with which I cut the rings off which I gave them afterward. Also, before we threw the victims into the ditch I saw how the Germans tore out golden teeth from the murdered ones. Because in some cases they did not succeed doing so, they trampled the teeth out by kicking with their boots. When we had completed with the first party of killed ones, we moved back at the double to behind the marksmen, and a second party was marched in which had been waiting behind the cornfield. The procedure with that one was in every way the same. I cannot recall how many parties were shot that day, but mostly there was one person to each stake.

Late in the evening we were brought back and all 40 of us were locked into a railroad car. Next day the entire group of 40 was brought back to Zasavica to the same location and the shootings began like on the day before. On the first day only Jews were shot. On the second day, however, there were more of our gypsies than Jews. During the whole period of shooting, the Germans took pictures of various moments, like: victims before the shooting, how they are marching to the stakes, the bodies lying next to the stakes, us, carrying the bodies into the ditch, the lineup of the marksmen and other moments.

I figured that in those two days at least 1,200 civilians were shot. The ditch was about 200 meters long and crammed full with the exception that at one end there was a hole about 5 meters long and 1.50 meters deep into which bags and other items were thrown. After the first day we left the ditch open. When we arrived the day after we found some dogs who had eaten part of some bodies and had carried away some parts. A German shot one dog and said, pointing at the ditch: "These too are dogs." Then pointing at the dead dog he said: "And this one is their brother."

Signed
MILORAD JELESIĆ

After the war, the bodies were exhumed, a passport was found on each of them, and the Yugoslav authorities in cooperation with the Association of Yugoslav Jews in Palestine, made a list of those slaughtered in the massacre. The list is now part of the archives of Yad Vashem in Jerusalem, the Israeli agency which is both a memorial for the 6 million Jews murdered in the Holocaust and a research institution dealing with all aspects of that shameful part of twentieth-century history.

Sime Spitzer was not among those killed in the massacre described by Milorad Jelesić. He was not murdered by semiliterate peasants in a field but "first class," in an automobile, by a Gestapo officer. The officer's name is known: it is Krieger. I found no record showing that Krieger was tried anywhere.

Though data regarding the scandalous outrage of the Kladovo massacre and what led to it are to be found in various records, the information is dispersed. Without having been pulled together the data have rested in various archives, under different headings—and in the minds of people who were not interested in publicity for the Kladovo scandal. Neither the Jews nor the British nor the Nazis yearned to have all the facts revealed which led to the slaughter.

Years after the war a claim was published that the Mossad, at the last moment, offered Spitzer the chance to bring the Kladovo people to Sulina with the help of Rumanian transit visas and that Spitzer refused to do so because this was supposedly too risky. It was even claimed that Spitzer refused to let the refugees make their own decision about whether they would, individually, make use of the alleged last-minute chance. We found no documentary evidence of such an offer, nor of any offer after the failure described in the December 31, 1940, report of the Association. Many doubt such a claim. Bata Gedalja, now in Jerusalem, thinks that such dictatorial behavior from Spitzer would not have been at all probable in view of his personality. He points to the fact that no record of any such offer exists, although the Association held official meetings every week or at least every two weeks.

And even if a last-minute offer had been made, we could well understand that, because of previous letdowns, the leaders of the Yugoslav Jewish community did not believe a word anymore which came to them from the original organizers of the transport. The conglomeration of obstacles, coupled with the accompanying British propaganda broadcasts, had done the job. This one illegal immigration action at least had been stopped at the source.

But for the British, the *Darien II* affair was not a success either. They had calculated everything in detail; the purchase of the ship, the gathering of the scrap iron, and the filling of it with explosives in Palestine, shipping all these "goods" first to Greece and from there as a new transaction via the Danube, supposedly to Hungary. They had seen to it that the conversion of the *Darien II* into a refugee ship encountered no difficulties in Athens, and they had procured all the necessary papers. They had not calculated on the refugees, however, because they expected no trouble from this quarter. The Jewish leadership, after all, was in on the plot. Because the British gave no thought to the escapees and the Mossad leaders were busy arguing in Istanbul, the refugees in Sulina took things into their own hands.

As soon as the *Darien II* laid anchor in Sulina, an event occurred which I had experienced several times before and could have predicted. The refugees who were standing on the pier stormed the ship and refused to leave it at any other place but Palestine. One hundred eighty had gotten on before the organizers and the police could stop them. And with these people on board, the whole explosion plan of course was off. Even if the British had tried to proceed and to blow up these 180 with the scrap iron, those who had escaped from the hands of Hitler and the Rumanian Iron Guard would have revolted had they seen the ship going back up the Danube instead of heading out to sea.

The British were furious. But they did not accept defeat. Those on board were Jews, after all, and the British had heavy—Jewish—ammunition to bring to this particular "front."

Unbelievably enough, their heaviest gun was Dr. Chaim Weizmann, president of the Jewish Agency.

Hacohen reports that from the moment he was told in Bucharest by British intelligence about the Balkan "assignment," they expected of him, he had discussed the British "request" not only with Sharett but also with Ben-Gurion, "and later with Dr. Weizmann" and that "without any further hesitation,"* these Jewish leaders had acceded to the British plan. Thus the British had Dr. Weizmann already involved on their side and they intended now to pressure him—and they did.

Dr. Weizmann was not only the almost undisputed leader of the Zionist movement. He was also a British subject who, as a Jewish leader, was eager to have the British favorably disposed toward the Jews.

But would he go along with the British and exercise pressure

*Hacohen, op. cit., p. 137.

himself to have the *Darien II* delivered "clean" to British intelligence?

As soon as problems over the conflict between the orders from above and the wishes of the Mossad members developed, Arazi was under definite orders from Hacohen to have the *Darien II* arrive at the Bosporus "clean." Under no circumstances were refugees to be on board, because the *Darien II* was by then actually owned by the British. When the intelligence services learned that there were close to "200 Jews" on board, Hacohen's associates in British intelligence in London blackmailed Dr. Weizmann. Hacohen reports that "friends" in the "top echelon" of the

> Special Department in London approached Dr. Weizmann and explained to him that not keeping this agreement between their people in Palestine and the Aliya Bet [illegal immigration] people, really showed that we do not deserve their trust; and responsibility for cancelling all cooperation would rest with us.*

Under this pressure, Dr. Weizmann sent a telegram to Shertok which read:

> DO NOT SPARE ANY EFFORT TO HAVE THE DARIEN COME OUT ABSOLUTELY CLEAN, EVERYTHING DEPENDS ON IT.†

Shertok, as Hacohen reports, answered without delay:

> WE ARE NOT SPARING ANY EFFORT TO GET THE DARIEN INTO A CONDITION WHICH IS ABSOLUTELY FAULTLESS. I AM CONVINCED THAT THE WHOLE THING WILL BE ARRANGED IN A SATISFACTORY WAY.‡

As unexpected as it may seem to learn that Dr. Weizmann sided in this matter with British intelligence and actively used his power to press for a success of the devilish British plan regarding the *Darien II*, we have to give credence to Hacohen's report. He was, after all, from long before the Kladovo disaster and after the war, closely associated with the top echelon of Zionist politics and a

*Ibid., p. 163.
†Ibid.
‡Ibid.

friend of those whose tragic involvement in the Kladovo catastrophe he reports. Hacohen published his autobiography only after much time had passed, years after the other prominent Jewish leaders named in *Time to Tell* had died. Whether one believes that he acted right under the circumstances or that he erred gravely, he was never described as irresponsible. Again and again, he was reelected as member of the Israeli Parliament where he served for twenty years. In his hometown, Haifa, he served for twenty-three years on the city council and was at times Haifa's deputy mayor. His last major contribution to Jewish life is his autobiography as it brings into focus for those able to assess the situation, the risk of trying to appease an unappeasable adversary, one whose policy is set, whether one does him "favors" or not.

Hacohen's report, specifically his and Arazi's role in pressuring the field workers of the Mossad, is largely corroborated by those whom he and Arazi tried to force into the handing over of the *Darien* to British intelligence for the described act of sabotage.

And as for Dr. Weizmann's role in all of this, we shall learn in the subsequent chapter from official British documents that the Kladovo affair was not the only one in which Dr. Weizmann functioned as a tool for the British. Another action he participated in against the interests of the refugees also had tragic consequences.

But despite Weizmann, Sharett, and Hacohen, the 180 from Rumania who had stormed on board the *Darien II* in Sulina did not budge. The British, desperate about the unexpected complication, now offered 100,000 pounds—half a million dollars—for a "clean" *Darien*, though they had purchased the ship from Hacohen for 15,000 pounds. Those on the ship did not know, of course, of this big game that was being played, but even ten times the amount offered would not have caused them to leave the ship. They knew that dead people do not need any money.

Now another similarly inhuman plot was devised with Hacohen's active participation: the refugees from Rumania, now on board the *Darien II*, would leave, thinking that they were going to Palestine, but would instead be put out on a Greek island, either Lemnos or Samothráki. From there the *Darien II* would return to Rumania as if it had already discharged its refugees in Palestine and would be ready for the planned sabotage purpose.

This plan, just as the intent to remove the refugees in Sulina from the ship, not only shows an utter disregard for the rights of the refugees to live but also demonstrates a total lack of knowledge of their psychology. Unless told that they were in Palestine and thus tricked into leaving the ship in Greece, no power on Earth would have been able to get them from the ship without killing each one of them first.

This latest plot was not just a vague plan. Concrete steps were taken to put it into effect. Although the invasion of Greece was imminent, Hacohen and two Britishers arranged for a meeting in the Greek Consulate in Istanbul where they obtained from the Greek authorities there the promise to permit the debarkation on Greek soil of the refugees from the *Darien II*. However, as luck would have it, before the okay for such an arrangement arrived from the Greek government in Athens, the German blitz had smashed into the Balkans, and under these circumstances, not even Hacohen wanted to go through with the plan which would have so obviously handed refugees over to the slaughterers.

The *Darien II* finally sailed with the refugees from Rumania to Varna in Bulgaria. There she was stormed once more by desperate Jews fleeing the Nazis, until the ship was crammed full. In Istanbul, she took on still more refugees and on March 19, 1941, she disembarked 878 men, women, and children in Palestine, all escapees from Hitler's plan for a "Final Solution" of the "Jewish Problem."

Another almost 900 saved.

But those of the Kladovo group for whom the *Darien II* had been destined were not among them.

---

chapter 5
SHIP AFTER SHIP

As the relentless manhunt in Nazi-held lands intensified, we could save only a very small percentage of those destined to be massacred, yet the small ships plying the Danube and the leaky crates stealthily plowing the waters of the Black Sea, the Marmara, and the Mediterranean had for us about the same meaning which the famous small craft of Dunkirk had for the British or the famous Paris taxis had for the French at the beginning of World War I. When the Germans invaded France and were marching on Paris, they engaged the French on the Marne in the great battle of that name. The French had not enough soldiers, not enough supplies, and, most important, not enough transportation. Thousands of Parisian taxi drivers, by shuttling back and forth with men and ammunition, helped to win the decisive battle. But our paddle-wheelers and creaking, coughing old freighters remained unsung heroes.

One group of 151 who had left Vienna by train on February 4, 1939, however, would have taken any such ship gladly. This group was referred to by us as, and laughingly called themselves, the "China group," because their final destination according to their visas was "China," and it seemed a joke to travel to China by train via the Balkan countries.

The group's leader, Emil Patlaschenko, kept a logbook of the China expedition's tortuous journey, although, for security reasons, the keeping of such logs was forbidden. He describes how after several delays en route, the group finally reached Constanţa, where they were temporarily housed in the same customs hall in which I had had my first encounter with the representative of Rumanian civil service bribery.

But the temporary stay in Constanţa was to become a much longer one than these hapless would-be voyagers first realized. Scarlet fever, then a dangerous, dreaded disease, broke out, and the contagion spread throughout the ranks of our group. If everyone could have come down with the disease at the same time, it would in the long run have made things easier. But the cases came in a trickle, and with each new case the stay of the entire group was prolonged by another six weeks—the incubation period. At one point Patlaschenko and his staff made a list of those in the group they felt would be of most value in building Palestine and who could withstand the physical and emotional frustrations of the final sea voyage in the hope that those at the top of the list could sail with another transport. But when the chance came and 25 were chosen to go on the *Gepo II,* just before sailing time one of the group came down with scarlet fever and all 25 of the "lucky ones" were sent back.

To boost morale among this group, we assigned Leo Guttenmacher, the most capable young man we had in Rumania, to our China project. He spent most of his time keeping the Rumanian authorities in good humor, straightening out the problems

Patlaschenko had with the increasingly unruly group, and maintaining contact with us in Bucharest.

Despite the moral support from Guttenmacher, the Constanţa Jewish community, and my visits, the distress of those in the China group heightened. The news of new pogroms on the continent and of war coming ever closer added to their mounting anxiety. It was particularly hard for them to have to sit by and watch as ship after ship left from the port, right before their eyes. They sadly watched as the *Astir,* the *Liesel,* and other ships sailed.

They also learned that the Revisionists had opened a new route from Marseilles and that the *Aghia Tzioni,* commanded by a Viennese known to most of them, Rico Schick, was on the way to Palestine. Hopes that Rico would come and pick them up were great, but proved in vain.

By the spring of 1939, other Zionist groups besides the Revisionists felt impelled to start organizing illegal transports, although the official Zionist policy remained firmly opposed to anything that would antagonize the British. Members of the He-Halutz and Hashomer Hazair Zionist-socialist youth organizations saw hundreds and thousands of Betarim leave for Palestine while their own members, following the promises and the dictates of the World Zionist Organization in London, were arrested and deported as they were waiting for the minute number of legal immigration entrance certificates. Following the pleading of their youth groups on the continent, some socialist Zionist leaders in Palestine, notable among them, Mr. Berl Katznelson, rebelled and began to follow in our footsteps. They too mounted an illegal immigration effort, and their ships in increasing numbers made their way down our proven Danube route and sailed from Rumanian ports.

Sunday, April 16, had started a particularly bad week for the China group. After a long pause, and when it had already been assumed that the scarlet fever epidemic had run its course, one more man was stricken with the disease. But there was even worse news than that for those who still had families in Germany or in German-occupied territories. That Sunday news accounts carried the following notice:

REICH HALTS JEWISH EMIGRATION AS WARTIME LABOR SHORTAGE LOOMS. Paris, April 14 (JTA)
The tense international situation has prompted the Nazi authorities to suddenly reverse the Jewish emigration policy. According to reli-

able information reaching Paris today . . . Jews are no longer given permission to leave the Reich, contrary to the previous policy of forcing Jews out of Germany, legally or illegally. . . .

This was Germany. Across the sea, another land greeted those who reached its shores, as it still does, with the words: "Give me your tired, your poor, your huddled masses yearning to breathe free." From that land of the "golden door," the following news item appeared just a few days after the above news from Germany:

> U.S. CONSULATES HALT ISSUANCE OF VISAS TODAY. REICH QUOTA FILLED. Paris, April 23. Issuance of visas to German and other refugees will be suspended by the American Consulate in Paris and Berlin, because the quota which ends June 30 is exhausted, . . . it was disclosed by the consulate here. . . . Consular authorities estimate that 30,000 applicants are now registered with the Paris consulate [alone] and new applicants of German origin will have to wait approximately six years for their turn to get visas. Applicants of Polish origin, even those who spent most of their life in Germany, will have to wait at least 50 years since the American Consulate in Paris cannot issue more than 15 visas monthly to those coming under the Polish quota.

Note that this halt in the issuance of visas referred to those privileged ones who had relatives or close friends in the United States who had supplied them with an "Affidavit of Support" guaranteeing that this would-be immigrant would not become a public charge. Those who had no relatives or friends in the United States were not even mentioned.

Today some Jewish leaders believe that the above announcement by the State Department was a trial balloon to see what the reaction of American Jewry would be. The reaction by American Jewish leaders was zero. No storm of indignation materialized, and within three days another shot was fired. It was the announcement not only that immigration to the United States was "temporarily suspended" (waiting time 6–50 years) but that issuance of *visitor's visas,* which was not under the vicious, antiquated quota system, was also being halted. And let us take note, it was not halted for all bearers of German passports, only for German Jews. Nazis were still allowed to visit the United States, but Jews with German passports were not. It sounds unbelievable today—but such was the U.S. State Department's decision, and America's Jewish leaders simply swallowed it. No mass demonstration was called against that inhuman, brutal, discriminatory decision, when on June 27, the media correctly reported:

U.S. HALTS ISSUANCE OF VISITOR'S VISAS TO REICH JEWS.

Of the world's numerous newspapers which carried the story, a few also ran simultaneously a small notice which referred to what I would call the Unknown Jewish Immigrant:

Jerusalem, April 23. The unidentified body of a German Jew was washed ashore today in the vicinity of Ashkelon. He had apparently been drowned while landing.

If this man had been a Nazi, he could have entered the United States as a visitor without formal difficulty.

After Czechoslovakia was handed over to Hitler, he began demanding Danzig, parts of Poland, and some of the British colonies in Africa. At this point, the British king and queen decided to visit the United States to gain much-needed support. To awaken American Jewry to British perfidy and to counteract the totally naïve "advice" of such American Jewish leaders as Rabbi Lazaron of Baltimore,* the Jabotinsky movement set about organizing a large-scale demonstration to be carried out in the United States by American Jews to coincide with the impending royal visit. Hearing of the plan, the British were quick to react. The British Embassy in Bucharest called me in and offered the following deal: they would "close their eyes" to the landing of our next three ships (representing about 2,500 people) if we would call off the American demonstration. I contacted Jabotinsky about the offer, but before we could even formulate a reply, I was informed that the offer had been withdrawn. I was puzzled until I saw the following news dispatch from New York:

ZIONIST COMMITTEE HITS CALL FOR DEMONSTRATION ON KING'S ARRIVAL. New York, June 1 (JTA). The National Emergency

---

*In a letter to the *New York Times* on May 29, 1939, Rabbi Lazaron exhorted Jews "not [to] spend time and substance in fighting a situation which is now irretrievable" and "to build economically" in Palestine! How many more lives would have been lost had we followed this advice!

Committee for Palestine, in a statement today, voiced "emphatic disapproval" of ... circulars calling for a demonstration against Britain's Palestine policy when King George and Queen Elizabeth arrive in the United States. "Resistance to the White Paper bears no relation whatever to the visit of the royal heads of Great Britain," the statement said.

I kept no record of the demonstration that was finally held, but most American Jews followed the ill-conceived advice of their leaders and did not demonstrate.

Thus encouraged by official Jewish attitude, British propaganda in the United States against the mass rescue action went on the offensive. On July 22 a confidential note was sent to all British consuls in the United States to help win support for the British point of view. The cynicism of that note (Colonial Office note: Foreign Office papers 371/24091) can hardly be topped: "The idea is fostered by Jewish circles that they are justified in trying to break the law by virtue of some super-legal morality, and in extenuation they cite the persecutions in Greater Germany, and the desperate plight in which many European Jews now find themselves. But in this view they, like many other lawbreakers, are thinking only of themselves, and fail to realise that what they are doing is fundamentally anti-social—as anti-social as the German persecution of which they complain."

The beleaguered China group finally saw an end, late in May, to their main problem—the scarlet fever subsided. By now, however, they had another serious obstacle before them. They had no money at all left with which to pay for a ship out. The situation was saved by the Jews on the island of Rhodes. I had contacted the Jewish community on Rhodes, and after several trips and arrangements, I succeeded in developing a plan whereby a contingent of the Jews on Rhodes would travel to Palestine by paying their own fare plus enough extra to finance the fares of the China group. On June 24, 1939, not an entire month after Rabbi Lazaron had sent his message of no hope to the *New York Times*, the China group set sail; after picking up those at Rhodes, they numbered altogether 801 immigrants (151 from the China group, 351 from Rhodes, and the remaining from various parts of Europe) aboard the S.S. *Rim*.

Their long voyage was not to be over, however. On July 3, at about three-thirty P.M., the *Rim* went down in a blaze near an uninhabited rock, probably the victim of arson by the crew. Fortunately all aboard managed to scramble onto the rock, and a short time later, they were all picked up by a passing Italian ship, the *Fiume.*

A ticklish situation thus developed as the Italians were Hitler's allies and did not know what to do with all these stranded Jewish escapees of Hitler's extermination campaign. I was arrested by the Italian authorities on Rhodes, and then released on the condition that I not leave the island. I was told to have all foreign Jews out in two weeks or I would be returned to jail. Keeping me on the island made it very difficult for me to organize any new transport; the problem seemed especially staggering because all my phone calls and cables had to be explained to the police. I called a friend in London, Mrs. Lola Bernstein, to come to our aid. She was Viennese, but as she had married a British citizen, she had a British passport that allowed her to travel freely throughout the Balkans and to keep our contacts open.

On August 10, only five weeks after the fire and shipwreck of the *Rim,* the entire group plus 8 more from Rhodes, boarded the *Aghios Nikolaos,* and one of the three smaller ships which the *Aghios Nikolaos* had in tow, and sailed off toward Palestine.

Unbelievable as it may seem, major Jewish organizations— though probably with the best of intentions—helped Britain to keep Jewish survivors from escaping to Palestine. In 1974, when enough time had lapsed so that the files of the British Foreign Office had become available, I found massive documentary evidence of this. The following correspondence about an earlier voyage of the *Aghios Nikolaos* is self-explanatory.*

From: Arthur Lourie,†
        The Jewish Agency for Palestine
        77, Great Russell Street,
        London W.C. 1.

To: Sir Herbert Emerson
        2, Knole Paddock,
        Sevenoaks

*All documents re: correspondence between Mr. Arthur Lourie of the Jewish Agency for Palestine, Sir Herbert Emerson, and the British Foreign and Colonial Office are from British Foreign Office File: 371/24091/2829.
†Mr. Lourie was then, according to the *Encyclopedia Judaica,* political secretary of the Jewish Agency in London under Chaim Weizmann.

26th May 1939

DEAR SIR HERBERT:

On looking through the correspondence regarding the
refugees on board the *Aghios Nikolaos* and the *Astir* totaling
1448 persons in all, I find that the 700 Jews on board the
Aghios Nikolaos are described as Czechoslovaks, and that they
were organised in Bruenn. I shall try to communicate with the
Jewish community of Salonica with a view to ascertaining the
origin of the other refugees and shall get in touch with you at
once as soon as I have any information.

Yours sincerely,

ARTHUR LOURIE

The eager Mr. Lourie had this one followed by another:

From: A. Lourie

To: Sir Herbert Emerson,
        High Commissioner for Refugees
        16, Northumberland Avenue,
        London, W.C. 2.

4th June 1939

DEAR SIR HERBERT,

With further reference to the two boats the *Astir* and the
Aghios Nikolaos I am now informed from Greece that the
former contains refugees from Danzig, the latter, as I
indicated in my previous letter, was a transport organised in
Czechoslovakia.

Yours sincerely,

A. LOURIE

No time was lost to get this valuable information from the
Jewish community of Salonica, into the hands of the Foreign and
the Colonial offices. The following communication dated June 5
from Sir H. Emerson was recorded in the British Foreign Office, as
received from another unwitting Jewish community, that of

Constanţa, and on June 7, it was relayed with the Number 8840-34 as follows:

F.O. 371 24091		W 8849
2829		34
1939	REFUGEES	7 Jun 1939

Registry W 8849/1369/48 number	*Illegal immigration into Palestine of Jewish refugees.*
From Sir H. Emerson, High Commissioner for Refugees under Protection of League of Nations. 80850 5th June 1939 7th June 1939	Transmits copies of letters dated (A) 26th May and (B) 4th June from Mr. Arthur Lourie giving information regarding refugees from Danzig on board s.s. [sic] "Astir" and from Czecho-Slovakia on s.s. [sic] "Aghios Nikolaos"
Refugees	
Last Paper.	
(W8830)	(Copy of (3) sent to Mr. Downie Colonial Office).
	(Signed) M. REILLY 9/6 (signature illegible) 9/vi

But such covert actions by the British were not all. They were complemented by the passivity of others who were "on our side."

As the pathetic "convoy" was making its way toward Palestine, the *Aghios Nikolaos* in the lead like a mother duck followed by three successively smaller boats, the immigrants on board who had brought along their crystal sets heard the following news item from Geneva:

In preparation for the World Zionist Congress meeting here, the powerful U.S. delegation adopted a program suggested by Dr. Goldman, President of the Zionist Organization of America, that the

Congress *not discuss proposals for illegal immigration,* but *first set up committees to study the advantages and disadvantages of these proposals.**

So: nothing at this Congress. The next one was not able to meet as scheduled two years later; it was able to meet only in 1946, 6 million dead Jews later. I wonder whether a committee is perhaps still somewhere studying the "proposals."

The Greek captain of the *Aghios Nikolaos* was, happily, not a committeeman. On August 20, after he had seen to the transfer of his passengers to the smaller ship, the captain was on his way back, steering his ship to her hideout in the Greek islands, while the newspapers in Palestine reported:

800 REFUGEES SEIZED IN THREE BOATS OFF PALESTINE COAST. Three vessels carrying 800 Jewish refugees were sighted Saturday morning off Netanyah and taken into custody by government forces. The vessels were a motor launch, a schooner, and a sailboat. The launch was beached by its crew and the other craft were escorted to Haifa.... Those taken to Haifa included 80 children and 50 women.... Later they were removed to Sarafand concentration camp.

Detained or not, they were home. Home after it all. And that's where they stayed. For good.

Of the other ships whose names belong in the history of free immigration to Palestine, there were three which we usually referred to as "the three *P*'s," because their names all started with that letter. They were the S.S. *Parita,* the S.S. *Patria,* and the S.S. *Pencho.* Contrary to the lack of publicity concerning what happened to the Kladovo people and the *Darien II,* the trials of the *Parita,* the *Patria,* and the *Pencho* gained much public attention. Yet the adventures and happenings associated with each of these three were entirely different.

Actually, there was at about the same time a fourth *P,* a ship with a very odd history.

While I was tied up on the Island of Rhodes, I learned in a telephone conversation with Bucharest that a travel agent there had chartered a small ship, the 232-ton S.S. *Mersin,* and was selling

*Author's italics.

spaces on it for illegal immigration into Palestine. To gain the confidence of those buying passage, he claimed that the entire undertaking was organized by me. Apparently he knew that I was far away and could not return any time soon. When my friends went to him to protest, he clinched the matter. He renamed the ship *Las Perlas*—the Perl people.

Although he demanded a multiple of what we were charging, he had, of course, no problem filling his tiny steamer to standing room. He loaded 370 refugees, and the *Las Perlas* steamed for Palestine.

The captain and the crew believed that there was a landing operation waiting for them and did not foresee any difficulties. After all, had they not seen other ships of ours go and come back to load more refugees? The *Las Perlas* headed for Netanyah, our most often used landing site, and expected to find there one or two small landing ships to which the passengers would be transferred.

The British had no doubt that the *Las Perlas* was one of our ships and considered it brazen provocation that—for the first time—we had renamed a ship in a way which openly indicated its function. They lay in wait for her. Her captain, completely unfamiliar with the experiences we had had, did not use any of our usual means of evasion, e.g., zigzagging in the area and around the Greek isles, heading from there south toward Alexandria and then coming up north from Egypt, etc. He did not even order the people below deck while passing through the Bosporus. With her name *Las Perlas* clearly visible, with hundreds of refugees jamming the deck and waving happily to the people on the banks, the ship sailed through the narrow straits. On the first of July 1939, as soon as she approached the Palestine coast in the vicinity of Netanyah, she was, of course, captured.* British marines boarded the *Las Perlas* and declared all arrested: the ship, the captain with his 13-man crew, and all the 370 refugees. The refugees were sent to an internment camp, but they were happy. Barbed wire or not, prisoners or not, there were no poison gas and no crematorium here. And best of all,

---

*The warship apprehending the *Las Perlas* was none less than the H.M.S. *Ivanhoe*, the destroyer which shortly after was to become a symbol of heroism to the free world. Ironically, the *Ivanhoe*'s fame derived from a combat action involving the liberation of 300 people held captive by the Germans on a prison ship. The Germans held 300 British seamen prisoners on the German S.S. *Altmark*, anchored in a Norwegian fiord. On February 16, 1940, in a surprise attack by the British in which the *Ivanhoe* distinguished herself, the captives were liberated, taken off the prison ship, and brought home.

they had arrived in their homeland. The fall guys in the whole undertaking were the shipowners (unless they had been paid more than the value of the ship for the voyage) and, most of all, the members of the crew, who had been obviously unaware that they were sailing straight into certain imprisonment. On August 8 the media carried the following news item:

> The Haifa Assize Court yesterday sentenced to a year imprisonment Mustafa Talay, captain of the Turkish steamship *Las Perlas* captured off Netanyah last month while trying to land 370 refugees. Thirteen of the ship's crew were sentenced to three months each and the ship was confiscated.

The story of the *Las Perlas* brought home to me once more how odd and unpredictable the ways of life can be. Here was a travel agent who, completely inexperienced and employing doubtful methods, had saved 370 lives. There too was a shipowner who had been looking forward to what was likely a large windfall profit and had lost his ship. And there was a captain and 13 crew members who had played the most active part in saving those lives but who were not honored for the feat as others who save lives are. They instead had to go to prison for it. And finally there were 370 refugees who had naïvely believed that they could simply buy a ticket for travel to Palestine—just like that—and whose belief had proven correct after all.

While the people in Bucharest were registering for the *Las Perlas,* our preparations for a transport which would involve the most photographed ship of them all, went into the final stage. My being prevented by the Italian police from leaving the Island of Rhodes was a handicap which could only partly be compensated for by almost daily phone calls from Rhodes to Athens, Bucharest, and London. It was Zeev Jabotinsky himself, the leader of the World Revisionist Organization and of the Betar, who now took a most active role in trying to arrange the escape of more Jews from Poland, particularly of as many as possible of our Betarim there. His son Eri, in regular contact with his father and with the headquarters of the Revisionist organization in London, held a Palestine passport which permitted him to travel in countries not yet held by the Nazis. Our mobility had by then been valuably increased by the fact that the Irgun commander, David Raziel, had appointed Dr.

Reuben Hecht, a human dynamo, to be Irgun representative for Aliya Bet in Europe. Dr. Hecht traveled on a Swiss passport. In Bucharest, Mila Epstein was the intermediary between London, myself, and Bucharest. Abraham Stavsky, who knew conditions in Poland better than most others and who had experience with illegal Aliya, having organized the *Astir* transport and having helped with the *Noemi Julia*, was a prominent part of the team. We had at that time even a group in Paris, and one of our ships, the *Har Zsion*, had sailed from Marseilles. It took on board 600 Jewish refugees who had been stuck in France and had brought them in a long trouble-filled voyage to Palestine. Communications between Rhodes, Bucharest, Athens, and Paris were difficult. Mail delivery was uncertain, and most of our communication as a consequence was done by phone. But using the phone created problems too. In addition to the technical deficiencies of the telephone systems in these countries at that time, we also had to deal with the likelihood that either the British, the Germans, or both might be listening in. When telephoning, therefore, we had to use a code for critical words. It could not be anything that would require much time for deciphering. Thus, we had to think up code words and anagrams which were easily remembered by those using them so that there were no suspicious pauses in the flow of our conversations. At the same time, these code words had to be readily understood at the other end of the line. Consequently, we employed ciphers which by some mental association would be easily remembered. When speaking of the Danube River, for instance, we used the name "Johnny" (association: *Johann* Strauss); baksheesh was referred to as "Holmes" (Sherlock Holmes lived on *Bak*er Street). Afterward, during the war, when the use of an English name was not advisable because it might have aroused German suspicions, the code word for baksheesh changed to the quite common Turkish name of *kebab (shish* kebab being a Balkanese and Mideastern dish). The police were referred to as "Mr. Tara" (the second half of the Hebrew word for police—*mishtara*). A riverboat was a "parcel"; a seagoing vessel a "consignment." Founded by Hillel Cook, a member of the Irgun in New York, the American Committee for Friends of a Jewish Palestine was "Mr. Neuer" (association: Neuer—*New* York). Jail was "Kuno," the name of a cousin of mine who, as most of our earlier workers knew, had been arrested and brought first to Dachau and then to the Buchenwald concentration camp. If to the given name

"Kuno" we added his last name "Walder," then it meant the step following simple imprisonment: concentration camp. The number of passengers or of any group of people generally was expressed in kilos.

There were altogether some thirty or forty key words which, all by similar mnemotechnic aids as those described, we had to remember in order to conduct a phone conversation in partial code. Thus, for example, the sentence: "The kids are all right, but Johnny has a cold. We called Dr. Neuer. He sent his assistant Dr. Holmes and now things should be all right with Johnny" meant: "There is danger that the Danube might freeze. We called the American Friends of a Jewish Palestine in New York. They already sent funds for baksheesh, and this should enable you to get the ship ready prior to the freezing of the Danube."

In a coded phone conversation with Paris, I gave to our people there the name of a Greek shipowner whom I knew to be ready to go into the Palestine blockade running business. Mr. Minakoulis had a forty-year-old cattle ship; it was quite small but not much smaller than most of our ships. His ship, the 563-ton *Parita,* was at the moment in Marseilles. At the suggestion of his father, Eri Jabotinsky and Stavsky took up negotiations with Mr. Minakoulis. Agreement was reached. To appear less conspicuous than she would have been in Marseilles, the *Parita* sailed for the small French port of Sète where she was transformed for our purposes. The usual platforms were hurriedly built into the holds with running boards and an assembly area on each "floor." Rows of wooden bunks were built and toilets were installed at the edge of the ship so that the urine and excrement would fall right into the sea. It was determined that the absolute "unchangeable" maximum that could be jammed into this ship would be 750 persons.

Although the work went on in secrecy and although the departure of such a refugee ship from Sète was not expected—neither by the British nor by the thousands of refugees in France—word had somehow leaked out to some of those who were desperately seeking some way of getting out of continental Europe and going "home" to Palestine. By the time the *Parita* sailed from Sète for Rumania to pick up those whom we had planned to smuggle on her to Palestine, there were already 80 Jewish refugees on board, most of them Austrian and German Jews, but also some from France. They enjoyed what could then have been considered a pleasure cruise, with plenty of space, and sufficient food and water, from the western Mediterranean, up the Marmara and Black Sea into Rumania.

It was all carefully prepared and was done with the precision of clockwork. Zeev Jabotinsky, due to his political connections in Poland, had procured there Polish travel permits. Our people in Rumania, with the help of the Jabotinsky connections and with the powerful aid of "Mr. Holmes," had obtained Rumanian transit visas. On July 9, 1939, the *Parita* arrived in Constanţa. On July 11, after the Polish and Rumanian authorities had received confirmation that the seagoing vessel was in port waiting for the immigrants, a sealed train with 600 left Warsaw. Again, Begin, working with Mordechai Katz, Aron Propes, Eisik Remba, and other Betar leaders, had done an excellent job of selecting and organizing. The Warsaw group was well briefed, ready to experience extreme hardships, and determined to make it to the homeland whatever the intervening misfortunes might be. It arrived in Constanţa on the night of July 12–13, and within the hour, the transfer of the 600 from the train to the *Parita* was under way. With the 80 who had come on the *Parita* from France, with the 600 from Warsaw, and with 120 more Betarim who had been taken on in Rumania, the ship boarded exactly 800. A few more hours, and by noon on the thirteenth of July, the *Parita* was on her way.

The composition of the passengers was an exceptionally favorable one as far as the expected maintenance of discipline on board and the readiness to undergo hardships went. Of the 600 from Poland, 400 were members of the Betar. The other 200 had been organized by the Warsaw Yiddish Daily *Inser Welt*—Our World. Of the 80 who had come from France, about 20 were Betarim, thus with the Rumanians, there were 540 Betarim on the *Parita*—two-thirds of all those on board.

Mr. Minakoulis, the *Parita*'s owner, had assured us that he had a most reliable crew; that the landing ship would definitely be on time at the appointed place; and that if we were ready to unload to the small ship, everything would go absolutely smoothly. He was confident that within five to six days the *Parita* would discharge her passengers and would be back in Rumania within twelve days. In fact, he urged us to have another 800 waiting for the *Parita* fourteen days after her leaving for the first voyage. Our landing organization—the landing detail of the Irgun—was by then well experienced, and we too expected this to be a smooth trip, and we loaded water and food for only six to seven days. It may be asked why we were not more careful and did not take more water and food along just in case. We answered such questions in our own minds by deciding in favor of people: one day's more supplies for 800 people meant that we would have to leave at least another six or seven immigrants behind.

Up to Cyprus everything went smoothly. The skies were blue, the crew friendly. Under the leadership of "Erwin" Leibovich, assisted by Yaakov Ariel and Eliyahu Even, the commanders of the tightly organized Rumanian Betarim, spirits were high. Songs were sung, the people climbed on the masts and hung from places where one could hold on long enough to make space on deck for the dancing of the horah. Daily physical exercise permitted relaxation of muscles otherwise strained in the crowded places. The taking of turns by the groups between being on deck and being below was effected without problems. The voyage through the Bosporus had apparently attracted no attention.

In Cyprus, in a secluded inlet sixteen miles from the small port of Kyrenia, the *Parita* was to rendezvous with the landing ship. The small ship was not waiting as it should have been. The *Parita*'s captain, a capable seaman well liked by his crew, waited for half a day. He then zigzagged in the area for two more days. No landing ship—and now two and a half valuable days had been lost. The captain, who was genuinely concerned for his passengers, discussed the situation with our leaders on board. Neither the *Parita* nor the smaller ship had a radio. Thus, both ships were isolated from each other and from the outside world. As the *Parita*'s coal and supplies were running low, she had to find a port quickly. Our people knew of the hospitality that the Italians had shown to the *Rim* on the Island of Rhodes when she burned and sank less than three weeks before. They knew too that I was there and could help with the authorities and establish contact with Rumania and Greece to find out what had happened to the landing ship. So, they decided to head for Rhodes.

At two A.M., on July 23, ten days after the *Parita*'s departure from Rumania, a knock at my hotel room door awakened me. I rose from a sweat-drenched sleep—air conditioning was unknown as yet—and climbed out of the mosquito netting. At the door was Giacomo, a hotel clerk who was on my baksheesh list.

"There is a ship with three thousand refugees in port. The police are boarding it."

"Three thousand, are you sure?"

"That's what a harbor policeman told a man who came running to tell me, and I gave him a tip for it."

I knew that the *Parita* had been scheduled to take 750; even figuring the usual last-minute increase, it could not be more than 820 or so. It must be another ship. But which one? In any case, I had to see what I could do for the people on board.

A friend of Giacomo's had a motorcycle ready, and we soon thundered on it through the sleeping town to the port. The ship was not in the port itself, but about a mile outside. I could make out nothing in the dark, not the size, certainly not the name. The policemen remained taciturn, as if a state secret were involved. Nights are short in July, and after two hours or so, one could see more clearly. The ship obviously could not hold 3,000. It could have been the *Parita* which should have been on her way back to Rumania now after having transferred her passengers to the landing boat. I had coffee in a little breakfast restaurant right in the port. At one of the four tables a harbor policeman was sipping his espresso. To gain relief from the heat, oppressive even at that early hour, he had the collar of his uniform unbuttoned. I started talking to him, and, as expected, I found that an unbuttoned collar makes even a policeman feel less like a stuffy official. He told me that "more than a thousand" Jews were on board, and that the ship's name was *"Patria."* It was now clear to me, it was the *Parita*. The name *Patria*, which both in Italian and Latin means "fatherland," was just the more likely one for the policeman. After ten minutes or so, another policeman joined the first officer. This one had been on board. The ship's name was *"Parita,"* he said; it was not allowed to land and was being held incommunicado.

The little restaurant I had chosen turned out to be the hangout of the various minor harbor officials. More of them came in for their morning espresso con latte and, well before any offices opened, I had much more information. The *Parita* was out of food, out of water, and short on—though not out of—coal. The captain had asked to get in touch with me, but a decision as to that request would have to wait until eight in the morning when the governor's office would open.

I went back to the hotel, shaved, and put on clothes which

looked more respectable than the hastily thrown on garb I had slipped into at two A.M. when Giacomo had awakened me. By the time I arrived at the governor's mansion, it was seven-thirty, and the lower-echelon staff was just opening up the building. I waited with much hope in the governor's anteroom. After all, this man had shown himself to be very human and helpful in regard to the shipwrecked passengers of the *Rim,* whom he was still allowing to live in tents—supplied at his own orders. Although they were not permitted to leave the vicinity of the camp, the *Rim* people were nevertheless treated by the soldiers like fellow humans.

But my hopes took a nosedive when two or three minutes later, the representative of the British Consulate entered. I knew why the man had come. When he sat down, it was not that he did not just look at me—as he looked around the room, his glance passed me and went *through* me as if I did not exist at all! With indescribable arrogance, probably acquired in years of serving in India or some other colony, he sat there, leisurely smoking a Balkan Sobranie cigarette, an expensive brand seen so often in these days in the mouths of those in the British diplomatic service. Looking at him, I had to think of the people who within an hour or two would be roasting in the sun, standing one pressed against the other on the scorching decks of the *Parita,* and of those who in the sufficating holds—doubly infernal when the ship was not moving—would be envying those whose turn it was to be up on deck. But obviously the British Consulate had been tipped off before dawn by one of its informers of the Parita's arrival.

Just before eight A.M., the executive officer came into the anteroom, apparently to wait there for his superior. From his behavior, I assumed that he knew why the two of us had come.

In less than five minutes, the governor's heavy step could be heard on the marble staircase. The executive snapped to attention and saluted. The Britisher and I rose. Nodding in recognition of our *"Bon giorno,"* he seemed surprised when he saw the Englishman and me next to each other in his anteroom. Apparently he did not know. Office hours had not started yet for the governor. The executive officer followed him into the inner sanctum, and after a short time the Englishman was called in—before me, of course.

He did not stay long, maybe ten to fifteen minutes. Then it was my turn. The governor was as friendly and warm as before—but while the tone of his voice was Jacob's, his hands, the action, was

Esau's, firm and rough. I had not to say much; he knew why I was there. With genuine warmth, he assured me of his compassion. But ... he had learned, he told me, that we intended to use his island as a kind of staging area for the "invasion of Palestine by tens of thousands of people." There could hardly be a coincidence in the fact that although Rhodes was not on the direct course, this was the second ship within less than three weeks that was trying to use his island as a point to recover from difficulty and from there to continue the trip.

I was truly unable to answer the governor's question why the *Parita* had come to Rhodes and suggested that I be permitted to talk to the captain who had up until then been kept incommunicado on the ship. The permission was granted, and in the presence of an Italian major and his adjutant, a young lieutenant, I spoke to the ship's captain, who was brought on land for that purpose. I suggested that he tell the truth—and he did. He explained to me the missed rendezvous and asserted his determination to leave as soon as he had loaded coal, food, and water. All this could be done by nightfall.

When the major and I returned to the governor's mansion, we were seen by the executive officer who took notes of our report but stated that the governor was sorry, he had checked with Rome in the meanwhile. He would go on helping the shipwrecked ones from the *Rim* but could give no help whatsoever to any other refugee ship in the future. Apparently the Englishman's assertion that we wanted to abuse his helpfulness and use his island as a "staging area" had hit home.

I immediately called Zeev Jabotinsky in London and suggested that somebody from the world headquarters of the Revisionist Organization fly in right away. The emissary from London, I stressed, would have to guarantee the governor that no other ship of ours would ever seek haven on Rhodes once the *Parita* had been permitted to fill its bunkers with coal and to purchase and load food and water. In that phone conversation, I learned what was probably the root of the failure of the rendezvous. My friends who had chartered the *Parita* had not at the same time made certain that the landing ship was owned by the same person or company. I knew that this was a must for success because only in case of the same ownership for both ships could one be certain that the small boat would be at the right time and at the agreed-upon location. The owner of the landing ship told us later that his boat did not show up because his crew had gotten drunk just before sailing for the rendezvous, had become involved in a fight in which there had been severe injuries, and had all ended up in jail.

In less than twenty-four hours after my phone call to London, Eri Jabotinsky flew in into Rhodes, and I saw to it that he met with the governor. Eri had, of course, a much higher standing in Rhodes than I had. He had come in by plane—then not yet a matter of course—"from London," his father's name Jabotinsky could be found in any encyclopedia, and Eri represented the Revisionist world organization, while my prestige had badly suffered from the *Rim* tragedy and from the fact that I was then, practically speaking, a prisoner of the Rhodes authorities.

Eri was almost able to swing the situation. Almost. He convinced the ever well-meaning governor that it would be good for Rhodes to obtain the assurance that we would unconditionally keep all our ships away from his island. The governor agreed to call Rome. There, the Ministry of the Interior immediately consulted with the Ministry of Foreign Affairs, and we knew that the latter would veto any help to the *Parita*. It did. And without food, without having received even water, with what coal was left—there was more of it than the captain had admitted—the *Parita* was ordered to set sail.

Prior to that order there was a tragicomic episode, however. A luxury liner on a cruise of the Mediterranean had just steamed into port. In all its shining glory and overwhelming majesty, it was anchored hardly more than six hundred feet away from the tiny, shabby, and crowded *Parita*. I thought that by chance there might be some influential person on board the cruise ship, who, seeing what was going on, might help us with the authorities. But the *Parita* continued to be held incommunicado, and I was not permitted even to enter the harbor area. However, in one of the stores in the city, I saw two American ladies from the cruise ship while they were shopping. I approached them, told them of the misery on the *Parita*, and asked them to help. They did not know of any prominent people on board but said they would ask the captain and make inquiries among the other first-class passengers. They would also try to get food sent on board.

Whether as a result of my talk with these ladies or because the cruise passengers saw what was going on, in the afternoon a small boat took off from the liner and brought several cases over to the *Parita*.

"You know what they sent us?" Eliyahu Evens told me years later. "Cases of beer and oranges. They wanted to help, but it was tragic to see the huge gap between our condition and what the people on the other side of the fence believed our needs were."

When the order to leave port without loading anything became definite, the captain refused to obey. Eliyahu Even continues to report:

> So Italian military sailors (six) were sent aboard. They spoke to our crew. The crew told them they could not take the ship out of the port "because we threatened them." So the Italians said they would bring the ship out into the sea. Actually we had not threatened them. The Italians said: you cannot, but we can. They were armed with rifles and submachine guns. So we sailed from Rhodes to Alexandretta which was Turkish, on the Turkish-Syrian border. I do not know about coal but do know that we were again not permitted to buy food, yet we did get water there. Several small boats with water came alongside. The Turks were sitting with their bare feet in the water which we were to drink. But who cared.
>
> From Alexandretta we again sailed for Cyprus. Again no landing ship. By now we were starving. We now—still no food, but fortunately water on board—sailed for Izmir. There we stayed several days. But in Izmir, too, the British had done their job well.
>
> The Turks refused to sell us food. Instead, they sent police to force us out of the port. There were demonstrations by Izmir Jews and some of our people threatened suicide. Some of the Turkish policemen who saw our plight cried.
>
> When the order to leave port was definite and about to be enforced, some of the crew refused to bring the ship, with many of the people half dead, out into the sea.

The next day the media carried the following wire dispatch:

MUTINY FLARES WHEN REFUGEE SHIP IS ORDERED TO QUIT SMYRNA. London August JTA. Dispatches from Smyrna said today that mutiny broke out on the Greek ship *Parita*, flying the Panama flag, when the Turkish authorities ordered the vessel to put out to sea with its cargo of more than 500 refugees.* The ship had been lying in

---

*The media always tried to estimate and usually underestimated the number of passengers.

Smyrna harbor since Tuesday, its passengers banned from landing. A fight broke out between mutineers and the remainder of the crew when the order to quit the harbor was served. The mutineers were aided by refugees. Turkish police were called by the ship's captain to put down the outbreak. The captain had been threatened with death if he carried out the Turkish order to leave the harbor.

But nothing helped. British diplomatic pressure on the Turks was too strong. The *Parita,* still without food* but supplied with water—on which a person can survive for many days—finally did leave, but, to the horror of the passengers, not in the direction of Palestine! Without food for the refugees on board, the ship could never have made it as far as Palestine without the certainty of many deaths. Some of the older people were already in very bad shape, and even a few of the younger ones were dangerously dehydrated by diarrhea. So instead of heading south toward Palestine, the *Parita's* captain headed north toward Istanbul. This was done in full agreement with us. We hoped that in the larger city the wider publicity about the atrocious conditions on board would force the Turks, notwithstanding any countermoves the British might make, to permit the bringing of provisions aboard—and also to obtain more coal. To intervene with the Turkish authorities, Zeev Jabotinsky sent Mr. Ben Horin, a member of the Revisionist Executive to Istanbul with funds collected in the United States by the American Friends of Jewish Palestine. Eliyahu Even's report describes the outcome of that mission:

> In Istanbul was Ben Horin and now we could buy food and medical supplies. As soon as those were on board we left. For the third time we headed for Cyprus. And again there was no small ship there.
>
> We now decided: we cannot go on like that; we just have to go straight for Palestine, whatever becomes of it.

The longer the trip lasted, the worse the deprivations became, the closer grew the relationship between the crew and the refugees. It was particularly Yaakov Ariel who had a knack to relate to the crew as if he were one of them. Several of them were married and

---

*Some soap had been smuggled to the immigrants, but this did not improve the unhealthy conditions aboard. Soap does not lather with salt water.

had children. As they experienced daily how the numerous children on the ship were suffering, the crew members identified with the children's lot and were really ready to take upon themselves even more hardships than this apparently never-ending voyage brought even to them. Several of the crew shared their rations with the children, and many of the sailors and also the officers felt almost as strongly as their passengers that the mission just had to succeed.

Again, we have to name one of those who in a time when everybody turned against the "outcasts of Europe" acted toward the refugees as if they each had been a relative on board or as if all aboard—crew and passengers—really did belong to the human race. It was the ship's second engineer, Mr. Serioja, a Russian, originally from Bessarabia, the part of Rumania which until 1919 had been part of the czarist empire and is now again a part of Russia. He was known among the passengers as "the angel."*

After the third attempt for a rendezvous at Cyprus had failed, there were no alternatives left. British warships shooting at the *Parita* or not, she had to break through the blockade boldly and without hesitation. Because this decision was made, the *Parita* was one ship for which the British were not lying in wait. They knew by then quite well that our ships circled and zigzagged in order to avoid them. They apparently knew that the landing ship would not be at the appointed place, and thus expected that the *Parita* would lose at least another two or three days because of missing her rendezvous. But such calculations were wrong. After failing twice, the *Parita* waited for the landing ship for only twenty-seven hours. She then set out for the Palestine coast by the shortest route possible. No zigzagging, no circling this time. This way she was approaching the Palestine coast much sooner than the British had anticipated. She did not go for one of our usual landing places either, nor did she remain at the usual safe distance. She headed straight for Tel Aviv, although that city has no port and no docking facilities!

When about twenty miles from the coast the entire ship started shaking heavily, those in the holds—as they knew less of what was going on than did those above—were worried:

---

*Unfortunately, contact with Mr. Serioja has been lost. Several who had been on the *Parita* and whom I interviewed in Israel while I was preparing this book voiced hope that this account might help to locate him as they would like to invite him and his family to Israel as their guests.

"What is it? It sounds as if the ship is going to explode!"

"No, it won't explode. The engines are just working at top capacity. We are sailing at the fastest possible speed for Tel Aviv."

"Toward Tel Aviv? But Tel Aviv has no docks!"

"Never mind, we are sailing into Tel Aviv."

"We will probably be shot at by British warships," the passengers were warned, "but we will go straight on, bullets or shells or not." A hurrah from hundreds of throats sounded.

"Better we die in battle than like hunted, exhausted animals!" a girl shouted.

"Yes, better to die in battle," a chorus replied. What a battle it was they anticipated! The *Parita* against. . . !

The "battle mood" rose to a pitch when the Panama flag at the ship's stern was lowered and the blue and white Zionist flag of the future State of Israel was hoisted. Not only those on deck but also those below in the suffocating holds stood at attention as soon as they heard the first bars of the Jewish national anthem which the Betarim on deck had started to sing. Parched, dehydrated, starved, many were so weak that they could not have stood up had they not been pressed one against the other. With feverish eyes, they scanned the sea as the expected warships were approaching. Yet defiant and jubilant, they were singing the song of eternal hope: "We have not lost the hope . . . to return to the land of our fathers . . . to the City of David."

A rabbi climbed up on a pile of ropes. Tall, thin, and emaciated, he looked both patriarchic and unreal, his long white beard matted, he cited the Scriptures:

> Thus says the Lord who created you, oh Jacob, and formed you oh Israel: Fear not for I have redeemed you; I have called you by name, you are mine. When you pass through the water, I shall be with you. . . . For I am the Lord, your God, the Holy One of Israel, your Savior. . . . Fear not for I am with you. From the East I will bring back your descendants, from the West I will gather you. I will say to the North: Give them up! and to the South: Hold not back: Bring back my sons from afar and my daughters from the ends of the earth.*

*Isaiah 43:1–3, 5–6.

The paroxysm reached a height when the coast came in sight, and shaking as if about to fall apart, the *Parita* continued full steam ahead to approach the all Jewish city. Now the houses of Tel Aviv had become visible. On went the *Parita*.

"Where to?!" asked some. "There is no port."

"Never mind. We are going home. Home." Three more miles. The ship headed straight for the center of the recreational area where today the five-star Hotel Dan stands, close to the present location of the U.S. Embassy. Two more miles, now one could see the cabanas, and the people running, waving wildly. The immigrants again intoned the Jewish national anthem. As if in furious defiance of those who tried to bar the children of Israel from the country of Israel, the foghorn started howling. Suddenly, a new sound, a grinding one. The *Parita* had run right up the beach and was aground in the center of the busiest bathing place of Tel Aviv!

On land, people embraced and kissed each other. Hundreds more have escaped! Have come right into our midst! Perhaps there are even some relatives or friends whom we have thought lost among them.

It was August 22 and the same day hundreds of newspapers all over the world printed the following wire story:

> 800 EXILES LAND ON TEL AVIV BEACH AS THRONG WATCHES. Tel Aviv August 22nd. The Greek steamer *Parita* flying the Zionist flag landed more than 800 Jewish refugees on the seashore of this all-Jewish city in full view of thousands of spectators. Police cordoned off the beach.
>
> The small 180-ton vessel has apparently successfully run the blockade of the Palestinian coastline maintained by the British Coast Guard and warships to keep steamers from illegally landing their refugee passengers.
>
> The *Parita* last week was reported to have tried unsuccessfully to disembark its passengers at Smyrna, Turkey, after having wandered the Mediterranean for weeks in search of a port that would accept them. A riot occurred on the ship when the Turkish authorities ordered it to put out to sea and three of the passengers were reported killed.

The news spread like wildfire through the city, through the country. It was a holiday, and thousands of sightseers came to the beach to see the ship which had braved all obstacles and had brazenly run itself aground right in the midst of town.

People were singing and dancing on the beach—on that part which had not been cordoned off by the police. With the news of the landing, of course, came the British police. But even an official British report states that 221 of the *Parita* passengers evaded arrest.

The arrested ones were brought to a detention camp in Palestine. Again they were behind barbed wire, but they were safe—and at home. After several weeks, they were released: humans again among humans.

This was almost but not yet entirely the end of the story of the *Parita*. Among those dancing and celebrating on the beach one started to whisper it into another's ear, and soon everyone was talking about it. The police and newspapermen were after an even bigger story: there was a rumor that the crew had been murdered by the refugees. They had been, the whisper said, thrown overboard as the ship approached the coast.

It was true that no crew member was on board, but the rest of the account was incorrect. The crew and passengers had been on good terms. As it was impossible to land the passengers otherwise, the crew at the pleadings of the Irgun and Betar leaders on board, had shown some of the people how to head the ship straight onto the beach. They had put the engines on full steam ahead and had themselves left in the two lifeboats a short while before the beaching. A meeting point had been prearranged with the Irgun. The Irgun would try to hide the crew members and to get them on some outgoing ship. Should they be caught, they would say that they had not been responsible for the illegal landing; they had been forced by the Betarim to abandon the ship. When questioned by the police, our people would confirm that story.

The members of the crew were hidden for a few weeks, but somehow, before they could be smuggled aboard a ship, the police found out about their hideout and arrested them all. Rumor had it that the British in order to avoid more unfavorable publicity about their failure to prevent such direct "assault" against the blockade, released the crew and sent them home under the stipulation that they keep mum. This rumor seems confirmed by the fact that none of those who were ready to testify that they had forced the crew members off the ship because the latter had refused to beach it was ever called to confirm this story. And so the *Parita* survivors are still looking for the helpful Greek sailors with whom they shared forty fateful days on a ship which *AF AL PI*—in spite of everything—made it.

The story of the S.S. *Parita*, whose voyage has just been described, and that of the S.S. *Patria*, which gained much publicity, particularly in the United States, and was heatedly debated in the House of Commons, are as diametrically different as possible, though the two ships with similar names were often confused with each other.

On September 21, 1939, the commander of the Reichssicherheitsdienst (the National Security Service), Reinhard Heydrich, sent out to all units of the Sonderdienst—the special formations of the SS whose almost exclusive job was "extermination"—an announcement of ominous portent for Jews. Heydrich informed the special SS units of the Fuehrer's decision to have all Jews still remaining under German rule deported to the east within one year. Those of our people in Vienna who were still there now went themselves "illegally" to Palestine, and more and more new people moved in. Few of them had the organizational and leadership abilities of their predecessors. Adolf Eichmann now appointed a man of his choice. Bernard Storfer, Jewish businessman, was put in charge. He was a *Kommerzialrat*. The title *Kommerzialrat* (commercial attaché) was an honorary one which had formerly been given by the former Austrian government to leaders of business and industry. Storfer was a Viennese Jew whose name was not known in Jewish circles as ever having been active in Jewish affairs before. He seemed to enjoy a relatively easy relationship with Eichmann, at least to the degree that any slave can "get along with" a ruthless master. Mr. Storfer was even suspected of wielding too much Gestapo influence, but suspicions of that kind were not uncommon in times loaded with danger, blackmail, and treachery. The facts remain that Storfer, who renamed the office Ausschuss fuer juedische Ueberseetransporte (Committee for Jewish Overseas Transports), was a capable organizer, got many thousands out and onto "illegal" ships, but in the end did not make it out himself and perished. He just disappeared without a trace.

On the third of September 1940, a little flotilla of riverboats, organized by Storfer, left Vienna. It was a warm day, and the sun was shining on the four boats led by the *Schoenbrunn*, named after the famous Hapsburg castle. The others were our old friends the *Uranus,* the *Melk,* and the *Helios.* On the *Schoenbrunn,* there were 600 people who had been released from Dachau as Storfer had guaranteed their immediate departure. Another 1,771 refugees were distributed among the other three Danube boats. They included a large contingent from Danzig and 700 young pioneers, who had been training in Austria and in Czechoslovakia for a future life as farmers in Palestine.

In Tulcea where we had first had the *Gepo* remodeled in 1938 and where many transfers had since been completed, the convoy which Storfer had sent down the Danube transferred on the eleventh of September to three seagoing vessels. All three of them, as usual, old and decrepit. The 800 from the *Melk* went on the *Milos.* The 1,000 from the *Uranus* transferred to the *Pacific,* which was probably the worst of the three ships. She had hardly any facilities for drinking water on board. The 1,700 who had come down on the *Schoenbrunn* and on the *Helios* boarded the *Atlantic.* This group included 300 old people and 150 children under 12.

The British, as usual, did their very best to prevent the departure from Rumania, but finally, on the seventh of October, the *Atlantic* with her 1,700 escapees, was allowed to leave Tulcea. The other two ships followed soon after.

To be less conspicuous, each of the three ships tried to make its own way. For each of the three, the trip took much longer than anticipated. Soon food and water ran low. The starvation, and—in the later part of the voyages—the total absence of water, and the lack of air in the overcrowded ships—particularly the suffocating conditions in the holds—would have made it impossible for almost anyone to survive the torment of day after day if one did not have hope. The hope that at the end of the voyage was freedom in one's own land and, in many cases, that there were relatives praying and waiting for one's arrival.

For the conditions on one of the ships, the *Atlantic,* there exists a description from an objective source, the British governor of Cyprus, where, although she thus blew her cover, the *Atlantic* had been forced to enter port. On November 18, 1940, the governor of Cyprus sent a telegram, classified MOST IMMEDIATE, to the Colonial Office in London with a copy to the high commissioner for Palestine. Obviously horried by conditions on board, he described vividly the suffering that those on the ships were undergoing and urged that they be sent at once to Palestine. The message stated that his director of Medical Services had visited the ship and had found conditions to be

> "indescribably shocking" . . . there was gross overcrowding; standing room on deck only; below lack of ventilation, light; no ablution or laundry facilities at all; . . . D.M.S. considers that every day's delay in taking passengers off increases risk already high of epidemic, death toll, which would probably be very heavy as passengers are suffering from exposure and hardship and are emaciated. Case of typhoid developed yesterday. . . .

On the other two ships conditions were similar. All three, the *Atlantic,* the *Pacific,* and the *Milos* were intercepted as they approached the Palestine coast.

But those escapees from Hitler's Final Solution who believed that with their arrival in Palestine their misery would be over were to have their hopes soon turn into despair. Britain was in those days certainly in urgent need of shipping. However, even more urgent than their requirement of bottoms for war purposes was their need for an effective means of warfare against the Jews. For that, they decided, they needed a large ship to deport a few thousand captured Jews to a place with deterrent influence. The "nowhere" they decided upon was to be the tiny Indian Ocean island of Mauritius. It was far enough and sufficiently fever-infested and epidemic-ridden to serve as a warning example. When France collapsed under the German onslaught, the British succeeded in getting their hands on some French ships before the Germans did. One of them, a real prize, was an 11,000-ton French liner, the *Patria.* It was that ship which was now going to serve as a prison ship for the internment of the Jewish refugees captured off the shores of Palestine and for the deportation of these wretched people to Mauritius.

The British, of course, knew that the refugees would resist deportation from Palestine and therefore would refuse to transfer to the *Patria.* But a good precedent had been set on how to avoid such undesirable annoyances. When the Nazi trains arrived in resettlement centers in Europe, the Jews were told on leaving the train that for "sanitary purposes" they would first all go into the shower room. Then there was the little change: instead of water, poison gas steamed forth from the faucets. In a way mildly reminiscent of the trick used by the Nazis, the passengers of the *Milos* and of the *Pacific* were lured into transferring peacefully to the *Patria* by being told that this was done for "sanitary reasons." They loved the incomparably better accommodations from which they hopefully would soon be processed to enter Palestine. It was clear that this big ship would in wartime not be sent to any German-occupied land.

Shortly afterward, 80 from the *Atlantic*'s 1,771 were likewise transferred to the *Patria.* Yet even now, although overcrowded for what would be normal conditions, the stay on the *Patria* seemed like real luxury. Most of all, the people were in Palestine, not outcasts anymore in a hostile country; 1 million welcoming hands were stretching out for them. They could see the lights of busy Haifa, the people in the port,waving to them, the cars rushing up and down Mount Carmel, and those who had by then relatives in Palestine knew that their families were waiting right there.

It was at that point that the first bomb hit.

On November 20, 1940, the Palestine government made its official announcement:

". . . His Majesty's Government are not lacking in sympathy for refugees from territories under German control. But . . ."

After some excuses, the statement goes on to say that illegal Jewish immigration is likely to prove a serious matter to British interests in the Middle East. They have accordingly decided that the passengers of the S.S. *Pacific* and the S.S. *Milos* shall not be permitted to land in Palestine but shall be deported to a British colony as soon as arrangements of safe transport and building accommodations can be made, and shall be detained there for the duration of the war."

But those who thought that this was all the British had in mind for them were in error. Even now while the war was still on (and was in fact to last for four and a half more years) the British told the hapless survivors of concentration camps and other Nazi persecutions that *even after the war* they would be barred from immigrating into Palestine. The above cited government announcement continues:

Their [the refugees'] ultimate disposal (*sic*)· will be a matter for consideration, but it is not proposed that they shall remain in the colony to which they are sent or that they should go to Palestine.

Similar action will be taken in the case of any further parties who may succeed in reaching Palestine with a view to illegal entry.

While the news came as a surprise to those on ships, Zionist leadership was well aware that decisions had been taken by the British government from now on to deport all Jewish escapees who reached Palestine and that their destination would be Mauritius.

For the Jews, this order was extremely provocative. It meant deportation from home where—after unbelievable suffering—the escapees had finally arrived, from home which they saw alive and pulsating right in front of them. It was deportation to almost the other end of the world to a steaming most unhealthy island. It was the announced intention of keeping them out of Palestine even after the war as a kind of life sentence punishment. And this sentence had a cruel symbolic meaning in addition to its cruel practical effect: there was not one who did not know that prior to the acceptance of the Final Solution, according to Nazi theory developed by the top Nazi theoretician Alfred Rosenberg, all Jews were to be deported to the faraway island of Madagascar.

Madagascar is a large island with a relatively healthy climate. The tiny miserable island next to it, is Mauritius. What difference between the Nazis and the British, the Jews asked themselves. There was of course a difference but not enough to prevent a real uproar among the Jews of Palestine.

But for the moment, only the Zionist leaders had learned that deportation plans were in the making. Without resistance, the unsuspecting escapees from the *Pacific* walked into the trap and were transferred to the *Patria* "for sanitary reasons." On November 11, the transfer from the *Milos* began without incident. On the seventeenth, however, when the *Patria* started loading coal for the long trip, the refugees became panic-stricken. No processing had as yet occurred for sending them to one of the detention camps in Palestine, and why was the ship now loading coal? And so much coal! Rumors started flying, and fear gripped those who had suffered so at the hands of the Nazi police, when, apparently without reason, 150 British policemen boarded the ship. This move was made in preparation for the triple bombshell: the announcement on November 20 of the deportation to Mauritius; the order to stay there for the duration of the war; and the proclamation of the future exclusion from Palestine—even after a victorious war.

When news of the announcement spread, the Jews of Palestine were stunned. Those on the *Patria* were terror-struck. They were certainly used to bad news and to the worst of deprivations, but now they had seen themselves at last able to start a new life in dignity. "It cannot be," said the prisoners on the *Patria.* "It must not be, it will not be!" shouted the crowds that gathered in the streets of Jerusalem, Tel Aviv, and Haifa.

In short sequence, 20 of the harrowed humans held captive on the *Patria* jumped overboard. Fifteen of them were fished out of the water. The fate of the other 5—whether they drowned or were saved and managed to evade the British in the heavily guarded port area, never became known.

The Revisionists in Palestine, and most of all the Irgun, their militant branch, called for mass civil disobedience. But they were a minority in the country. The Zionist leadership on the same day, the twentieth of November, called for a countrywide strike but stressed that it should be peaceful. All the Jewish businesses remained closed; workers did not show up that day—but this is about as far as the action went. Unless one considered the government's promise to permit two Zionist leaders to make a visit on board the *Patria,* before her departure a success, but depart she would.

The Revisionists, being on the outs with the British, did not know the details, but they had known that something of the kind was in the making. As they had realized that London would hardly be influenced by demonstrations in Palestine, they were preparing a massive campaign in the United States because England then more than ever needed American goodwill and help. The inflaming deportation order would lead to mass demonstrations before the British Embassy in Washington and before the British Consulates in New York, Chicago, and Los Angeles. The speakers not only would demand cancellation of the brutal deportation order but would expose to the American public Britain's policy of having—contrary to her obligations of the Balfour Declaration and of the Mandate— barred Palestine to those of Hitler's victims who succeeded in getting out of the Nazi hell.

This put Britain in a most undesirable situation. In their desperate need for American aid—and finally for America's entry into the war—they had to counteract creation of anti-British sentiment. On the other hand, Americans would not like it if Britain mixed into what was going on in America.

Fortunately for the British, they had people, Jews, whom they could let do their dirty work, thus saving Britain from having to soil her hands.

These people whom the British were going to use were none other than Dr. Weizmann and Moshe Shertok (Sharett).

The following cypher telegrams are self-explanatory. Because of their extremely delicate character, they were—quite unusual—classified not only SECRET but also MOST IMMEDIATE and PRIVATE and PERSONAL.

To High Commissioner—Sent 17th of November 1940—1600 hrs.

Illegal Immigrants. I saw Weizmann on 14th November and explained to him why we considered it absolutely essential in existing circumstances to proceed in manner proposed. He admitted force of arguments and expressed willingness to do his best to damp down Jewish agitation. He has now asked to give him facilities for telegraphing to Shertok and to his friends in U.S.A. in following terms.

Begina [sic] Lord Lloyd informs me ships now at Haifa are being followed by another contingent about 1800 refugees now at sea which may be followed by yet others. Government opinion is that this action may be prelude to wider and more systematic efforts by Nazis now in control of Rumanian ports. This aims first at getting rid of Jews. Second at embarrassing Britain creating conflicts between Government and ourselves by introduction of German agents provocateurs, and using this for propaganda among Arabs. Doing my best to obtain alleviation of situation. You must try prevent rise of feeling which may complicate situation. Cable your own suggestion. *ENDS.*

I am giving Weizmann non-committal answer for the moment. Meanwhile, I should be glad to learn with least possible delay whether you consider that message on above lines would be useful to you as tending to allay Jewish excitement and to facilitate task of Palestine Government. I do not overlook risk that by encouraging Weizmann's cooperation in this matter we may be laying up embarrassments for ourselves hereafter if and when we have to take measures (e.g. implementation of White Paper) to which Jews will raise strong objection. Immediate needs of the moment have to be weighed against these wider considerations. Please telegraph your views urgently.*

*FO371/25242 76021/40 288.

That Weizmann in his eagerness to please the British was ready to let himself be used as a tool and "to do his best to damp down Jewish agitation" was evident to Sir Harold MacMichael from the communication above. But the high commissioner did not like even "the appearance of making use of Weizmann as a favor." He wanted it to be absolutely clear that the Jewish leaders recognize their collaboration in the vicious British scheme not as a favor but as a duty and therefore they would have to accept the idea that they were not entitled to anything in return. He replied with the following telegram to the minister in London:

> CYPHER TELEGRAM from High Commissioner—Palestine—D. 18th November, 1940—R. 16th November, 1940—12.35 hrs. MOST IMMEDIATE and PRIVATE and PERSONAL SECRET.
>
> Illegal Immigrants. Your telegram of 17th November. At the moment Jews are apparently quiescent though pamphlets are being circulated. They are apparently awaiting reply to their representations conveyed in my telegram No. 1161.
>
> 2. I do not much like appearance of making use of Weizmann as a favor and so increasing obligations which will of course be cited later. Moreover I have been holding up issue of notice regarding absence of October-March quota until departure of *Patria* and its issue would be represented as a poor return for favors granted.
>
> 3. On the other hand we have represented to Jewish leaders here that it is their duty to assist in preventing disturbances, etc. and same applies to Weizmann ex officio. I suppose that we cannot expect him to advise support of the government but assuming his desire to carry out what is his duty with arrière-pensée he could well cable to Shertok advising against any anti-government action in respect of these illegalities. I should strongly deprecate citation of yourself or request for suggestions to be cabled. There is less justification for telegraphing to America in the sense suggested by Weizmann.*

The next telegram, again SECRET, IMMEDIATE and PRIVATE and PERSONAL, allayed the high commissioner's fears. *Nothing at all was promised to Weizmann* in return. The British manufactured it in such a way that they just "raise no objection" to Weizmann's intervention with the Jews in the United States. The British made certain that if anything were to go wrong they could wash their

---

*FO371/25242/1817/289.

hands of it, and Weizmann would be the villain. This is the telegram sent to the high commissioner of Palestine in reply to his telegram cited above:

> Your private and personal telegram of 18th November, I decided on further consideration to raise no objection to Weizmann sending telegram to Shertok and to his friends in U.S.A. in terms quoted in my private and personal telegram of 17 November. The censorship authorities were advised accordingly.
>
> I should explain that it was made clear to Weizmann through medium of a telephone message that while he was at liberty to send telegram on his own account, I had no particular desire that he should do so at this particular moment, and must not be understood as asking or inviting him to take any such action. On the other hand, if he specially wished to proceed as proposed, there could be no objection on my part.
>
> In other words, Weizmann has sent his message on his own initiative and not at my request or suggestion, and I do not consider that I have placed myself under any obligation to him in the matter.*

Under these circumstances the planned storm in the United States never materialized, and as the peaceful demonstration in Palestine was—peacefully—over, as the British were now certain of no further complications, they gave the green light for the departure of the *Patria* for November 25.

On that morning, the *Patria*'s engines had already been started, but she was still stationary, when, eleven minutes after nine A.M., a terrific blast shook her. Within seconds, in view of thousands of horror-stricken spectators, the *Patria* exploded.

She sank rapidly. Within twelve minutes, she settled on the bottom of Haifa harbor.

Those below deck never had a chance. Men and women tried to climb through the portholes. But the portholes were too small. Some victims remained stuck and went down this way with the ship. Their bodies were recovered months later in that position when the wreck was lifted. Parents pushed their smaller children through the portholes, but even of those children who made it, many drowned as they were sucked under by the waters of the sinking ship.

---

*FO371/25242/1817/290.

Most of those on deck jumped overboard. But dozens of these were also pulled down with the *Patria* as she sank to the bottom.

The horrified crowd, massed in that part of the port which had not been cordoned off, and those standing on the slopes of Mount Carmel—which rises steeply right next to the port—saw scores of humans go under and not come up again. Even had there been time to help, the onlookers would have been helpless as the entrance to the immediate port area had been barred by rifle-bearing British guards.

Among those who saw the horror was a young man, Eliyahu Hakim, who later, partly driven by what he had witnessed on that November day, was to become the assassin of the man, who on the highest level, was responsible for British Mideast policy, Lord Walter Edward Guinness Moyne.

Two hundred and fifty-four souls perished in that catastrophe, and 209 bodies were recovered. After all they had gone through, they had become victims of the four-front war. The youngest of the dead was only four days old. A native of Palestine, a baby boy, born in Haifa, on the *Patria,* on November 21, 1940.

Even wartime censorship could not keep this tragedy out of the news. A huge headline on the front page of the *New York Times* of November 26 read: "REFUGEE SHIP OFF PALESTINE IS SUNK BY BLAST: CASUALTIES FEARED AMONG 1,771 HOMELESS."

The Associated Press from Haifa stated:

> Haifa, Palestine, Nov. 25. The refugee steamer *Patria,* packed to the gunwales with 1,771 wandering, homeless Jews, exploded and capsized in Haifa Harbor yesterday with an undetermined but possibly heavy loss of life . . . an official stated that "some casualties" are feared. . . .

The following day, the *New York Times* reported 22 dead and 254 "missing."

For many years, well into the postwar period, the cause of the explosion remained a mystery. With good reason, nobody suspected the British of having blown up the ship themselves. The catastrophe had generated much publicity, all of it adverse to the British. There were two theories. One was that the refugees, in the Masada tradition, had decided to die in sight of their own land rather than to be deported from it. The other, closer to the truth, held that our

Irgun, to incapacitate the ship and thereby to thwart the deporta-tion, had planted a bomb on the *Patria* but had underestimated its strength. Actually, it was not the Irgun, the much more militant underground group, which had placed a bomb on board. It was the Haganah, the military arm of the Zionist establishment, that had done it. They expected that the *Patria* would not sink but would merely be damaged as a result of the explosion and would be unable to sail. A young Haganah member, Munja M. Mardor, was in charge of that operation which he described in detail—with the names of all those involved—in a report published in Hebrew in 1957 and seven years later in English.* He described how the bomb was produced and how, with the active help of desperate refugees already on the *Patria,* it was smuggled aboard. The error, according to him, was not in the strength of the bomb but in the fact that the ship's bolts were so badly corroded that the effect of the blast was far greater than anticipated.

Most of those who had survived the disaster had lost members of their family or at least friends. Still under the shock of what had happened—dripping wet and shivering from the icy water, the cold air, and the after effects of their shattering experience—the *Patria* survivors were brought by the British to the Athlit detention camp. The majority of the *Atlantic* passengers were also herded into Athlit. Only 100 of these had been on the *Patria.*

Those who may have believed that the torment was now over for these hunted ones—who had escaped but were continually rejected everywhere—were mistaken. The British could no longer deport those who had perished in Haifa harbor, but they insisted that those who had managed to survive the catastrophe were still to be deported to Mauritius! At the very hour while the survivors were being flung into trucks to haul them and those who were still on the *Atlantic* to the detention camp, the British were already preparing two more prison ships for the voyage to Mauritius. These were the *New Zealand* and the *Van de Witt,* two Dutch ships the British had gotten hold of when Holland fell to the Nazis.

With the news of the deportation on the heels of the *Patria* tragedy, expressions of utmost disgust came in from many places in the world—including from members of the House of Commons. Mr. Shertok met with the high commissioner, Sir Harold

*Munja M. Mardor, *Strictly Illegal* (London: Robert Hale, Ltd., 1964).

MacMichael, who stipulated that not only those who had been on the *Atlantic* and had therefore not been themselves victims of the explosion but also those who had been merely witnesses to it would be deported. Those who had been on the *Patria* and survived the explosion would also be deported to Mauritius! With the flare for understatement typical of his class and generation, Sir Harold MacMichael stated: "Governments sometimes have to face unpleasant situations." He did not say whether he thought it also "unpleasant" for the refugees, but deported they all would be.

It all worked out outrageously enough but not as entirely heinous as the high commissioner had planned. Colonel Wedgwood, the British Labor leader with whom I had kept in contact during our entire operation, led an attack in the House of Commons against the happenings which had resulted in the *Patria* tragedy. Other members of Commons joined him; others opposed him. Churchill himself was known not to be any particular friend of the tough Palestine policy practiced by his various departments. Yet there was a war on, and he favored the principle of letting people on the spot make their own determinations when the decision seemed not to be of critical importance. With Weizmann's reported intervention against agitation in the United States, no major embarrassing mass demonstrations by New York's 2 million Jews were carried out in front of the British Consulate there; no attempt to storm the British Embassy in Washington was made, or the like. The issue had not become a major one, and on November 22, two days after the deportation order had been given, no major trouble had erupted. Churchill had a note delivered to the colonial secretary, in which he stated that the deportation would have to take place, "but the conditions in Mauritius must not involve these people being caged up for the duration of the war." Churchill did not trust colonial authorities and so his message continued: "The Cabinet will require to be satisfied about this. Pray make me your proposals."

A few months later Churchill repeated the expression of his feelings that the prejudice of his Mideastern Command was vehemently and without good political reason heavily directed against the Jews. In March 1941 Churchill wrote regarding the hostile attitude against the Jewish refugees exhibited by the commanding officer of the British Mideastern Command, Sir Archibald Percival

Wavell. When Wavell suggested the deportation from Palestine of all "illegal" escapees from Hitler's slaughterhouses, Churchill stated:

> General Wavell, like most British military officers, is strongly pro-Arab. He sent a telegram not less strong than this, predicting widespread disaster in the Arab world, together with the loss of the Basra-Baghdad-Haifa route. The telegram should be locked up and also my answer in which I overruled the General and explained to him the reasons for the Cabinet decision. All went well and no dog barked.

Finally, most of those who had been on the *Pacific,* the *Milos,* and the *Atlantic* were deported. The number of those who after that torturous voyage had reached Palestine had now been reduced anyhow by those who had been killed on the *Patria.* As to the remaining one, the "fair" compromise decided upon by the British and announced on December 4 as "an exceptional act of mercy," was to deport to Mauritius the entire group of 1,800 who had not been "in" on the explosion. Those who had actually been on the *Patria* at the time she blew up and who had survived, however, would not be deported. Yet not only those who had been on the *Patria* had lost part of their family in the disaster. Many who had remained on the *Atlantic* had seen part of their family transferred to the *Patria* "for reasons of hygiene" and had lost them. To complicate the situation further, some of those who had been on the *Patria* and survived had the rest of their family on the *Atlantic.* The survivors would now see their parents, or one of them, their brothers or sisters, or one of their children who had stayed on the *Atlantic* deported, while they, being *Patria* survivors, had been pardoned and would stay behind in Palestine. How humane a "compromise" to let the actual *Patria* survivors stay and to deport all the others!

Rumors among the survivors had it that large-scale demonstrations by New York's influential Jewish minority were under way. However, with the help of the Jewish leadership, any such vehement reactions in the United States had been stifled. But in Palestine too many Jews had witnessed the catastrophe; too many had friends and relatives now in the Athlit detention camp to take the deportation order in stride. It was not only that after all their sufferings and after reaching the Promised Land these brothers and sisters were to be deported to some faraway island. They had reached Palestine and to every Jew forceful deportation from the land promised to him by God was a total negation of Jewish rights, of British obligations, and was sacrilegious. Palestine's Jews were ready for an open revolt against their colonial rulers when the order to deport the 1,800 from Athlit to Mauritius was announced. And this time it was not only the Irgun who were ready to use civil disobedience methods and even to resist the deportation with force. A plan was worked out by the Haganah for masses of people to block the streets through which the deportees were to be hauled to the prison ships and not to give way, even to engage the armed convoy in "battle" if necessary. But although Haganah leaders pleaded for permission to have this plan put into effect in cooperation with other groups, the Zionist leadership, in its continual endeavor to appease the British, insisted on only a token demonstration. It was to be restricted to the port area of Haifa; nobody must carry even a stick. The protest had to be absolutely peaceful. This was exactly what the British wanted: hush the thing over in the United States and have just a peaceful protest in the immediate embarkation area in Palestine. They could now go to work on the refugees. And they did.

Their military and police conferred and agreed that whatever the Zionist Executive might wish, the refugees would not allow themselves to be hauled without a fight from Palestine soil to the prison ships waiting for them in Haifa port. The British firmed up their "battle plans." Military preparations were accordingly made.

First of all, the final decision and the date of deportation had to be kept secret to prevent early preparations by the "enemy." The date of the operation was set for Monday, December 9. But in the course of the preceding day, the interned ones could not but notice that something was in the air, and that it was nothing good either. The British police who until then had guarded those detained at Athlit were withdrawn and replaced by a new police unit which had the reputation of being particularly tough and cruel. Obviously, it was feared that those who had guarded the refugees so far had seen too much of their plight, that they had developed some compassion for them. The whole action was prepared and proceeded in proper military fashion, as taught in the military staff schools. Control posts were set up in various sections of the sprawling camp, manned by men carrying rifles and Bren guns. A number of Jewish assistant policemen had previously been assigned to the camp to serve as a liaison with the refugees, as many of them did not speak English. These Jewish policemen were now withdrawn. In the fields adjoining the camp, those behind the barbed wires saw one armored carrier after another drive up and get into position. "The British have learned in France and in Dunkirk what encirclement means; they are practicing now on us," one of the refugees remarked bitterly.

Soon after darkness fell on Sunday, the refugees were told that they would "continue their voyage" and were ordered to pack their belongings. That they had no belongings was irrelevant; somebody who did not know better had issued the order.

"We shall not go. We shall fight," shouted the young ones, but many of the older refugees said: "Fight with what? We do not even have broom handles left; they took the brooms away." "We will undress and fight with our trouser belts. We will lose the fight, but we will not go without defending our dignity as humans," announced one young man who went from hut to hut to urge the others on.

The British noticed that there was a communication between the huts and locked each hut, hoping thus to prevent a "conspiracy." Men and women were held prisoners in different parts of the enclosure, and so husbands and wives could not even experience together that night so filled with anxious suspense. This was particularly hard on several couples who had arrived on the *Atlantic* but whose children had been on the *Pacific* or the *Milos* and had died in the sinking of the *Patria.*

The British went into action at six A.M. The entire procedure was under the personal command of the inspector general of the Palestine police, Mr. Sanders, known among Palestine's Jews as one of their worst enemies, a colonial officer loyal to the Crown with little understanding for troublesome natives.

The refugees had barricaded their huts from inside, but it was of course easy for the men in uniform to push in the doors and knock them open. Inside they found men as well as women lying naked on the floor and refusing to get up and to leave. This was something the police were not used to—they stalled and waited for orders. The orders came quickly. Billy clubs—not an unfamiliar sight to many who had been beaten by the SS—were to be used to make the naked get up. The police, it was later reported, were amazed how much beating it took to get those on their feet who had experienced even worse beatings and mistreatment in Dachau or Buchenwald. The pleading, screaming, and crying of men and women mixed with the terrified shrieking of small children who saw their mothers and fathers being clubbed and starting to bleed. One man, a cripple, defended himself with his crutches; some naked women fought literally tooth and nail as they resisted being wrapped into blankets and being carried to the waiting trucks.

To the credit of the British, it must be noted that, although this was a specially selected police unit, a number of men disobeyed their orders and stood by passively during the battle. The refugees remember that one constable, called "Taylor" by the others, openly defied his orders. On the other hand, one of the officers, seeing the hesitation in some of his men, shouted: "Get on with it, chaps. There's work to be done. Roll up your sleeves and let them have it!"

Many of the refugees think that a good number of the police-men were drunk. This could account for the brutality. Then too, the police may not have found it difficult to be brutal when these refugees from Nazi Germany cursed the British and shouted at them "Storm troopers," "Where are your swastikas?" and other insults. But in their despair, the deportees cursed the Jews of Palestine too: "Where are our brethren? You have shamefully abandoned us!"

The refugees were not the only eyewitnesses. The Jewish "su-pernumerary" policemen who had been relieved of their duty for that day had been detained in a separate hut from which they observed how inexorably the military got the upper hand in this ignominious encounter.

The resistance was such that in spite of all preparations, the operation was not completed until two P.M. The time gained thereby saved 45 of those to be deported from sharing the fate of the others. The physicians in the detention camp declared them too sick for any kind of voyage; they would almost certainly die in the trucks or on the trip. The British did not want the "unpleasantness" of any additional unnecessary deaths and so, after some bickering and formalities, they left the 45 behind.

The other 1,584 were finally thrown into the trucks like cattle being brought to the slaughterhouse, in a scene reminiscent of what was happening to those they had left behind. The entire post area was closed to the public, but nearby thousands of Jews—as ordered by the Zionist leaders, eager to dampen down Jewish agitation—staged a proper and peaceful, and, accordingly, unimpressive demonstration. Yet relatives of those being deported tried to incite the crowd into attempting to free the prisoners. However, generally the decorum was maintained—and no high-positioned Jews in London had to be ashamed of any excessive emotional outbursts. Although the prisoners themselves were disappointed by this lack of support, they put up another fight when they were unloaded from the trucks and hauled on board the two ships which were already under steam and ready to go. But the spirit of the deportees was now broken. Within a few hours they saw the coastline of the land which they had undergone such inhuman hardships to reach slowly disappear. They were on the way to the Indian Ocean.

The way the British announced the deportation shows that they did not dare to stand up before the eyes of the world for what they had committed. This is the announcement as printed in the *New York Times* of December 19, 1940.

> Jerusalem Dec. 18. It is revealed that 1,584 illegal Jewish immigrants who reached Palestine from Europe aboard a small vessel, the *Atlantic,* sailed from Haifa Dec. 8 in two modern vessels placed at their disposal by the Palestine Government by the British Ministry of Shipping [sic]. Their destination is a British colony where they will remain until the end of the war.

Thus the British made it appear as if they had helped the refugees who had arrived in a "small vessel" by placing "at their disposal" "two modern vessels." The announcement did, of course, not mention that the refugees were deported to the epidemic-stricken island of Mauritius.

There was no announcement by the Jewish Agency, no press conference, no leaking of information to be published that the immigrants had to be clubbed into the prison ships and that the above announcement was entirely misleading. The British had made good use of their Weizmann connection without incurring any obligation.

Churchill's demand that the refugees should "not be caged up" was not known to Jewish leaders, and in the fast-developing events of the war those who should have remembered conveniently did not do so. In fact, immediately upon arrival at what the refugees called Devil's Island, they were caged up in an old French prison. As befits criminals in a prison, men and women were separated. The men were committed to cells. The women were herded, in groups of 24, into corrugated huts, where the heat was unbearable. For two hours, three times a week the women were permitted to see their husbands, other male relatives, and if one could prove one's engagement, even a fiancé.

The Jewish Agency asked the British government for permission to allow the Mauritius deportees to volunteer in the Palestinian Jewish units of the British Armed Forces. Oh no, not these people! Permission denied. The request was repeated. Permission again denied. In the meanwhile, these people, who had been criminal enough to try to save their lives, were wasting away on that horrible island. More than three years later, when in the House of Commons, several British statesmen again voiced their concern about these abuses of colonialism, the under secretary of the colonies claimed to have no information about how many, if any, of the refugees perished on the voyage itself, but he admitted that within less than nine months of their arrival, by September 30, 1941, 54 of the refugees had succumbed. Twenty-six of them "due to infectious or contagious diseases"; the others had died due to "other" causes.

The following excerpts from a comprehensive British report are self-explanatory:

> TYPHOID OUTBREAK IN THE CAMP. The detainees brought this infection with them, the first case being admitted into the hospital on December 28, 1940, i.e., the day after their landing. Their general health was poor on arriving owing to the extreme privations they had suffered on their journey. They reached the colony at the height of the hot season, when flies are extremely active; hence the spread of the disease in the early days of January. . . .*

> MALARIA. Following an exceptionally hot and rainy season, cases of malaria were detected on the 13th of January, 1941, the epidemic spreading rapidly by the end of January.†

*Government report to Jewish Agency SF 427-41 Feb. 1943. Central Zionist Archives, Jerusalem S25/2634.
†Ibid.

But the stricken ones had nothing to worry about. They were well cared for by real experts whose qualifications are named in the official report which continues as follows:

> On the 25th of January, a special malaria ward was opened and placed under the control of Lady Clifford, President of the Local Branch of the Red Cross Society. Lady Clifford and a great number of V.A.D., many of whom belonged to the best Mauritius families, worked day and night with great devotion and skill. . . .*

No doubt, that these ladies belonged to the "best Mauritius families" was a source of great consolation for those who had lost most of their beloved ones in German-occupied lands, on the voyage to Palestine, on the *Patria* catastrophe and/or still others in the typhoid outbreak on Mauritius itself.

They did stay, as initially ordered, to the end of the war, or almost to the end. When approximately three long years after the deportation, on October 22, 1944, the *Palestine Post* announced that close to 100 of the refugees had perished in Mauritius (there were actually more), their case started moving again. When Allied troops were already fighting well inside Germany, and Berlin was about to fall, ten weeks before Germany's surrender, the British government became suddenly magnanimous toward the prisoners on Mauritius. But the rule that they would have to stay for the duration of the war continued in force. On February 12, 1945, the governor of Mauritius announced that "the Jewish refugees now in Mauritius will be allowed to enter Palestine." This sounded good—after more than four years—but the proclamation continued. "No promise can be made as to when that will be . . ." Four months later, in June 1945, one month after Germany had surrendered, eight new deaths among the Jewish refugees were recorded. This time the killer epidemic was infantile paralysis. Altogether, according to British records, 126 of those who had escaped Hitler did not escape Mauritius and are buried there.

The inhumanity with which the British proceeded is probably best exemplified by the case of little Heinz Hirschmann, then ten years old. After a tortuous voyage he had arrived in Palestine. His

*Ibid.

mother and he were clubbed into the prison ships and deported to Mauritius; his father was left behind in Palestine. In Mauritius his mother died of typhus on January 5, 1941, and his father tried now to gain his son's release from captivity in Mauritius. Lengthy correspondence between the Jewish Agency—which wanted to help the father—and the British authorities ensued. The high commissioner remained adamant. Heinz could not join his father. Finally, after continuing interventions from many sources on behalf of little Heinz, on September 2, 1942, almost two years after his mother's death, the Colonial Office in London magnanimously changed its mind and permitted the child to join his father in Palestine "as soon as shipping facilities are available."*

Hardly less tragic, though not standing alone because many of the captives on Mauritius were in a similar situation, was the case of Mrs. Mirjam Gruber, a widow. While she was held at Mauritius, her son in Palestine had joined the British forces and had hoped that this would cause the British to let his mother out and to join the rest of the family in Palestine. Her son was killed in active service, but in 1944 Mrs. Gruber was still being held in Mauritius. We have no information as to her further fate.

Had the Jews deported to Mauritius been German prisoners of war, the British would have had to treat them incomparably better. Germany would have protested with justification that deportation to that epidemic-infested island was a violation of the Geneva International Convention on Prisoners of War, and, in fact, no German prisoners of war were forced to suffer a similar fate.

Among the last ones to die on Mauritius was a woman in her fifties who had contracted malaria there. Her sons were residents of Palestine and had all volunteered for the British army. They had made one appeal after another seeking permission to allow their mother to join them, the more so as the father had been killed by the Nazis. The requests had all been denied.*

Thus, in a way, the story of the *Patria,* which had started so hopefully with Mr. Storfer's flotilla gliding down the Danube in October 1939, ended only after the war was over—at least for those who had managed to overcome in turn each of the "fronts" in our

---

*Central Zionist Archives, Jerusalem S25/2635 2B.
†Ibid.

four-front war: the Nazi front, the British one, that of the Jewish establishment, and finally the front posed against us by nature itself—rough seas, bad climates, and the epidemics of Mauritius.

Certainly the stories of the *Patria,* and *Parita,* and the *Las Perlas* were quite dissimilar from one another. Yet even more markedly divergent from the adventures of any of the "four *P*'s" is that of the S.S. *Pencho.* Not only the experiences on the voyage and its aftermath, however, make the story of the *Pencho* unique. The ship itself deserves description because it is doubtful whether any contraption like it ever sailed the high seas.

Late in 1939, when Poland had already fallen and the Einsatztruppen, whose main purpose was mass executions, were busy all over the Nazi-held territories, the Revisionist scouts—whom we had everywhere looking for ships—learned of a small ancient Italian paddle-wheeler, the *Stefano.* It did the odd jobs on the Danube that nobody else wanted, functioning partly as tugboat and partly as ferry for short runs on the Danube. From today's perspective it seems like madness to have considered that ship for a sea voyage, but those were days in which people might well have tried to rescue themselves on a float of reeds. We decided, at any rate, that whether we wanted to take the risk or not, we had to.

In the Nazi puppet state of Slovakia, persecution was particularly cruel and relentless. I knew personally that the little town in eastern Slovakia from which my paternal grandfather had moved to Prague, the town of Zborov, had proudly announced that it was the first one which, following governmental orders, had "rid itself" of all of its Jews. Because of conditions in Slovakia, the Betar leaders there, our old friend Citron and our Betar office in Prague, run by Eliyahu Gleser and Emil Faltyn, insisted that the Slovakian Betar had to be immediately evacuated. We therefore decided to cram as many Slovakian Betarim as possible on the *Stefano* and to try to have her paddle our people all the way down the Danube, through the Black Sea, the Marmara and the Ionian and the Mediterranean, all the way to Palestine. This was a great risk, of course, but we knew that the alternative was "extermination."

First we had to change the ship's flag. Italy was Germany's ally, and the western Mediterranean was then still—although not for much longer—controlled by the British. With the extensive help of "Mr. Kebab"—baksheesh—the transfer was effected. At that same time, the name of the ship was changed to *Pencho*—why just that name, nobody seemed to know even then. When I asked, "Why *Pencho?*" I was told, "If we called her *Spinach,* people would think she ought to be green."

The little thing had to be remodeled for carrying passengers— and plenty of them. After she had been "transformed" for the sea voyage, our *Pencho* looked like a toy put together by an eleven-year-old with tinker toys or an erector set. Eri Jabotinsky described the *Pencho* as follows:

> The whole contraption looked like a cross between a flea and a submarine . . . a roof and walls were built around its upper deck. Accommodation was made for 400 passengers.*

The boat was so old and "unriverworthy" that it was not even commissioned to travel the entire length of the Danube. In particular, there was one narrow spot on the river, the "Iron Gate"—the location at which the British and with them some Jewish leaders planned to blow up the *Darien II*—at which the water flowed quite swiftly. Even before we acquired the *Pencho,* the river authorities had limited her travel only up to the Iron Gate because the boat's sides were considered too weak to withstand the pressure of the stronger current at that point.

A man in the office having the power to change the restriction became, under the influence of baksheesh, a genius of a nautical engineer. He suggested that we "strengthen the sides of the ship by putting heavy rocks inside it." These rocks would press against the outside and thereby "counter" the pressure of the swiftly flowing river. His suggestion was adopted, and as we were now to obtain a new license anyhow, we convinced the Commission of the Rumanian Office of Marine Navigation to issue us a certificate that the *Pencho* was capable of sailing from Bratislava just forty miles down the river from Vienna—to Haifa!

But we had not paid in full for the ship. Members of the Betar came usually from the poorest families. The Slovakian Betar was particularly poor; hardly any one of the 300 Betarim whom Faltyn and Gleser evacuated had any money. Besides, money was of no

---

*Eri Jabotinsky, *The Sakarya Expedition* (Johannesburg, S.A.: Nero Press and Publishing Co., 1945), p. 14.

value unless it could be transferred into foreign currency—an undertaking illegal in all Balkan countries and punishable by death in Nazi-controlled areas. Yet we had to make these illegal transfers continually because only free currencies, English pounds and American dollars, were acceptable in the people-smuggling trade. Time and again I crossed borders with illegal money in the highest possible denominations stuffed into my specially made hairbrush, where it was hidden between the bristles and the wooden back. If that space in the hairbrush was insufficient in spite of the large denominations used, I had the balance sewn into my belt which was cut open at the place of arrival. I am still amazed that I was never discovered smuggling foreign currency. As I became better known to the authorities in half a dozen Balkan countries, however, we began using unsuspected third persons for such currency transactions. Unfortunately, on two occasions, these people "transferred" the money to themselves, and there was nothing we could do about it. Surprisingly, neither I nor anyone I knew about was ever apprehended smuggling currency. This was partly due to the high percentage of illiteracy in these countries. For smuggling we usually chose remote little-traveled outposts. Our names were, of course, on the lists of those who were to be thoroughly searched, but most border guards in the sticks had trouble reading. But even those who could read found it hard to locate a name in the alphabetical order on the voluminous lists each border station had.

Though the Slovakian Betarim had hardly any money, we finally did manage to pay for the *Pencho.* As we had arranged before, we had some refugees come along who could pay the fares for others who were unable to. In addition, Zeev Jabotinsky and Hillel Cook's American Friends of a Jewish Palestine Committee succeeded in collecting the remaining money we needed to get the people on the *Pencho.*

Finally, on May 18, 1940, at a time when the French defense line had already collapsed before the German onslaught, our contraption left the Danube port of Bratislava with 414 Jews, most of them from Slovakia. At Bezdan, the first Danube port in Yugoslavia, 100 more refugees were crammed into the old tugboat. From Bezdan, the *Pencho,* passing Belgrade, went down to Moldavia, but there she was stopped. The Rumanians, under heavy British pressure, had announced that no passage through Rumania could be granted. The Balkans had not yet then been invaded by the Germans, Britain had an embassy in each of the Balkan capitals, and every one of these embassies did its best to block the escape route of our ships. The people on the *Pencho* felt that this was particularly cruel because since early in May, after France, Holland, and Belgium had fallen, practically all of the European continent was in Nazi hands and now more than ever flight to the East via the Danube was the only remaining chance for escape. From Moldavia the *Pencho* with her 514 on board had to turn back to Yugoslav territory.

In Yugoslavia, the 514 were held up for seventy days. The financial report for 1940 of the Association of Yugoslav Jewish Communities lists among the expenses: "Provisioning for 70 days the 514 people on the *Pencho.*"

The Yugoslav government finally helped them to get as far as the feared Iron Gate. There the emigrants were taken off and transferred to a motorboat supplied by the government. They stood on the banks praying that their ship, their only hope, would not be crushed right before their eyes. It was not, and they could board it again and continue their trip to Vidin in Bulgaria. But there the Bulgarians did not permit them to drop anchor. When our people wanted to buy food and coal, this request was also denied. The British would view this as "aiding" illegal refugees. As the *Pencho* people could not obtain any provisions in Bulgaria, they sailed on to Rumania to Gurghiu. And there—as nothing with these illegal transports could ever be predicted—the Rumanian authorities who had before taken such a firm stand against the *Pencho* were now compassionate and helpful! On September 11 we received permission for the *Pencho* to load coal, food, and water and to continue the voyage down the Danube to Sulina. On September 21, 1940, exactly on the anniversary of Heydrich's announcement a year earlier that the fuehrer wanted all Jews "resettled" within a year, the 514, after three months and three days on the Danube, were able to leave port for the intended sea voyage.

As this caricature of a ship paddled its way out into the open sea, intent on making it to Palestine, seamen in the port, dock workers, and fishermen stood there and shook their heads. "They will not make it even ten miles out." Besides all the obvious technical shortcomings of the boat, the war had then been on for over a year, Italy had entered on Germany's side more than four months earlier, and the Mediterranean was a battleground, swarming with Italian warships, with British warships and with submarines from Britain, Italy, and Germany. Then too there were the minefields. Yet just as if this freakish vessel were meant to be nothing more than a float loaded to the railings in a carnival parade, music could even be heard from the departing ship. There were several musicians among the refugees; two of them had brought their violins along and one his French horn, and the little band played gay songs as the *Pencho* moved farther and farther away from the mouth of the Danube River. "They will never even get through the Black Sea. She cannot. Not a chance in a hundred," was the consensus of a group of sailors from another ship seeing the *Pencho* depart.

They were all wrong. As unlikely, as impossible as it seemed, the people on the *Pencho* did reach Palestine. But it took them a long, long time, and they underwent enough adventures and experiences to fill a book or make a spell-binding movie.

She was such a monstrosity, apparently because she looked ready to topple over or to sink at any moment, she found it easier than other refugee ships to obtain permission along the way to procure enough provisions and coal to paddle to the next place. Most of the passengers had never been on any ship and were not aware what, nautically speaking, the *Pencho* was undertaking. Morale on the ship was relatively good, partly due to the large percentage of well-disciplined Betarim on board, partly because of the effective leadership of a member of the Irgun whose certainly unenviable job was the obviously impossible mission of getting the people to Palestine.

The *Pencho* had been less than a month on her way and "already" in the Mediterranean, near the Turkish-Syrian border, when she was accosted by Italian torpedo boats. When she was first spotted by one of these warships, its officers did not know what kind of thing it was that they saw floating on the sea. They found it hard to believe their eyes when they came close and boarded the *Pencho*.

"Where do you think you are going?" Our people were afraid to tell the truth.

"We are going to Paraguay. Here are our visas." The Italian officers were stunned.

"To Paraguay—and you are here, do you know where Paraguay is?" Finally our people had to tell the truth. The Italians were still suspicious.

"How could you get here, the sea is full of mines, we know

where our minefields are, the British know theirs, you claim you know none. How is it possible that none of the magnetic mines hit you?"

Jokingly the leader of the transport replied: "Maybe because we did not know about them, they did not know about us." But this turned out not to be a joke as the naval officers determined right afterward. The one who had gone below deck came up with the answer: "This thing has so little displacement—it is almost flat—and it has so little metal on it, that it did not attract the magnetic mines."

The Italians escorted the *Pencho* to the nearby small island of Stampalia. There the story was all taken down in detail, typed in triplicate, the ship and all the refugees were searched. Nothing was found to contradict their story. True to the spirit of helpfulness the Italians had shown toward the *Rim,* they permitted the *Pencho* to load food supplies, water, and coal, and with the wishes of scores of sailors who were waving to the departing *Pencho,* she sailed off once more. Again the little band played its tunes, as, on the pier, the islanders and the military men watched them with astonishment—and pity.

This incident might sound like a lighthearted episode, but it was not one for those on the ship. When they had first spotted the Italian warships approaching, they feared that the torpedo boats—which, to them, appeared as "huge battleships"—were British and might open fire on them. When it became clear that these were Italians, the refugees were afraid that they might be handed over to the Germans.

But though it had all ended well, a major catastrophe was just ahead of them. In fact they sailed straight into it. No torpedo, no minefield, no warship, "it" was a storm. The *Pencho* people describe it as a kind of hurricane, but actually it would not have taken much of a gale to incapacitate this little boat which had so far luckily encountered only good weather. In the storm that ensued, the paddle-wheeler spun around, out of control. When, to gain more control, the crew speeded up the engines, the next catastrophe hit. A pipe which fed the steam boiler blew up. Disabled, the ship started to take on water as wave after wave hit it. Fortunately, however, as the wind picked up, it drove the *Pencho* ahead—and now good news again: an island had come into sight. No, it was not an island, just a large rock, no house, no tree, not even a trace of shrubbery. But before the people on board had time to do much thinking about the "island"—the *Pencho* had been driven against the rocks. And on this unnamed, uninhabited island, the life of the courageous little *Pencho* came to an end.

The passengers all managed to scramble ashore. But there was no water, no vegetation. Fortunately, after the people had been saved, some of the supplies still on board the wreck were salvaged, too. Using the sails and tying women's clothes together, the shipwrecked ones made large SOS signs. They also lit wood saved from the *Pencho* to attract attention. But no ship, no plane noticed them.

Five men volunteered to take off in the only lifeboat, to try to reach some inhabited island in order to alert the people there. The five set out. None of them returned. All the *Pencho* people thought that the five had drowned, but years later, after the war, they learned that the five would-be rescuers had been picked up by a British warship and brought to a hospital in Alexandria, Egypt, from where they finally made their way to Palestine.

Those who had stayed on the rock island had in the meanwhile consumed what little food they had saved from the *Pencho* and had begun eating snails and seaweed. Lack of water constituted the worst problem. A few fish were caught, but the weaker passengers began to fall ill from the lack of water and food.

A few bottles that had been on board were sent out with messages describing what had happened and giving the location of the wreck. A raft was made and sent out with the same message.

On the tenth day of their being stranded there, October 18, a warship appeared on the horizon. Was it Italian or British? It was Italian, and again, true to previously shown compassion, the Italians helped these refugees once more. They gave their water supplies to the shipwrecked, they fed them, and because wine belongs with an Italian meal, they even served them wine. Again, within an hour or two, fate had reversed itself. Hell had changed into paradise.

The warship took the refugees to the nearest Italian port—which just happened to be the Island of Rhodes. There, the *Pencho* people were housed in the same tents in which those who had seen the *Rim* burn and sink had been quartered.

The Jews of Rhodes outdid themselves in their concern and help for the marooned ones of the *Pencho*. Their efforts were ably coordinated by the community's chairman, Mr. Franco, and a younger relative of his, the indefatigable Mr. Soriano, both of whom had been most helpful with the *Rim.*

The shipwrecked ones were most restless, and rightly so. The Germans had by then conquered Poland, Belgium, Holland, and France. Italy was in the war. The Germans were expected to invade some of the major islands of the western Mediterranean any moment. Again every day counted, and urgent letters and telegrams went out from individuals as well as from the Rhodes Jewish community stressing to Jewish organizations in the free world the pressing need for a ship. Money too, was needed, but only a ship could save their lives.

The Jewish Agency had an office in neutral Switzerland, in Geneva, specifically for the purpose of aiding refugees from Nazi persecution. A German Jew, Richard Lichtheim, an old-time leader of German Zionism, was in charge of coordinating escape efforts of European Jewry. Naturally his office became a central point for pleas for a ship. But we have no indication that any effort was made by the Jewish Agency to engage in something as improper as saving fellow Jews "illegally." To the contrary. In a letter dated October 29, 1940, marked RL/LU A 4d, and addressed to New York, to Mr. Henry Montor of the United Palestine Appeal,* Mr. Lichtheim shows himself in good humor as to the efforts to save Jews by free immigration. He derides us as—how funny!—*"Jewish admirals."*† After having received desperate letters from Rhodes, he wrote to the United Palestine Appeal in New York as if he had never heard of the tens of thousands whose lives had by then been saved with the help of "illegal" shipping:

> I have not the slightest idea what can be done besides sending money which should be sent from America to the Jewish Community in Rhodes.

And striking a humorous note, which he apparently felt was a more proper thing to do than taking any illegal action to save lives, he later in the letter continues, after mentioning the British fleet:

> ... they simply do not allow these refugee-boats to approach the Palestinian waters after having passed through the Dardanelles. So

---

*Then the name of the multimillion-dollar United Jewish Appeal.
†Author's italics.

the boats have to tramp along in the Aegean Sea, waiting for some opportunity to land somewhere or to fool the British Navy which is not as easy as our "Jewish admirals" believe it to be.

Yet while this "humorous" letter was crossing the ocean, the Germans were already preparing the invasion of Rhodes. In the face of this tragic lack of understanding on the part of the man in charge of just the office which was supposed to help, it is heartrendering to read the letter the Jewish community of Rhodes wrote to that same Jewish Agency office on December 6, 1940: written in French, the language used in these days in Europe in international communication, it begs the "dear coreligionists" not to abandon them. It mentions the need for money but stresses:

> *Encore une fois nous vous prions de prendre serieuse en consideration, tout ce que nous avancons, qu'independent des envois* plus copieux *de l'argent qu'il nous faut, vous vous préoccupiez et c'est le seul salut qui existe, DE LEUR ENVOYER LE BATEAU, LE BATEAU SAUVEUR, qui doit les emmener dans le pays de leur destination.**

The letter is signed by Mr. Franco, the self-sacrificing, ever-caring chairman of the Rhodes Jewish community who was himself to be murdered not much later in Auschwitz. But it met with little understanding at the highest level of the Jewish establishment's office for refugees. It was unfortunate that the recipient of that letter had to be the same official who had wisecracked about the "Jewish admirals" who were hallucinating about how "to fool the British Navy." Yet it would have been so easy for the relatively well-to-do UPA to buy an American ship, not just one small one, but several ships, and to have them sail into the areas where they were so critically needed. America was not in the war yet, not for another year. The British, in dire need of U.S. aid, would certainly not have dared to shoot at U.S. ships. The Germans and Italians, eager to keep America neutral as long as possible, would not have

---

*"Once again we beg you to seriously consider, that all we are putting forth, aside from sending *much more* money that we need, is that you give primary consideration—and it is the only salvation that exists—TO SEND THEM THE SHIP, THE SAVIOUR-SHIP, which must take them to the country of their destination."

interfered either. Tens of thousands more could still have been saved at that late point. But: "I have not the slightest idea what can be done . . ." and a joke about the "Jewish admirals" was the Jewish establishment's attitude.

When it became clear—at least to the Italian hierarchy—that the Germans were going to take over the major islands in the western Mediterranean,* the governor of Rhodes had his Jewish refugees all transferred as "prisoners of war" to the Italian mainland. It was due to that move that the *Pencho* people avoided sharing the fate of the Jewish community of Rhodes. As soon as the Germans were in control on Rhodes, the entire Jewish community, which had not previously escaped on the *Rim,* was shipped off to Auschwitz. Only a few who had the means to bribe some officials and the luck to find functionaries who let themselves be bribed survived. All others, including the community's chairman, Mr. Franko, and the aged, revered rabbi, were murdered in the gas chambers.

Our *Pencho* people, safely out of Rhodes, prior to the deportation of the Jews who so short a time ago had been so much better off than the shipwrecked 514, were now in Italy itself. Although confined, they seemed safe. Then came the bad news. The Gestapo had taken upon itself to "solve the Jewish question" in allied Italy. October 11, 1943, is known as the Black Sunday of Rome. After well-planned preparations, all the Jews of Rome whom the Germans and the Italian Fascist police could round up, were arrested, dispatched to Auschwitz, and immediately murdered. This included members of well-known Roman families who had been active in the Catholic Church but who themselves or whose parents or grandparents had been born as Jews. At the same time, it became known to the *Pencho* people in their camp at Feremonti that the action in Rome had been preceded by a similar one in Trieste on October 9. In spite of all endeavors for secrecy, news spread unbelievably fast in the totalitarian oppressive setting. The *Pencho* people learned that on November 3 the Jews of Genoa had been hunted down and deported to Auschwitz; November 6 those of Florence; November 8 was the day for Milan; the day after for Venice. The Jews of Ferrara were hauled away on November 14, and the Jew hunt continued all over Italy.

---

*The bloody German invasion of Crete and its capture, which were soon to take place, would remain one of the fiercest battles of World War II.

But as miraculously as that good old caricature of a ship, the *Pencho,* had made it down the Danube, the Black Sea, the Marmara, and the Aegean Sea through the minefields, well into the Mediterranean, just as miraculously as its refugees had evaded the fate of the Jews of Rhodes, they now also were able to escape the fate of the Jews of Italy, even though they, as fugitives from Germany, would have normally been considered a prime target. The saving factor might have had something to do with the fact that at one point they had been designated as "prisoners of war," but certainly this alone would not have saved them from the Germans. A Jew was a Jew whoever he was. The whole voyage of the *Pencho,* in spite of all the sufferings, must have somehow been blessed with—relatively—good luck. Or, as the more religious stated: "The Almighty must have decided from the beginning: I will save these people who are daring oceans and war with that boat."

The *Pencho* people stayed in Italy all through the war; they were liberated by American troops and could finally, six years after they set out to reach Palestine, arrive home there, find alive and well the five scouts whom they had considered dead, and tell their unbelievable story.

chapter 6

THE *SAKARYA* EXPEDITION: THE LARGEST VENTURE OF THEM ALL

Plans for the largest single venture of them all were conceived more than a year and a half before their fruition. It was the undertaking that was to become the one with the most unexpected ending. In August 1939, after the departure of the *Rim* people from Rhodes and their safe arrival in Palestine, the Italian police in Rhodes finally returned my passport to me. The next day I flew back to Athens, and it was on that flight that the plan was born.

Leaning back comfortably in my seat, happy in the knowledge that the *Rim* people, after all their trials, were now at their destination, I relived much of their odyssey. The thought came to me that the problems arising from such a transport did not grow in proportion to the number of immigrants on board. Why, then, I thought, should we not charter a really large ship, organize a really mammoth transport. Instead of planning for the usual 800 to 1,200, we should try for a ship that would save 2,000 or 3,000 people on one voyage.

In Athens, I soon found out that, although the theory might be correct, one problem was much harder to solve in planning such a large transport: how could one find a shipowner who would risk such a large ship? Most of those already in the Jew-smuggling trade—or willing to enter it—had only small ships. Smugglers must unload their cargoes fast, therefore they shun larger ships. No large ships came from Greece, nor did telephone calls to Varna in Bulgaria net me a ship as large as I had hoped to find. Germany's "non-aggression treaty" with the Soviet Union now became known, and as a German attack against the West was expected any day, bottoms were very much in demand. Even smaller ships were becoming harder for us to obtain. Why should a shipowner risk confiscation for smuggling Jews if he could make almost as much money by legitimate trade.

Among the many people whom I contacted was a shipping agency in Galatz, Rumania. Months before, Popescu had brought to my hotel a tall, heavy-set Jew whose name was Rand and who owned the shipping agency of Rand, Shneer and Co. in Galatz. Rand's brother-in-law, though from an old Rumanian family, was a citizen of Iran (for tax reasons, no doubt), and thus had business connections there and in Turkey. Rand had at that time told me that if we ever needed to transfer a ship to an Iranian or Turkish flag, he could quickly arrange it. It occurred to me now that he might be able not only to help us arrange the transfer of a ship to a Turkish or Iranian flag but to come up with a ship from one of those nations. I contacted him and he said he could get us a Turkish or Iranian ship large enough to carry 2,000 or more.

This news reached me just one day before war broke out: August 31, 1939. Because the outbreak of war had long been expected, I had made my preparations in advance and so was not only ready—but able—to leave on the next train. From the day of the announcement of the Hitler-Stalin treaty, I had booked reservations for a seat on the Orient Express for every single day of the coming week. A "contribution to the living expenses" of a man working for the Wagons Lits Company took care of all the details connected with it. Every morning he cancelled the reservation for that day and added one for eight days ahead, while keeping in force the reservations for all the dates in between. Thus, the morning Germany invaded Poland, I had a valid reservation for that day's train on which the sign read: SALONIQUE, BELGRADE, MILAN, PARIS, LONDON.

No description of the Athens railroad station on that day can do justice to the bedlam there. Everyone who could afford to flee to the West tried to catch a train out. The environs of the railroad station were clogged with automobiles loaded to the brim inside and with boxes on the rooftops, with fiacres, and in between goats and donkeys that had become caught in the stream of automobiles and horse-drawn vehicles converging on the railroad station.

If I had not anticipated just such a situation, I would probably have stayed behind just as hundreds of others did, whether they had valid tickets or not. But it had been clear to us that with the outbreak of war, to keep up our offices in the warring nations, we would need a coordinating office in a neutral country. The intelligence community also knew that one neutral country in the heart of Europe would be needed by German, French, and British agents alike to coordinate actions, to gather—even to exchange—intelligence data. Switzerland had been able to keep out of wars for hundreds of years and had been an intelligence clearinghouse in World War I. Everything pointed to its serving this function again. Well before the outbreak of the war, therefore, we had decided that when war was declared, I should get myself to Zurich as fast as possible.

But first I had to get to the railroad station. And then onto the train. As expected, all civilian aviation had stopped for the moment. In anticipation of the rush to the railroad station, and two days after the announcement of the Hitler-Stalin treaty, I had bribed a dispatcher who worked for the rescue squad. He was not used to bribes and therefore agreed to a ridiculously small sum. The man, whose name was Kyrimakis, received 2 pounds (about $10) with the arrangement that whenever I required transportation by one of the rescue squad vehicles, one would be ready and available to take me for a trip within ten kilometers of the rescue station. The railroad station was much closer than that, but I did not want him to know my destination. Otherwise he might have guessed the purpose, might have sold the same service to others, and, in the end, left me behind. On boarding the ambulance, I would hand over another 2 pounds and on arrival another 3.

I thought that I had prepared for everything, but I had not. When I learned on Friday morning that war had broken out, I was out of my room within less than twenty minutes. But I had not thought of paying my bill each night in advance, and the cashier's desk was beleaguered by frantic guests who were also trying to get away as quickly as possible. Instead of getting in line, I first decided to put in a call to my man at the rescue squad, and he assured me that the ambulance would meet me at a nearby corner in exactly one hour. When I returned to the cashier's cage, the line had not grown any. It seemed that most of the people who wanted to leave were already through as I took my place at the end of the line. It moved very slowly. After ten minutes, a few people had paid their bills, had left, and there was still nobody behind me. I was now fairly confident that not many more would come. I had more than fifty minutes' time before the ambulance would come, and I decided to make a phone call to Salonica, to a man who was to help our ship *Noemi Julia,* then en route, in case she might need help. After several minutes, I returned without having reached the man. The phone operator could not get a single long-distance call through, all lines were busy and reserved for government calls. When I got back in line, I discovered that another eight persons had lined up in the meanwhile and were now standing between me and the man who was originally in front of me only a few moments ago. I am not by nature a patient person, but I had learned to be patient in the work I had by then been engaged in for two years. However, the impatience I experienced as I saw the line in front of me move with agonizing slowness was not just unbearable, it was consuming. I wondered why people—most of whom were probably quite well off—did not just tell the cashier: "Here, take so and so much—this is certainly more than my bill could be. Keep the rest." To the contrary, however, several of them checked each item on the bill meticulously. One man argued about or claimed an error of a few drachmas. Others paid in foreign currency for which complicated receipts had to be written. I had no idea what my bill could be and was ready to pay twice the amount, but I could not estimate it because of the many long-distance calls I had made.

While I was waiting there in line, my Wagons Lits man showed up in the lobby. Naïvely I thought he had come to assure me—for additional baksheesh, perhaps—that my seat was still reserved. Actually he was there to obtain money from everyone in the lobby in exchange for seats on the train. People were pushing toward him as if he had the means of their salvation in his hands—which, at that point, he really seemed to have: if Italy entered the war before the Orient Express had passed through it, Europe would be split down the middle all the way from the Baltic to the Mediterranean by Germany and Italy—the Axis—and citizens of Western countries would be cut off from their homeland. All during the time that my line was inching along so excruciatingly slowly, the fear of being cut off was also on my mind. Suddenly a bus drove up, driven by an enterprising bus owner who, anticipating the difficulty of catching a taxi, brought his bus around and demanded for the ride to the station what would normally be the fee for a two-day sightseeing tour. His bus filled up and left before I had moved one inch nearer to the cashier's cage. The hotel had by now put two cashiers to work as the line behind me grew longer and longer.

Finally, finally, when I was near to exploding with impatience, my turn came. I paid and ran to the appointed place. I was concerned that the Wagons Lits man, who was stuffing money into all his pockets, would be stuck there and with him my reservation. I told him that I had "special transportation" to the station which he would otherwise be unable to reach.

So, as I raced to meet my ambulance, he puffed along behind me. But would the ambulance be there?

I was already ten minutes late, yet no ambulance. But within a few moments, we heard it coming from a distance. Howling and blowing its siren, it came racing down Panepistimiou Street— University Boulevard—and screeched to a halt at the appointed corner. My dispatcher friend had come himself and was sitting next to the driver. I paid the 2 pounds due then, the Wagons Lits man and I jumped in, and we raced away with all the noise, all the wailing and howling which the ambulance, equipped to top the already loud street noises of Athens, could produce. In spite of all the excitement, I was aware of the humor of this situation as I saw policemen a long way ahead already clearing the road crossings and waving excitedly to coachmen or those riding donkeys to get out of our way. The dispatcher sat next to me, and eager to come as fast as possible into possession of the rest of the "fortune" awaiting him at the railroad station, he urged the driver to make more noise and to go even faster. As we approached the station, traffic became heavier and heavier, but we swept through it all with the help of our three powerful noisemakers: the siren, the ambulance's horn, and an ear-splitting whistle which my dispatcher blew continuously—obviously with much enjoyment.

The streets close to the station were almost completely blocked by the converging traffic. A policeman was busy beating a donkey, which, poor animal, reacted to the excitement around by stubbornly refusing to move at all. Other policemen tried to regulate the flow from the side streets into the main access route but were quite ineffective because so many people had had the same thought: avoid the main access and try to make it via the less-traveled streets. In the traffic jam, stalled between the taxis, private automobiles, fiacres, and hand-pulled delivery carriages, I also saw the bus which had left the Grand Bretagne Hotel so much earlier. We were no longer able to whisk through traffic in that last section of our trip, but with the help of our furious noisemaking and the excited policemen, we did make steady progress forward while others remained mired in the snarled-up traffic that the police, not at all trained to face such a situation, seemed unable to disentangle.

On arrival, I handed the ambulance dispatcher the promised balance, 3 pounds. Knowing the shabby way underlings were treated in the Balkans, I suspected that the driver might receive little or nothing of it, and so I gave him most of the Greek money which I still had on me—about 1 pound. The anxiety and impatience I had felt while in line at the hotel had been—it turned out—suffered needlessly. I was one of the first passengers to arrive at the station; my seat was reserved, and I did not need my Wagons Lits man anymore.

But the anxious times were not yet done with. Though seated and ready to go, I along with the others who had managed to board the train had a new worry. The train's departure time was delayed. After the first hour went by, the waiting time was filled with growing anxiety. I had gone through many more threatening situations but could not entirely escape the nervousness and heightening tension felt by the other passengers when the rumor circulated that the delay was caused by Italy's having entered the war and that the train might not leave at all.

One hour. An hour and a half. Two hours. Finally, when every single place had been taken and the aisles filled up with people who had no seats but had bribed their way into the wagons, we started to move. As we slowly pulled out of the station and the train began to gather speed, I was keenly aware that a new period had started in the life of most of those on board and in the history of all of Europe.

After we had passed Salonica and were approaching the Yugoslav border, a new rumor spread through the cars: the Germans had invaded Yugoslavia, and the train would end its voyage short of the border of that country. I recognized this "news" as the nonsense it was. Why should the Germans, who now needed their troops in Poland and in the West, invade Yugoslavia at this time? The rumor, however, was of help to me. I was so untouched by the resulting fears that it now became clear to me to what an irrational, illogical degree I had allowed myself to be infected by the overall hysteria. True, I had not been as panicky as most of the passengers were, even those who pretended to appear calm. Yet I had become to some degree a part of the frightened mass. The anxiety which the illogical Yugoslav-war rumor caused in them helped me to separate my reactions from theirs and to view more calmly the situation in general, and also my own personal situation and that of free immigration to Palestine. We had prepared for the eventuality of war, which had now occurred. And I, after all, had a nearly priceless visa in hand.

Only those who lived and traveled in those days know how hard it was then to obtain any visa, especially for someone holding a passport marked with a large letter *J* for *"Jude."* To obtain a visa to Switzerland or any other relatively safe country with such a passport was almost impossible. Yet I did have a Swiss visa in my passport, and the way I received it is a story in itself.

Before leaving from Rumania for the Island of Rhodes in the last days of May, I had appeared at the British Consulate in Bucharest—right in the lion's den—to the great surprise of the staff there and applied for a visa to England. The man I was let in to see turned out to be an acquaintance of mine: he was not a regular consular employee but one of the consulate's intelligence staff. I made notes after the visit.

"Mr. Perl, you are the Dr. Perl who is engaged in illegal immigration to Palestine, aren't you?"

"I am not. I am the Dr. Perl who is engaged in free immigration to Palestine."

"Is this not just a play with words? You are breaking our laws, and you really want to visit our country? Can't we talk things over openly?"

"We not only can, we should. I am, the way we see it, not breaking the laws of your country—you are breaking them. You are breaking your obligation made in the Balfour Declaration to work toward the reestablishment of the Jewish National Home in Palestine, and you are breaking the League of Nations Mandate according to which you are obliged to do just that: aid us in the reestablishment of the Jewish National Home, in our ancestral homeland. In our eyes there can be nothing more legal than to help people escape from torture and murder and help them to go home to the land promised to them not only by you and the League of Nations but, more important, in the Bible by God. As you can see, I am not holding back. This is the way you want our talk to go, is it not?"

"Quite. You are of course organizing the flouting of our laws, but as you are not using subterfuges, may I ask why do you want to leave the Balkans and visit England, just as your work is going bloody well?"

"We need money. There are some very wealthy British Jews whom, I think, I can swing to support us."

"Why would your friends in London not be able to do it just as well? They have better connections and are not needed here."

"I believe that only I who have seen the misery of those who are trying to get out, a Jew who himself has already had part of his family killed can do it."

"And how about your work here?"

"It will go on for a short while without me. I admit it is not an easy decision; I am needed in the work. But money is needed too as the Jews on the continent are being robbed of everything. My friends in London will use their connections with rich Jews to introduce them to the man who has shown that he can bring many to safety."

"Your request for a visa is quite extraordinary, is it not?"

"We live in extraordinary times."

He tried then to pump me for information, and I told him that I had been fully frank with him and did not want to lie. He would do best, therefore, not to probe me any further. When I left, he was obviously impressed with the openness with which he felt I had behaved in the meeting. He told me that it would take a week or so to decide upon my application.

I knew that the decision would not be made by the Consular

Department but either by Sir Reginald Hoare, the British ambassador to Bucharest, or more likely by some intelligence agency in London. In approximately a week, the desk clerk at the Majestic handed me a message that the British Consulate wanted to see me. I went immediately, and my German Jew passport, still in my possession, shows the unbelievable entry, a visa, dated 31 May 1939, granted to me by the British Embassy in Bucharest: "Good for a journey to the United Kingdom. Visa valid for single journey only." Added to the regular form are the words: "Pleasure visit only." These words are handwritten in red ink, and I assume they were the catch. I had no doubt that the visa was granted with the intention that I be arrested in England in order to put me out of circulation and our work into jeopardy. The British had added the words "Pleasure visit" in red, although the rest of the visa was in black. As I would not use my visit for pleasure, there would be a good reason to arrest me for fraudulent entry.

But I had not the slightest intention to travel to England; I knew I could never get out. The British, in their conviction that they were so much more clever than we, had fallen for a trick. The British visa in my passport was a real bonanza. First of all it "proved" to everybody to whom I wanted to prove it that the British were actually working with us and not against us. Hesitating shipowners who feared for the security of their ships and Jewish leaders who regarded our undertakings as "too dangerous" were impressed when told in confidence that I would soon "again" visit England to discuss matters of free immigration with the Foreign Office. Impressed, yes. But they doubted whether this could be true. At that point, I told them I could show them something but only if they swore to secrecy. Their appetites thus whetted, they did. I would then pull out my passport, and there was the British visa. That it said "Pleasure only" confirmed the mutual conspiracy. Of course, the British Embassy in Bucharest knew that I was not a pleasure-seeking tourist. Once a shipowner, to reassure a nervous crew, asked me to show my visa to his captain and the first mate. He had not told them about it because of his oath—he claimed—but he wanted me to show them the visa. I did, but told the men that the game was being played in such a way that, in spite of our actual "cooperation" with the British, risks would still be involved. Yet seeing the visa did much to allay their fears and thereby helped us to get the ship.

The other big hit achieved with the British visa was that with such a desirable visa, it was incomparably easier for me to obtain other visas. The reasons most countries gave for refusing visas to Jews was that they were without means and had no possibility to leave. Now, with my visa to the United Kingdom in my passport, smaller countries did not have to worry that I might be stuck there without their having a place to deport me to if I was stranded without funds. Besides, to travel to England from Bucharest, I had to pass several countries, and I therefore applied for transit visas. Thus it came that I had a transit visa for Italy and also one for Yugoslavia and also one for Bulgaria in my passport. The French had refused to give me one, in spite of my visa to the United Kingdom. I had not applied for a Swiss visa before leaving for Rhodes—there had been no time for that anymore. But now in Athens, I could apply for one. As I claimed that I was traveling on a newspaper assignment—my passport gave my occupation as jour-nalist—the visa I obtained was even given free of charge.

It was a good feeling to sit in the Orient Express with a visa for Switzerland in my pocket.

But for the moment, although I was smoothly rolling through Greece and the eastern part of Yugoslavia, I was not in Switzerland yet. I had two more borders to contend with before I would be in Switzerland, the one into Italy and the Swiss border itself. Although visas for both these countries were in my passport, I decided that I had to get off the Orient Express before it crossed into Italy. If Mussolini joined Hitler in the war before the train reached Italy, this would most probably result, I figured, in a simultaneous order to have all Jews declared enemy aliens and deported to Germany for further "disposition." Therefore, I decided that Switzerland, just like Italy, would have to be entered with the least possible delay at remote crossing points which were used almost exclusively by the local population. Such places in the woods had no telegraph com-munication with the capital, and new directives—if any—would most probably arrive after a delay of a few hours—or maybe even a couple of days. By then I would have passed that border crossing point.

For these reasons I determined that I had to leave the fashion-able Orient Express at Ljubljana, Yugoslavia, and to rough it from there on.

After receiving help from friends of my father's in Ljubljana—a couple named Milorad and Nadia Djudjic—I made my way up to a remote checkpoint near the Isonzo River. As expected I had little trouble at this out-of-the-way place, as the border guard did not feel that he was to guard anything. He welcomed the chance to chat with anyone passing through, thereby relieving the monotony of that little trodden mountain pass.

Renting taxis for various segments of the trip, I finally arrived in Milan—at the home of Major Carpi, the leader of Italy's Revisionists.

When my old friend saw me descend from the taxi, his mouth fell open as if he were witnessing a miracle. He had on his desk a letter he had not yet completed in which he urgently requested Mr. Jabotinsky's help in getting in touch with me because, due to Italy's "new economic conditions, large-scale export was a necessity." He was, he told me later, unbelievably impressed with our efficiency! The war and with it the increased danger to Italy's Jews was only a few days old, and here I was already.

We withdrew to another room. He was badly disappointed that I had not come to organize a large-scale emigration immediately. I promised him that I would see to it from Switzerland that Jews from Italy would come along on the next transport if possible. But for the moment, I needed money for the taxi and Carpi's help to get into Switzerland. He sent his wife to a neighbor as he did not have enough money at home to make up the difference between what I had left and what I owed the driver.

After the driver had been paid and sent away, we had a real good long talk. First of all, I obtained from Major Carpi a complete rundown on the situation in the world as it was known from both Italian and foreign broadcasts. Italy had not yet entered the war. It seemed that Mussolini was waiting for Poland's collapse to make certain that the Nazi troops were fully ready to fight the French and the British before Italy, bordering France, would enter the war. There was no fighting yet on the western front, nor in the air. Carpi had heard the rumors about Berlin having been almost leveled by the Royal Air Force, but the BBC had confirmed nothing of that. In Poland, the Luftwaffe had rained thousands of explosives and fire bombs down on Warsaw and other major cities, which were now in flames and largely destroyed, as claimed by the Germans and confirmed by the BBC. The Nazi tanks were advancing into Poland, and the Poles were fighting the steel monsters in the most gallant but old-fashioned manner: with cavalry attacks. Carpi's neighbor had heard on the radio that prior to the charge a regimental commander had exhorted his troops with the words from Tennyson's "The Charge of the Light Brigade": "Theirs not to reason why, theirs but to do and die." Most of Poland's aristocracy was serving in those exclusive cavalry regiments and were perishing as they brandished their sabers against the oncoming tanks. No special regulations regarding Jews, passports, or border crossings had been announced by Italy and none by Switzerland. Nor had he heard any rumors of such measures.

Carpi again came back to the need to evacuate as many of Italy's Jews and the German Jewish refugees now in Italy as fast as possible. Once Italy entered the war, the younger Italian Jews might no longer be allowed to leave; they might be used not for military duty but for digging trenches and other menial and dangerous defense work. Again, in all our operations, we were racing against time. I discussed with Carpi what we could do for Jews in his country, but I also made it clear that considering the attitude of the Italian people with whom many Jews could find hiding places, right now those in Eastern Europe would have to be given priority. Yet in every transport possible, we would take along especially endangered Jews from Italy if they could reach the place of the transport's or ship's departure.

As to my getting into Switzerland, he suggested that I drive up to Ponte Tresa, a small resort on the Italian side of Lake Lugano and cross from there to Lugano on the Swiss side. He made a quick inquiry about when the first boat for Lugano was to leave Ponte Tresa. Six-thirty A.M. The passport control was on the ferry. It would probably be best to take that one. The checkpoint procedure was quite informal anyhow, and we figured that even border police would not like to become involved in complicated issues when still half asleep. Next morning at four A.M. I left for Ponte Tresa with a Jewish friend of Major Carpi. It was raining and I wondered on the fifty-mile-long trip to the ferry if I would get past the Swiss border guard.

Contrary to my expectation, the Swiss official in his heavy gray raincoat did not check the passports right away. Still half asleep when the boat arrived with just two passengers from the Swiss side, he continued to slouch in a corner, apparently completely unconcerned with anything but his repose. We were now halfway across the lake. Rain was falling lightly but steadily as we approached the shore. When we were about a mile away, this man whom I feared so much rose leisurely, and he seemed more alert than I had thought. Although I was sitting on a bench with three persons on one side and one person on the other side, he walked straight to me and asked in Italian for my passport. I gave it to him with the page open that carried the Swiss visa. He read it carefully. This was a good sign. No general cancellation apparently. He then turned the pages and looked at the first one. Good! He checked my face against the man in the photo. "Anything to declare, cigarettes, liquor, or anything else?" "Nothing." I was through!

We were landing. I stepped onto the boat dock and then onto the cobblestones of the square. I was in Switzerland! Free. After so long a time, again in a country where law prevailed, where I could not be arrested at the whim of some official. I was here on a legal visa, in wartime, in the one country which would almost certainly stay neutral and be saved from Nazi invasion, bombings, and destruction. I could go to sleep not fearing any surprises for the first time after what appeared now an endlessly long period in countries in which I never knew whether I would next night be sleeping in a luxury hotel or on a flea-ridden cot in some jail. I knew I would not stay for long in Switzerland; I would have to return to the Balkans, but for the moment I was free and safe.

Pension Renée, which housed our Swiss headquarters, was located in 14 Schuetzengasse, an inconspicuous side street of Zurich's main avenue, the Bahnhofstrasse. It was owned by an elderly, heavy-set lady, Mrs. Luedi, who ran the establishment in typical Swiss fashion—efficiently and with an iron hand. This was where I met Yerushalmi again. It was his code name, meaning "the man from Jerusalem." His real name was Dr. Rudi Hecht. I had known him before from Revisionist congresses and similar Jewish gatherings as the leader of our movement in Switzerland. From the first moment of our now-close cooperation, we hit it off exceedingly well. In the following months, a friendship developed between the two of us which is today as deeply founded as it was then. As we worked together day and night for four months on the same problems, shared the same worries, and had to find impossible answers to one apparently insolvable complication after another, we became a nearly perfect working team. We began often to guess each other's thoughts before they were expressed or to come up with an answer which the other could not have found alone.

Rudi, who later changed his first name to the Hebrew "Reuben," combines an innovative, imaginative approach with extraordinary organizational talent. He has proven this in the postwar area too, by becoming one of the leading industrialists, archaeologists, and art collectors in Israel.*

Early in 1939, the commander of the Irgun, David Raziel, appointed Hecht to work for the Irgun in matters of free immigration and asked him to proceed for that purpose to Europe. It was then that Hecht chose the code name Yerushalmi. Hecht, then in Palestine, held Swiss citizenship, which added to his value to the organization. He was another one who even in wartime would be able to travel much more freely than most others, as Switzerland was a neutral country. Also, as Hecht came from a family well known in Switzerland, he would be able to help with Swiss authorities. These assets became increasingly valuable because many of the financial transactions forbidden in Germany and the Balkans had to be undertaken via Swiss accounts. In addition, as a Swiss citizen, Hecht could use his connections regarding German refugees in Switzerland who wanted to get to Palestine. The Swiss Jewish communities might be inveigled to pay their expenses—and to do so in the valued Swiss currency. Moreover, in addition, our Swiss office could work in wartime with our representatives in England and France as well as with those under German rule.

Hecht's role as coordinator was needed for another reason too. Quarrels had developed in our own ranks, as might well have been expected when a decision often involved the lives of hundreds if not thousands. At times, each side was convinced that it had the only answer to save the endangered lives and that the other's solution would only lead to disaster. Dr. Hecht was on good terms with everybody and thereby excellently qualified not only to coordinate all activities but to get us together again—as he did—on so many problems.

One of the first things I did after my arrival at the Pension, after greeting Rudi, was to put in a person-to-person call to Vienna for my aunt, Mrs. Liesel Sonnenkind-Kant. My aunt, then in her early forties, was a very efficient and attractive woman who knew

*Dr. Reuben Hecht is known not only in Israel but to tens of thousands of tourists as the founder and owner of that landmark of Haifa, the "Dagon," Israel's largest—and up to a short time ago only—grain elevator, whose pleasing architectural design blends so well with the lovely contours of the Carmel Mountains sloping down to the sea.

better than any woman I ever met how to use her feminine charms to handle men. She was working in our Vienna emigration office and was invaluable there for the good connections she had established with the DDSG, the Danube Steamshipping Company. Often when people had to leave immediately, we did not have the money to pay right away. Liesel more than once obtained credit for us—which was an unbelievable thing for Jews—with the arrangement that payment would follow with the next ship. It always did, and Liesel Kant was trusted by the DDSG directors to deliver as promised. With her help, we even obtained certificates from the DDSG that listed such and such person as scheduled to leave with a DDSG steamer for abroad on a certain future date. With these certificates, we achieved the release of hundreds of people from Buchenwald and Dachau concentration camps. In these cases we could present to the Gestapo not only our own "certificates," stating that a certain person would be leaving for abroad on such and such a date, we also supported it with the official document adorned with swastikas and the rubber stamps of the DDSG confirming the booking.

Liesel, because she was associated with our Vienna office, was at least for the time being exempted from the threat of deportation to the East. If possible, the Nazis wanted to get rid of the Jews in a manner which did not tie up the German railroad system. And those working for the emigration to Palestine, which by then had already gotten tens of thousands out, were as a rule left to do their work.

Liesel's full name was Liesel Kant and when I used the name "Sonnenkind-Kant," in making a person-to-person call to her home, I was employing a ruse. Actually *Sonnenkind*—"sun child"—was the name used for my wife Lore—and Liesel understood well: she would summon Lore to her house, and Liesel would be ready for the call only after she had gotten Lore there too. As Sonnenkind sounded very much like a Jewish name, it would not indicate to the listening censors a conversation between a Jew and one racially not Jewish.

While I waited for the call, I received the latest status report from Dr. Hecht. He told me that the Germans were breaking through everywhere in Poland, and that it was rumored—and later confirmed to be true—that a provision of the recent German-Soviet pact called for the Soviet armies to invade Poland from the east once the Nazis had penetrated from the west to a certain point. He also gave me the particulars of the Swiss office he had established, data which I had known in broad outline only.

There were several hundred Jewish refugees—if not several thousand—in Switzerland who had entered the country illegally by now. Because Switzerland was small, well administered, and did not have much tourist trade then, many of the illegals had been caught and arrested. Others were hiding, all of them in mortal fear of being sent back to Germany. Hecht had provided protection for some 700 by assuring the Swiss authorities that these illegals would leave Switzerland for Palestine with one of our transports. Our record showed that we could do that, and some of the high Swiss officials, particularly Dr. Briner, the city president of Zurich, showed themselves quite sympathetic. The Swiss Jewish communities were financing this effort.

In this endeavor one of our main problems was that Switzerland is landlocked. No transports were then leaving from neighboring Italy or France. Therefore those ready to take the risk had first to be brought to a place from which they could get on a riverboat or seagoing ship. The latter was almost impossible because it would have involved the granting of a whole series of transit visas. Of course, no Jews would return to Vienna, then an integral part of the German Reich, but we were surprised how many were not just ready but implored us to take them to Prague to join one of the Revisionist transports from there. Czechoslovakia, after having abandoned its Sudeten region to the Nazis in the fall of 1938 was not yet formally occupied by the Nazis when Hecht started working on a Swiss evacuation project. Czechoslovakia was then a satellite run by a government subservient to Hitler but not yet a "German protectorate." Looking back, one must wonder about the eagerness of so many to leave Switzerland to be flown to Prague for illegal immigration to Palestine. For many it was the attraction of "returning" to what they felt to be their homeland, but the fear of being extradited by the Swiss to Germany was a strong supporting factor for most, the main or even sole motivation for others. At any rate, Dr. Hecht, working rapidly as always, had by early March 1939 organized a large-scale exodus from Switzerland, consisting primarily but not exclusively of those refugees who had entered Switzerland illegally. With the financial help of the Swiss Jewish communities, and a contribution made by the city of Zurich, Rudi had chartered seven planes from Swiss Air which were to bring on March 15, 1939, Jewish refugees from Switzerland to Prague, where they would join one of the transports organized there by the Betar. But the saying that fate often plays odd tricks had, for our ventures, to be modified. So much could go wrong in our undertakings that fate did not often, but almost regularly, contrive to interfere with seemingly well-worked-out plans. On the very day of the scheduled departure from Zurich airfield, the Germans invaded the truncated remainder of Czechoslovakia and began marching on Prague. The Prague airfield was of course closed, and, for the moment at least, our refugees, of whom many had surfaced solely because the Swiss authorities would not interfere with their departure, were left stranded with only their knapsacks and their hopes. There was one good aspect to this latest tragedy, however: Swiss authorities, although at that time deporting back to Germany other Jews whom they caught crossing over illegally, did not clamp down on those of whose existence they had not known before and who reported their presence only in order to leave Switzerland for Palestine.

Just as he told me many details of the Swiss operation that first night, so I took him into many of the facets of the activities in the field, and we each gained a much better picture of the particulars involved in the overall undertaking. We sat and talked till the windows showed the grayish light of the awakening new day. The person-to-person phone call from Vienna had still not come.

I had slept only a few hours when I was called downstairs to the telephone. Vienna. Liesel. She told me about the need to get more people out—and to do so fast. They had numerous people lined up in Vienna, many released from concentration camps because of the promise of early departure. The DDSG, though shipping was scarce, would provide a riverboat, but as long as there was no seagoing vessel waiting, there could, of course, be no ship for the Danube part of the voyage. I held the "business" part of the conversation short; I told Liesel that I was preparing a really large transport, 2,000 or more people, and that prior to leaving Athens I had initiated negotiations and would call the shipping agents in Galatz tonight and call her back tomorrow or the day after with whatever news I had. She told me that Mirjam wanted to say hello to me too. *Mirjam* was not an "Aryan" name, and it would not appear suspicious if a Jew, after a very legitimate conversation with his aunt about an issue important to the Nazis—Jewish emigration—also should speak about private matters to what was apparently another member of the household. "Mirjam" was, of course, my wife, whom Liesel had fetched in the meanwhile and who had been waiting with Liesel for several hours for the call to come through.

Just to hear her voice again after so long a time made me feel like another person. I was suddenly not the planner of complex and risky schemes, not the man hardened enough to say "no" to people who were imploring him not to leave them and their families behind, not the one who was threatening some Greek or other Balkan underground figure that unless he stuck to an agreement we would not protect him from the wrath of our well-disciplined Betarim who—I would indicate—had been trained to take care of situations exactly like the one at hand. I was not the Dr. Perl who was the subject of dozens of British intelligence documents nor the Jew who had defied Eichmann and gone over his head to authorities in Berlin. I was just a young man in love, who knew of nothing at that moment and did not want to know of anything else but that he heard—and thereby felt close to him—his loved one. Lore, who had so much to tell me was in a condition similar to mine, only more so. As I learned later she had made notes of what she wanted to tell me, but she did not speak about a single one of these issues so important to her. They involved the need of this or that person to be taken along on the next transport. All Lore could say was how happy she was to be able to feel so near to me and, most of all, to know that I was in neutral Switzerland. I did not tell her that I had no intention of remaining there and would soon return to Eastern Europe. There were long pauses in our conversation, but neither she nor I felt that we were not using to the full the chance to talk. Lore did not have to tell me that she too felt that during these silences we were talking to each other more fervently than had we used words. Toward the end of the phone call she had to share with me two thoughts that were foremost in her mind. Her mother was very sick—so sick that she was, although Lore did not know it then, soon to die. And: "Aunt Elsa was very happy for the parcel you sent her through me. She took it along on her vacation; she said the sausage and the cheese were really delicious." I had no Aunt Elsa; neither did she. The meaning of the message was clear: send me food parcels from Switzerland; I will give them to those who are "going on vacation"—being deported—they need it badly. Lore did not know that the food would not have to last longer than for the voyage east itself. Of course, I sent parcels to her, one every week as long as I was in Switzerland. More would have raised suspicions as to the use of "all that food."

After the phone call, Dr. Hecht wanted to continue our planning session, but I was unable to return right away to the hard realities. To his surprise and open displeasure with my selfishness, I told him for that day this was all I could do and I retreated to my room.

The next morning the real work started. A phone call to Mr. Rand in Galatz, which I had also placed the night before, came through shortly before noon. Rand had worked fast. On the strength of my phone call from Athens after my arrival there from Rhodes, he had, he told me, already been assured the use of a Turkish ship which could easily take 2,000 and even more persons. I do not recall anymore the price which he then mentioned, but it had been reasonable. However, he informed me that the Turks had made a demand which was not usual. As a rule, we paid as the people boarded. The owner of the ship Rand was to get for us demanded 2,000 pounds—$10,000—as pay in advance. This was to be given not just to start the remodeling but to send the ship from Turkey to Sulina for remodeling there and for the subsequent voyage. This condition was contrary to the rules of the game, but with the war on and shipping almost not available for our work, and with dangers to the refugee ships from both sides opposing each other in the war, I had to agree to the demand.

But the Balkans are the Balkans, and I could not trust Mr. Rand enough to send him one penny of irreplaceable foreign currency from refugee sources on the basis of such vague information. I wanted to know the name of the ship, its present location, and when it would be available. In the phone call I made from Zurich to Galatz, Rand told me that the ship was the S.S. *Sakarya,* presently in Smyrna. The owners, he said, were Turks who had heard how some Greek shippers had made fortunes in the Jew-smuggling trade and were eager to please us, but the down payment was a must. I went to the Zurich Public Library and looked the *Sakarya* up in Lloyd's Register. A ship of that name did exist. It was some forty years old. Very old as far as old freighters go, but not older than most of our ships so far had been. She was Turkish-owned and this was an advantage. Because of the strategic importance of the Bosporus and the Dardanelles, Britain was most interested in keeping Turkey neutral. Thus, a Turkish ship was less likely than, say, a Greek one under a Panamanian flag to be shot at by the British. The Germans too were competing for Turkey's friendship, and it was not likely that their submarines would attack a ship flying the Turkish flag even if she was carrying 2,000 or more Jews to Palestine. And, most of all, her size made the *Sakarya* exactly what I had been looking for. The *Sakarya* was shown to have a net tonnage of 1,645 tons. We usually figured that we could easily put as many persons on board a ship as it had net tons. The larger the ship the less relative space was "lost" for all she needs to keep her going, machine room, storage space for tools, fuel, space for the crew's quarters, etc. We would be able to put more than 2,000 on this one ship alone.

The moment I had finished talking to Galatz, I called the operator and asked her to get me Vienna Number U 21-2-30, the Ausschuss fuer juedische Ueberseetransporte—Committee for Jewish Overseas Transports. Person-to-person for Mr. Storfer. Although the negotiations regarding the *Sakarya* were still quite up in the air, I had to let him know as fast as possible that a concrete possibility existed, because on the strength of the expected departure, he might be able to prevent the deportation of persons scheduled for "resettlement." He might even be able to take first steps toward getting a number of people out from Dachau and Buchenwald concentration camps, if he announced that there was a chance for them to leave the country in the near future. Storfer wanted to know the day the *Sakarya* would be waiting in Sulina so that he could start preparing. I told him that work on the matter had hardly started but that my target date for Sulina transfer was about six weeks from then, the second half of October.

Next we had to get the money for the first down payment of 2,000 pounds. While I discussed this problem with Hecht, a person-to-person call came for me from Robert Mandler of the Prague Ausschuss fuer juedische Auswanderung. He had already learned from Liesel Kant in Vienna that I was in Zurich, where I could be reached, and that I had concrete prospects for getting a large ship to Sulina.

Robert Mandler was quite an unusual person, in many ways different from any of the others working on free immigration into Palestine. When I think of him and the various other people who "did the job," I am impressed with the diversity of characters whom our work attracted and who dared to engage in it. To act efficiently in our ever-changing circumstances, however, certain traits were an absolute must: determination not to accept any "no"—even if a situation seemed hopeless; the ability to be firm, because amid pressures from opposing directions, decisions which involved the lives of many had to be taken almost as a routine; the ability to play one opposing force against the other was required; one needed imagination and innovation but most of all guts. One had to be ready to fight the Germans, the British, the Jewish establishment, the Jews who could not be taken along and tried to force their way into a transport, and even those who were coming along, maybe even already on a ship but suffered there more than they were able to take and tried to organize mutinies.

Robert Mandler, who was to play an important part in the organization of free emigration, had all these qualities, yet because he was made of stock quite different from all those who had so far worked with us, he in some ways did not fit well into the picture. An experienced businessman in his forties, he was much older than most of us. Mandler had not been a Revisionist; a Zionist he was but not an active one. An impressively good-looking man, always impeccably dressed, he was able to handle functions which the younger ones could not fulfill as effectively. Most of all, he was a go-getter if there ever was one. He had fled with his family to Prague after the Germans had marched into Austria. I knew of Robert's qualities because he was a cousin of mine, and I felt that his abilities might be used by our friends in Prague. He took a look at how we were working there—and felt that he could organize things better than "the kids." He was above all certain that one could achieve the most with authorities if one did not function as a political group, as we Revisionists no doubt were doing. Robert felt that we should also open an office of a more general character in Prague. Because Mandler was not a Czech citizen, he asked two brothers Frantisek and Karel Gross, residents of Prague, to lend their names for all the applications to be filed with the local authorities. The Gross brothers, distant cousins of his—and mine— lent their names for the various formalities, but they also proved themselves able young men, and Mandler soon had an efficient organization. As it could at times call upon sources which were closed to the Betar, Mandler's outfit complemented the Revisionist organization well. Just as there were stories about Mr. Storfer in Vienna, so rumors about Robert Mandler's cooperating with the Gestapo spread. As in the case of Storfer, from my own experience I do not know whether these rumors were justified. Of course, to get people out, one needed the permission of the Nazi authorities, and this was a time filled with suspicion, distrust, and frustration. I do know, however, that due to Mandler's unbelievable efficiency, hundreds of lives were saved; that he cooperated in the saving of thousands; and that after he had helped so many to live, he, his wife, Martha, and his fifteen-year-old daughter, Rita, were all murdered by the Nazis.

When Mandler called me now in Zurich, I confirmed what he had already heard from Vienna, that we would have a ship available which could carry more than 2,000. But also that the shipowners would not start moving until they had received a huge down payment: 2,000 pounds.

If my news was good news for him, his reply was one that almost swept me off my feet. "Two thousand pounds?" he said. "We have it." Just like that. Over the phone, no doubt listened to by the Nazis, he told me that he had now, while the war with Britain was on, 2,000 pounds. Before I could ask more questions, he added: "I obtained from the Czech authorities with the full concurrence of the German supervising offices the permission to exchange local currency up to twenty pounds for each person leaving. Since war broke out in the meanwhile, this can be paid only in the currency of a neutral country, but it will be a free currency, e.g., Swiss francs."

I do not know why he had not let me know before of this permit, but though I could hardly believe it, I had to: now in wartime we would receive foreign currency from the Germans to get Jews out!

As I am writing this, I have in front of me that amazing document, properly adorned with impressive rubber stamps. The document is dated Prague, June 15, 1939—three months after the occupation of Prague by Nazi troops. The notarized translation from the Czech, equally ornated with rubber stamps, shows the date of June 17, 1939. The document issued by the Prague Ministry for Social Welfare and Health, showing the ministry number R 413-1506, states that Mr. Frantisek Gross is granted permission to charge for emigration to Palestine the amount of 6,000 Czech crowns per person plus 200 crowns for "administrative expenses" per person and that for that purpose, for the emigration group under the leadership of Frantisek Gross, the amount of 20 English pounds on the average is granted. The document concludes: "All these decisions are valid only if your emigration is permitted by the German authorities." It is signed: "For the Minister: Dr. Kotek." The final sentence was a formality; of course, no such authorization would have been granted without prior consultation with the German occupiers. And no organizing of any group of even a small size was possible under the watchful eyes of the Gestapo—unless permitted.

This document probably more than anything else brings into focus the oddity of the entire situation. On ships of neutral countries, young Jews of many nationalities were traveling with our organization to British-held Palestine, where they would undoubtedly join the British forces to fight the Nazis. The British tried to prevent this. The Germans not only permitted it; they aided the undertaking of providing the British with young soldiers who were doubtlessly well motivated to fight the Nazis. The Germans let the people out who would otherwise have been able to perform slave labor in factories. The Nazis supplied the riverboats, and they even granted the right to exchange local currency into foreign currency so needed by the Reich.

Dr. Hecht's and my delight over Mandler's ability to obtain foreign currency was so great that another bit of news could not do more than cast a temporary shadow over our euphoria. At that moment we had the *Noemi Julia* with 1,136 immigrants on the seas, another one of the ships organized largely by our Abraham Stavsky. She had passed the Bosporus safely, but we learned that she had for some unknown reason missed the rendezvous with the landing ships. This made us worry not only for the *Noemi Julia* but for the *Sakarya* as well. If the *Noemi Julia* were caught by the British and the capture were to gain enough publicity to become known in Istanbul, the *Sakarya*'s owners might change their minds about chartering her to us because of the risk involved. Several days later when Athens reported that the *Noemi Julia* had not shown up for the alternative rendezvous either, our fears for the future of both ships' expedition rose. After a week of worry, a phone call from Bucharest turned our anxieties into relief and easy laughter. The ship's captain, a Russian by the name of Michail Alexandrovitch Glinsky, cleverly radioed on the day the war broke out—and his ship was off the coast of Turkey—to the British Consulate in Izmir that he had 1,200 young people on board who wanted to volunteer for the British forces. He asked whether he should land them in Izmir and bring them to the British Consulate there. He did, of course, not indicate who these "volunteers" were. All the British offices must have been crowded and bustling with activity that day; cables were no doubt flooding in and being sent out, inquiries coming from and answers going to British subjects in the area as to what to do and how to get home the fastest, etc. If there was one thing the Izmir Consulate did not want, it was some 1,200 foreigners descending on its modest offices to enlist in the British forces. Somebody in the busy consulate got hold of that foolish captain's telegram and answered: "No, under no circumstances should any volunteers be brought here to Izmir. Take them to a British port."

The captain did. He brought them to Haifa! On its arrival there, the ship was immediately confiscated, and its crew and the 1,136 passengers were arrested. But the captain produced the exchange of communications with the Izmir Consulate. All his passengers had volunteered to join the British army. He had no doubt that this desire was genuine; after all, they were Jews and wanted to fight the Nazis. Furthermore, a British office had instructed him to bring them to a British port—and that was exactly what he had done. He and his crew had to be freed, the confiscation order against the *Noemi Julia* lifted, and not much later the passengers were also released.

The rescue of another 1,136 and the early safe return of the *Noemi Julia* would enhance our status in the eyes of shipowners generally. The night we learned that those on the *Noemi Julia* were safe in Palestine, Rudi Hecht and I went out for the first time since my arrival at the Pension Renée to take in some of Zurich's wartime night life.

Things were going well now, but I was only too used to an unexpected downturn just when everything was "in the pink." An obstacle always seemed to come along just at such times. To make it as definite as possible that we would really have the *Sakarya* at our disposal if we lived up to our part of the deal, I asked Mrs. Lola Bernstein, who had proved so helpful in the *Rim*-Rhodes crisis, to make the voyage to Rumania. There she was to make certain that the *Sakarya* would really come up to Sulina when we forwarded to Rand the 2,000 pounds he had asked for. In addition, details of the contract had not yet been worked out, and she would have to do this on the spot. Mrs. Bernstein, carrying a British passport, could not as easily be put under pressure by the Balkan authorities as I could or most of the others of us who had German-Jew passports or were citizens of some smaller Eastern European country. Any shipowner or shipping agent—anybody, in fact—could put us under pressure by bribing some police official to have us arrested. To arrest a subject of His Majesty's was not a matter to be taken lightly. The British Consulate would not have intervened in case of arrest—it did not when Mrs. Bernstein was once arrested in Greece —but most people in the Jew-smuggling trade did not know that. We had truly made them believe that the high British authorities, despite their actions, actually were working with us.

Mrs. Bernstein's going to Rumania meant expenses again. And I was already deep in debt with Mrs. Luedi, the owner of the Pension Renée. Fortunately at this point, some money started flowing in from Vienna and some from Prague. The funds from Vienna were actually not being sent from there. Mr. Storfer had arranged that some people in Vienna, who were registering for our next voyage and who had relatives abroad, ask those relatives to pay 20 pounds on their behalf to a special account in Switzerland. With that sum, the relatives had paid in full for the trip for one person with the next transport.

With the money coming in now to Switzerland, I could pay the bills—especially for our costly long-distance calls—at Mrs. Luedi's and even arrange for Mrs. Bernstein's departure to Rumania. Italy had not yet entered the war, and Mrs. Bernstein could travel via Italy to Yugoslavia to reach Rumania.

Soon, in addition to the smaller amounts for administration expenses, the 2,000 English pounds from Robert Mandler in Prague arrived, officially transferred there from a Czech bank to a Swiss one. Robert implored me in several calls to make certain that the money not be paid until all arrangements were definite. I shared his fears. I knew that if we were swindled, not only would the foreign currency be lost and the Jews left behind, but everybody connected with the undertaking would be slaughtered. Robert did not verbalize this fear on the phone, however. He told me only that Eichmann had personally said to him that if he "suspected any kind of Jewish monkey business or bag of tricks" he would hold the Jews collectively responsible for it. At the same time, he threatened that unless the Jews were out by October 1, he would demand the foreign money back. All this placed us in Zurich in a seemingly unresolvable situation. The *Sakarya*'s owners would not move until they received a down payment—a fact confirmed by Mrs. Bernstein's call from Rumania. Once we had paid them, we were in their hands. What if they pocketed the money, and the *Sakarya* did not come? But if we could not assure Eichmann that the people were to leave in the immediate future, they would be lost anyhow. I discussed the matter with Dr. Hecht, but the decision had to be mine because it was I whom Mandler knew and trusted. Knowing that I was not deciding for me only but that a wrong decision might cost many lives, perhaps in the thousands, I decided that we had to take the risk. Mrs. Bernstein had by then made all the arrangements with the shipowners' representatives, the Rand shipping company in Galatz. But contracts were worth little in Rumania. What if Rand or the shipowners did not deliver? A lawsuit would last for many months, if not years, and would probably be won by the party who paid more baksheesh to the judge, anyway. By that time, all the would-be emigrants would be dead. No, the value of our agreement was not in the written contracts but in our capacity for enforcement. Fortunately, the Betar had the reputation of being able to "persuade" shipping agents who defaulted. It was on the strength of that and on the conditions in Prague and Vienna that I decided to send the 2,000 pounds to the Rand Company. The *Sakarya,* according to the agreement, was to be in Sulina, if at all possible, by November 4 but in no case later than November 18.

On October 10, while I was at breakfast, the waitress came in. "Dr. Perl, a person-to-person call from Prague."

Robert Mandler was on the phone. He had just been informed by the authorities that his group would be leaving the day after tomorrow. There was some problem with the railroad scheduling. Departure might be delayed two days to the fourteenth, but more likely it would be the twelfth.

I was aghast. "But we have no ship ready yet," I told him. "I do not expect the *Sakarya* prior to November 18 and have ordered the riverboat to be ready for boarding your people in Bratislava on November 19." "We are leaving the day after tomorrow anyhow," Robert replied. "If we cannot leave for Bratislava, we will leave in another direction." This was clear-cut language. I told Robert that under those circumstances, they would leave for Bratislava, and I

would try to get the Jewish community there—or whatever remained of it—to take care of the Mandler group until it could leave
by paddle-wheeler. Bratislava was not a part of the Nazis' "Bohemian-Moravian Protectorate." It was the capital of the Nazi puppet
state of Slovakia, which Hitler had carved out of truncated Czechoslovakia and which was ruled by Tiso, a Hitler appointee and as
virulent an anti-Semite as any Nazi. His Hlinka Guard was as
feared, as brutal, and as ruthless as the SS. By sending them to
Bratislava, Eichmann had gotten the Jews off his neck and had left
it up to his Slovak friends to do with them as they pleased. The only
fortunate element in the situation was that there were no large-scale
deportations to the east for "resettlement" from Slovakia at that
time.

Within minutes after I had finished talking to Mandler, I
called Vienna and asked Liesel Kant to procure from the DDSG a
certificate confirming that we had chartered a boat from them
which would be in Bratislava on November 20. It should also
state—without mentioning specifics—that it would board "to fullest
capacity" all the Jews who were waiting in Bratislava for transportation to Sulina. In the phone conversation with Mandler, I had not
dared to ask whether the order to leave by October 12 applied to the
Gleser-Faltyn group, too. The Bohemian-Moravian Betar had organized a group independent of Mandler's. Their people were almost
exclusively Betarim; they were young and had been preparing
themselves for a long time for life in Palestine. As valuable as each
human life is, the loss of this group would have been especially
crushing for us. When I hung up after talking to Mandler, I did not
know what was to be the fate of the Betar group, but in the evening
we had a phone call from Bucharest. Faltyn had called Eri Jabotinsky there and told him: ship or no ship, they were leaving on
October 12 for Bratislava. Same story! Would the Slovaks put them
into a detention camp or just continue the train to the Carpathian
Mountains and kill everybody off there in the woods. The Betar
group was in even more danger than the Mandler group. Mandler's
group and the people from Vienna would, with the help of Aunt
Liesel and the DDSG, be able to show the Slovaks that a German
riverboat would take the Jews out of Slovakia by November 20.
That was the date I had contracted with the DDSG, because the
Sakarya was due in Sulina on November 18 at the latest, and I
knew from experience that there would be easily a few days' delay.

But Faltyn's group could not present such a swastika-stamped letter, and the Slovaks knew only too well that there was no boat on the entire river large enough to transport all of them, Storfer's people from Vienna, the Mandler group, and the Faltyn group. Besides, there was also a group being formed in Slovakia itself under the leadership of the young but capable Mr. Citron. Mr. Jabotinsky in London had appointed Citron leader of the Slovakian Betar when Slovakia became separated from the rest of Czechoslovakia. Activities between the Bohemian-Moravian and the Slovak Betar were ably coordinated by Eliyahu Gleser, who had been the leader of the entire Czechoslovakian Betar prior to Czechoslovakia's partition.

Within the hour after I received Mandler's catastrophic message, Rudi Hecht and I went to the Zurich Jewish community and were given an appointment with its leader for the afternoon. This was just a day and a half prior to the one on which all the people registered in Bohemia-Moravia for free emigration were to be shoved into trains. At our request, the Zurich Jewish community called the one in Bratislava. They asked the Jews in Bratislava to do their utmost to prevent further deportation and assured them that they, the Swiss Jews, would do their best to help defray the expenses of the stay of those in Bratislava. The expected influx of Swiss francs, Hecht and I hoped, might help with the Slovak authorities and thereby enable the Prague Jews to wait it out in Bratislava.

As I had feared, the Slovak authorities did not fall for our claim that all these people would board the *Saturnus.* That paddle-wheeler, a luxury boat and the pride of all Danube shipping, was well known to the Slovaks, as it went up and down the river all the time. Yet the *Saturnus* was not that large that it could take all the people who had arrived from Prague and who by their mere presence were delaying the Tiso government program of making Slovakia rapidly *judenrein.* The promise of the Swiss Jewish community probably did help to prevent immediate shipment into the woods of the Carpathian Mountains. However, the Slovaks did not want to wait until November 20 for the *Saturnus* to take at least some of the Jews "off their necks." And even less did they want to wait for those for whom there was no German ship coming in the near future.

The adventures of the two groups from Prague differed in the beginning when they were both pushed out from the German

"Bohemian-Moravian Protectorate" onto the equally hostile Slovaks. To understand their divergent experiences one has to realize that certain differences existed in their organizational setup and composition. For Mandler, just as for the Betar group, youth, health, and anticipated morale during the voyage were essential criteria for acceptance into the transport. But Mandler also insisted that the prospective traveler pay for his voyage the modest amount of 6,200 Czech crowns, equivalent to 20 pounds. There were exceptions, but these were not numerous. For the Betar group, the person's value in building the future State of Israel was judged to be of so paramount an importance that its members, although of course encouraged to pay, were taken along even if they had not a penny. As the Betar was a youth organization rooted mainly in the poorest strata of European Jewry, exceptions to the rule were much more numerous in the Faltyn than in the Mandler group.

The Betar group was thus an excellently disciplined unit with high morale. The morale in the Mandler group was not as high, yet it could and did help the Faltyn group because of the Mandler group's more efficient bureaucratic and financial setup.

To start out with: Robert Mandler had, from the beginning of his activity, an Aryan appointed to be the government's official of the newly founded Committee for Jewish Emigration. That man, a Mr. Strunz, was most helpful to the entire undertaking. Whether this was so because Mr. Strunz wanted really to help, or whether Robert gained his cooperation in some other way I do not know. Certainly from what I know about Mandler, he would not have been afraid to try bribing an official, though this was not the Balkans. Under the Nazi regime officials could not, as a rule, be bribed—and if one reported that a Jew had tried to bribe him, the Jew would live only as long as an interrogation with torture took to find out whether he had bribed or tried to bribe anybody else. In any case, this Mr. Strunz proved most valuable to us. He could go to the various offices, to the police, the bank, the bureau for food control, etc., and could talk to the people on the same level. He initiated his interventions with "As you know, the fuehrer wants the Bohemian-Moravian Protectorate *judenrein* as fast as possible, and I need your help for that." After some time Strunz was replaced by a Mr. Sykora. The new kommissar was tougher in the beginning than Strunz had been, but it did not take Mandler long to turn Sykora into another valuable instrument for getting things done for the transport. Finally Eichmann, not trusting any of these Czech kommissars, put the Ausschuss fuer juedische Auswanderung directly under one of his trusted SS officers. Obersturmfuehrer Guenther was put in charge of the newly founded Zentralstelle fuer juedische Auswanderung—Central Office for Jewish Emigration. That office handled all Jewish emigration matters in the "protectorate." By the time of Guenther's appointment, however, many gains had already been made and useful connections established. Although direct supervision by the Gestapo constituted a daily threat, in retrospect it had some advantages, too. There were contrasting tendencies within the German power structure as to the policy on free emigration to Palestine. The Nazi party wanted to get rid of the Jews by any means. The German military, however, viewed it as a foolish party action to let Jews by the thousands out to Palestine where they would only augment the numbers of those who were fighting the German Reich. Fortunately, with Guenther in charge of the Zentralstelle, there was little risk of interference from German sources.

Mandler thus had permission to carry out foreign currency exchanges, and although it was granted to the Betar too, Mandler had the most cash because almost all of his people had paid. In fact, he told me over the phone that he wanted the entire *Sakarya* for his group; he had no problem getting his 2,000 people together and all fully paid. This would have been an easy and fast solution. Certainly Robert's request was alluring enough, but I could not leave the Betarim behind just because they had less money. The Betar had no other ship ready to make the voyage to Palestine.* I told Robert that I realized that if I took only his people, it would greatly simplify my dealings with the Turks. But I could give him only about 600 spaces, about 200 to the Vienna group he worked closely with, and the rest would have to go to the Betar. Robert did not like this decision, but 600 people was not a small number. He knew that this was three-fourths of what we usually could take on for an entire ship. With the Viennese group, the number of these non-Betarim constituted 800 people, or an entire usual shipload.

---

*While I had been in Rhodes, Mr. Jacoby of the Revisionist World headquarters in London, an able and most devoted man but not experienced in the Jew-running trade, had chartered a French ship, the *Nalco,* which was to smuggle 1,000 Betarim to Palestine. Unfortunately, as the ship was French it was requisitioned by the French at the outbreak of the war.

The Faltyn group left on the fourteenth of October. They went by train to Bratislava. Mandler was able to delay the departure of his group till October 28. In an unbelievably short time, Gleser and Faltyn were able to charter two small Slovak riverboats, which were to tow behind them two small barges. This convoy was to transport the Betar group down the river and out to Slovakia. They would then be transferred to a Rumanian barge provided by the combined efforts of the Prague and the Slovakian Betar offices and the London and Paris headquarters, together with our main Aliya Bet office in Bucharest.

The Mandler group was interned on arrival in Bratislava in a building called Svobodna. It was partially a school and partially a home for destitute men. There they were guarded on a twenty-four-hour basis by the infamous Hlinka Guard, whose members stood outside and in the corridors armed with rifles and submachine guns, ready to shoot anybody who was suspected of escaping. Nobody would have dared to, and there was no place to run to anyhow. But with these trigger-happy pogromists around, one was never certain whether or not one of them might start shooting just for the fun of it. Mandler had tried to obtain from the Nazi authorities in Prague the permission to have one of the Gross brothers stay with the transport until its departure with the *Saturnus*. The permission was first refused. In spite of the letter from the DDSG that the *Saturnus* would call for that group on November 19, the Slovaks threatened to send the transport back to Prague unless it left within ten days. It could not do this, and so Karel Gross was given permission to leave the "protectorate" and to travel "abroad" to Slovakia. He was told that, unless he returned, his entire family and his friends would all be "held responsible." This pressure on Karel Gross to return was exercised to assure smooth functioning of the emigration office. It indicated how eager the Nazis were to get the Jews out and how many more could have been saved if only the countries which prided themselves on fighting for human rights had let them in.

In Bratislava Gross did succeed in having the term of the stay extended till November 19. However, on November 3, Dr. Hecht and I were rendered a double blow. Bucharest called me in Zurich and advised me that the *Sakarya* might be "somewhat delayed." Yet I knew that I could not alter the departure date for the *Saturnus* without the risk that all those registered for the trip and still in Vienna or Bratislava would be deported for "resettlement."

Besides, I knew from experience that once a ship was reported "slightly delayed," it might be delayed much longer because something had gone wrong.

The other blow was not less severe. I learned that the Betar group's money was being slowly "eaten up" by expenses for the riverboats, the barges, and food, to such a degree that by now there was only a sum of 6 English pounds per person left, an amount which was steadily being reduced. Eri Jabotsinky in his description of the *Sakarya* expedition confirms that amount of 6 English pounds. That figure was so low that though the Mandler group was financially much better off, it would not leave us with enough money to pay for the *Sakarya*.

There is a certain breaking point for everybody. My hardest moments were when I learned in Rhodes that the *Rim* had burned and sunk—and now in Zurich when it seemed that the *Sakarya* was to be late and that when she came, we would not have the money to pay for her. One of the few uncoded entries in my diary was written on that day, November 3: "For all future catastrophic happenings my leitmotif must be: take it easy. Otherwise the burden of worries will crush me."

Hecht and I had a conference. I had an idea which had worked before when those stranded in the Constanţa basement had been left without a penny and, worse, without a ship. It was the *Rim* strategy. I had organized the transport from Rhodes where people were able to pay more than the actual cost and thus achieved an average that permitted us to charter a ship for both, the 151 in Constanţa and those who wanted to emigrate from Rhodes. Jewish community leaders from all over Europe were writing and cabling to me, pleading and entreating me to come to their city and take at least some of the Jews of their community along on our next voyage. I took out the "Miscellaneous Communities" folder: the Agudath Israel in Budapest seemed the one to pick in this instance. The Agudath people were not the most disciplined, and as they were orthodox Jews, their feeding complicated the issue, but still for the sake of the future state they were valuable. To them Palestine was not just a temporary haven, it was the land toward which they literally turned three times a day when they prayed to the Almighty to help them back to the City of His Glory. Another vital consideration was that Budapest, Hungary's capital, is on the Danube River, on the way from Bratislava down to Rumania. The people from

Budapest could easily be picked up in a short stop without delaying the voyage.

That night Dr. Hecht and I decided to go to Budapest to organize a transport there as fast as possible. I myself might experience difficulty in crossing Italy. I did have an Italian transit visa, which I had obtained upon my arrival in Switzerland. As I had the last time passed through Italy within twenty-four hours and still had my British visa in my passport, the new Italian transit visa had been granted without many questions. But at that time the Italian Consulate in Zurich had not known who I was. The border authorities, on the other hand, might by now have received instructions not to let me in—or to let me in and arrest me. The motivation behind such Italian antagonism toward our activity would be rather complex. The Italians were relatively friendly to the Jews. But Mussolini, who referred to the Mediterranean as *mare nostrum*—our ocean—had designs on Palestine. After a victorious war he wanted Palestine for Italy, and the Jews, he knew, would not be good "pliable" colonials.

Too many worries. I could hardly stand it. I called Vienna, Mrs. Sonnenkind-Kant. Speaking to my wife would bring some relief. I could not call often; that might have caused the Gestapo to take a closer look at that "Mirjam." But today I felt so low I had to talk to her. Again hearing her voice was happiness itself. It made me forget that I was in Zurich, and she in Vienna with the most forbidding border in between. For a short while there was no stranded group in Bratislava, none on a barge in the middle of the Danube waiting for a *Sakarya,* which might never come. It was Lore and I, and only someone who has been separated for a long time from the one he loves can know how close a phone conversation could make us feel. But only up to a certain point could I—and could Lore—feel that happiness. I then committed the stupid mistake of telling her that the next time I would probably be calling her from Budapest where I had to go "for business." First there was no reply. Then crying. Lore did not want to dissuade me from doing what I felt I had to. She saw too much of the misery of those who were being carted away to be murdered in the east. But she asked: is it really necessary? You are living now in Switzerland, a neutral haven in the midst of war. Going back into the Balkans—she said openly over the phone—might make it impossible for me "to return to the family in Switzerland if Italy should enter the war in the meanwhile," and I might not be able to move. What she meant was that I would fall into the hands of Eichmann. She knew that although Eichmann was following policy from higher up to get the Jews out and therefore did not put obstacles in the path of our work, he had it in for me personally since a certain phone conversation between Bucharest and Vienna some seven months before. This was when our transport of 151 was hopelessly stuck in Rumania, and there were problems in our Vienna office because most of our old people had by then left. At that point, I received a phone call from our office, which was then being "inspected" by Eichmann. After I talked to our men, Eichmann came to the phone.

"Eichmann speaking. You better come back here and straighten things out yourself or else your people are in trouble." I answered that I, being Jewish, would of course not return to Vienna and would try as best as I could to get everything done from Bucharest. "I'll grant you safe conduct if you come here," Eichmann said. To this I replied: "I appreciate your offer, but I am a free man here and do not ask for nor accept any free conduct." I did not then consider this a provocative reply, just a natural and perhaps proud response, but Eichmann had obviously viewed it as impertinent. He answered, "We will still get you, Perl," and hung up. Lore knew about that remark of his. She had also indicated to me that the way I had filled out the lawyer's questionnaire before I had left was considered by the Nazis an insult. Shortly after Hitler's march into Vienna, lawyers, like all other professionals, had received a questionnaire which was to indicate whether they would be able to continue to practice their profession. There was an entire page in the questionnaire just for filling out the names and places of birth of one's ancestors, to find out whether one had any Jews in one's parentage. I had not filled out that page at all. Instead I had written large across it: "Not relevant in my case because I can prove that for the last four thousand years I have been of pure Jewish ancestry." In the rush of the thousands of questionnaires coming in, the only result was that I was one of the first ones to be stricken from the list of lawyers. But when the whirlwind of the annexation of Austria subsided, my questionnaire received more attention, and the "provocative impertinence there" had been mentioned by one of the Nazi officials with whom our office had to deal. So Lore's worry about my falling into Eichmann's hands was not unjustified.

When I heard her cry over the phone, I felt like a heel. Depressed—more than that—shaken up by the news of the *Sakarya's* delay and the rapidly sinking funds of the Betar group, I had, like a little boy who runs to Mommy, called my wife to find consolation in talking to her. And I had not given a thought to how much it would upset her when she learned that I was leaving Switzerland to return to "fieldwork."

The day had really been a trying one. Even while slowly falling asleep I could still hear Lore's quiet weeping. She was obviously certain that in going into Eastern Europe again, clearly an early target for Nazi attack, I would not survive.

The next few days Dr. Hecht and I completed my most urgent business in Zurich, with a view to my not coming back again to Switzerland. Dr. Hecht was to follow me in about a week, and he would be back in Zurich two or three weeks later. As it turned out, I, as expected, did not return. Rudi Hecht did return but only after three eventful months.

My trip to Budapest was routine. No trouble on any border. On arrival I was met by a delegation of the Agudath Israel. They brought me to the Bristol Hotel where I had stayed before under the title Herr Konsul.

A carnival atmosphere pervaded the brightly lit streets and boulevards of the inner city, and gay music wafted from the numerous cafés. Now in its dying days, Budapest was filled with people who tried to experience life to the fullest, before it would be all over for good, as if they sensed that the anticipated rule of the goose-stepping Nazis would not be replaced by the return of freedom but by another dictatorship.

Having seen and lived the misery of those already under the German heel and of those on the refugee ships, I found it hard to become part of Budapest life in these days, yet I had to. Austria-Hungary had been one country not so long ago, and the old Austrian habit of doing business in coffeehouses still prevailed in Budapest. If I wanted to make any arrangements for the ships, I had to do it where there was music, entertainment, and rich food. Sitting in some plush place with waiters rushing and bowing around me, I felt almost a traitor to our refugees as I thought of the conditions of those in the Bratislava detention building and of those on the Danube barge.

The whole atmosphere had an unreal quality about it, yet the business I had to conduct was real enough. The Agudath Israel had informed me in a call to Zurich that they could pay only in pengös—the local currency. No official transfer in Hungary. Prior to my leaving Switzerland I had therefore made preparations to smuggle the pengös out of Hungary. In the Pension Renée I had met an American physician from Boston. Dr. Pat Cline was Jewish, and his passport was, of course, the best one could have these days in Europe. He volunteered to come to Budapest and to smuggle the pengös I would give him into Zurich, where they could be traded on the open currency market. The Hungarian Betarim soon learned that I was in Budapest, and they had people whom they wanted to send along—almost all of them without money. The purpose of taking people from Hungary, who were then still less endangered than those in Vienna or Prague, was to have the Budapest part of the group pay for what the Czech Betarim did not have, the rest being paid by the Mandler and the Storfer groups. On the other hand, I could not be in Budapest, organize an Agudath Israel exodus, and leave our own Betarim behind. A compromise had to be worked out. If paying fully, the Betarim always had preference. Of those who paid less than a certain amount, a somewhat larger percentage could be taken along, of those who paid less or nothing, an even smaller number would travel this time from Budapest. The pressure was not as bad as it first seemed to be. Many Betarim had joined the Gleser-Faltyn transport and were now waiting on a barge in Sulina to continue their voyage. I do not recall the percentage of the space distribution, but I believe that of the 180 I was to take from Budapest, one-fourth would be Betarim.

In addition, my diary entry of November 30 shows that I had determined to take along "11 Schoenfeld people," who would not pay. I am not certain anymore who those Schoenfeld people were, nor who Schoenfeld was, but they must have been the people from the Budapest jail, and Schoenfeld was most likely that spectacled, stout, and fast-talking man who had come to the Bristol and insisted that I take some of the people along who were in jail. They had crossed the border illegally from Austria into relatively safe Hungary and had been caught or betrayed at the crossing.

I will never forget my visit to that jail early one rainy morning. There were the two youngsters, brothers about sixteen and seventeen years old, whose family had been told to report in Vienna for "resettlement." The parents and a sister had obediently come to the collection point, but the two boys had decided to run for it. They had crossed over safely but had been apprehended near the next Hungarian village when they had been chased by dogs and had thus attracted the attention of the local policeman. The two had not a penny, but there was no question in my mind: I had to take both along. I also remember the haggard, disheveled, tall man with a graying beard who had his prayer shawl around his shoulders, his *tefillin* on his left arm and head, and a little prayer book in his hand. As important as my visit was to him, he did not stop praying because this prayer was one which must under no circumstances be interrupted. He had lived in a small town, more a village, in eastern Slovakia. With his wife and ten-year-old daughter, he had fled when the Hlinka Guard staged a little pogrom there and had killed several Jews, among them his father-in-law. The three had crossed woods and mountains and finally made it into Hungary but were caught in Budapest by a suspicious plainclothes policeman to whom the shabby people looked "foreign." I was about to tell the man that he and his family could come along when he made the fatal mistake. He told me that unless I took them, the wife would doubtlessly die here in jail. She was suffering from a lung disease and had been spitting blood recently. With a sinking feeling I went to the women's part of the jail to see the wife and verify the story. At my request she showed me her hankie. It was bloody. She believed that this would clinch it for them. Poor people. We could not have any sick ones on ships on which even the healthiest could hardly survive. Looking back I wonder how I had the strength to leave such people behind. But I had to. One had to be as hard as iron in the face of all we had to contend with. Many had to be sacrificed in order to save many more.

The same day in which I entered into my diary the little note on the "11 Schoenfeld people," I also wrote: "Another day of . . . historical importance. Helsinki was bombed by the Soviets." It was the day the Soviet Union, backed by its non-aggression treaty with Germany and certain that England and France would not move, invaded Finland.

Against that background of war, invasion, and the death of thousands in the Karelian lakes in Finland, and with the picture in my mind of the family I had just in effect sentenced to die, I had to sit in Budapest in the middle of a fool's paradise with gypsies fiddling at my table. I am not the nightclubbing type at all, and least of all was I longing for "night life" in these weeks in Budapest.

Never before and never after was I as much in the midst of it. Wherever one went, there was music, dancing, singing. Every entertainer and would-be entertainer was working till the small hours of the morning, and nearly every little eating place had turned into a *café dansant* or a cabaret. Morals were loose —I heard there for the first time of the then in Europe unheard-of custom of wife-swapping. Prostitution flourished. But not only prostitution. One night a woman knocked at my door. A young lady. She told me she was in town with her husband, a prominent physician in Hungary's second largest city. He was attending a medical convention, and they were to be here for several days. The night before, he had not come home until very late. Tonight, he had told her, he was staying at some modern hospital too far out of town to return to Budapest. From the hall porter she had learned what kind of work that young man was doing who seemed always beleaguered by desperate-looking people. I was a foreigner and my work demanded discretion. She could be safe with me knowing that no one in Budapest, where she was born and well known, would learn about "the effect loneliness had" on her. One must recall how Europeans looked down on the idea of a woman taking the initiative in sexual matters to realize the atmosphere which prevailed in these last weeks of a dying world.

One evening Dr. Hecht and I were having a late supper in one of the better café restaurants on the riverfront. An American singer was performing. She was supposedly well known in the States, and from her name—which I have since forgotten—both Rudi and I were certain that she was Jewish. The café was warm, full of people, full of smoke, and an atmosphere that seemed one of a desire to live it up—quickly. At some of the nearby tables, there were German officers, and the singer, obviously catering to them, sang several German folk songs. The slightly inebriated Germans were loudly singing along, which inspired the entertainer to switch from folk tunes to German patriotic songs. The Germans were now singing even more loudly; some were roaring in befuddled enthusiasm. After long and loud applause by the Germans, the entertainer smiled at them. During the short silence which anticipated the beginning of a new song, Dr. Hecht's voice broke in.

"You should be ashamed of yourself," he shouted aloud in German, "that you, a Jewish woman, are catering to the Germans in times like these." For a moment there was dead silence. Some people moved their chairs, ready to flee from the expected brawl, when the singer switched her entertainer's smile from the Germans to Hecht and me and started singing a Yiddish song, "A Yiddishe Mama." There were other Jews in the café, but Rudi and I were the only ones who applauded; in fact we rose doing so. Hecht and I rarely have a drink. We may have had a glass of wine with our meal that night, but I believe that our behavior resulted simply from indignation and youthful impulse. When the song was over, the singer came to our table and sat down with us. She told us that she was not Jewish and was sorry to have hurt our feelings. She was a fine woman who, being an entertainer, had without much thinking responded to the chance to have her performance liked by some of the obviously important guests.

And the Germans? As with so much that happened to us in free immigration, this incident too ended in a completely unexpected way.

It is often hard to understand the words of a song, and it took the Germans quite some time to realize that the new song was not set in some German dialect but that it was pure unadulterated Yiddish! It was only toward the end of the song that the highest-ranking of the Germans present, a major at the table nearest ours, called aloud for the waiter. The Germans put their heads together, paid, and left without a word. At first Hecht and I were baffled. Then we had to laugh. The explanation was obvious. They had to steal away; they could not afford to do anything else. Imagine what would have happened to them had the Gestapo found out that all evening long they had been listening to a *"Jewish"* entertainer, had publicly and enthusiastically applauded her, and—the ultimate ignominy—had sat in uniform through the singing of a Yiddish song!

In that whole climate of unreality, our negotiations with the Agudath, the Hungarian authorities, the DDSG, and Mr. Storfer in Vienna continued.

But dealing with the intricacies of how many to take of each group, how to arrange for the involved currency matters, and arrangements for supplies to be delivered to the riverboat were simple matters and almost a relaxing part of the work when compared to handling the truly nerve-wracking, catastrophic news from Rumania and from the DDSG in Vienna. With German punctuality, the *Saturnus* had left Vienna on November 19. It brought to Bratislava 211 free immigrants instead of the agreed-upon 200. In Bratislava another 600, Mandler's Prague transport, boarded the

Saturnus, and with its 811 rescued out from under the swastika, the *Saturnus* paddled down the Danube and arrived in Sulina on November 23 to transfer the passengers there to the *Sakarya.*

Only, there was no *Sakarya* there.

Our people called me from Sulina and Bucharest and told me that they were beginning to doubt Rand's honesty; they were starting to wonder whether the *Sakarya* existed at all, and if so, whether she would really come or not. I told them that she did exist, as I had seen her name in Lloyd's Register, and that they would just have to put pressure on Rand who had weeks before received the 2,000 English pounds as prepayment. When I told Sulina about the pressure which had to be put on Rand, Eri Jabotinsky answered that this was just the right time to "talk turkey" to Rand, of whom he was most suspicious. Every day Rand or his partner had informed our people in Rumania that the ship had just left Istanbul for Sulina. Just before my phone call Eri had learned that the *Sakarya* had truly left Istanbul but not for Sulina. She was just then sailing in the opposite direction, to Smyrna with a load of coal. Eri reports:

> I . . . rang up the agent at Galatz and told him that if the ship was not there on the tenth [of December] I would consider that he had cheated us. There were 500 Betarim on the *'Spyroula'* who would be exposed to the direct hardships of wintering on a frozen barge because of this fraud, but the Betar would know how to avenge itself. 'What do you mean,' he asked. I answered that he probably knew what was usually done to traitors. I hung up before he could answer me.
>
> The next day a letter came wherein the agent informed me that if he were murdered, the police would know who the murderer was. He had sent a complaint to the Ministry of the Interior to the effect that I had threatened him. His wife had listened to our conversation and was witness to my threats and so on. . . .*

Eri was certain that his threat had convinced Rand and that the *Sakarya* would now definitely arrive on the tenth.

But even if the *Sakarya* would arrive on December 10, those on the *Saturnus* and the barge *Spyroula* would together not have the money previously agreed upon for the *Sakarya*'s charter. They all

*Eri Jabotinsky, *The Sakarya Expedition* (Johannesburg, S.A.: Nero Press and Publishing Co., 1945).

had to wait until I got my Hungarian transport down from Budapest, and notwithstanding the hectic pace in which work at Budapest proceeded, this might take another week or ten days. This was
if all went smoothly.

Yet I am reporting here only the major complications and
problems which arose with this, or any other, transport. Every day
new difficulties arose, and they were usually the least expected.
Most of them were quickly taken care of, but each one constituted a
danger to the entire project. While matters in Budapest itself proceeded relatively well, we had never before even tried to organize a
transport that fast. But in spite of our race against time, one day
after another in Budapest passed, and we had no ship yet to bring
the newly organized people from Vienna and Budapest down to
Sulina. The great obstacle was, of course, with the DDSG. The
Saturnus was supposed to have unloaded her 811 Jews in Sulina on
November 22. Yet the DDSG boat was still stuck there because the
seagoing vessel had not arrived. The DDSG did not want to send
down still another ship, prior to the *Saturnus*'s transfer. Every day
from the eighteenth of November on, the day scheduled for the
Sakarya's arrival, the DDSG representative in Sulina reported to
his company in Vienna: no *Sakarya* yet. After a week, his reports
expressed doubts whether she would ever arrive. When she finally
came, on December 10, twenty-three days after the scheduled date,
we did not have the funds to pay for the *Sakarya* transfer. It was a
vicious circle. No transfer without first paying. No first paying
possible without the Budapest transport. And every day, every
hour, counted because any time now the Danube could freeze over
and the *Saturnus* would be locked in ice in Rumania—and this in
wartime when she was urgently needed in Germany.

It was under those circumstances that I was to persuade the
DDSG to send us yet another ship down the Danube. Now, in
December! And for such a long voyage, too, to bring some 200
escapees down from Vienna and to take 300 more in Budapest all
the way through southeastern Europe down to the Black Sea. It
seemed an impossible task to swing such an okay from the DDSG.
It would have been impossible but for the work of my Aunt Liesel
Kant, today a healthy eighty-five years of age and living in Chicago.
She had, as mentioned before, established excellent connections
with some of the DDSG bigwigs. One of them helped us to such an
extent that he—though a member of the Nazi party—risked not

only his position but also his life. He was Director Schaetz, the one whom the company had put in charge of all that "Jew business," and his name should be inscribed in the book of those Gentiles who in Nazi times rescued persecuted Jews. Before he came to Budapest, I thought that mere infatuation with my aunt had so far caused him to be as helpful as he had been all the time. Any relationship between the two not exclusively on a business level, the mere suspicion of *Rassenschande,* would have, if found out, resulted in her being killed right away and in his being sent to a concentration camp. But when Mr. Schaetz now came to Budapest to learn, as he expressed it, "from the horse's mouth" what the true story of the *Sakarya* was and what could be done to have the *Saturnus* return immediately, I saw that he, no doubt influenced by Liesel Kant, was truly intent on helping. He felt genuine compassion for the sufferings of the Jews generally and—most of all—he was ready to stick out his neck to save those on the *Saturnus.* He came to Budapest in the first days of December with orders from his company to have the *Saturnus* return to Vienna unless transfer was possible within three days. He left Budapest with the promise that he would do his best to keep the *Saturnus* in Sulina up to and including December 10—the last date set by Eri Jabotinsky in his "ultimatum" to the Rand Company. More than that: he told me that he could not promise but would do his best to have the *Grein,* a smaller paddle-wheeler which we had used earlier, leave Vienna for Sulina as late as December 11. The condition was, of course, that by then the German DDSG agent in Sulina had confirmed to him that the *Sakarya* was there and ready to board immediately the people from the *Saturnus* and those to be newly dispatched with the *Grein.* This arrangement with Director Schaetz was an almost unbeliev-able achievement. To send a new ship down the Danube as late as December 11 was a request which I had made but never expected to be fulfilled.

In the first week of December I learned from Bucharest that the British had increased their pressure on the Rumanian authori-ties not to permit any transfer from the *Saturnus,* the *Spyroula,* or from the other paddle-wheeler soon to arrive. They wanted Ruma-nia to insist that the ships all go back up the Danube, as the British demanded "deportation" of the escapees. We were thus in about as much trouble as one could be. No ship yet, the people on the ships eating up the money needed to pay for the seagoing vessel and the

British threatening the Rumanians with dire consequences if a transfer took place at all.

Mrs. Bernstein called me from Bucharest and described the depressing situation. When I asked her whether my going there might be advisable, I learned that the Rumanians had bestowed upon me the honor of making me the bone to be thrown to the British lion. They had promised that the moment I showed up in Rumania, I would be arrested, kept in jail until the next riverboat left for Germany, and at that time I would be put on board and thus deported "home"—to Vienna. Mrs. Bernstein insisted that I was most needed in Budapest for getting the Hungarian transport out and for the negotiations with the DDSG. I therefore decided to ask Dr. Hecht to leave right away for Rumania to strengthen our hand there and to make sure that when and if the *Sakarya* arrived on December 10, twenty-two bitter cold and worry-filled days after the latest date agreed upon, everything should go as fast as possible.

As promised to Eri after his threat, the *Sakarya* did arrive in Sulina on December 10.

Jubilation. The uninformed ones, those freezing twenty-four hours a day on the *Saturnus*, on which they had been since November 19, and the 530 shivering unremittingly in the even icier hold of the *Spyroula* believed that they would now sail within a couple of days. But they had to be warned not to expect anything like immediate departure.

I was informed by phone of the *Sakarya*'s arrival and alerted those who were to lead the Budapest section of the transport that they would be leaving within two or three days. I called the DDSG and Storfer in Vienna to get the *Grein* ready, which, I had agreed with Mr. Schaetz, would bring a total of 530 down to Sulina. Every few minutes, while I was phoning, I glanced out the window to see whether the gray sky had become any grayer and whether there were—God forbid—any snow flurries noticeable. We had often raced against time, but now on December 11 the race against winter seemed hopeless. We had the *Saturnus* with 811 in Sulina, and the 530 from Vienna and Budapest had not yet even boarded the *Grein,* and we still had the long trip ahead to the Black Sea.

I had just finished phoning Vienna and had received the assurance from Schaetz that unless the weather changed he would send the *Grein* down on December 12, when I was again called to the phone. Sulina. The news was catastrophic. A bombshell.

On the *Sakarya* her two owners had come along, both young men. Avni Bey was twenty-eight. His cousin, Kemal Bey, was twenty-four. In his matter-of-fact way, Eri described the first meeting with the two Turks as follows:

> ... the owners said that having arrived they could see that we had been swindled.... The ship had been chartered to transport 900 'legal' immigrants to Palestine. They were to be provided with visas for Palestine. The owners were to be paid L.St. 3,750 which was still due to them, within 12 hours after their arrival at Sulina and they were to be able to return within four days. If any of these conditions were not filled, the owners were at liberty to consider themselves freed from the contract and were not obliged to refund any sum they might have received up to date.*

Mrs. Bernstein told me over the phone.

The Turks had not received a penny yet from Rand. And this was not even everything. The Gleser-Faltyn group, which had informed us before that they had eaten up everything except 6 English pounds per person now admitted that they did not have even that. By the time the *Sakarya* would be remodeled and ready for sailing, in spite of all the support coming in from the Rumanian Jewish community—itself hard pressed—the Gleser-Faltyn section of the transport would have only 1 pound per person ($5) left for the entire sea voyage.

I was stunned by the apparent swindle perpetrated on us—including the threatened loss of Mandler's 2,000 pounds—and also by the news that the Prague Betar group had almost no money left.

"Where do we go from here," Mrs. Bernstein inquired.

"To Palestine, of course," I answered.

"You are crazy. We have no ship and no money."

"We are going to Palestine, with more than two thousand people, and do you know why? Because there is no other way. You keep the ship there, negotiate with the Turks. Make a contract directly with them, the best possible one. But if it is a bad contract, make it anyhow, as long as they will keep the ship there. We have to get the *Grein* down first. Otherwise the people in Vienna—for having misinformed the authorities—will all be immediately shipped out for extermination. Likewise, if the *Sakarya* leaves

*Ibid.

Sulina, the *Saturnus* with its eight hundred eleven on board will be
ordered back right away by the DDSG. Keep the *Sakarya* in Sulina,
whatever the conditions. Don't abandon the ship. I shall try to get
Mandler out of Prague and down to Sulina. He is a wizard in
financial matters and will help you all to pull through."

"We do not need a wizard, we need a magician."

"We have a magician—God."

Almost all the bad news possible was now known; just one
more thing might still hit us: the Danube could freeze over in any
part of the river between its upper reaches in Austria and the Black
Sea. But in at least that way the Great Magician was clearly with
us. Although it was December, the sun was shining every day, and
though that could change at any moment, the forecasts spoke of
continued good weather.

Two steps had to be taken. I had to get Mandler down to
Rumania. And I had to get the *Grein* passengers in Vienna, and the
remainder in Budapest to Sulina before the weather changed. Both
seemed impossible. Mandler was the one whom the Nazis held
mainly responsible for the currency which had left their treasury—
would they let him travel abroad? And despite all the goodwill on
the part of Mr. Schaetz, would he really take it upon himself to send
the *Grein* down the river that late in the season? He knew, of
course, that it was not our group. But because they could not get a
seagoing vessel, the Zionist-Socialists Hashomer Hazair had for the
past two months a transport stuck on riverboats in Kladovo. With
the *Saturnus* not yet unloaded, Schaetz was afraid that the *Saturnus*
and the *Grein* might, just as the three Yugoslav ships now in
Kladovo, be unable to transfer their passengers to a seagoing ship.
To assuage these worries at least partially and to cover himself to
some degree, he needed a confirmation from the DDSG agent in
Sulina that the *Sakarya* was ready to have that transfer accomplished. She, of course, was not. The owners had just told our
people, as reported by Eri, that we had been swindled. In spite of
it—I do not know how our friends in Sulina accomplished it—the
DDSG agent did inform his company in Vienna that the *Sakarya*
would take the people. Thus, as far as the DDSG was concerned,
the weather was the element that remained our worst danger. In the
meanwhile, Schaetz and the people in Vienna and in Budapest
prepared for the departure of the *Grein*. On December 17, a week
after the *Sakarya* had arrived in Sulina, the *Grein* left Vienna with

226 free immigrants, most of them members of the Orthodox Agudath Israel. Next day the *Grein* paddled into Budapest and took on 309, thus having on board altogether 535 passengers. Of the 309 who boarded the *Grein* in Budapest, 185 belonged to the Agudath, 105 were Betarim—most of whom had paid little or nothing—and the remaining 19 included those we had taken out of jail. This last was not only a humanitarian act but also one which had helped us with the Hungarian authorities.

After all the worries as to whether I would be able to organize this transport so rapidly, it was a festive day when I again stood on the gangplank and saw man after man, woman after woman, and, most of all, when I saw our youngsters from the Betar step onto the ship. At every such previous occasion, and now again, I had to think as I saw them make that decisive step: most likely he—or she—is this moment escaping death and moving toward a new life.

Yet as I saw the *Grein* slowly disappear into the foggy late afternoon, I was only too keenly aware that the *Sakarya* was now in Sulina but that we had paid in advance a huge amount to the Rand shipping agency that Rand had not delivered to the shipowners. We had no contract for the *Sakarya* and, even with the now-improved finances, not enough money to pay for her. I recalled Lola Bernstein's recent question on the phone, and to boost my own courage, I said to myself aloud: "Of course we are going to Palestine!"

"What did you say?" asked the Budapest DDSG man next to me. I repeated it, and he answered: "Of course, we know they are all going to Palestine." But was his "knowledge" correct? Would our people in Rumania be able to have the *Sakarya* really take on our immigrants and transport them?

The prime objective in negotiating with the Turks was to keep them there. Under no circumstances must they leave. If necessary, we had to promise them the moon. Thus we negotiated a contract with the shipowners which doubtlessly was most desirable to them. It started:

> The undersigned Mr. W. Perl, represented by Mrs. Lola Bernstein, whose present address is c/o "Romania" Official Rumanian Tourist Agency, Doamnei Street 1 Bucharest and Messrs. Avni Nuri Meseregi and A. Sadicoglu, owners of the ship Sakarya have agreed upon the following charter agreement. . . .

The contract then stated—and this was an ingenious move intended to make sure that the *Sakarya* did not leave—that I charter the *Sakarya* for altogether four voyages. The total amount for all four trips was to be 48,700 English pounds, or $243,500. This was several times the value of the ship and a most enticing lure. It was truly a *chutzpah*—an almost impertinent daring—to negotiate in terms of such huge sums when we did not have the money to pay for even *one* trip! Besides, it was clear to me that particularly in wartime a ship as large as the *Sakarya* could not be used for more than one trip. She was a target that would be too easily recognized a second time by the British. To dispel any doubts on the part of the Turks that our negotiation on that basis was serious, we insisted on such clauses as: installation of a water tank capable of holding 170 tons of drinking water; heating in the holds and electric lights there. The Turks insisted that the amount for all four trips be deposited in advance in a bank so that the bank guaranteed payment. After a long apparent hesitation, our people gave in to that condition, knowing, of course, that we could never fulfill it but always having in mind: "under no circumstances must the *Sakarya* leave." We had to get the people on the *Grein* down first before we could seriously start discussing even one voyage. Without the *Grein* people, we had far too little even to begin talking seriously. Even with the *Grein* people we were still short of what we would have to expect as a final charter fee. Our situation was complicated by the fact that more and more of those who were hanging around in the various Rumanian ports had to be taken along. Many of them were from countries already occupied by the Nazis, others were Rumanian Jews who saw the handwriting on the wall, and, of course, whether they had money or not we had to take along a good number of Bertarim from Rumania.

Certainly on paper all our rescue actions had appeared impossible from the beginning, yet finally they had worked out. This one, however, seemed absolutely hopeless. From all rational viewpoints it was, but we refused to listen to logic and proceeded on the basis that: they will sail because they must sail. And they will land because they must land.

In the meanwhile, Mrs. Bernstein, in my name, supported not only by Dr. Hecht but also by several devoted Rumanian Jews, negotiated an agreement which was—though we were ready to accede to anything—not bad at all for us as far as the price for the charter was concerned. In fact, it was much less than we had ever paid to any of the Greeks. The charter fee would be 17,000 pounds for the first trip, and this would permit us to bring 2,600 people on board. The amount, which was also the guideline for the second, third, and fourth trips, was arrived at as follows: 6 pounds for each one of the first 2,000 people. This made 12,000 pounds. For the next 600, 4½ pounds a head, which made 2,700 pounds. Together this was 14,700 pounds. The remainder of 2,300 pounds was to be an advance payment for the second voyage. For all the other trips, the minimum charter fee was to be 12,000 pounds for 2,000 passengers, and if we wanted more on board, up to an additional 600, we would have to pay 4½ pounds for each. For all future voyages, the contract also included clauses penalizing the shipper for each day the ship was late in arriving and penalizing us if the ship had to wait for the arrival of the passengers. It was a good, fair contract—the only joker in the game: we did not have the money!

In the meanwhile, while the contract was being negotiated, the *Grein* was paddling downriver. We hoped that Mandler would be down by then; we needed him for dealing with the shipowners, but also because his group was the main source of our finances, and his people, having almost all paid in full, were complaining bitterly about being held back by those who had no money.

When I called Mandler and told him that his presence in Rumania would be imperative, he wanted to go but wondered whether he would receive permission to leave. It would be easier to send one of my other cousins, Frantisek or Karel Gross who were working with him and were capable too. I told him that the situation was more intricate and more difficult to resolve than that of any of our previous ships and that his personal push, energy, and financial wizardry were a must. I asked him whether or not he could leave his wife and daughter as hostages guaranteeing that he would return. In words that were at first obscure to me but whose meaning I later on understood, he indicated that my thinking made no sense under existing circumstances: should he get permission to leave, he would have to put up his family as hostages as a matter of course. Yet if things went badly, and if an international scandal resulted because the Jews were not able to leave, the German authorities would hold him plus his family responsible, if he were there. If he did not return, they would have only his family—and Eichmann himself might be blamed for having let him get away.

That he would not return if things went wrong because the family would be lost in any case was a possibility the authorities would doubtlessly consider. Therefore he believed his chances to get to Sulina were minimal.

But Mandler could almost always do the impossible. He convinced Eichmann that without him the transport would never leave Sulina, the Jews would freeze to death, and unfavorable publicity for Germany would result. The Nazis assured him that if the transport did not leave, and if—whatever happened to the transport—he did not return, his family would have to pay. As Robert told me when we met in the Balkans, he had been told that if he did not return—whether the transport left or not—his family would not just simply be "resettled." They would first experience daily "special interrogation" until he returned.

Bad news rarely came singly, but the same was true of good news. The day the *Grein* loaded and left Vienna, Mandler called me from Prague and told me that Eichmann had given permission for him to travel to Rumania in order to "better straighten things out there." Apparently the Germans figured that, with the *Grein* added to the other undertakings, there was now too much at stake to hold Mandler—whose ability to disentangle complex situations they knew—in Prague. A major scandal in Rumania would get the Nazi Ministry of Propaganda up in arms, and Dr. Goebbels was even for Eichmann far too formidable an opponent. On the day the *Grein*, now carrying the full load of 535 free immigrants, left Budapest, Mandler called me again at the Bristol there. He was just about to leave for Rumania.

Although I did not see how the *Sakarya* could be made to sail with all the people who expected to travel with her, I was in a much more hopeful mood than I had been for weeks when I left Budapest the day after we had dispatched the *Grein*. My next destination was Italy. When I had traveled through Italy in the first days of the war, I had promised to try to get Jews out from there too, and an unbroken chain of letters had since reminded me of the promise. Italy does not border Hungary; I had to go through Yugoslavia, and all I could obtain from the Yugoslavs was a transit visa which specifically stated that no stay whatsoever was granted, just permission to travel through. Yet I had to meet with some of our friends. The Dragoner family for many years had been devoted disciples of Zeev Jabotinsky, and I knew them from various Revisionist congresses. They were eager to help Jews get out of Yugoslavia, especially veteran Revisionists and Betarim. I wanted to discuss these possibilities with them, but I also wanted to talk with them on how we could counter some of the British pressure exercised upon Yugoslavia to block transit and transfer on the Danube. Mr. Dragoner had good connections with the Yugoslav government, and I thought he might be able to help us just as we might be able to get some of his people out.

Fortunately there was no direct train from Budapest to Italy. I had to change trains in Belgrade. But unfortunately the wait involved in changing trains was less than two hours. This would not give me enough time in Belgrade, especially as I also wanted to talk to the local DDSG representatives there. I had spoken to these people over the phone several times but wanted the personal contact. This would also keep me in touch with developments regarding the *Saturnus* in Sulina and the *Grein,* now on her way down. If there was any complication, I had to know. I could not possibly sit still in a train for so long a time when the weather might change at any hour. I decided that in Belgrade I would simply slip away from the station, instead of waiting for the next train, and take care of my business for a day or two. When on leaving Yugoslavia I would show my passport and the border control would discover that I had overstayed my visa—so what? I would be at the Italian border at that point anyhow. None of the European countries was then interested in keeping any foreign Jews in its jails, which were usually overflowing with illegal refugees.

Well, that was my plan, but it did not work out that way. When we crossed into Yugoslavia from Hungary, the border control officer, noticing that no stay was permitted me, took my passport and told me it would be given to the passport control on the train with which I was to leave and I would get the passport back as soon as that train reached the Italian border. This was to make sure that I did not disappear while I was waiting for the train to Italy.

That certainly upset my calculations. I could not, a foreigner in wartime, run around the city without a passport, unless there was legitimate reason for doing so. But there was none. Therefore I had to invent one. On arrival in Belgrade, I left the platform with the crowd, hopped into a taxi, and told the driver to bring me to the city's best hotel, the Srbski Kral—the King of Serbia. But though I took the least-expensive room, the address was still that of the city's swankiest hotel, and this might help with the police when the bubble burst. One treats a guest of the Srbski Kral differently from an obviously penniless refugee. At the desk I filled out the form with scrupulous care, and when the man asked me for my passport, I told him—truthfully—that it was with the police. To forestall further inquiries on his part, I added—less truthfully—that the police would bring it to him tomorrow—"in the course of the day." That would give me probably two days to work without being found out and hauled to jail or to the next departing train. Like any other respected guest, I was shown up to my room by the bellboy.

I called the Dragoners and also a young Gentile woman, Milana Duduković, whom I had known in Vienna in my student days. She was a Serbian patriot and might have connections which would prove helpful. I also called the Belgrade DDSG and made an appointment there for the next morning. Next I called Mr. Schaetz in Vienna. It was good to hear that the *Grein* was well on her way down with no new complications. "If only the weather holds," he added.

The ruse with the passport and the excuse I had given the hotel worked. Of course, as soon as the police found out that I was not on the train that was to bring me to the Italian border, they began searching for me everywhere. I am certain that they also checked all reports from the hotels that noted new arrivals. But the Srbski Kral had not reported my checking in; they were waiting there for the police to bring my passport in so that the hotel could fill out the data which I claimed I did not know by heart, such as the number of the passport and where, when, and by whom it had been issued. Thus, every time I passed the reception desk I smiled as I saw in the pigeonhole beneath my room number the white slip which contained my registration.

The ruse enabled me to discuss everything I had to with the Dragoners. Two phone calls to Sofia helped to coordinate actions with Bulgaria where Dr. Confino had been most successful in Aliya Bet. I also checked daily with the DDSG about the situation of the riverboats. I even went to the German Legation, met there with an attaché, a Mr. Puhr, and tried to have him counter some of the British moves aimed at preventing the DDSG from using the Yugoslav leg of the Danube voyage for bringing down our emigrants and thereby fulfilling the DDSG contract. The *Sakarya* had been in Sulina now for more than ten days, and the *Saturnus* was still unable to perform the transfer. I did not tell Puhr that this was due mainly to lack of funds but ascribed the difficulties entirely to British machinations. He knew of British interventions in Belgrade and was furious because of the danger to the German ships. He said he would try to counteract British moves regarding transit of our ships, but when I asked him to help me with the Yugoslav police so that I could stay a few more days, he refused.

In the meanwhile Mandler had arrived in Sulina. With Hecht, Lola Bernstein, and members of the Bucharest Jewish community, he concentrated on one effort: to get the Turks to agree to having the people from the *Saturnus* and the *Grein* transfer to the *Sakarya* on the basis of a partial payment because the rest of the money was on the way "from America and South Africa," and if the DDSG ships return with their passengers, not only would the Turks have lost the business of this trip and the following three, but they would also have lost all the time which they had so far invested in it. Yet the shipowners refused to let anyone go on board until payment for the entire trip was either received or guaranteed by a bank.

I was daily informed in Belgrade of the status of the negotiations in Sulina and Bucharest, but I never knew whether a phone conversation I had started would be interrupted by my arrest or not. It could not last much longer. On December 24 in the morning I learned from the DDSG that the *Saturnus* had received orders to return that evening, because the freezing of the river was anticipated. I called my Aunt Liesel. Schaetz could do no more than he had already done. The ship would go back unless—Schaetz had said—I could get the Belgrade DDSG office to confirm that the weather forecast for the lower part of the Danube had changed. Of course, they would not do that.

In the lobby of the Srbski Kral, I was just waiting for a call from Bucharest when my time ran out. Two men came toward me, with the firm step and serious expression of plainclothes police. Milana was with me and started crying when they arrested me. Before taking me away they wanted an explanation. The police thought I had bribed the people at the desk and were after them, too. I explained that I must have misunderstood the police on the train. I had spoken to them in my native Czech, and they had spoken Serbian. As both languages are Slavic and thus somewhat similar, I believed that we had understood each other, but apparently there had been a misunderstanding. My explanation got the hotel people off the hook, and the fact that I was a guest at the Srbski Kral prevented these detectives who had finally found out where I had been all these days from treating me roughly.

They even permitted me to send a telegram which, I hoped, might keep the *Saturnus* and the *Grein* another day or two in Sulina. In a hurry I composed a cable which I gave to Milana to dispatch. As this was early afternoon on December 24, Christmas Eve, all offices and shops closed and business came to a halt at that time in that part of Europe. The sun sets early at that time of year, and I was certain that nobody would be in the DDSG office in Vienna or in Belgrade at that hour either. I sent the following identical cable to the DDSG in Vienna, to the DDSG representative in Sulina, and to Schaetz personally:

ALL WEATHER FORECASTS PREDICT WARMER WEATHER DUE ON DANUBE. PROGNOSIS SUNSHINE, WARMER. STOP. NO PRECIPITATION FOR COMING WEEK. SIGNED: PUHR, ATTACHÉ GERMAN LEGATION, BELGRADE.

At the same time, I instructed Milana that she had to put in an urgent call to my Aunt Liesel, tell her to call Schaetz at home, and tell him of the "German Legation" telegram. I figured that Schaetz, although he knew that Puhr was involved with our work, might have doubts regarding the authenticity of the telegram. But Schaetz wanted to help, and if he had a document to back him up, Liesel might move him to suspend the order that the *Saturnus* and the *Grein* had to return immediately.

As much as I pleaded with Milana to rush to the telegraph office and to make the phone call, she insisted on accompanying me to the railroad station. "With me around, they won't do anything more to you than just put you on the next train leaving for the border." She cried again when the policeman, the moment we were out of the hotel lobby, put handcuffs on me. They did not want to take any risks with that guy who had evaded them so long. For me the handcuffs meant little, but I was embarrassed for the girl as we left the taxi and walked through the crowded station toward the platform. The next train was to leave in only a few hours, and I finally persuaded Milana to leave me and go to the post office and make the call.

While I was rolling toward the Italian border, the telegrams and the phone call did their work. The DDSG agent in Sulina, confused, tried to contact the Vienna home office. No one at that hour, of course, could be reached. Neither could he reach anyone at the German Legation in Belgrade. Now he did not dare to send the ships with the Jews back. That Jews involved politics, as the German Legation had cabled, was all the more apparent in this case. A citizen of an authoritarian state heeds a suggestion by his government, even if an order of his own company demands the opposite—in this case immediate return. Naturally, the effect of the trick was of very limited duration. But it was in these subsequent hours that the breakthrough with the shipowners was achieved. On the evening of December 25, they agreed to have the people from the DDSG ships transferred to the *Sakarya* in exchange for partial payment. On December 26, the transfer was effected, and minutes later the *Saturnus* and the *Grein* were on their way back.

That the shipowners changed their mind during these critical thirty-six hours and agreed to the transfer was at least to some degree due to the influence of a girl. When Avni Bey and Kemal Bey had arrived in Sulina with the *Sakarya,* they had brought with them a tall, stunningly beautiful blonde who was introduced as their cousin. Leyla, twenty-three, played an important part in all the negotiations, because she was the only one of the Turkish group who spoke and understood a language other than Turkish. Up until then, languages had never been a problem for us. When I started the rescue work, I spoke German, Czech, French, English, and Italian fluently, and also some Greek. In the course of our work, I also become proficient in Rumanian and Portuguese. In addition, my knowledge of Czech helped me to understand other Slavic languages fairly well, such as Serbian, Polish, or Russian when they were spoken slowly. Eri knew at least one or two more languages than I did; Hecht spoke several languages fluently, and so did Mrs. Bernstein. But who in the world spoke Turkish unless he was a Turk? Leyla's knowledge of French and German was the communicating link between our people and the shipowners. This gave her— fortunately for those on the ships—an important role in the negotiations. She had been on the *Saturnus* and the *Spyroula* and was deeply impressed with what she had seen there. Whenever she could, she used her influence in favor of those whose plight had affected her more than it had the businessmen with whom she had come to Rumania.

I was already in Italy when I received the happy news of the transfer of all passengers from the *Grein* and the *Saturnus* to the *Sakarya*. For two days I stayed in Venice and then proceeded to Milan. There I met again with Major Carpi; with him were three or four other leaders of the Revisionists of Italy. Poland had by then completely collapsed, and Italy had not yet entered the war. The news about mass killings in Poland made our hair stand on end, and we all agreed that Jews from Eastern Europe would have to have priority, but that the Italians would investigate the chance to get a ship in Italy and to organize a transport from there directly. We would advise them and take care of the landing in Palestine.

In Rumania, the worst pressure of time had been removed with the transfer of the passengers from the *Grein* and the *Saturnus*. Now all the people from the Mandler transport and all those Storfer and his most efficient co-worker Moritz Pappenheim of the Agudath Israel had first assembled in Vienna in cooperation with Mandler were on the *Sakarya* and also 535 from Budapest and Vienna whom Hecht and I, working from Budapest, had organized rapidly into a transport. The *Sakarya*'s owners had realized that unless they let them board without another hour's delay, these people would all be on their way back and thereby lost as potential passengers. But the Turks—understandably—refused to let the 500 Betarim from the *Spyroula* on board unless and until the money for the voyage had all been paid. Although now the pressure of time was not as threatening as before, it still existed because of the conditions on the *Sakarya* and the *Spyroula*. Winter, which had been late in coming, suddenly came with a vengeance as if to make up for its delay in arriving.

Notwithstanding the worries and the living conditions, morale on the *Spyroula* had been incredibly high. A messianic atmosphere prevailed among the young people. The *Spyroula* was for these 500 not just a rusty old barge. It had turned for them into a symbol: the determination to hold out, whatever the circumstances might be, to make life even on that barge livable and to accept the suffering as something they had to overcome to make the Aliya, the ascent to the land promised to them by God. Idealism, however, would not have sufficed. Efficient organization of daily life on the barge was necessary, and with the help of most of those on board, Gleser and Faltyn, the leaders of that section of the *Sakarya* expedition, turned the existence there into a well-structured daily regime.

The barge had no motor. It was built to be towed only and was little more than a king-sized floating tub. The barge consisted of two large holds, each covered with tarpaulin, and each of the holds housed 250 people. Built into the holds were, as on all our ships, wooden galleries which provided "bed space" of about the width of one's rucksack. The distance between one such layer of bunks and the one above—or below—was two feet only. One could therefore barely sit up in one's allotted space. There were three platforms—or "stories"—in each hold. To move from one floor to the other, one had to use a ladder or a rickety staircase.

Yet leadership over those in these cramped quarters was firm and well respected. The following episode, described by Eri Jabotinsky will throw light not only on the morale on the barge but also on the reason why, under such harrowing conditions, discipline could be maintained.

> I was once present when the young people on the barge misbehaved. It was at a wedding which took place on board. A special wedding cake was prepared and divided among 500 guests. Towards the end of this distribution it appeared that some mathematician had miscalculated and 50 of the guests were going to remain without a cake. A small scuffle ensued. The Mifquada (leadership) immediately retired for a consultation and after a quarter of an hour issued a statement to the effect that as there was no one to punish for this indelicate incident which had spoilt the happiest day of the young couple's life, the Mifquada was going to take the responsibility and punishment on itself. As punishment the Mifquada was not going to get any dinner. The immigrants assembled in the forebunker to discuss this development and decided to fast that evening, out of solidarity with the Mifquada. Instead of dinner we had an evening of music. There were some excellent musicians and several instruments and songs. Then I told some stories about Palestine and the evening ended on empty stomachs but with hearts brimming with that sweet sickness that the French call 'Nostalgia.'*

There was organized active social life on board. For certain hours, part of one platform was reserved for the "*Spyroula* Kindergarten." There were also classes in Hebrew, in Jewish history, and there was music and group singing. Even when conditions worsened with the advent of the increasingly colder weather, one of the

*Ibid., p. 15.

passengers, Mr. Klapper, a Viennese entertainer, performed miracles in keeping up the morale. On the way down the Danube he had organized cabaret performances in which he not only used his own remarkable ability but also drew upon the talent of the passengers themselves. His performances regularly involved audience participation, particularly in the singing parts. In fact, a visiting Rumanian journalist once wrote a feature article referring to the *Spyroula* as The Singing Barge. As the situation worsened, the "Cabaret Viennois" performed almost nightly. All this helped those who were suffering from the biting cold to gain a sense of perspective about their plight.

Those on the ship were able even to get many a good laugh out of a situation in which one could find not only tragedy but, if one looked at it with Klapper's eyes, also humor. One funny occurrence concerned a man who had somehow gotten into that group and was a "revolutionary." He, not an unusual character type on any of the transports, was constantly complaining about the people who had so poorly organized the whole undertaking. He always found some followers among the 5,001; after all, they were not all angels. When everybody was frustrated enough anyhow, this man whom we'll call Mr. M., gave incendiary speeches that drew a good gathering, the more so as there was little to do. When we asked him to refrain from spreading unrest in an already tense setting, he reacted by giving even more inciting speeches. One afternoon after one of his truly inflammatory tirades he was cheered by a fair number. The Mifquada met to discuss what should be done to stop him. Various punitive steps were suggested. None of them was accepted. But next morning Mr. M. found his set of false teeth missing. After several days the teeth showed up again, but Mr. M. had somehow lost his desire for public speaking.

The Cabaret Viennois did more than just entertain for a few hours; it helped to create a tendency to express one's emotions in ways other than by complaints, self-pity, or being cantankerous. New songs were created on the *Spyroula*. Songs of hope but also of sadness, songs full of fighting spirit but also of worry about those left behind. These tunes spread to the *Saturnus* and from the *Saturnus* and the *Grein* people to the *Sakarya*. Soon they were sung and hummed also by the refugees who were hanging around in the port hoping to get on the ship.

There were happy events too. Two children were born on the

Spyroula. The first one, a girl, was named Mirjam Spyroula. Almost half of the Jews of Braila, the nearest larger Jewish community, came to celebrate the event on the windswept singing barge. Within a week there was another birth. This time it was a boy. A rabbi came down from Bucharest to perform the prescribed circumcision. In his speech he referred to the spirit prevailing on the barge and to the birth as one of God's signs of how much He loves life and wants the Jewish people to go on living.

But as days and weeks went by, and more weeks, and as the Rumanian winter hit with full force, suffering on the *Spyroula* as well as on the *Sakarya,* the latter not at all ready to leave, became more than flesh and blood could bear. Eri reports:

> The river froze and the *Spyroula* slowly turned into a block of ice. The respiration of 500 condensing on the walls, covered them with a sheet of ice which became thicker every day. Outside the thermometer descended to many degrees below zero.*

Being anchored outside the harbor to save on the accumulation of harbor fees, the *Sakarya* had the additional problem that she had to be reached by launches in order to be supplied with food. Endeavors to do that often had to be abandoned because of the raging seas. For days those on the *Sakarya* remained without meals because even the small quantity of provisions destined for them could not reach the ship. Eri describes one such vain attempt:

> The weather became terrible and the *Sakarya* with all its souls aboard became difficult to reach from the shore. Food ran short. Once I tried to reach her with stores on board the tug, the *'Maria,'* but the sea proved too strong. I was standing on the captain's bridge when just after leaving the mouth of the canal, the *Maria* dived into a wave. I got completely drenched and was almost thrown off the bridge. Several seconds later we dived into a second wave. Gasping, the captain said he could not do it, and returned into the canal. A sharp cold wind was blowing, and I suddenly saw that my overcoat had become one sheet of ice. That day and the next day the *Sakarya* remained without food.†

On January 4, 1940, Sir Reginald Hoare, the British ambassador to Bucharest, had sent a coded telegram dispatched—as the

*Ibid., p. 35.
†Ibid., pp. 35, 36.

official record shows—at 8:50 P.M. and received at the Foreign Office at 9:20 P.M.* He states in the telegram:

HIS MAJESTY'S CONSUL GENERAL GALATZ REPORTS THAT CONDITIONS ON SS SAKARYA ARE APPALLING AND THAT LIGHTING AND HEATING HAD BEEN CUT OFF. THERE ARE ALREADY SEVERAL CASES OF PNEUMONIA. HE HAS BEEN INFORMED THAT THE VESSEL WILL NOT LEAVE SULINA UNTIL THERE ARE 2,000 JEWS ON BOARD. THIS APPEARS DIFFICULT OWING TO THE CLOSING OF THE DANUBE TO RIVER STEAMER BY ICE.

In reply, the Foreign Office answered on January 7,† also in code, that the ambassador should publicize the plight of the refugees to stop a further attempt to reach Palestine illegally and adds:

The plight of the passengers appear [*sic*] to be the responsibility of the Rumanian Government and it is hoped that it will serve as a deterrent. A reference to the conditions on ship will be included in BBC foreign language broadcasts.‡

In these days of paralyzing, demoralizing cold, with difficulties ever evolving, and during these nights when the exhausted ones had finally fallen asleep but awoke again quickly because it was just too cold to sleep, morale of some even on the *Spyroula* plummeted. One of the men on board stated that it would have been better to be killed in Germany fast than to freeze slowly to death on a filthy old barge in the wastes of the Danube delta. He was applauded by many and his words circulated. This called for some action on the part of the leadership to help the marooned ones to keep their perspective in spite of that trying Rumanian winter.

The following morning, according to Gleser's suggestion, the Order of the Day consisted only of one sentence. "The Jews said unto Moses: are there not enough graves in Egypt that thou hast brought us to die in the desert?" The reading of that Order of the

---

*F.O. 371/25238/1809

†Ibid.

‡Notice: The Foreign Office ordered the BBC to broadcast the plight *only abroad*, clearly in order to discourage "illegal" escape from Hitler's extermination units. There was no need for the people in Britain to know the inhumanity of British policy.

Day was followed by silence. By a meditative silence. The people on the *Spyroula* had gained their perspective and were ready to go through even more torments in their wandering to the Promised Land.

In the meanwhile, in the grimy hotel rooms of Sulina and in the much better but not less smoky hotel rooms in Bucharest, negotiations went on and on. The shipowners had raised the price originally agreed upon and pointed to the loss which they were suffering because their ship was anchored outside Sulina waiting for the payment. Every day lost, they rightly claimed, was a loss of money for them. Besides, prices on the shipping market went up daily as the warring powers needed every available bottom. And as the prices went up, we had even less money because every day those on the *Spyroula* and those now on the *Sakarya* ate up more of the funds. The shipowners stated that if the ship's safety could be ensured and if we could obtain a British permit which made that one transport legal, they could take us for the little money we had. To obtain such a permit appeared, of course, impossible. But by the end of January, the suffering of those who by then had been marooned on the *Spyroula* for a quarter of a year and of those who had spent a freezing month on the stormswept *Sakarya* had attracted some publicity and criticism in England. As no stone could be left unturned, an appeal was made to the British. On January 20, Zeev Jabotinsky in London undertook that desperate attempt. He wrote the following letter to the Right Honorable Viscount Halifax, Secretary of Foreign Affairs, Downing Street SW 1 London. Simultaneously an identical letter was sent to every other member of the Cabinet.

MY LORD,

I appeal to you to save 2,000 refugees marooned on small barges in the ice on the Danube. Their agony is indescribable, and now that a German move into the Balkans is expected, they will not even be able to try to escape.

All the causes of their plight are subsidiary to the paramount cause: shipowners are threatened with confiscation of steamers and imprisonment for masters and crews, if captured near the Palestine shore.

It would be cruelly futile now to argue whether these refugees were "right" or "wrong" trying to escape from hell. They *have* tried, in the only direction they or you, or anybody

could think of. Today they must be saved, and as Rumania
will not allow them to land, the only way to save them on the
brink of a hideous hecatomb is to lift—for them at least—the
Palestine ban.

No argument of "policy" can be invoked in the face of
such misery, where only the argument of humanity has the
right to be heard.

I am,

my Lord,

your obedient Servant,

V. JABOTINSKY

Well, the unturned stones—now turned—proved to be just
stones; the hearts of the British policy makers could just not be
reached by Jabotinsky's appeal and by "the argument of humanity."*

The rejection of the plea did not come unexpected. But the
cynicism of the reply, which amounts to plain mockery of those
shivering on the frozen Danube, is noteworthy. Viscount Halifax's
reply to Mr. Jabotinsky reads:

SIR,

I am directed by Viscount Halifax to reply to your letter
of 23rd January concerning 2,000 refugees marooned in ships
frozen in the Danube.

It is understood that these unfortunate people were
induced to embark upon their present journey by
unscrupulous tourist agents who concealed from them the fact
that persons not having immigration permits are prohibited
from entering Palestine. . . .†

---

*Researching British government archives, I found that our visaless immigration had caused
the British even to consider the granting to the Jews of some British colony as a "second
Jewish national home." F.O. file 371/29161 HN 06526 reveals the following consideration,
dated December 28, 1940: "The only way of stopping illegal immigration would seem to be to
give the Jews themselves responsibility for administering the immigration policy of some area
of the world's surface which so far as immigration is concerned they can call their own.
Alternatively a second Jewish national home could be set up somewhere else than in Palestine
as suggested. . . ." Special consideration for such possible second national home for the Jews
was given to the British colony of Guyana in South America, but not even that was ever
offered.

†F.O. Registry No. W1316/38/48 354.

The letter concludes that to prevent similar happenings "His Majesty's Government have [*sic*] therefore taken steps to warn intending immigrants . . ."

While the British secretary of state did not feel embarrassed to claim that those crammed into the holds of the barge and of the *Sakarya* believed that they were embarked on a legal voyage to Palestine and that "unscrupulous tourist agents" were behind it all, the same secretary of state sent a letter to another British statesman, Sir A. Sinclair, in which the viscount states the exact opposite of what he wrote to Mr. Jabotinsky. This letter, naturally classified "Confidential," states of Mr. Jabotinsky:

> . . . he and his friends are themselves largely responsible . . . The Colonial Office and ourselves have information which leaves no doubt that *the New Zionist Organization, otherwise called the Revisionists, over which Mr. Jabotinsky presides, is itself the chief organizer of the whole traffic. . . .*

But while our position was desperate, the one of Avni Bey and Kemal Bey was not enviable either. We had persuaded them to take the 811 passengers of the *Saturnus* and the 535 of the *Grein* on board the *Sakarya*. The first time Mr. Avni Bey mentioned that he would have to "unload" his ship, we asked him whether he thought that those on board would follow such an order, if we were to issue it. He realized they would not; he could only "unload" in Palestine.

In the final negotiations with the shipowners, the Rumanian Jewish communities and its leaders proved of utmost help. Mr. Aronson and Dr. Filderman of the Bucharest Jewish community especially were ready to help, by day and by night, with money, advice, intervention, or whatever else we requested.

As a result of endless negotiations, in which Dr. Hecht played a major part and which seemed to break up a dozen times, the final contract was signed in Bucharest on January 22, 1940, forty-three days after the *Sakarya*—delayed by twenty-two days—had arrived in Sulina. The contract stated that the shipowners had by then received 7,050 English pounds and would be paid another 6,150 pounds plus the expense of 75 tons of coal, plus 1 million lei, which was the equivalent of 500 pounds. The document also stated that

*Author's italics.

the amount paid by Dr. Willy Perl to Rand be ceded to Dr. W. Filderman because he, for the Jewish community, advanced that money and would try to recover it from Rand who had not handed it over to the shipowners. The contract is signed by Lola Bernstein, Robert Mandler, and "Arslan Sadicoglu Aaavni, Galata Kucuk Kan" and by the co-owner "Meseretei Oglu."

This contract enabled us to take the 500 Betarim of the *Spyroula* along practically free. One pound a person—$5—was all the fee for that group. Moreover, it had to take upon itself some other obligations including the supply of lumber for the additional accommodations. Eri writes about it:

> We were to pay a pound per head plus the price of the necessary accommodation for 500 men on the *Sakarya* and also our part of the food for the journey. We would also undertake the responsibility for the landing of the whole transport. To me this looked almost too good to be true. This was salvation.*

But even with that arrangement there was not enough money to pay the shipowners the "irrevocably" agreed-upon fee. Fortunately Mr. Jabotinsky in London procured a donation from South African Revisionists and the Betar borrowed 500 pounds from friends in Bulgaria. Still we were 500 pounds short to make the payments. At that point a donation was received from Hillel Cook's American Friends of a Jewish Palestine, and all seemed set.

Since Mrs. Bernstein and Mandler had signed the final "irrevocable" agreement with the shipowners on January 21, day and night hammering, sawing, and loading of wood and supplies went on aboard the *Sakarya*. This time we had such a large number of people waiting that we could recruit the work force from among our own travelers.

Everything now appeared to be all right, but it was not. This time two barriers arose to stall the departure. One was a demand by the Sulina port authorities that the *Sakarya* prior to leaving pay 800 pounds in duties as a port tax for the immigrants she had taken on there. This demand was fully justified by the port rules, yet the money was not available. Avni Bey went to Bucharest and saw the Turkish ambassador about that fee. I suggested over the phone that he must not plead with his ambassador but rather use the political

---

*Jabotinsky, *op. cit.*, p. 22.

situation to gain his—and our—ends. Specifically, I recommended that we utilize the British pressure on Rumania to make the Rumanians write off our debt with them. The Rumanians had promised the British not to permit any transfer of potential illegal immigrants in Rumanian territory. Fortunately, the Rumanians were humane enough not to stick to that promise. The British believed that the lack of Rumanian cooperation was entirely due to our having bribed them. How would it look to the British if it would appear that the Rumanians demanded payment of 800 pounds before granting a permit which they were not supposed to grant? I was informed that Avni Bey, the older of the two Turkish shipowners, did use that argument. Whether the Turkish ambassador applied the same reasoning when he intervened with the Rumanian foreign minister, I do not know. But the fact is that within forty-eight hours after Avni's visit to his ambassador the Rumanian authorities advised us that the embarkation tax had been written off upon "orders from Bucharest."

But still another difficulty was to show up. It was the question of the number of immigrants who could be boarded. The Turks insisted that no more than 2,011 be taken aboard because—and they were correct in this claim—there was lifesaving equipment only for that many. We had to agree to that figure. But we had so many more whom we just had to take along. These were mostly Rumanian Betarim but also other Jews from Rumania whom we had promised to take along in small repayment of all that we owed to the Bucharest Jewish community for aiding us in every way possible. We were by then old hands in getting around rules, and many were smuggled aboard. Some of them slipped through at the counting, but most of the additional ones came as "provisions," packed into crates and sacks which supposedly contained potatoes, flour, and other bulky goods. Our people managed to have it arranged that those items which were best suited to serve for that smuggling were loaded at nighttime. In a rickety shack, in a dark corner of the port, a "sewing factory" had been set up, and on the nights during which the loading of the "illegal" illegals took place, that shack was buzzing with hectic activity. Unfortunately, those smuggled aboard that way could not wear any heavy coats because of the space limitation. We had the choice between coats and humans. As most people had only one overcoat, usually a heavy one, they had to leave it behind unless an arrangement to have it brought on the ship separately had been worked out. In any case they had to remain in the subzero temperature, without moving, for often many hours, protected only by a large bag of heavy paper or sack cloths.

The unloading of these "provisions" had to be well coordinated during the loading, or else it could have happened that some of those bags containing precious "cargo" might have been thrown down too hard or that other goods loaded on top would have caused injury or even death to the person inside. The Turks found out that the Rumanian guard personnel could be bribed and had given baksheesh to several of the guards to make certain that not more than the 2,011 went aboard. Yet we were a step ahead. Our people had bribed the same guards not to reveal to those who had bribed them that we were indeed smuggling passengers on board! The difficulty was less with the watchfulness of those who were checking than with the long time it took to have a person sewed into a sack or bag. This part had to be done well because the Turkish crew was not on the take and must not find out what was in those sacks of "potatoes," "beans," and "sugar." Unbelievably enough, this subterfuge gave an extra 165 persons the chance to escape. The *Sakarya* ended up with 2,176 instead of the 2,011 for whom lifesaving equipment was available.*

The British intelligence services were soon to send out coded cables with the exact figures and with amazingly correct data about the composition of that transport. They numbered the passengers as

... 2,176 of whom 1,375 are men and 801 women and children. ...
The passengers comprised 4 groups.

(1) 600 persons from Prague and 211 from Vienna under Gerhard Glesinger. Prague was left by rail 28th October for Bratislava where they were joined by party from Vienna. After 14 days in Danube steamer *Satbus* [sic] for Sulina. Both parties were organized by Robert Mandler of Emigrations Hilfe of Prague.

(2) 530 persons in charge of Emerich Falti [sic] and Eliahua Glesser [sic] the majority of whom left Prague on 14th October for Bratislava. The corrupt group [sic] was organized by the Transport Bureau of Prague directed by Harous Borjas of New Zionist Organi-

---

*Our people had believed that many more had been smuggled on board; they thought that they had close to 2,400 on board, and at one point it was even assumed that there were 2,800. Somehow with all the activities going on in the last days and hours prior to the departure some miscalculation had occurred.

zation. Over two thirds are members of Revisionist Party traveling in uniform of Betar. They include Patr [sic] Jabotinsky, son of the Revisionist leader.

(3) 530 persons including 225 from Vienna and 135 from Budapest. This group was . . . organized by Auswanderungsbureau for Overseas Transport managed by Komercialrat Storffer and Doctor Willi Perl now in Budapest.

(4) About 300 persons drawn from various parts of Europe some of whom are traveling independently. Some were expelled from Bulgaria and Rumania and put on board by the police at Sulina. . . .*

From appearances it was an odd group which sailed into the Black Sea. A British intelligence report accurately described some of their travel documents as "Visaed chiefly for Bolivia, Liberia and China."† For some the official destination was even a country whose only ports are in the southern Pacific: Ecuador. Again others held Panamanian, Uruguayan, and Paraguayan end visas. One and the same ship carried people who were supposedly traveling via the Black Sea to South America, to East Asia, and to Africa! And it still had not occurred to anyone that the visas for Bolivia and Paraguay were not what the British demanded as "end visas," because these countries are landlocked and to get to them, transit visas from one of their neighbors would have been necessary. Yet whether "bound" for Bolivia, China, Liberia, or Ecuador, the group had one burning aim—to reach that one country not mentioned in any of the documents: Palestine.

Eri was not supposed to go along. We needed him for the work in Europe, and there was no doubt that in Palestine—if he were not arrested on arrival—authorities would start a manhunt to get him behind the thick walls of the Acre prison fortress. Just when the ship was about ready to sail, the shipowners received from some "friendly" source the "reliable" information that we had no intention of really disembarking the passengers clandestinely but intended to run the ship aground on the coast of Palestine as we had done with the *Parita*. The Turks were truly worried about that possibility. To make certain that this would not happen, they told Eri: "We know that you would be a prize catch for the British. With you in their hands, the British could exercise pressure on your father to stop the transports. If you come along we will feel

*FO371/2540 276 4588.

†F.O. W5383 69. Memo to J. E. Carvell, "reference to Mr. Downie's letter 76021/11/40."

confident that your people would under no circumstances let the ship be caught." Eri knew well enough that even if he were to be caught and have threats made against him—his father's only child—Zeev Jabotinsky could not be pressured into anything he thought would be damaging to Jews. Courageous and resolute as he was, Eri agreed without hesitation to go along. He took over the command of all four groups aboard and formed them into one organized unit with centrally controlled subgroups.

As the *Sakarya* was slowly moving out of Sulina, the joy of those on board was tempered by the scenes of despair of hundreds of persons on the pier who up to the last moment had not given up the hope of somehow being taken along. This time the concern with those who could not come was particularly deep among Rumanian Betarim. A group of most capable young people had been left behind who commanded every priority for being among those sailing. They were fifty young Betarim who had helped to prepare the Rumanian part of the transport, who had aided in the negotiations with Rumanian authorities. They knew what to expect from whom, and it was felt by those in Sulina who made the final decision that the fifty had to stay behind to organize the next transport. On board the *Sakarya* was our old friend Guttenmacher who, had he stayed behind in Rumania, would not have been able to help us as he would have had to serve in the Rumanian military. His younger and only brother Nachum Guttenmacher was one of the fifty who must have had very mixed feelings when they saw the *Sakarya* disappear. Would they be able to organize another transport? Would they themselves be able to get out with the hundreds or thousands they were expected to rescue?

As soon as the *Sakarya* was out on the sea, a memorial service was conducted on board for those who had set out on the voyage but had not lived to see the departure. Considering the inhuman deprivations and the large number of persons involved, the toll was small. Two men had died on the *Saturnus,* and an eight-month-old baby had perished on the *Sakarya* while the ship had been anchored all those weeks outside Sulina. There was one more fatality; this one occurred during the sea voyage. A woman who traveled with her husband died of heart failure.

Eri describes the funeral:

> The burial took place by night. After midnight the lady was lowered into the sea. One of the most fantastic moments of the

voyage was when Ernst Hartman brought the two sugar sacks into which the Mifquada had decided to sew the body, together with some bricks as a weight. Those were ordinary sacks with the name of a Bucharest firm of sugar merchants printed on them in black. After being sewn in, the body and the sacks were enveloped in a big straw mat, to which a plank gave the rigidity of a coffin.

It is usual to stop a ship for a burial. The Mifquada decided that a Free Immigrant ship could not be stopped. The body was not thrown overboard. It was lowered by two cords till it almost touched the raging water. Then we let go the cords and it disappeared into the black chasm. We had not informed the ship of the funeral, so that only two or three hundred people were present. A rabbi of the Agudath Israel said a prayer. There were no speeches. None of us had ever assisted at a funeral so impressive in its starkness.*

Shortly afterward, the *Sakarya* developed engine trouble, and one evening the engines stopped entirely. For that night, the ship was completely at the mercy of the waves and the wind, and there was hardly one immigrant who was not seasick. But to the cheers of those on board the engineer succeeded in making the engine splutter to a halting start, and not much later it was working again.

After a few days the weather improved. Sunshine, real sunshine! After all the ice and snow in Sulina, it made the whole world appear like paradise, and one felt as if one were already close to the final goal, to warm, sunny Palestine.

But how about the British? What trouble was to be expected from them?

Orders had gone out to the British navy to intercept the ship, and from the moment she left Sulina, a continuous flow of cables kept the commander of the British fleet in the Mediterranean informed of her whereabouts. This one, the largest transport of free immigrants ever, must not slip through. Because of the despair of those on board and because of their large number, the British considered armed resistance a possibility. On the other hand, they did not want to provoke a clash by too provocative a display of force on their part; after all, these people had nothing to lose. As soon as the *Sakarya* was out of the Dardanelles, between the island of Tenedos and the Turkish coast, she was intercepted by a British

*Jabotinsky, op. cit., 40.

warship which was laying there in wait for her. It was His Majesty's Ship *Fiona*.

The warship ordered the *Sakarya* to stop. At first the *Sakarya* refused to obey. But after she was shot at—with blank ammunition for a warning—she stopped. Backed by the H.M.S. *Fiona*'s guns, which were aimed at the refugee ship and carefully watched by the rest of the warship's crew, a heavily armed guard, consisting of two officers, one petty officer, a sergeant, two corporals, and ten "other ranks" of the 2nd Battalion Royal West boarded the *Sakarya*. Using Leyla as interpreter, they asked the captain for his destination. He answered that he was bound for Alexandrette. "You will not go to Alexandrette; you are herewith ordered to proceed to Haifa." The captain was flabbergasted! But he quickly understood what had happened. The navy had received orders to intercept the ship. These were not people who were thinking in political terms. To their straight-thinking, simple military mind, it appeared natural that a captured ship full of Jews be brought to Palestine and handed over—ship, crew, and passengers—to the naval authorities there. The captain saw his chance. He refused to go to Palestine unless ordered in writing to do so. Without any suspicion, Lieutenant J. B. Sillitoe signed a paper stating that the captain had refused to proceed to Haifa and had stated that he would do so only at the order of the Royal Navy.

The news—"we are going straight to Haifa"—spread like wildfire throughout the ship. From the holds the people came up and crammed the decks to the last inch. The boarding party noticed the excitement and expected trouble. The men had their hands ready on the trigger, when to their surprise they heard, faintly at first, from the deck below the bridge the opening bars of a familiar tune. Soon the voices swelled into a song, louder and louder, everyone was singing—and the Britishers did not believe their ears. This supposedly hostile crowd was singing "God Save the King!" As prescribed, the armed guard saluted to the singing of their national anthem, while the crowd was having its fun. God Save the King for the blunder of his Royal Navy!

Like an ocean liner which on its maiden voyage enters New York to the blowing of its foghorn, so the *Sakarya* entered Haifa Bay in triumph. She had left Constanța on February 1, 1940. She arrived on Tuesday, February 13, at two-thirty P.M.

In their initial fury, the Palestine authorities declared the ship confiscated, its crew of 28 and all the passengers under arrest. But this decision soon had to be changed. It could be proven by documentary evidence that the ship had been forced to Haifa by orders of the Royal Navy. The British obviously had no intention of publicizing that whole case even more, particularly because a neutral power, Turkey, intervened in the matter in which the British were clearly in the wrong. The ship, her crew, and even the passengers, first the women, and a few weeks later the men, were all released, safe and now legally in Palestine. The *Sakarya* expedition, the largest single-ship rescue action during the entire Nazi era had come to a happy end. And another 2,175 people could start life anew.

chapter 7

COFFINS AFLOAT

By late 1940 the persecution of Jews had turned into mass extermination. SS murder companies were busy in Poland every day. As the Germans achieved successes on the battlefields, first in Poland and then later in Belgium, Holland, and France, the leaders of the racist anti-Semitic movements in the Balkans saw their chances rising. Ever since the collapse of Poland in September 1939, the Jews of Rumania lived in a state of growing alarm. As they saw the paddle-wheelers and barges coming down the Danube, loaded to the rim with Jewish refugees, and as daily the anti-Semites in Rumania became louder and more brutal in their actions, an increasing number of Rumanian Jews saw the handwriting on the wall.

Panicky, they tried to flee—but where to and how? From the Baltic down to the Mediterranean, Germany and Italy divided Europe in half. With countries around them under the control of Germany, or allied with her, there was only one route open: the Black Sea. Thus illegal immigration to Palestine was the only remaining chance to escape.

Whether a ship was seaworthy or not, the Jews had to choose between the Devil and the sea.

Yet even the chance to escape by sea was further reduced with the entrance of Italy into the war in May 1940. The Mediterranean had become a battleground, and ships had become very scarce.

The frantic Jews, although completely inexperienced, tried, in their despair, to organize rescue ships on their own. They grasped for straws. And straws they proved to be. "Travel agents" appeared who promised to find them the necessary ships. Some of these "agents" just took the money and were never heard of again.

The *Salvador*—also known as *El Salvador*—was a rotting wooden sailboat that had a small auxiliary motor. She looked heavenly to the Jews, most of whom had never seen the ocean before. The Bulgarian authorities refused to let such a ship sail under the Bulgarian flag. How unhappy a complication for the Jews this seemed. But with some more money, they succeeded in having her transferred to a Uruguayan flag, and the Bulgarians washed their hands of it.

The boat weighed sixty tons and for a short trip along the coast, she could have taken up to 30 or 40 passengers. Instead, 327 refugees were stuffed into her. Most of them were Rumanian citizens. Under Nazi pressure, Rumania had ceded a part of her territory, the Dobruja, to Bulgaria. Bulgaria was at the time under full Nazi control and expelled the Dobruja Jews—into Rumania! And in Rumania, the Iron Guard—the Rumanian full equivalent of the German SS—was "taking care of the Jewish problem." No wonder the *Salvador* looked superb, even though she had neither bunks nor, of course, cabins. That she had no compass and no barometer, the refugees did not even notice. She had hardly any provisions, but Istanbul was not so far, and once abroad, away from the SS and the Iron Guard, provisions for the rest of the trip could be obtained there.

When she was already crammed so full that there was hardly even standing room, the Bulgarian authorities, eager to get rid of the Jews who had suddenly become "foreigners," stuffed even more human cargo into the hold. One passenger, a journalist, described what happened.

> The Bulgarian authorities insisted on our departure and refused to allow us time to prepare for the voyage . . . Cramped one against

the other, we were driven aboard, towed out into the Black Sea by a tug and abandoned to our fate. Fortunately, we were driven into Turkish waters and a passing motor boat towed us into the Straits. At Istanbul we stopped for a while but eventually the captain gave the order to weigh anchor and we headed for the Sea of Marmara.

Suddenly a violent shock aroused us. We had been hurled onto a reef. The ensuing scenes were terrible. Prayers and shrieks mingled with the howling of the gale, and in the pitch darkness the white-crested waves broke over us and water poured through thousands of fissures as the ancient craft began to break up. There were hardly any life belts [sic—"life preservers"] on board and they disappeared instantly. There was one small rowing boat aboard and we were 300. Suddenly the vessel broke its back and precipitated every one into the raging sea.*

Two hundred and four humans who thought they were on the way to the Promised Land drowned. This number included 66 children. One hundred and twenty-three "survivors" were brought to Istanbul, but the Turkish authorities did not permit them to stay. Sixty-three "survivors" were deported back to Bulgaria and never heard of again.†

Seventy succeeded somehow in hanging on in Istanbul. They were picked up by another "refugee ship," into which already 723 others, mostly Rumanian Jews, had been sardined. When those boarding that ship in Istanbul saw the ship's name, it did not tell them anything. Little did they know that this ship, the *Darien II* had been a central element in the ignominious Kladovo Intelligence Plot; that in Yugoslavia, shortly to be invaded by the Nazis, more than a thousand fellow refugees were with growing anguish waiting for this ship, which though destined for them and promised them

---

New York Times, December 16, 1940, 4:4.

†Notes in F.O. file 371/25244 HM 06447, commenting on the sinking of the *Salvador,* state: "*There could have been no more opportune disaster* from the point of stopping this traffic. . . ." (Author's italics.) They suggest to use that sinking for publicity via the BBC to deter refugees "from setting out for Zion." For more complete exploitation of that "opportune disaster," the F.O. sent a cypher telegram (No. 1565 18 December 1940 1:45 A.M.) to the Honorable Adrian Knatchbull-Hugessen, British ambassador to Turkey, asking him to "press Turkish Government to do everything possible to prevent the survivors from attempting to reach Palestine by overland or other route." But this sinking offered more opportunity. The cypher cable continues: "Turkish aide-memoire of the 16th August 1939 only mentioned restrictions imposed upon Jews of German, Austrian, Italian, Roumanian and Czechoslovak origin. Opportunity may be taken to extend these to Jews of Hungarian and Bulgarian origin, if they have not already done so, and also to Jews of Polish origin if you see no objection."

again and again would never come. The *Darien II* and the 793 on
board were "captured" by the British near the Palestine coast on
March 19. The prisoners were brought to the infamous Athlit
detention camp near Haifa. Seventeen months they spent there
behind barbed wire before they were permitted to become humans
again.

As bad as the conditions were on the Black Sea, there was one
word of hope which the Jews from Hamburg down to Rumania
whispered into each other's ears: Constanţa. Families took off with
what they could carry. They swam through rivers and waded across
marshes, but these were not the most feared parts of the trip. It was
the borders where most of the danger lay. Most of those who took
off for Constanţa never arrived there. Yet, as early as February
1939, an Associated Press dispatch from Constanţa reported that
2,000 Palestine-bound immigrants were stranded in the port. And
by March 2, the media carried the following report:

> Constanţa . . . resembles a refugee camp with hundreds of Jews . . .
> forming queues in front of travel offices. Allured by agents of racke-
> teering shipping companies, hundreds drift to Constanţa with the
> hope of finding a way to emigrate, and find themselves penniless and
> stranded. Faced with the problems of hundreds of hungry and des-
> perate Jewish youths, the Constanţa Jewish Community is warning
> Jews not to be misled by false emigration proposals. A delegation of
> Jewish leaders has left Bucharest for Constanţa to investigate the
> situation. The Palestine office at Czernowitz and the Zionist Revi-
> sionist party had also made statements warning against racketeering
> travel agents.

In Constanţa more and more Rumanian Jews joined those who
had made their way down from Czechoslovakia, Poland, Germany,
and Austria. Later in 1941, when the Jew hunt all over Europe had
reached a new height, after the Soviet Union had been invaded by
her up-to-then Nazi allies, when the SS in the occupied territories of
the Ukraine and White Russia had slaughtered hundreds of thousands of Soviet Jews, the panic among the Jews in neighboring
Rumania reached a peak.

It was under those circumstances that the 50 Betarim who had
first been scheduled to leave on the *Sakarya* but had stayed behind
in order to organize the next transport were preparing the rescue of
another 800. They and the few adult co-workers whom the Revi-

sionists still had in Rumania encountered fewer difficulties on the part of the authorities than we had to overcome at previous transports because the Rumanians were eager to get rid of the foreign Jews and also of their own Jews who had turned Constanţa into one huge refugee camp. The main problem was that of finding a ship. The war had by then been on for two years. The Mediterranean was a battleground, and agriculturally rich Rumania was obliged to deliver to Germany large quantities of cattle and wheat. For this purpose the Germans had taken over practically all ships. They were most interested in those traveling the Danube to bring foodstuffs up to Germany. Yet the Germans had not requisitioned a small, old cattle boat which, rickety and ramshackle, was rotting on a Danube dock. Its name was *Macedonia,* and it had seen better days. The Germans did not want it—too risky to entrust it with cattle for the trip up the Danube.

The Jews in their justified panic got hold of the *Macedonia.* No nation would have permitted putting any passengers on board. The Jews congratulated themselves when they succeeded in getting the boat reregistered under the flag of Panama, which apparently did not care or did not know the condition of the "ship." She was renamed *Struma.* Officially she was fifty-six feet long; according to an editorial in the *New York Times* on March 13, 1942, only fifty feet. It sounds unbelievable. But 767 (seven hundred and sixty-seven) human beings were packed into this fifty-six-foot-long boat, which had been built ages ago for transporting cattle on the Danube River. And the 767 set sail to cross the seas, hoping to reach the Promised Land.

The *Struma* had not a single toilet. Its "cabins" consisted of barred cages for the cattle. The "mechanic" on board was not familiar with the *Struma*'s little engine. It cannot be understood how such a number of persons, among them many professionals and business executives, would engage in such a trip, nor how it was possible that so many herded themselves into such a small space, unless one knows what had happened in Rumania prior to the departure.

This was December 1941, and during the entire year there had been rapidly increasing harassment and persecution. Rumania had been forced to "cede voluntarily" the provinces of Bessarabia and Bukovina to the Soviet Union; they are now the Moldavian and part of the Ukrainian Soviet Republics. The dissatisfaction at the loss of

these provinces had found an easy scapegoat in the Jews. Within a
few weeks after the loss, the Bucharest Daily *Curentul* warned that
"parasite" (Jewish) industries must be eliminated. The Iron Guard,
dissolved in November 1938, had been reinstated. And a pro-
German, anti-Semitic cabinet had been installed. The month before
the *Struma*'s sailing, R. Mironovici of the Iron Guard had been
appointed police prefect of Bucharest. And the Jews knew that this
meant the police would be in on any future pogroms.

On Tuesday, January 20, 1941, Rabbi Gutmann of Bucharest
had gone to bed worried about the fate of his community. He lived
in the center of the Jewish quarter, which stretched around Calea
Vacaresti and Calea Dudesti. The rabbi was a simple man, deeply
religious, well versed in the Torah, but he knew little about the
world. One thing he knew was that a pogrom was in the air.

All Iron Guardists arrested after the attempted coup in 1938
had been freed in April 1940. The same day all "foreigners" were
ordered to deposit their passports with the police. Most of these
"foreigners" were Rumanian Jews who had been deprived of their
citizenship. In August 1940 all Jews had been ordered to register for
compulsory labor service. They had to report for duty September 1,
equipped with clothing and food for three days. At the same time
ghettoes were being instituted with severe penalties for Jews who
left the enclosures without authorization. On December 4 the Greek
Orthodox Church of Rumania had jumped on the bandwagon. The
Holy Synod of the church had pledged loyalty to the Iron Guard.
Two days later a decree forbade Jews to fly the Rumanian flag.
And like all Jews, the rabbi was aware that two days before,
January 18, 1941, the Iron Guard paper, *Cuvantul,* stated that King
Carol's "persecution" of the Iron Guard in 1938 had been orga-
nized by Jewish financiers in London. The same day, the Labor
Ministry announced that no more work certificates would be issued
for Jews and that all outstanding work permits will be "revised."
And finally, yesterday, January 19, Iron Guardists in fifty identical
speeches given all over the country had blamed "international
Jewry" for the war and for the difficult conditions in which the Iron
Guardists found Rumania when they took power.

That night the rabbi was awakened by shouts for help and
rushed outside, but the Jews who had been beaten had already been
carted away. The coming two days proved to be the most awful in
the history of Rumanian Jewry.

The Iron Guard, not satisfied with its ministerial position, staged a revolt against the military dictator Antonescu. The military was loyal to Antonescu, and even before starting to shoot at each other in their struggle for power, both factions started shooting Jews.

The massacres of Jews and pillaging began in Bucharest but, according to Reuters, quickly spread to the provinces. The same Reuters dispatch reports thousands of Jewish families slain and that the pogroms in the provinces were particularly severe.

Of the many accounts published in Western newspapers and wire services, we have chosen the following report about what happened in these two days, including the fate of Rabbi Gutmann.

SOFIA, Jan. 29.—This, I believe, is the first eyewitness account to reach the outside world of the Iron Guard horror in Rumania.

It was necessary for this correspondent to come to Sofia to send out details of the revolt because the Bucharest censorship refused to pass anything but milk and water versions of the insurrection and banned any mention whatever of the well-organized anti-Jewish pogrom carried out simultaneously with the disorders last week.

Of the 4,000 or more lives lost in Bucharest approximately 2,000 were rebel guardists, 600 soldiers and 1,400 civilians. At least 1,000 of the latter were Jews who were murdered by one Iron Guard Army while another battled the khaki-clad Rumanian army in the center of the city. Jewish leaders believed that dead throughout the whole country would exceed 2,000.

Unknown hundreds of Jews will never be found, however, because of the manner in which they were put to death. The spectacle of thousands killing and being killed in a fight for political· power is terrible enough but the spectacle of thousands of non-combatants tortured and murdered only because of their race or religion is far worse.

... This correspondent, like most newspapermen, always has been unwilling to place credence in atrocity stories but, after what I saw ... I am forced to admit that atrocities can and do occur and that those which occurred at Bucharest far exceeded in bestiality anything that might ever be imagined.

Dozens of Jews—women and children as well as men—were literally burned alive. I am not speaking of those who were burned to death in hundreds of buildings to which Guardists set fire, after shooting and beating the inhabitants and looting the contents of their homes. I am speaking only of Jews who were beaten senseless on the streets, robbed, then doused with gasoline and set afire.

In the Bucharest morgue yesterday a military surgeon showed me the charred bodies of nine persons, burned beyond recognition. All of them, he assured me, had been picked up in the streets of the Jewish quarter following the most frenzied stage of the pogrom, last Wednesday.

Trusted friends have told me, and officials have confirmed, numerous cases of Jewish women whose breasts were cut off, not to mention sadistic mutilations like gouged-out eyes, brandings and bone-breakings.

Perhaps the most horrifying single episode of the pogrom was the "Kosher butchering" last Wednesday night of more than 200 Jews in the municipal slaughterhouse.

The Jews, who had been rounded up after several hours of Iron Guard raids, were put into several trucks and carried off to the slaughterhouse. There the Greenshirts forced them to undress and led them to the chopping blocks, where they cut their throats in a horrible parody of the traditional Jewish methods of slaughtering fowls and livestock.

Tiring of this sport after a few score had been thus dispatched, 40 to 50 armed legionaries, mad with hate, beheaded the rest with axes and knives. Some mangled bodies were disposed of by pouring them down manholes to the sewers usually used to carry off animal remains.

What this correspondent does not report is that many of the bodies so slaughtered were hung up in the slaughterhouse on meat hooks, and signs reading "KOSHER MEAT" were put on these headless torsos. Nor does he describe how, before they left this gruesome scene, the murderers scrambled for the severed heads lying scattered on the bloody floor, competing with each other for the gold teeth the dead mouths might contain.

On January 31, the same correspondent smuggled out his second eyewitness account.

SOFIA, Jan. 30.—Storming through the Jewish quarter to a mad orgy of killing and destruction, armed Guardists gangs killed or beat up every person they saw who appeared to be Jewish. The test seems to have been merely whether persons encountered by the frenzied gangs were willing to participate in the massacre. If they were willing they were considered "Aryans" and not attacked, if otherwise, they were instantly killed.

The pogrom, which cost the lives of at least 1,000 Jews in Bucharest, was not accidental but an integral part of the Guardist insurrection and had been prepared long in advance. It was designed, in case things went wrong, to deflect the attention of the populace and convert the uprising into a wholesale massacre of Jews. It was a massacre of Jews but instead of infecting the populace the action caused revulsion among the people and several hundred Christians lost their lives vainly seeking to protect the Jews from the Guardists.

... The pogrom lasted continuously until Thursday midnight— approximately 36 hours. In this brief period the Greenshirt gangs devastated the entire Jewish quarter, destroying nine out of every 10 shops.... It was a significant point in Greenshirt psychology, however, that the Guardists never set fire to any building without first removing everything of value and hauling it away to Legionary hideouts in stolen military trucks mobilized for this purpose....

The *New York Times* was even more specific about the looting. It reports that seventy large truckloads of stolen goods of all descriptions, mostly taken from wrecked Jewish shops during the mass murders of Jews, had been sorted by the police.

The eyewitness account reported above, continues:

What happened to the Spanish temple was typical of what happened to three other synagogues destroyed by flames—the Emigratului, Atena and Amare synagogues.

In the attack on the Spanish temple, a mob of several hundred Greenshirts, mostly under 25, stormed the building with clubs and stones. After smashing windows and breaking down the doors, the Guardists went inside and systematically destroyed all but certain items of furniture. Everything of intrinsic value was piled outside and hauled away to Legionary warehouses. All the ritual objects, altar vestments and books were gathered in another pile which was soaked in gasoline and put to the torch. While some went inside to sprinkle gasoline over the synagogue's floor, preparatory to firing the building, others outside formed a circle and capered in an "Indian dance" around a bonfire fed by Torahs [Holy Scrolls], Talmuds [commentary on the Bible], altar benches and tapestries. Still others fired guns into the air or shot any stray passersby, whether Jewish or not, who happened to come within range.

As a last act in the hideous ceremony—before the synagogue was set afire—20 to 30 Jews were rounded up and made to dance to the tune of bullets fired by the Guardists, after which they were shot and killed or beaten into insensibility. Gasoline was poured over several of the latter and they were roasted alive. Meanwhile, the synagogue went up in flames, creating a pillar of fire and smoke visible from all points in the city.

Four days later, on February 3, another eyewitness account reached the West. It includes the story of Rabbi Gutmann.

SOFIA, Feb. 2.—Rumanian peasants, defying Iron Guard marauders with rabbit guns, clubs and stones, transformed their little village of Dudesti Cioplea into a safe haven for an estimated 1,000 Jews during the Bucharest pogrom last week.

The village is on the outskirts of Bucharest, not far from the periphery of the Jewish area of the capital. It is populated by peasant dairymen whose wives come into Bucharest on little troikas every morning to distribute milk throughout the city.

On Wednesday night the inhabitants of the village sent emissaries into the Jewish quarter with offers of sanctuary to anyone able to escape. This correspondent was unable to learn how many Jews were able to take advantage of the villagers' offer but their number must have been near a thousand.

Not a single Jew who sought refuge in the village came to any harm. The milkmen and peasants, armed with shotguns customarily used for shooting rabbits, formed a cordon around the village and resolutely refused to let any Guardists enter it.

The Jewish hero who towered above all others was a Rabbi Gutmann, who refused to be cowed by the Guardists and stood in the doorway of his house, thundering warnings of God's wrath.

His wife being absent, he picked up his two young children and holding them in either arm appeared fearlessly in his doorway when the Guardists approached the house. The mob was taken aback for a moment when the huge, bearded man began to scold them for their folly showing no interest whatever in his own safety.

The rabbi failed, as did [others], to bring the mobsters to their senses. After a brief period of hesitation, Guardists fired several shots at Gutmann but when he failed to fall the mob became confused and left without ransacking the house.

Reliable witnesses of the incident told this correspondent that an old woman, who had been caught by the mob hysteria and had trailed along with the Guardists, suddenly fell to her knees at the sight of the venerable rabbi upbraiding the throng before her eyes.

Apparently confusing the rabbi with an orthodox priest—both wear beards and similar vestments—the crazed old woman cried out, "Father, don't condemn us all. We are not all guilty."

Gutmann, himself half-crazed with emotion, staggered back into the house where he discovered that the Guardist bullets had killed both of his children but only creased his body in several places.

Refusing to succumb to his grief, the rabbi then became the Moses of the Jewish community, visiting stricken homes and giving comfort to the victims. Last Friday, Saturday and Sunday, after quiet had been restored, it was this rabbi who officiated at most of the Jewish funerals. On Friday he read the funeral service at the burial of his own little sons.

Horrible as these Rumanian massacres were, every new refugee arriving from Poland, the occupied Soviet territories, or else from Nazidom, brought reports of even more carnage in their hometowns and the lands they had crossed on their flight to the "haven of Constanţa." Only when one knows these facts can it be understood why the 767 dared the trip on the *Struma*, and how it could be possible that such a number could be crammed on and into a fifty-six-foot-long boat. Those on board included the Betarim who, originally scheduled to leave on the *Sakarya*, had stayed behind to organize further rescue action. One of those Betarim who himself had been instrumental in the rescue of thousands was the brother of our old friend Guttenmacher. It was unbelievable that the *Struma* carried so many. Even more incredible, that she did succeed in limping into Istanbul on December 16, 1941, after four days at sea. But this was all she could do.

The Turks did not permit anyone to disembark. It was obvious that this ship could not continue anywhere, and the Jewish Agency tried to persuade the British to admit at least the children into Palestine. At the same time, Lord Moyne, British deputy minister of state for the Middle East—later assassinated by the Jewish underground "Stern Group" for this and other "humanitarian" actions—pressured the Turks to send the *Struma* out into the open sea. The British stretched out the negotiations. And this was December and January. Winter. The refugees on board, with hardly standing room and no toilet, were in a condition to which no animal on the *Macedonia* had ever been subjected. A minimum of food was supplied by the Istanbul Jewish community, which was all the comfort the refugees obtained.

The Turkish authorities were embarrassed. But not enough to permit disembarkation. They started negotiations with the British, but each time it took days before an answer was received. And then it was dilatory. On January 19, 1942, the captain of the *Struma*, a Bulgarian, wrote a letter to the port commander. "My ship flies the flag of Panama. As a state of war exists between Panama and the

Axis, the voyage through the Mediterranean is very dangerous and I cannot assume the responsibility of traveling these waters with the transport which was put under my command." He refers to the fact that the *Struma* left Constanţa five days after Pearl Harbor, and meanwhile, Panama, joining the United States, had declared war on the Axis powers. But the captain's appeal failed.

Shortly after the *Struma*'s arrival in Istanbul, the Jewish Agency had asked Britain to admit to Palestine all persons on that boat, and to charge the number of immigrants against the quota of official immigration certificates which was allowed annually. The British refused this request and gave two reasons. One, there could be German spies on board. Two, Palestine was too full already. As to the first excuse, the Jewish Agency agreed to internment of all *Struma* refugees in Palestine, close scrutiny of each, and detainment to the end of the war of anyone who was suspicious. In response to the claim of possible spies on board the *Struma,* Lord Wedgwood stated in the House of Lords, March 10, 1942:

> ... the Jews have certainly more cause to hate Hitler than anybody else in this world. In Palestine you have the additional argument that Hitler can get Arab agents more easily and cheaply than anybody else. That allegation regarding the Jews is a bare-faced excuse which supplies fresh evidence of Anti-Semitism on the part of people who admit quite openly "We do not like Jews."

The second excuse for the refusal of admittance, that Palestine was too full already, was countered by the American Joint Distribution Committee, which offered to train *Struma* refugees at its own expense, in productive occupations. All younger men would happily join the British forces to fight the Nazis.

When the Jews asked that at least a part of the 767 on the cattle boat be saved, the British came up with still another objection which hardly deserves comment. To choose some, they said, would be too cruel to those who had not been chosen.

As conditions on the boat worsened and disease spread, as the Turks' pressure to rid themselves of the *Struma* increased, the Jewish Agency in London and Jerusalem literally begged to save at least the children. Finally a promise was obtained from the British to admit to Palestine the *Struma*'s children under sixteen years of age and to inform the Turks, so that the transit could be arranged.

Parents of such children on the boat were jubilant. At least the children would live! But the British had not been "precise." Only children between ages eleven and sixteen would be admitted. Well, to the parents of these children, the British lack of precision was not just a trifle. It meant in many cases that the baby in the family, or several of the smaller ones who had already been seen as saved, were again condemned. Or that all the children of a family would perish with their parents.

Days passed and the Turks did not receive any message, not even one regarding the eleven-to-sixteen-year-old children. The British Embassy in Istanbul claimed to know nothing. A delegation of the Istanbul Jewish community went to the British Embassy and asked that London be contacted. The officials promised to do so, but days went by and no answer came from London. Parents from the *Struma* pleaded for permission to go ashore to state their case in person. Permission refused. The Jewish Agency intervened in London and Jerusalem. London repeated the promise but still did not inform either its embassy in Istanbul or the Turkish ambassador in London. The British just bided their time.

And all these weeks, altogether more than two months, the 767 remained imprisoned on the little boat. No one was allowed to leave, and the choking stench from urine, feces, vomit, and filth, besides being degrading to the extreme, was literally suffocating. There was no possibility of washing; many would have been ready to die if they would just have had the chance to take a bath or shower first.

Of the many pregnant women on board, one Mrs. Medja Solomonowitz, apparently dying in childbirth, was permitted to be carried ashore. The baby was born dead in a Turkish hospital. Mrs. Solomonowitz was still in the recovery state when the frightful news arrived.

The rest of her family and all aboard the *Struma* learned, on February 23, 1942, that the captain had received the final order to leave immediately. They tried to prevent the crew from casting off. At first they were successful. Then 80 Turkish policemen clubbed their way on board. The refugees fought them with bare hands. Literally crawling over the shoulders and heads of the solid human mass on deck, the policemen reached the docking lines, cast off, and a tugboat towed the *Struma,* with all the children, all the women and all the men, into the Bosporus.

Today on the Bosporus stands the Hilton-Istanbul Hotel, and here and there elegant villas and little castles adorn the shore of this beautiful stretch of water. On the twenty-third of February 1942, the sight was different. Seven hundred and sixty-six human beings, screaming for help, guilty of nothing, were being towed to their deaths. Out of many shirts, they had made huge banners reading "S.O.S.," but nobody who heard them or saw these signs saved them. All murdered yet still alive. They were towed out from the Bosporus five miles into the Black Sea with the thought that they should try to reach Rumania. Rumania! Of the mass pogroms!

In the Black Sea the *Struma,* this shame of civilized society, was left helpless. The captain still hoped that there was a very slim chance to reach by sail a Bulgarian or Rumanian port.

He hoped in vain. On February 24, at nine A.M., an explosion occurred which tore the floating coffin into pieces.

Of the seven hundred and sixty-six children, women, and men on board, only one survived. He was David Stoliar, a twenty-one-year-old Rumanian Jew, an expert swimmer. Four had almost made it to shore, holding on to the same piece of floating wreckage as young Stoliar. But after several hours of clinging to the flotsam, the other three, one by one, froze to death. Stoliar, now completely alone, kept alive by treading water constantly.

At about the hour the waters closed over the last ones struggling to live, permission arrived in Istanbul to admit the children on the *Struma* to Palestine. Those between eleven and sixteen, that is.

This was not the only humane act by the British in the tragic story of the *Struma.* On March 23, they announced that David Stoliar was being granted admission to Palestine. This permission did not include his family. They were on the bottom of the Black Sea.

The cause of the explosion will never be known. It could not have been caused by the tiny auxiliary motor. A mine was unlikely at that stage of the war, in that location of the Black Sea. A German submarine was a possibility. A British submarine could certainly not be excluded. If not even one had survived, there would have been no further scandal. Other ships too that had been turned back had never been heard from again, and there was no publicity.

But there was one survivor, and on the morning the sinking of the *Struma* became known to Palestine, the streets were plastered with posters, which read:

MURDER

SIR HAROLD MAC MICHAEL

KNOWN AS HIGH COMMISSIONER FOR PALESTINE

WANTED FOR MURDER

OF 800 REFUGEES DROWNED IN THE BLACK SEA ON THE

BOAT STRUMA

From that day on, the Jewish underground began an all-out war against the British. British terror was countered by Jewish acts of terrorism. As news of gruesome persecutions, of torture and mass murder, arrived in almost daily reports, as Britain continued to pursue those who had fled the Nazi massacres, the ardor of the underground Jewish freedom fight spread. More and more young people joined the underground forces. In more and more basements, secretly the hymn was sung:

> *These are the days of wrath, the nights of holy despair.*
> *Fight your way home, eternal wanderer*
> *Your house we shall repair*
> *Relight the broken lamp.*

How religious fervor merged with militant action is probably best expressed in a short poem of Yair Stern, the leader of the most radical of the Jewish underground organizations.

> *My teacher carried his prayer shawl in a velvet bag*
> *to the synagogue.*
> *Even so I carry my sacred gun*
> *to the synagogue.*
> *That its voice may pray for us.*

But not only the militants, the entire Jewish population of Palestine was aroused to fury by the death of the *Struma* refugees. Large demonstrations swept the country. Celebration of the Purim festival, the most joyous one among the Jewish holidays, was forbidden by the Vaad Leumi, the official representation of Palestine Jewry.

The Palestinian Jews lived under the British whip and gun. In what way did the Jews in the free countries, in the United States and Britain, react to this repetition of mass murder by drowning?

Before describing their reaction, I should relate a dream I had while I was imprisoned in a Salonika dungeon, one of the many times the British had succeeded in pressuring a Balkan government to immobilize me at least for some time. I had never been to America and knew New York from books and movies only, but from thoughts I had before falling asleep, the dream had created a most vivid picture.

I was dreaming that word had gotten through to New York about the torture and murder of Jews in Hitlerlands, including Rumania. I saw thousands and thousands of Jews streaming down into the streets of New York City. Like in one of the ticker-tape parades I had seen in newsreels, throngs filled the canyons of lower Broadway. And more people amassed, furious and shouting for revenge. At the end of the street, across it, stood a large building, the British Embassy. The masses stormed it and hung from the balcony two flags, one next to the other—the Swastika and the Union Jack. The two were connected by a rope from which hung the same elderly man whom I had seen dead in Rumania when he hanged himself with his suspenders after the loss of his family. I was standing between the flags and explaining to the multitude below that nobody but they could help. They should stage demonstrations like this one in every country; in every city where the Nazis or the British had any kind of representation, hundreds of thousands should demonstrate. Jews, but also Christians who wanted to awaken the world to its responsibilities. Only powerful, dramatic expressions of "No, not in my time" would break the silence with which the atrocities were met, would bring the news of the suffering from the back pages of the papers to the front. As the crowd hailed my words, suddenly flames burst out all around me. Somebody had put the building—in the dream it had become both the British and the German embassies in one—to the torch. I leaped—and woke up.

Actually, the free Jews in the Western countries could have helped. They were numerous and powerful enough to arouse the conscience of the world and to force the British government to end its conspiracy with Hitler's extermination plans. Maybe American Jews would not have been so complacent if they had realized the full extent of the plans which the Nazis were so painstakingly and so effectively turning into reality all over Europe. On March 10, 1942, newspapers brought a little story from Nazi-occupied Russia.

> ... The Jews of Shamkovo were harnessed to coaches in place of horses and were forced to haul their executioners to the place where the entire Jewish population of the township was shot by firing squads after being forced to dig their own graves. Following the two mass executions at Borisov all three Nazi newspapers published in White Russia—one in the Russian and two in the White Russian language—cynically reported that "the Jewish problem in White Russia is now solved, *but there are still five million Jews alive* in the United States!"*

But even in the wake of the *Struma* disaster, which itself followed the *Salvador*'s, nothing at all happened, neither in England nor in America. Nothing which could have moved the British to change their Palestine policy. Nowhere in America, in spite of its "still five million Jews alive" was there even a ripple in the daily routine. The day the *Struma* catastrophe was published in New York, the Metropolitan Opera played *Tosca*. In Carnegie Hall a gala night was celebrated. A full house listened in delight to a violin recital by Josef Szigeti. All the proceeds of the performance were to go to Britain for British War Relief. The Jewish Theatre played the successful *Should I Tell My Mother?* Doubtlessly numerous Jews also crowded gay Collins Avenue in Miami at that height of the season. But nothing happened. Not even a voice was heard demanding that the proceeds from the gala concert in Carnegie Hall be diverted from Britain, to be shared by the few survivors of the *Salvador* and by Mr. Stoliar and Mrs. Solomonowitz. Within the halls so holy of the British Embassy in Washington not one demonstration occurred, none in any of the numerous consulates and missions in the United States. Neither were there demonstrations in or in front of the Turkish missions. No Jewish leader called a spade what it was, nobody thundered his *"J'accuse,"* accusing the British of being flagrantly Hitler's executioners. And it would have been

*Author's italics.

just that unfavorable large-scale publicity in America, which Britain, so dependent on American aid, could not afford. Instead, the Jewish leaders called memorial services and minced many words, couched in diplomatic form. Meetings were called for more words to be spoken. Oh yes, even carefully formulated written protests were delivered to fill the wastepaper baskets of the British, actions just as world-shaking as the "protest" which the American Jewish Congress and the World Jewish Congress "submitted" to the Rumanian minister in Washington on February 4, denouncing the January pogroms.

A delegation of five even went to the U.S. State Department, and asked, in the proper form, for intervention with the British. This was the same State Department which had not granted visas to the damned of the *St. Louis* and the *Salvador,* nor to the *Struma* refugees during the months they had been waiting in Istanbul; the same State Department which had already on April 24, 1939, announced that no more immigration visas for refugees could be issued and, three days later, extended this rule to visitors' visas; which, since then, had admitted only the most carefully selected few, and which had, in my own experience, still in 1940, Czech quota numbers available in Johannesburg, South Africa, while refugees from Czechoslovakia were perishing on the Danube, in the Black Sea, and at a hundred different places.

Quiet diplomacy. A silent game played with those who used this silence for more murders.

No wonder that with so little public reaction to persecution, the *Struma* outrage did not rate more than a report on page 7, four paragraphs, when it was announced in the *New York Times.** Just a news item about the sinking and the death toll. Not one word that in this Nazi-originated massacre, the British—and, under pressure from them, the Turks—had acted as Hitler's henchmen.

No wonder either that as not even the *Struma* atrocity had caused anything even approaching an uprising by the Jews in the free world, the later loss in the Black Sea of still another floating coffin received even less attention. The sinking of the *Mefkuri,* with 350 refugees on board, did not rate page 7 and not even four paragraphs anymore. No major protests—the world had become used to the fact that Jews were being killed. The loss of the *Mefkuri*

New York Times, 25 February 1942, 7:2.

rated only page 8* and one single paragraph in the *New York Times*, with two more short notices later, when it was found that not all 350 on board had perished. Five survivors had shown up in a Turkish fishing village.

But between the drowning of the 765 of the *Struma* and the 345 of the *Mefkuri,* developments took place which were followed by some softening of the British policy of keeping the gates of Palestine barred to the escapees from the Nazi massacres. It was a typical case of too little and too late, yet it permitted those working on free immigration to Palestine to tear from the jaws of the Holocaust Moloch still another 2,006 humans and bring them to Palestine.

Faithful to the poster "WANTED FOR MURDER," the Irgun and the Stern groups made several attempts to avenge the death of the *Struma*—and other victims of the "barred escape gate" policy— by assassinating Sir Harold MacMichael. He, it was felt, was to blame for deliberately delaying the information to the Turks that the children between eleven and sixteen on the *Struma* could be admitted to Palestine. In the last of these assassination attempts the high commissioner escaped only by a hairsbreadth. On that occasion he was in his car on the way from Jerusalem to Jaffa when the automobile had to slow down because of a dangerous curve. Suddenly seemingly from nowhere, Geula Cohen, a stunningly beautiful girl of nineteen, and a young man named Eliahu Hakim stood there and opened up on the car with submachine guns. Sir Harold was hit, but the attackers had misjudged the speed of the car, and the high commissioner received two flesh wounds only. Yet the incident was enough to cause the British to order Sir Harold's transfer to Malaysia. And also to consider some steps which might tend to reduce the growing inclination of Palestine's Jews to revolt against the British rule.

In Britain itself the atrocity committed against those on the *Struma* caused many who had kept quiet until then, to speak up against their government's Palestine policy. A heated debate in the House of Commons, spearheaded by the great humanitarian Josiah G. Wedgwood, was paralleled by one in the House of Lords in which Lord Davies openly accused the Palestine authorities of having obstructed the London-made decision to admit at least a

New York Times, 7 August 1944, 8:8.

certain category of children. Britain, traditionally not fast in changing established policies, did at first continue with unaltered attitude
and actions. But as the revolutionary mood in Palestine grew, as
revolutionary acts increased in number and intensity, and as in
Britain itself criticism of the refugee policy became more outspoken,
a minor concession was finally made.

In August 1943, when the Nazi murder factories were already
working day and night; when almost all still surviving Jews were
"safely" contained in ghettoes, "stored" there for the shipment to
extermination camps; when travel to the Constanţa "paradise" had
become hardly more than a dream, Lord Cranborne, minister of
state, informed the British Embassy in Ankara that those who
succeeded in making it to Turkey "on their own steam" would be
admitted to Palestine.

Fortunately, by then the long-overdue cooperation between the
various Jewish groups who were working on free immigration to
Palestine had been established. Our own group—the Revisionists—
the Mossad, representing both, the Zionist Socialist groups and also
the Zionist establishment, and representatives of orthodox Jewry,
were all working together on making the best of the tiny loophole
the British had opened. Probably to the surprise of the British they
succeeded in sending six smaller shiploads of those who had still
survived the Holocaust from Rumania to Istanbul from where they
were then brought by train, via allied-occupied Syria to the haven of
Palestine.

The group in Istanbul was run primarily by the Mossad,
although our Josef Klarman—supported by Eri Jabotinsky, who
had come for that purpose to Turkey—was recognized to be a most
valuable team member. It was the Mossad which provided the
funds required for the operation, and it was also the Istanbul group
which, on the strength of the new British promise, obtained from
the Turks the necessary transit visas and arranged for rail transportation from Istanbul to Palestine. In Rumania the responsibility to
organize the transport, to find and provide ships, and to obtain the
required Rumanian exit permits was primarily the responsibility of
the Revisionists, but here too all activity was performed in team-
work fashion. Our Lipa Chaimovic was the director of Orat, the
travel agency which had been purchased and under whose name the
evacuation from Rumania to Turkey was conducted. Lipa was
assisted by Dr. Enzer, Dr. Meissner, and Dr. Geiger, the represen-

tatives of the other Jewish organizations. The Bucharest group had dug up a Greek shipowner, Mr. Pandelis, whom they viewed as a full-fledged member of the team. Pandelis, it was clear, was in it not for profit only. He enjoyed the adventure and also his role in the rescue of so many fellow human beings. Pandelis helped not only in procuring transportation but also by negotiating with those authorities which could not as easily be approached by Jews.

At that time Rumania was already fully under the Nazi heel, and Jews were drafted by the military to dig ditches and for other forced-labor purposes. By summer of 1943 large portions of the Soviet Union had been conquered by the Germans, and Jews were murdered in the newly occupied Soviet territories by the tens of thousands. Rumania's borders with the Soviet Union were tightly closed, and anyone found crossing over was shot on the spot. Yet a trickle of Jews succeeded in getting into Rumania usually by swimming across the Dniester River at night from a lonely spot along the shore. Lipa Chaimovic had a special arrangement with the authorities regarding these refugees from across the border. If they were not shot while crossing, they were arrested and shipped to one of the labor battalions. This was so arranged because our friends in the Orat office had an agreement with the military which complemented the one which they had with the police. If the Orat certified that a certain person had been accepted for a certain transport to Palestine and that he would be leaving Rumania within not more than a week, the military discharged him from the labor battalion.

The attitude and actions of Mr. Petrica Stanescu provides a good example of the kind of Balkan official with whom we had to deal in these days. Petrica was a higher-ranking police officer. He was the one who had to decide what to do with Jews who had illegally crossed over from the Soviet Union. For each person he decided to send to the military, he was, according to the arrangement, to receive a certain amount of baksheesh. At a time when Orat was in a bad money squeeze, Petrica was asked to wait for the money due to him. He had called several times to report that he already had so and so many under arrest on the border and that he had no facilities for keeping more there. One day after an urgent call from Petrica, Lipa Chaimovic, who did not expect funds in the near future, decided to tell the police official the truth. Petrica shouted at Lipa, threatened to have all the people—there were close to 200 by then—sent back to Russia where the SS would take care of them, unless at least half of the baksheesh due to him was paid within forty-eight hours. Lipa, in despair, told him: "Dod [Uncle] Petrica. I have bad news. We do not have any money and, frankly, do not expect any in the near future. As unhappy as we are, we cannot prevent the sending back of these people." In response, much to Lipa's astonishment, Petrica shouted angrily, "What do you think I am? I am not a monster. Nobody will be sent back. I am trying to make an honest living, but I am a human being. They all will still be transferred today to the military."

At this time the voyages planned were just passage through the Black Sea and the Bosporus, short trips for which truly small ships could be used. In fast succession the Bucharest group sent out the *Milka* with 410 Jews mainly from Rumania, followed by the *Maritza* with 244 who had survived the Nazi massacres in Poland and in the then-German-occupied parts of the Soviet Union. This number included several who had escaped from the infamous Warsaw ghetto. The Istanbul group had obtained the Turkish disembarkation permits. And it had made all the arrangements which brought the *Milka* and the *Maritza* passengers by land from Istanbul to Palestine.

As soon as the *Milka* and the *Maritza* had unloaded, they returned to Constanţa and brought refugees once more to Istanbul, this time 433 and 266 respectively. As they debarked in Istanbul, the train was already waiting for them. Because these voyages were short, with apparently not much risk involved, our people were able to get hold of three more small ships, the *Morina,* the *Salah A Din,* and the *Bulbul.* The *Morina* brought 218, the *Bulbul* 410, the *Salah A Din* 547 survivors from Eastern Europe to Istanbul.

Then, in August 1944, the catastrophe of the recently chartered *Mefkurie* put an end to further organized efforts to use the lately opened escape route to Turkey. The *Mefkurie* with 350 passengers on board did not just sink. Her crowded deck was machine-gunned; the ship was torpedoed; and the survivors were again machine-gunned as they swam in the water. Three hundred and forty-five out of the 350 escapees from the Nazi hell were killed.*

The nationality of the warship which fought this gallant naval

---

*According to the *New York Times* the 345 killed included "sixty orphans from Transnistria and forty other children traveling with their parents." *New York Times,* 17 August 1944, 9:1.

action with the *Mefkurie* remains to date a mystery. It could have been a German warship, and those who believe it was cite the fact that the *Mefkurie,* together with the Red Cross flag, flew the Turkish flag. Turkey was then still neutral, but shortly before, the Turks, now thinking that Germany would likely be defeated, had broken diplomatic relations with Germany. Unusual for the Nazis, the German High Command issued an announcement as to the *Mefkurie,* stating that no German units were then operating in the area in which the *Mefkurie* was attacked. It could have been a ship of the Royal Navy. The British had fired on refugee ships before and killed survivors of the Holocaust. Rumor had it that it was the British who torpedoed the *Mefkurie* in order to stop the influx of young Jews into Palestine, who might later demand freedom from the colonial yoke. It could even have been a Soviet ship; Soviet naval units were active then in the Black Sea, and the USSR was then vying with the Germans as well as with the Western powers for position among the Arab countries.

Whether the ship that torpedoed the *Mefkurie* and machine-gunned the survivors of the blast as they were struggling in the water was German, British, or Russian, the action had to be seen as a warning by one of the major powers. The Jews were now entirely bottled up in Europe. The last-known escape hatch had been closed. Some 40,000 had been saved "illegally," 20,113 of them counted by the British and showing up in their official statistics. But as to the millions who had been trapped in the Nazi inferno. . . .

EPILOGUE

While trying to arrange another large transport in Athens, I was arrested in March 1940 by Greek authorities under pressure from the British. Placed on a train headed for Berlin, I decided that rather than be delivered alive to Eichmann, I would commit suicide. Just before the Yugoslav border, I was given permission to go to the men's room; locking the door, I made two deep incisions in my left wrist. The guards noticed the blood coming from under the door and broke it down. I was carried off the train and placed in the hands of a sympathetic Yugoslav physician who took it upon himself to convince the Yugoslav border guards to refuse me permission to enter the country. As the Greeks had been under strict orders to deport me, they would not permit my reentry into Greece. The decision was made to allow me to recuperate in the home of a local Greek farming couple in the town of Idomeni, where I stayed for two weeks.

Mrs. Bernstein, hearing of my plight, flew in and arranged for me to be transferred to a jail in Salonika to convalesce. With the help of Father Richard Liebel, ironically the Father Confessor of the German Legation in Greece, I was further aided to obtain a visa to Portugal in time to escape the imminent invasion of Greece by Germany.

After many nightmarish brushes with unwilling authorities in Fascist Italy and in Portugal, including new arrests and near deportations, I finally made it to Lisbon, only to be told again that my papers were not in order and that I would have to be sent back to Italy from where deportation to Germany would have been certain. Another suicide attempt—although this time not a genuine one—landed me in the care of another friendly medic, in the Sintra hospital near Lisbon. The medic convinced the authorities that my superficial wound was too dangerous to allow me to be moved.

Having recovered a second time, I again set out to organize transports to Palestine, now from Portugal. Shortly afterward, however, a British intelligence agent observing my movements threatened me with immediate deportation by plane to Germany if I engaged in any more negotiations for transports.

Seeing that my usefulness on the continent was at an end, I decided to try the impossible—to enter Palestine myself, but via the "back door," around Africa and up the Red Sea. I obtained a visa to Shanghai and began the long sea voyage to Mozambique aboard the S.S. *Mouzinho*. On my lengthy cruise, however, I had a change of heart after many long conversations with Moshe Smilansky, a large landowner in Palestine. Smilansky, who had fought with Jabotinsky in the Jewish Legion in World War I to liberate Palestine from the Turks, was also the writer of Hebrew articles, poetry, and political books, and had an astute grasp of the situation in

Palestine. He convinced me that somewhere along the way, in Africa, in Cairo, but surely in Palestine, the British would track me down and arrest me. The Irgun would have to spend some of its much-needed resources in helping me rather than others who needed it more. Thus I decided upon landing in Mozambique to apply to the American Consulate there for a visa to the United States.

After much red tape, the consul finally succeeded in getting me a temporary visa to the United States.*

Finally, on the S.S. *Mary*, I reached Sparrows Point, Maryland. After many further visa complications, and only after the American authorities had been convinced into believing that, although really penniless, I was a man of means, was I granted permission to stay in the United States "for the duration of the war."

The day after Pearl Harbor was attacked, I tried to enlist in the U.S. Navy. Not being a citizen, I was turned down but was finally able to become a member of the military after having volunteered for an early draft. In the army, I was sent to the Military Intelligence Training Center at Camp Ritchie, Maryland, where I became an instructor.

In the spring of 1944, I was commissioned a second lieutenant and, at my request, was shipped overseas, where I interrogated newly arrived high-level German prisoners of war at the Combined Services Detailed Interrogation Center (CSDIC) in England. The camp, ironically for me, was run chiefly by my old antagonists, the British.

My outfit was not far behind the American Army's advanced line when Germany fell.† Being not too far from the Austrian border, I had great hopes that I could make a search to see if my wife Lore was still alive. My last letter from her, written in code and mailed via a mutual friend in Switzerland, told me that Lore had been called in for questioning by the Gestapo for aiding Jews. I did

---

*To my horror, I discovered that there were many unused Czech quota numbers available in Johannesburg and other such unlikely places where it would be highly improbable that any Czech Jew, like myself, could ever take advantage of them.

†Some of my intelligence assignments on the continent resulted in my being awarded four battle stars.

not write again for fear of bringing her more trouble. Despite my proximity to Austria at the end of the war, however, I found that my plan was hindered by the army's ironclad nonfraternization order on all U.S. troops stationed in Germany. This led me to organize a work slowdown in my unit, which was composed mostly of other German and Austrian Jews who like myself had joined the U.S. Army and were now desperately making inquiries about their families. To make an exception in my case, the army went so far as to allow me to take a jeep to the APO closest to Austria. Taking the lead, I drew up false "orders" for a nonexistent "hush-hush" mission which fooled both sides and got me through the American and Russian checkpoints and into the strictly forbidden Russian zone to Vienna to make my search for Lore.

Lore had last lived on Rosenhuegelstrasse, the Street of the Hill of Roses. On June 22, 1945, as I drove down the street toward number 31, I passed a girl, who in the short moment I had to glance at her, seemed to resemble Lore. She was carrying a baby in her arms.

What if Lore, from whom I had not heard for three years, had. . . . Please God, just let me find her alive; nothing else matters in relation to that, I thought.

I stopped at number 31. More a shell than a house, it had been badly bombed out. The house across the street was a total ruin; apparently the bomb which had destroyed it had badly damaged Lore's house. The windows were all boarded up, the plaster was gone from most of the walls, broken tiles lay everywhere, yet many houses looked no better and still people were living in them.

I got out of the jeep and hammered at the heavy gate. No reply, but I heard the shuffling of feet. There were people inside.

"Open up," I shouted. No reply.

"Open up or else we will break the gate open." With that I hit the gate with my .45. I heard the bolts being removed, and then a tiny, elderly woman stood before me.

"Where is Lore Rollig?" I did not dare to ask for her by her married name. The woman hesitated. In the next few seconds I would know whether Lore was alive or dead.

"Lore is not in right now," she said.

Alive! She's alive! I thought. "Where is she?"

"She went to take care of some orphaned children." Alive, alive! was the only thing I could think, but even before the fact had fully penetrated my thinking and feeling, I heard a shout. I turned and down the street came a girl running—no, flying—and with her hands stretched out, she was shouting: "Willy! Willy!" She was the one whom I had passed a few minutes before. Laughing, talking incoherently, Lore lay in my arms. Seven years and thirteen days, each day filled with so many happenings, had elapsed since we had said good-bye to each other on the Vienna airfield.

She then explained to me what had happened to her: "I was in the concentration camp at Ravensbrueck."

"We will try to make up for all that has happened—not one day more will separate us," I said, kissing her, breathing her, knowing that this was the happiest day I could ever possibly live to see.

Lore had been turned in by a Nazi neighbor for helping Jews and trying to care for Jewish children left behind when their parents had been shipped out. Because she was still regarded an "Aryan," she was allowed to receive some of the food parcels sent to her in camp from a friend. Although this helped to see her through the ordeal, she spent four months in a hospital recuperating after we were reunited. I was assigned to the War Crimes Branch and became a member of the prosecuting team in Dachau at this time.

Soon after we arrived in America, a son was born to us, and then a few years later a second son. But the story was not complete.

The events recorded in this book ran their full course when, in 1960, the man who headed the list of most wanted war criminals was apprehended in Argentina.

On March 21, 1963, I received the following cable from Jerusalem:

YOUR EVIDENCE EICHMANN CASE STOP COULD YOU COME JERUSALEM END APRIL STOP EXPENSES COVERED BY US CABLE ANSWER G. HAUSER ATTORNEY GENERAL.

The story was now complete.
The circle had been closed.

APPENDIX

List of Voyages

NAME OF SHIP	DATE	APPROX. NO. OF IMMI-GRANTS	EMBARKATION AND DEBARKATION POINTS	ORGANIZER	REMARKS
1. *Kosta*	3-37	16	(Vienna) Athens–Beach near Haifa	Revisionists	Sailboat with auxiliary motor. Wading ashore. No landing organization yet.
2. *Artemisia I*	8-37	68	(Vienna) Athens–Tantura Beach	Revisionists	First time aid of landing organization. *Artemisia* net tonnage: 115
3. *Artemisia II*	12-37	120	(Vienna) Korinthos–Tantura	Revisionists	
4. *Artemisia III*	6-38	386	(Vienna) Inlet near Athens–Tantura	Revisionists	
5. *Draga I*	9-38	246	Susak–Tantura	Revisionists	Mordechai Katz's group plus those who had escaped to Fiume and Susak landed on Yom Kippur. *Draga* net tonnage: 277
6. *Draga II*	11-38	544	(Vienna) Galatz–Netanyah	Revisionists	*Draga II* and *Ely* carried the survivors of Arnold-stein transport plus additional immigrants.
7. *Ely*	11-38	620	(Vienna) Galatz–Netanyah	Revisionists	*Ely* took *Draga II* passengers aboard, prior to landing procedures.
8. *Gepo I*	12-5-38	734	(Vienna) Tulcea–Netanyah	Revisionists	Smooth sailing and easy blockade breaking. Arrived, landed, December 18.
9. *Katina*	1-18-39	775	(Vienna) Balchik–N. of Netanyah	Revisionists	
10. *Gepo II*	2-20-39	750	(Vienna) Balchik–N. of Netanyah	Revisionists	*Gepo II* sinks in Mediterranean. *Katina* rescues all on board and lands them near Netanyah.
11. *Astir*	3-6-39	720	(Danzig) Varna–Al Jura, Palestine	Revisionists	Transferred to & debarked by S.S. *Marsis*.
12. *Atrato I*	3-9-39	386	Bari–Palestine	Mossad	
13. *Sandu*	approx. 3-15-39	269	Constanţa. Captured off Palestine coast on 3-23	Private	Ship captured by British. Left Palestine 3-26. Arrived Constanţa with all aboard 4-2-39.
14. *Assimi*	3-20-39	260	Constanţa–Palestine	Members of Mizrachi & Ha Noar Ha Zioni. Ship "adopted" by Haganah.	Captured by the British (4-1). Turned back. Returned Palestine and landed June 7.

NAME OF SHIP	DATE	APPROX. NO. OF IMMI-GRANTS	EMBARKATION AND DEBARKATION POINTS	ORGANIZER	REMARKS
15. *Aghios Nikolaos*	Late March 39	750	Constanța–Palestine	Private (Mr. Flesch)	Fired at by British patrol. One passenger killed. Immigrants landed anyway on 4-39.
16. *Atrato II*	Late March 39	400	Susak–Palestine	Mossad	Immigrants first embarked on S.S. *Colorado;* then transferred.
17. *Aghia Zioni*	Late March 39	600	Marseille, Fiume–Near Rehoboth (Palestine)	Revisionists	420+ evaded arrest. 173 arrested "near Isdud," of whom 44 escaped after arrest. (Landed 4-22-39)
18. *Panagai Conasteriu*	Late March 39	80	Korynth–Palestine	Revisionists	Jews from Austria & Germany who were stranded in Greece after having escaped individually to Athens.
19. *Aghios Nikolaos II*	4-20-39	600	Burgos–Palestine (Haifa)	Private (Mr. Flesch)	Passengers transshipped to S.S. *Nichola*. Landed by *Nichola* 5-19. Arrested & later released: 308.
20. *Atrato III*	4-39	400	Susak–Palestine	Mossad	Passengers first embarked on S.S. *Colorado*. Then transferred to *Atrato*. Short voyage, fast, successful landing.
21. *Liesel*	5-17-39	906	Tulcea–Palestine	Maccabi-Revisionists	Captured by British 6-2; Master of *Liesel:* 9 months prison; crew acquitted; passengers released in Palestine 6-4.
22. *Atrato IV*	5-20-39	430	Constanța–Palestine	Mossad	Captured 5-28-39 by H.M.S. *Sutton*. Passengers released in Palestine after short detainment.
23. *Colorado I*	5-19-39	266	Constanța–Palestine	Mossad	Was observed by British intelligence passing Istanbul 5-22, yet succeeded; landing undetected.
24. Unnamed sailboat	Late May 39	26	Yugoslavia–Palestine	Private	Landed 6-7, near Akko.
25. *Berlitsa Maria*	5-27-39	350	Burgos–Palestine	Revisionists (Confino)	Landed 6-8.
26. *Frossoula*	5-29-39	658	Czechoslovakia, Sulina–Palestine	Private	Long Odyssey. Epidemic on board. Ship fumigated in Beyrouth. From there stranded passengers taken aboard & landed by *Tiger Hill*.
27. *Aghios Nikolaos III*	6-39	693	Varna–Palestine	Private	Landed 7-3-39 by transfer to landing ship *Nicola*.
28. *Rim*	6-26-39	801	Constanța–Rhodes. See remarks.	Revisionists	Ship caught fire July 4 off Rhodes. All aboard saved. Passengers taken aboard & landed by *Aghios Nikolaos IV* near Netanyah, 8-20-39.

368

NAME OF SHIP	DATE	APPROX. NO. OF IMMI- GRANTS	EMBARKATION AND DEBARKATION POINTS	ORGANIZER	REMARKS
29. *Las Perlas*	Late June	370	Palestine	Private	
30. *Dora*	7-39	500	Holland– Palestine	Mossad	Mainly German Jews who had escaped to Holland and were evacuated before German invasion of Holland.
31. *Parita*	7-8-39	800	(Poland) Galatz–Tel Aviv	Revisionists	Ran straight through the blockade, up the beach of Tel Aviv. Beached there (8-23-39).
32. *Colorado II*	7-14-39	266	Varna– Constanţa– Palestine	Mossad	Captured on July 28.
33. *Rudnichar I*	8-1-39	305	Varna–Palestine	Revisionists	Passengers landed 8-10.
34. *Aghios Nikolaos IV*	8-8-39	809	Constanţa– Rhodes– Palestine (near Netanyah)	Revisionists Agudat Israel	After loading immigrants at Constanţa, ship picked up the shipwrecked from *Rim* in Rhodes. Landed all 796 by landing ships *Tassos* and *Rosetta*.
35. *Tiger Hill*	Mid- August 39	1,417	Constanţa– Beyrouth–Tel Aviv	Mossad	Included in the 1,417 when landing were passengers of the *Frossoula* (see *Frossoula*, No. 26). While breaking the blockade, the *Tiger Hill* was, on 9-1-39, fired at and two of the immigrants were killed.* Repeated the *Parita* feat. Beached in Tel Aviv.
36. *Krotova*	8-20-39	650	Fiume–Palestine	Revisionists	Relatively smooth sailing.
37. *Syros*	8-22-39	593	Fiume–Palestine	Revisionists	Last transport sailing from Italy before outbreak of war.
38. *Noemi Julia*	8-29-39	1,136	Constanţa– Palestine	Revisionists	September 19, '39 ship sailed openly into Haifa and demanded admission for those on board. With war on, in wake of furor over British killing of *Tiger Hill* refugees, British hesitant to shoot at *Noemi Julia*.
39. *Rudnichar II*	8-30-39	368	Varna– Constanţa Burgos–Palestine (near Herzliya)	Revisionists	All aboard landed by landing boat S.V. *Bapha* and 4 small wooden boats 9-19-39.
40. *Rudnichar III*	10-27-39	457	Sulina–Palestine (Sydne Ali, near Tel Aviv)	Revisionists	Passengers transshipped for landing to schooner *Kooperator* and small boats.
41. *Hilda*	12-9-39	729	Balchik–Sulina– Palestine (Haifa)	Mossad	Ship captured 1-24-40 by Royal Navy. Brought to Haifa. Passengers first detained, then released.

*They were the first persons to be killed by British bullets after the outbreak of World War II.

NAME OF SHIP	DATE	APPROX. NO. OF IMMI- GRANTS	EMBARKATION AND DEBARKATION POINTS	ORGANIZER	REMARKS
42. *Delpa*	12-24-39	224	Constanţa–Varna–Palestine	Revisionists	A youth transport, almost all Betarim from Hungary, Poland, Rumania, Bulgaria.
43. *Sakarya*	2-1-40	2,175	Sulina–Palestine (Haifa)	Revisionists	Captured by H.M.S. *Fiona* and escorted to Haifa 2-13-40. Largest ship, largest load, fastest trip of all. Ship seized but later released to owners due to legal quirk. Passengers to detention camp. Released 8-12. Eri Jabotinsky, the *Sakarya*'s C.O., brought to Akko fortress, imprisoned there till death of his father, Zeev Jabotinsky, 8-6-40.
44. *Pentscho*	9-21-40	514	Sulina–Mytilene (Greek island, Stampalia, Rhodes)	Revisionists	Ship faltered near Kamili Island (actually uninhabited rock). After almost perishing of hunger, picked up by Italian warship and taken to Rhodes, then Italy. Interned but miraculously survived the war and returned to Palestine.
45. *Libertad*	5-40	390	Burgos–Palestine (Zikhron Ya'acov)	Revisionists	Bulgarians, mostly, with some Yugoslavs, Rumanians.
46. *Atlantic*	10-7-40	1,771	Tulcea–Sulina–Cyprus–Haifa	Mossad	Those arriving in Palestine on the *Pacific* plus 80 from *Atlantic* were transferred by the British to their S.S. *Patria*. The *Patria* blew up and rapidly sank in Haifa Harbor. 254 perished in this catastrophe. 1,584 survivors, most from *Atlantic* and *Milo*, were deported to fever-stricken island Mauritius. Survivors of this climate and epidemics received permission to enter Palestine five years later.
47. *Pacific*	10-11-40	1,000	Sulina–Haifa	Mossad	
48. *Milo*	10-19-40	880	Tulcea–Haifa	Mossad	
49. *Salvador*	12-40	[327]	Burgos–Istanbul sinks in Sea of Marmara.	Private	204 died as *Salvador* sank. Survivors reached Istanbul. From there on 3-19-41 the *Darien*, another refugee ship, picked them up and landed them in Palestine.
50. *Struma*	12-11-41	[767]	Constanţa–Istanbul. Turks towed the unseaworthy ship out into the Black Sea on 2-23-42 where she sank 2-24.		One sole survivor. All others drowned. Militant Irgun Zvai Leumi declared this sinking to have been "murder" and initiated violent actions against the colonial power.

370

NAME OF SHIP	DATE	APPROX. NO. OF IMMI-GRANTS	EMBARKATION AND DEBARKATION POINTS	ORGANIZER	REMARKS
51. *Darien II*	2-19-41	878	Constanța–Varna–Palestine	Mossad	Ship sailed from Constanța with 380. In Varna 370 more board. In Istanbul 128 survivors of *Salvador* boarded.
52. *Vitorul*	9-42	120	Constanța	Private	The 60-ton unseaworthy ship is not known to have arrived.
53. *Euxenia*	4-42	12	Sulina–Casne (Turkey)	Private	Sailboat with auxiliary motor. Foundered in Aegean Sea. All 12 saved; land in Turkey.
54. *Milka I*	3-44	410	Constanța–Istanbul. Continued by land to Palestine	Mossad-Revisionist cooperation	Due to *new* policy, those who on their own craft reached neutral Turkey could from there legally enter Palestine by land.
55. *Maritsa I*	4-44	244	Constanța–Istanbul–Palestine	Mossad and Revisionist cooperation	See remarks re: travel from Turkey, above.
56. *Maritsa II*	5-44	266	" "	"	"
57. *Milka II*	5-44	433	" "	"	"
58. *Morina*	7-44	308	" "	"	"
59. *Maritsa III*	7-44	318	" "	"	"
60. *Bulbul*	8-44	410	Constanța–Istanbul–Palestine	"	See remarks re: travel from Turkey, above.
61. *Salah A-Din*	8-44	547	Constanța	"	
62. *Mefkurie*	8-44	[350]	Constanța (torpedoed)	"	Ship torpedoed, survivors machine-gunned in water. 345 perished.

*Total number of those tabulated who reached Palestine**

*Tabulation of Aliya Bet shipping constitutes a most intricate task, as reports about ships, dates, number of passengers vary widely. When in doubt we accepted the lower figure. Besides, contemporary news reports and intelligence dispatches mention more names of ships carrying "illegal" refugees than are tabulated above. Careful scrutiny reveals, however, that a good number of these communications erred. The blockade-breaking ships often had their names changed. Thus a dispatch might name a ship as loading refugees in some port. Another ship with refugees crammed on board, flying a different flag and showing a different name might be reported passing the Bosporus. Again another ship was related as hiding in one of the numerous inlets of a Greek island. Still another ship was written up as unloading visaless immigrants in Palestine. Yet it was always one and the same vessel.

On the other hand, as the Jew hunt in Europe increased in intensity, a growing number of individually organized small vessels, mainly sailboats, set out for the only possible point of escape. Those who made it to Palestine had landing organizations waiting for them. Their arrival was not recorded and they mixed as fast as they could with the population there. The total number of visaless Jews reaching the country during the Nazi reign therefore exceeds the number tabulated above.

INDEX

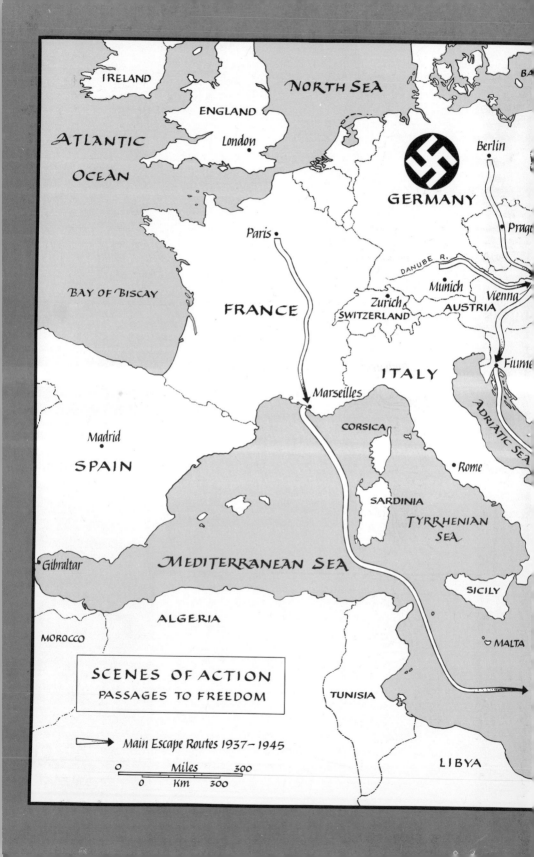